"These nineteenth- and early-twentieth-century biographies, now republished by Chelsea House, reveal an unsuspected significance. Not only are a good many of them substantively valuable (and by no means entirely superseded), but they also evoke a sense of the period, an intimacy with the attitudes and assumptions of their times."

—Professor Daniel Aaron

Copyright, 1902, by Rockwood, N.Y.

Other titles in this Chelsea House series:

HENRY WARD BEECHER
LYMAN ABBOTT

INTRODUCTION BY
WILLIAM G. McLOUGHLIN

American Men and Women of Letters Series

GENERAL EDITOR
PROFESSOR DANIEL AARON
HARVARD UNIVERSITY

CHELSEA HOUSE
NEW YORK, LONDON
1980

Cover design by Stanley Dunaj

Library of Congress Cataloging in Publication Data

Abbott, Lyman, 1835-1922.
  Henry Ward Beecher.

  (American men and women of letters)
  Reprint of the 1903 ed. published by Houghton
Mifflin, Boston; with the omission of "Tributes",
quotations by Beecher, and a chapter by S. R. Halliday.
  1. Beecher, Henry Ward, 1813-1887. 2. Congre-
gational churches-- Clergy--Biography. 3. Clergy--
United States--Biography. I. Title.
BX7260.B3A65 1980 285.8'32'0924 [B] 80-19338
ISBN 0-87754-163-9

Chelsea House Publishers
Harold Steinberg, Chairman & Publisher
Andrew E. Norman, President
A Division of Chelsea House Educational Communications, Inc.
70 West 40 Street, New York 10018

TO PLYMOUTH CHURCH

IN APPRECIATION OF THE KINDLY WELCOME
AND CORDIAL SUPPORT EXTENDED TO ME,
WHEN, ON THE DEATH OF MR. BEECHER, I WAS
CALLED TO SUCCEED HIM IN THE PASTORATE,
THIS VOLUME IS GRATEFULLY DEDICATED.

CONTENTS

CONTENTS

CHAPTER XII

CHAPTER XIII

CHAPTER XIV

CHAPTER XV

CHAPTER XVI

CHAPTER XVII

APPENDIX

LIST OF ILLUSTRATIONS
FOLLOWING PAGE 222

General Introduction

THE VISITABLE PAST
Daniel Aaron

THE TWENTY-FIVE BIOGRAPHIES of American worthies reissued in this Chelsea House series restore an all but forgotten chapter in the annals of American literary culture. Some of the authors of these volumes—journalists, scholars, writers, professional men—would be considered amateurs by today's standards, but they enjoyed certain advantages not open to their modern counterparts. In some cases they were blood relations or old friends of the men and women they wrote about, or at least near enough to them in time to catch the contemporary essence often missing in the more carefully researched and authoritative later studies of the same figures. Their leisurely, impressionistic accounts—sometimes as interesting for what is omitted as for what is emphasized—reveal a good deal about late Victorian assumptions, cultural and social, and about the vicissitudes of literary reputation.

Each volume in the series is introduced by a recognized scholar who was encouraged to

write an idiosyncratic appraisal of the biographer and his work. The introductions vary
in emphasis and point of view, for the biographies are not of equal quality, nor are the
writers memorialized equally appealing. Yet a
kind of consensus is discernible in these ran-
dom assessments: surprise at the insights still
to be found in ostensibly unscientific and old-
fashioned works; in some instances admiration
for the solidity and liveliness of the biographer's prose and quality of mind; respect for
the pioneer historians among them who made
excellent use of the limited material at their
disposal.

The volumes in this American Men and
Women of Letters series contain none of the
startling "private" and "personal" episodes
modern readers have come to expect in biography, but they illuminate what Henry James
called the "visitable past." As such, they are of
particular value to all students of American
cultural and intellectual history.

Cambridge, Massachusetts
Spring, 1980

INTRODUCTION
TO THE
CHELSEA HOUSE EDITION
William G. McLoughlin

The Genius of Henry Ward Beecher

"The life of such a man is the life of his epoch."
—Lyman Abbott

"Our age is more and more marked as a period of
change. The questions of our day are questions of
reorganization—of progress of reforms. The spirit of
our people, and I think God may say, the public
spirit of the world, is for amelioration and expansion
and growth toward individual and social excellence."
—Henry Ward Beecher

WHEN HENRY WARD BEECHER was about
to be sued for adultery by the husband of
Elizabeth Tilton in 1875, the lawyer he hired
to defend him did everything possible to prevent the suit from coming to trial, not because
he thought Beecher would lose but because he
thought "The scandal would tend to under-
mine the very foundations of social order."
Beecher was more than a popular preacher; he
was a national institution. Abraham Lincoln

could find no more fitting person to deliver the oration reuniting America after five years of bloody civil war; he chose Beecher to speak at the raising of the nation's flag once more over Fort Sumter in 1865. To have assailed Beecher's career in 1875 would have been like firing on the flag, so deeply had he come to symbolize the ideals for which America stood.

To understand Beecher's life and philosophy is to understand the way we were in the middle of the nineteenth century. Beecher's pulpit in Plymouth Congregational Church in Brooklyn Heights was the spiritual center of the republic for almost half a century. Millions heard him speak; millions read his works; millions believed that in him they had a leader and a spokesman who understood their hopes and fears, who upheld their moral and spiritual values. Although the Founding Fathers had officially separated church from state, it was the genius of Henry Ward Beecher to put the two back together. He preached that America was not only a Christian nation but an evangelical Protestant nation. Moreover, the future of Christianity rested with the future of the United States of America because evangelical Protestant Americans were God's chosen people. God tested America with a great civil war to purge it of the sin of slavery and thereby perfect His vehicle for the ultimate redemption of mankind.

Earlier in the century Americans had been less sure of themselves. Between 1813, when Beecher was born, and 1837 when he began preaching, the United States seemed in danger of falling apart, of becoming a materialistic, disintegrated, seething mass of conflicts and contradictions. The sense of civic virtue and self-sacrifice for the common good that had brought the nation through the Revolution and the shaping of the Constitution had evaporated in a wild scramble to make money. A richly endowed country waited to be exploited by aggressive self-made individualists shouting, "Every man for himself and Devil take the hindmost." There seemed to be no center, no unity, no order. A burgeoning welter of denominations, sects, utopian communities, and cults divided the ecclesiastical order. New parties, factions, and interests divided the political order. Wildcat bankers, entrepreneuers, land speculators, cotton planters, textile manufacturers, corn and wheat growers divided the economic order. Westward expansion brought sectional disorder; increasing wealth brought class divisions.

People seemed to have no clearly defined core of beliefs and values to provide stability and direction to their lives, no sense of social duty. The older philosophies of Calvin, Locke, and Jefferson had lost their hold on men. Calvinism seemed too pessimistic, rigid, narrow;

Locke and Jefferson too simplistic. The new nation needed a new philosophy that was Christian, democratic, optimistic, and libertari- and yet at the same time provided stability and a check upon human greed and rapacity.

It would be too much to say that Henry Ward Beecher single-handedly provided this new philosophy. Perry Miller has pointed out how the Second Great Awakening produced a sense of overarching unity within Protestant- ism. John William Ward has shown how Andrew Jackson provided a charismatic symbol for American politics. Albert Weinberg has ex- plained how the concept of Manifest Destiny provided a sense of national purpose. Other historians have described how Emerson's self- reliance, Webster's constitutionalism, Charles Grandison Finney's pietistic-perfectionism, and Francis Wayland's laissez-faire capitalism pro- vided key elements for a new democratic faith. But how were these diverse concepts correlated and molded into a consistent, coherent ideolo- gy? In retrospect Henry Ward Beecher appears to deserve more credit for this process than any other single figure. Though in no sense a pro- found or original thinker, Beecher was a genius at synthesizing prevalent ideas and articulating them in terms the common man could un- derstand and appreciate. More clearly than Abraham Lincoln or Ralph Waldo Emerson, Beecher stands out as the preeminent spokesman for his age. It was his version of romantic, evangelical Christianity that carried the nation into the Civil War and reunited it through liberal Protestant evolutionism after Lincoln's death. He started his career in 1837, the year Jackson left office, and died in 1887, when the Victorian era was at its height. He saw America transformed from a nation of farmers and planters into a mighty urban-industrial empire, and he inspired that transformation. Within that half-century, as Lyman Abbott glowingly wrote, "It cannot be questioned that no other man exerted so wide and profound an influence on the progress of thought, moral, political and religious."

Beecher's moral influence included the promotion of a host of humanitarian reforms (temperance, antislavery, women's rights) and the redefinition of a coherent private and social ethic for the middle class. Politically he supported the Republican ideology of free soil, free labor, and free men. Rejecting the "alleviated Calvinism" of his father's generation, Beecher formulated an optimistic interpretation of Christian theology that put God and man in partnership for the redemption of the world. God loved man for his potentialities and offered all kinds of incentives, persuasions, and assistance to better his condition and thereby to reform him. Clifford E. Clark, who has written the most astute analysis of Beecher's thought, identified in Beecher's preaching and writing four dominant central themes that "became a central part of the Victorian cultural ethos"—"the creation of a moral code based on the internalization of values and peer-group pressure, the establishment of the reform ideal of the disinterested, non-partisan public critic, the emphasis on a massive appeal to the common man through tracts, newspapers and lyceum lectures, and the easygoing, highly naturalistic Christian doctrine that made religion a matter of common sense for the average citizen." Beecher made the industrious, frugal, pious, charitable individual the center of a concentric network of institutions that reinforced the ideas of progress, public spirit, amelioration, expansion and prosperity.

In formulating the cultural ethos of Victorian America Beecher altered the profession of the ministry and the role of the church. He successfully defused the challenges of science (first in geology and then in biology) to religious faith. He successfully showed Americans how to find freedom as self-reliant individuals and still cherish the family, the church, the school, the government as institutions essential for order, growth, and security. He told them how to reconcile life in the city with the virtues of life in the country. He explained how class divisions, though seemingly inegalitarian, were justifiable as long as equal opportunity prevailed and those who rose to the top did so by honest toil and Christian character. He even demonstrated how a life of luxury and conspicuous consumption could be a means of lifting the poor to a higher esthetic and moral plane. As a consequence of his skill in resolving national doubts while keeping himself always at the forefront of changing political reforms, Beecher received the highest salary of any minister in America and lived a life of solid comfort, respectability, and prestige equal to that of the merchants, bankers, and businessmen who ran the country. His words, explained as God's Word, gave meaning and justification to Americans' actions.

Beecher's contribution to theology lay in explaining Christianity in terms of the idealistic philosophy of romantic poets and philosophers like Wordsworth, Carlyle, and Coleridge. God's spirit was not outside this world but dwelt within it. God's presence could be felt and seen in nature—in a sunset, a thunderstorm, a field of daffodils, a blade of grass. Creeds and doctrines were not important, nor were the disparate rituals of different denominations. God gave every man, woman, and child something of Himself and the inward eye to discern truth intuitively. One could come to God through nature as well as through revelation. Best of all, one could rest assured that since God was in the world, all was right with the world. Slowly but surely God was working out His will in history. Evolution was "God's way of doing things" on earth, guiding the laws of spiritual growth toward ultimate perfection.

Beecher sometimes appeared to be radical, as when he raised money to send Sharpe's rifles to Kansas to help antislavery emigrants to that territory fight off proslavery emigrants, or when he advocated votes for women so that their superior moral temper and refinement might assist in reforming the nation. But in fact he seldom got out of step with the mood and temper of the churchgoing middle class. He disliked extremists like William Lloyd Garrison, Henry David Thoreau, John Brown, Thaddeus Stephens, and Terence V. Powderly. What was good for the middle-class American was always in Beecher's view best for the nation. Foreigners were to be given equal opportunity to acculturate to American beliefs and values but could not be wholly trusted until they were safely inside evangelical churches. Freed slaves were told to lift themselves up by their own bootstraps; women were to play their part in the domestic sphere. Though claiming to be a spokesman for democracy, Beecher shared much of the elitism and paternalism of his New England forebearers.

Lyman Abbott, as Beecher's assistant pastor and ultimately his successor in Plymouth Church, paints in this volume a glowing portrait of Beecher. To Abbott, Beecher was the herald of a new and brighter day for Christianity and for America. He did not see how narrowly Beecher's philosophy was integrated with the interests of the particular class for whom he spoke and the particular political economy that class found useful in developing the nation's resources to its own advantage. Today it is easier to discern Beecher's faults—his smugness, complacency, elitism, and chauvinism. It is easy to criticize his facile accommodation of Christian transcendence to cultural relativity. But it is also important to see him as his contemporaries saw him. He was a giant in his day. No other American—politician, poet, novelist, preacher, reformer or philosopher—spoke so perfectly for the mind and mood of Victorian America from 1837 to 1887.

Providence, Rhode Island
April, 1980

NOTE ON THE CHELSEA HOUSE EDITION

THIS EDITION of Lyman Abbott's biography of Beecher contains all that Abbott wrote but omits material by others that was included in some editions. Abbott first wrote this "portrait" in 1882, five years before Beecher died. Upon republication of the book in 1887, Abbott added four chapters called "Closing Years," one of which consisted of an autobiographical sermon by Beecher, omitted here. The edition of 1887 also contained 175 pages of "Tributes" by various contemporaries, 110 pages of quotations from Beecher's works, and a long chapter of reminiscences by Beecher's pastoral helper, S. B. Halliday; these too have been omitted in this edition.

William G. McLoughlin

AUTHOR'S PREFACE
TO THE
1903 EDITION

In 1854 I entered the law office of my brothers in New York City, and went to live with the older of them in Brooklyn. He was attending Plymouth Church and I naturally went there with him. He was a son of New England, a Puritan, though of liberal temper, and a Webster Whig, and therefore originally had a triple prejudice against the young preacher who had recently come to Brooklyn, and who was in manner a Westerner, and in theology and politics a radical. But my brother had characteristically resolved to listen to six successive sermons from the preacher before finally deciding about him, and, as a result, was already a sympathetic listener and a devoted friend. I was not yet twenty years of age, and the defects and the excellences of Mr. Beecher appealed alike to my boyish nature: his exuberant life, his startling audacity, his dramatic oratory, his passionate fire, his flashes of humor, his native boyishness, all combined to fascinate me. But this superficial enthusiasm soon gave place to a deeper feeling. I had constructed for myself a crude theology, doubtless largely bor-

rowed from others, but for which I ought not to
make others responsible. That theology may be
briefly described in a sentence thus: I had inherited from a depraved ancestry a depraved nature; I had broken the laws of God, and deserved
punishment; God was a just God, and justice
compelled him to insist on the penalty; but Christ
had borne the penalty that the law might be justified and still God's justice maintained; if I accepted
Christ as my Saviour, the law would be honored,
God could be merciful, and I could be released
from the penalty. For me, religion was acceptance
of this mercy, and obedience to the laws which I
had before disobeyed; the Bible was the source of
my knowledge of those laws; the Holy Spirit was
a helper to enable me to keep them. I was afraid
of God, I was attracted to Christ, and, partly impelled by the fear, and partly inspired by aspiration,
I wished to listen to conscience, to obey the law,
to do my duty; but I had no assurance that I
could, or perhaps I should rather say, that I would
do either persistently.

Mr. Beecher revolutionized my theology by
revolutionizing my life. I obtained through him a
new experience of God, of Christ, of salvation, of
religion: I began to see that Jesus Christ was
what God eternally is, that his laws are the laws

of my own nature; that I have not more truly inherited disease than health, depravity than virtue,
from my ancestors; that salvation is life, and that
Jesus Christ came into the world to give me life;
that God is my Father and my Friend, and that
my fellowship may be with him; that the Bible is
the record of the experiences of men who knew him
and his love and his fellowship, and who narrated
their experiences that others might share them;
that religion is not the obedience of a reluctant soul
to law, but the glad captivity of a loyal soul to the
best of all loved friends. As this new life was
born in me, there was born also in me the strong
desire to impart it to others; and after long hesitation, and much debate with myself, I abandoned
the profession of the law in which, at the age of
twenty-two, I was already successfully engaged as
a member of the New York bar, thanks to my two
older brothers with whom I was associated. After
a year of special study, with some accompanying
experience in preaching to a village congregation in
Maine, I gave myself to the work of the Christian
ministry. From that day to this my desire has been
by voice and pen to give to others the life which
had been given to me when I learned that God is
love and Jesus Christ is love's interpreter, and
therefore God's interpreter.

In 1858 I left Brooklyn, and therefore Plymouth Church, and did not return until 1887, when, on Mr. Beecher's death, I became his successor. During those nearly thirty years of absence from Brooklyn, I rarely heard Mr. Beecher preach or lecture. I was at one time intimately associated with him in preparing a special edition of his sermons, and in the work of preparation examined with care several hundred of them ; and later I was in constant fellowship with him as his associate in the editorship of " The Christian Union." But during these years I was less a pupil of Mr. Beecher than a critical student of his work. For guidance and inspiration I went less to him than to those to whom he had gone : first of all to the Four Gospels ; next, to the Epistles of Paul ; then to those teachers in the Church, from Clement of Alexandria to Robertson and Maurice, who had seen in religion a life rather than a law, in God a Friend rather than a Judge, and in salvation character rather than destiny. I went back also to the instructors of my childhood. I read again my father's " Young Christian," from which I had received the first conscious impulse which any voice or pen had given me to the Christian life. I followed the clue which Mr. Beecher had given me, and I lived and honored him none the less for the discovery that the Church had never been without witnesses to a faith and life like his. That faith and life were not new except as the song of every bird is new, though the same note has been sung by a thousand ancestors. But they were new to me when in my youth I heard them and accepted them in Plymouth Church. To Mr. Beecher I am indebted for a new interpretation of and a new impulse to the life of faith and hope and love. So, when the publishers of this volume asked me to prepare it, I acceded to their request in the hope that it might serve to bring to others, through the story of Mr. Beecher's life, that conception of Christian truth and that experience of Christian faith which Mr. Beecher had brought to me. Nearly half a century has passed since from the young preacher of Brooklyn I received the impulse which sent me into the ministry, the message which subsequent study has done much to develop, but nothing to contradict, and the faith which life has never disappointed, but has constantly enlarged and enriched. That half century has been largely spent with other masters, and I believe that I am now far enough from the spell of Mr. Beecher's personal presence to estimate justly his life and character. Certainly this volume will not be coldly critical; I do not mean that it shall be indiscriminately eulogistic.

Generally the preface to a volume is the portion last written. Before I set pen to paper on the substance of this volume, I write this preface to make clear to myself, and I hope also to others, my purpose. It is not to tell the full story of Mr. Beecher's personal life: that has already been done by his wife and son and son-in-law, in a volume which is essentially autobiographical and to which I could add nothing. It is not to write the life and times of Mr. Beecher: he was so identified with all the great events of his time that to write such a volume would be to write the history of the United States in what is perhaps the most critical and certainly the most dramatic period of the national life. In this volume, I, his friend, who gladly acknowledge my own indebtedness to him, seek to interpret the life and character of a man of great spiritual and intellectual genius, whose faults were superficial, whose virtues were profound, whose influence will outlive his fame, and who has probably done more to change directly the religious life, and indirectly the theological thought in America than any preacher since Jonathan Edwards.

LYMAN ABBOTT.

CORNWALL-ON-HUDSON, N. Y.

BIBLIOGRAPHY

[Prepared by Rev. W. E. Davenport.]

Cincinnati Journal. Edited in part by Henry Ward Beecher. Cincinnati, O., 1836–37.

Sermon on the Occasion of the Funeral of Noah Noble, late Governor of Indiana. pp. 27. Indianapolis, 1844.

Seven Lectures for Young Men. Indianapolis, 1844; Salem, 1846 ; Boston, 1849, '51, '53, '55, '63, '65, '68, and '69 ; New York, 1851, '53, '60, '73, '79, '81, '84, '93, '98 ; London, England, 1851, and many reprints ; Philadelphia, as Industry and Idleness, 1850. Copyright expired 1895, and since that published by Henry Altemus, Philadelphia.

A Dissuasive from Moral Intolerance. Address by Henry Ward Beecher, at Bloomington, Ind. Indianapolis, 1845.

Indiana Farmer and Gardener. Edited by Mr. Beecher. Indianapolis, 1845. 24 numbers.

Western Farmer and Gardener. Henry Ward Beecher, Editor, 1846. Indianapolis, 24 numbers.

A Discourse Delivered at Plymouth Church, Thanksgiving Day, November 25, 1847. Cady & Burgess : 60 John St., New York, 1848.

Address before the Society for Promoting Collegiate Education in the West. (In annual report of Society, 1848.)

Plymouth Church Manual. New York, 1848, '50, '54, '67, '74. One in 1848 and one in 1850 printed by Henry Speer, 78 Wall St., by vote of the Church.

The Independent, Star Contributor, beginning October 18, 1849.

Sermon for Thanksgiving Day. Hunt's Merchant Magazine, December 12, 1850. New York, 1851.

Two Papers on Politics and the Pulpit. New York, 1851.

BIBLIOGRAPHY

National Anti-Slavery Standard (Sermons and Addresses in). New York, 1851.

On the Choice of a Profession. Address by Henry Ward Beecher. 1851.

Book of Eloquence, by Charles Dudley Warner. Selections from H. W. B. Cazenovia, 1853.

Pulpit Portraits of American Preachers, by John R. Dix. Chapter on H. W. B., with portrait. Boston, 1854.

Off-hand Takings; or, Crayon Sketches of Noticeable Men of Our Age, by G. W. Bungay. (Article on H. W. B., and portrait.) New York, 1854.

Autographs of Freedom. (Includes portraits of and sketches by Lewis Tappan, H. B. Stowe, and Henry Ward Beecher.) Auburn and Rochester, N. Y., 1854.

Star Papers. J. C. Derby: New York, 1855, '59. Enlarged edition, 1873.

The American Portrait Gallery. (Portrait and Sketch H. W. B.) New York, 1855.

The Plymouth Collection of Hymns and Tunes. Preface H. W. B. A. S. Barnes & Co.: New York, 1855, '56, '59, '62, '67, '68, '83.

Bartlett's Distinguished Modern Agitators. (Article on H. W. B.) New York, 1855.

Fowler's American Pulpit. (Includes able article on H. W. B.) New York, 1856.

Man and his Institutions. An address to the Society for Promoting Collegiate Education in the West. Delivered in Boston, May 28, 1856. American Journal of Education, July, 1856. Republished, New York, 1856.

Defence of Kansas. By Henry Ward Beecher. Washington, D. C., 1856. Buell & Blanchard, printers.

Banner of Light. Includes sermons by H. W. B. Boston, 1856.

Social Reform Tracts, No. 5. The Strange Woman of the Scriptures described and the young cautioned of her wiles and of their dangers, being a lecture addressed to young men by the Rev. Henry Ward Beecher, U. S. (brother of Mrs. Stowe). Edited by J. Harding. London: Simpkin, Marshall & Co., 1857.

BIBLIOGRAPHY

Inquirer and Chronicle. Includes sermons by H. W. B. New York, 1857.

American National Preacher, No. 1, vol. xxxi. Sermon by H. W. B., on Christ Knocking at the Door of the Heart, January, 1857. New York, 1857.

The Baptist Collection. Being the Plymouth Collection adapted for Baptist use. New York, 1857.

Social Reform Tracts, No. 6. The Home of the Harlot, its description, character, and tendencies as seen under the Scripture lamp; being the concluding part of the celebrated lectures to young men by the Rev. Henry Ward Beecher (U. S.), brother of Mrs. Stowe. Edited by J. Harding. London: Simpkin & Marshall, 1857.

Life Thoughts. Extracts from extemporaneous discourses, edited by Edna Dean Proctor. Boston, 1858, '59 (30th thousand). Large paper edition, 1860; London, 1860; New York, 1860, '69, '71, '80.

Life Thoughts. Henry Ward Beecher. Complete edition. London, 1858: Hamilton & Adams Co. Alexander Strahan & Co.: Edinburgh, 1859.

Life Thoughts, by Henry Ward Beecher, with a biographical sketch. London: Simpkin, Marshall & Co., 1863.

Life Thoughts, gathered from the extemporaneous discourses of Henry Ward Beecher. London: Wardlock & Tyler, Warwick House, Paternoster Row.

God's Seal and Covenant, with a list of members of Plymouth Church. Brooklyn, 1858.

Revival Hymns, by Henry Ward Beecher. Boston: Phillips, Sampson & Co., 1858.

Letter to Messrs. Brown & Co., Boston, recommending the torches manufactured by them. 1858.

The New York Ledger (many contributions). New York, 1858.

The Power of the Spirit, by Henry Ward Beecher. London, 38 Ludgate Hill.

Men's Excuses for not becoming Christians, and Discouragements of the Christian Life. Two sermons by Henry Ward Beecher, with portrait. New York, 1858.

How to become a Christian. A tract for the times. Boston.

BIBLIOGRAPHY

How to become a Christian, by Henry Ward Beecher. New York, 1858, '62 ; Brooklyn, 1862. Revised by the author, and published by the American Tract Society of Boston, 117 Washington St.

A Narrative of Remarkable Incidents, by W. C. Conant, with introduction by H. W. B. Derby & Jackson: New York.

Sermons by Henry Ward Beecher (12mo). One sermon in each number, published weekly. London: J. Heaton, Norwich Lane, Paternoster Row, 1859.

The Telegraph and Fireside Preacher. (Includes sermons by H. W. B.) New York, 1859.

Memorial of the Revival in Plymouth Church, Brooklyn, in 1858, comprising incidents and fragments of lectures and sermons by the pastor. By a member of the Church. New York, 1859.

William Lloyd Garrison, Henry Ward Beecher, and Theodore Parker. Boston, 1859. pp. 15.

Articles on T. Parker ; An Explanation of Views on Total Depravity. Printed by authority of the Fraternity Course Lectures Society, Boston. A. Williams & Co., 1859.

Notes from Plymouth Pulpit. A collection of memorable passages from the discourses of Rev. Henry Ward Beecher, with a sketch of Mr. Beecher and of the Lecture-room. By Augusta Moore. New York: Derby & Jackson, 1859. New edition greatly enlarged, Harper & Bros., 1865.

Pulpit and Rostrum. (Includes sermons by Mr. Beecher.) New York, 1859.

Who is our God : the Son or the Father ? By Rev. Thos. J. Sawyer. A reply to Henry Ward Beecher's articles on Theo. Parker.

Vagabondia, by Adam Badeau. (Includes articles on H. W. B.) New York, 1859.

Chronicle of the Hundredth Birthday of Robert Burns. (Includes oration by H. W. B.) Edinburgh, 1859.

Plain and Pleasant Talk about Fruits, Flowers, and Farming, by Henry Ward Beecher. Derby & Jackson: New York, 1859; Boston: Brown, Taggard & Chase, 25 & 29 Cornhill, 1859 ; London, 1859.

Pleasant Talk about Fruits, Flowers, and Farming, by

BIBLIOGRAPHY

Henry W. Beecher. New edition, with additional matter from recent writings, published and unpublished. J. B. Ford & Co.: New York, 1874.

New Star Papers; or, Views and Experiences of Religious Subjects. Derby & Jackson: New York, 1859, '69. Published as Summer of the Soul, London.

Address on Mental Culture for Women, by H. W. B. and James T. Brady, in Pulpit and Rostrum. New York, 1859.

Echoes from Harper's Ferry, by James Redpath. Includes pp. 257–279, sermon by H. W. B. preached in Plymouth Church, Sunday evening, October 30, 1859.

Italian Independence, by J. P. Thompson. (Includes address by H. W. B.) New York, 1860.

Woman's Influence in Politics. An address in New York, February 2, 1860. Boston, 1860, '69, '71.

Civil War : Its Causes, its Consequences, its Crimes, and its Compromises. Series No. 1, by Henry Ward Beecher and Archbishop Hughes. Published by Reuben Vose, New York, 1851. 8vo. pp. about 24. Pamphlet appeal against Mr. Beecher and in favor of stopping "this horrid war"; quotes from Mr. Beecher's addresses.

Remarks by Henry Ward Beecher, at the funeral of Edward Corning, Plymouth Church, Thursday afternoon, January 31, 1861. For private circulation.

War and Emancipation. A Thanksgiving Sermon preached in Plymouth Church, November 21, 1861. Philadelphia, 1861.

The Independent. Edited by H. W. B., December 19, 1861, to December 21, 1862.

The Love Element of the Gospel. H. W. B. Printed at request of Father Cleveland, Boston.

Crime and its Remedy. H. W. B. Issued by the Howard Association, London.

Fast-Day Sermons ; or, The Pulpit on the State of the Country. Peace be Still. H. W. B. pp. 265–292 ; Rudd & Carlton: New York, 1861.

Sermon before the Thirty-fourth Annual Meeting of the New York and Brooklyn Foreign Missionary Society. Published with the Proceedings. New York, 1862.

BIBLIOGRAPHY

Eyes and Ears, from the New York Ledger. Boston, 1862 ; London, 1862 ; Boston, 1863 ; (3d edition) Boston, 1866, '67 ; New York, 1887. Printed in England as Royal Truths.

Eyes and Ears, by Henry Ward Beecher (author of Life Thoughts). London: Sampson & Co., 1862.

The Methodist. (Includes sermons by H. W. B.) New York, 1862.

Royal Truths, by Henry Ward Beecher. (6th thousand.) Alexander Strahan & Co.: Edinburgh ; Hamilton Adam & Co.: London, 1862.

Freedom and War. Discourses on Topics Suggested by the Times. Boston: Ticknor & Fields, 1863.

American Cause in England. Address at Manchester, England, October, 1863. James Redpath, Boston, 1863 ; New York, 1863.

American Rebellion. Report of Speeches of Henry Ward Beecher delivered in England at Public Meetings in Manchester, Glasgow, Edinburgh, Liverpool, and London; and at the farewell breakfasts in London, etc. Manchester, England, 1864 ; London, 1864.

Sermons by Henry Ward Beecher. (15 nos.) London: J. Heaton & Son, 42 Paternoster Row, E. C., 1864.

Sermons of H. W. Beecher. 2 vols. Dickinson: London, 1864.

Aids to Prayer. New York: A. D. F. Randolph & Co., 1864, '66, '87.

Our Minister Plenipotentiary, by O. W. Holmes, in The Atlantic Monthly. Boston, 1864.

Universal Suffrage. An Argument by H. W. Beecher, including report of conference between Secretary Stanton, General Sherman, and Freedmen in Savannah. Delivered in Plymouth Church, Sunday evening, February 2, 1865. Printed by William E. Whiting, New York, 1865.

Trip of the Oceanus. Address at Fort Sumter, April 14, 1865. New York, 1865. Also reprinted as an Old South Leaflet, Boston.

Sermon on Lincoln's Death. New York, 1865.

Universal Suffrage and Complete Equality in Citizenship.

BIBLIOGRAPHY

Discourses by H. W. Beecher, Andrew Johnson, and Wendell Phillips. Boston, 1865.

Reports of the New England Society of New York. (Include addresses by H. W. B.) See Reports for 1866, '67, '71, '72, '73, '74, and '83.

Presentation Memorial to Workingmen. Oration at the raising of the old flag at Sumter, and sermon on the death of Lincoln, with sketch of Lincoln. Manchester, England, 1865.

Letter to the Soldiers and Sailors. New York, 1866.

The Political Status of Women, by Henry Ward Beecher, in The Friend, vol. i. New York, 1866.

Address at the Anniversary of the American Missionary Association, 1866.

595 Pulpit Pungencies. G. W. Carleton: New York, 1866; London, 1866.

Address at National Woman's Rights Convention, May 10, 1866. Reprinted as Woman's Duty to Vote, 1866. Reprinted, 1898.

The Methodist. Has fortnightly sermons by H. W. B. New York, December 8, '66, to February 13, '69.

Norwood, a novel (from New York Ledger). New York, 3 vols., by Scribners, 1867, '68, '80, '91. J. B. Ford, 1874 and 1898; London, 1867; Sampson, Low & Co., 1887.

Address at Laying Corner-stone of Adelphi Academy, Brooklyn. Brooklyn, 1867.

On Health. An Address delivered before the New York Medical Students' Union, Brooklyn. Brooklyn, 1867.

Royal Truths, by Henry Ward Beecher. Boston: Ticknor & Fields, 1867.

Prayers from Plymouth Pulpit. Stenographically reported. A. C. Armstrong: New York, 1867; Scribners' seventh edition, 1868. Armstrong, 1895.

Famous Americans, by James Parton. Chapter on H. W. B. and his Church. 1867.

Article on Plymouth Church, The Atlantic Monthly, Boston, 1867.

Sermons by Henry Ward Beecher. Edited by Lyman Abbott. 2 vols. Harper & Bros.: New York, 1868.

BIBLIOGRAPHY

Prayers in the Congregation, by Henry Ward Beecher, D. D.   Strahan & Co.: 58 Ludgate Hill, London, 1868.

Putnam's Magazine (sketch of H. W. B.).   New York, 1868.

Sunshine and Shadow in New York.   Chapter on Beecher and Plymouth Church, by Matthew Hale Smith.   Hartford: T. B. Bun & Co., 1868.

Men of our Times, by H. B. Stowe.   (Includes chapter on H. W. B., and portrait.)   1868.

Illustrated Bible Biography.   (Introduction by H. W. B.)   Boston, 1868.

Plymouth Pulpit, New York, September, 1868, to September, 1873.   J. B. Ford & Co.

Gnaw-Wood ; or, New England Life in a Village.   A satire on Norwood.   New York: National News Co., 1868.

Sermons, by H. W. Beecher.   Dickinson : London, 1869, and thereafter to 1886.

Oratory, Sacred and Secular, by Wm. Pittenger.   Includes note on and sketch of H. W. B.   New York : Samuel R. Wells, 1869.

The Funeral Service of Mrs. Lucy W. Bullard.   Address by H. W. B.   Worcester, 1869.

How Beecher Makes his Sermons, by Ralph Meeker.   Packard's Monthly, March, 1869.

The Overture of the Angels, by H. W. Beecher.   J. B. Ford, 1869.

The Great Metropolis, by J. N. Browne.   Chapter 27 on H. W. B.   Hartford, 1869.

The Christian Union.   Edited by Henry Ward Beecher, January 1, 1870, to November 2, 1881.   New York.   Now The Outlook.

The Potato Book, by G. W. Beat.   Includes article on the Potato Mania by H. W. B.   1870.

Familiar Talks on General Christian Experience, by Henry Ward Beecher.   London : Nelson & Sons, Paternoster Row, 1870 ; Edinburgh and New York.

Lecture-Room Talks.   A Series of Familiar Discourses on Themes of General Christian Experience.   J. B. Ford & Co., 1870.

BIBLIOGRAPHY

O. P. Morton's Oration. Prayer by H. W. B. 1870.

Henry J. Raymond and the New York Press, by Augustus Maverick. Includes Mr. Beecher's funeral sermon. Hartford, Conn., 1870.

1000 Gems from the Sermons of Henry Ward Beecher, by the Rev. G. D. Evans, Victoria Park, London. Hodder & Stoughton: 27 Paternoster Row, 1870.

Common Sense for Young Men on the Subject of Temperance. A sermon by H. W. B., in Plymouth Church. New York: National Temperance Society, 1871.

Address at Semi-Centennial of Amherst College, July, 1871.

On Labor; Popular Errors in the Education of American Youth. By H. W. B. Baltimore, 1871 and 1872.

The Unity of Italy. Includes address by H. W. B., at Academy of Music. New York, 1871.

My Summer in a Garden. Charles Dudley Warner. Introduction by H. W. B. Osgood: Boston, 1871.

My Summer in a Garden. Charles Dudley Warner, with an Introduction by Henry Ward Beecher. London: Sampson & Low.

Morning and Evening Exercises. Edited by Lyman Abbott. Being selections from the published and unpublished writings of Henry Ward Beecher. Harper Bros., 1871.

The Heavenly State and Future Punishment. Two sermons by Henry Ward Beecher. New York, 1871.

The Life of Jesus the Christ, by Henry Ward Beecher. One vol. J. B. Ford & Co., 1871. Large edition, New York, 1872. Completed in two vols. by his sons, 1891. Reissued by E. B. Treat, 1896.

The Life of Jesus the Christ, by Henry Ward Beecher. London: T. Nelson & Sons, Paternoster Row, 1871. Also issued in Edinburgh.

Successful preaching, by J. Hall, T. L. Cuyler, and Henry Ward Beecher. American Tract Society: New York, 1871.

Forty-eight Sermons preached by Henry Ward Beecher previous to 1867. London: R. D. Dickinson, 1871.

Great Fortunes, by John B. McCabe. (Includes chapter on H. W. B.) New York, 1871.

BIBLIOGRAPHY

Una and her Paupers. Memorials of Agnes E. Jones. (Introductory preface by H. W. B.) New York, 1872.

Remarks and Prayer at the Funeral of Elizabeth Cripps. 1870.

Records of the Proceedings at the Unveiling of the Franklin Statue at Printing-House Square, New York City. (Includes an address by H. W. B.) New York, 1872.

A Day in Plymouth Church, — Henry Ward Beecher's. S. W. Partridge & Co.: London, 9 Paternoster Row, 1872; Glasgow: Thomas Murray & Son, 1872.

Popular Lectures on Preaching, by Henry Ward Beecher. Glasgow: Joseph Man & Sons; London: Simpkin, Marshall & Co., 1872.

Should Libraries and Public Reading-Rooms be opened on Sunday? Address delivered by Henry Ward Beecher at the request of members of the Mercantile Library Association of New York, at Cooper Union Hall, Monday, April 22, 1872. Phonographically reported by T. J. Ellinwood.

Contemporary Review. Sketch of H. W. B., by H. R. Haweis. London, 1872.

Temperance Sermons, No. 10, Liberty and Love. An Appeal to the Conscience to Banish the Wine Cup. New York, 1872.

Men of our Day, by L. P. Brockett. (Includes portrait and chapter on H. W. B.) St. Louis, 1872.

Scribner's Monthly. Article by A. McElroy Wylie. New York, October, 1872.

The History of Plymouth Church, including Historical Sketches of the Bethel and the Navy Missions, by N. L. Thompson. J. W. Carleton: New York, 1873; London, 1873.

New York Tribune Extra, No. 2. Lecture by H. W. B. on Compulsory Education.

Yale Lectures on Preaching, by H. W. B. 3 vols. J. B. Ford & Co.: New York, 1872–74, also 1881 and 1893; Three vols. in one, 1900. London, 1872.

The Present Fearful Commercial Pressure. Discourse by Henry Ward Beecher in Plymouth Church. London: W. Howell & Co. Price, one penny.

BIBLIOGRAPHY

Letters on the Future Life, addressed to Rev. Henry Ward Beecher by B. F. Barrett. Philadelphia : Claxton, Remsen & Hafflinger, 1873

Duyckinck's Eminent Women and Men of America and Europe. Sketch and portrait of H. W. B. 1873.

Plymouth Pulpit (New Series). New York : J. B. Ford & Co. Begun September 27, 1873 ; ended September 18, 1875 ; 4 volumes. Reprinted, 1891.

New York Tribune Extras, Nos. 6 and 7. Yale Lectures for Ministers, by Henry Ward Beecher.

Account of Services of Silver Wedding Week at Plymouth Church. Edited for Committee by H. C. King. New York, 1873.

Sketches of Representative Men, by Augustus C. Rogers. Portrait and sketch of H. W. B. Atlantic Pub. Co.: New York, 1873.

Proceedings at the Farewell to Professor Tyndall. (Includes address by H. W. B.) New York, 1873.

William H. H. Murray's The Perfect Horse. Introduction by H. W. B. Boston: James R. Osgood, 1873.

Memorial of Horace Greeley. Funeral address by H. W. B. New York, 1873.

The Discipline of Sorrow. H. W. B. J. B. Ford, 1874.

Proceedings of the Evangelical Alliance. (Includes address by H. W. B.) New York, 1874.

Clergy of New York and Brooklyn, by J. A. Patton. Sketch of H. W. B., and portrait. New York, 1874.

A Summer Parish. Sketch and Discourses of the Morning Services at the Twin Mountain House, N. H., 1874. New York: J. B. Ford, 1875.

Great Modern Preachers. Sketches of Spurgeon, Stopford Brooke, and Henry Ward Beecher. London, 1875.

Truth and Candor Vindicated from the Assaults, and Christian Ministers Vindicated from the Compliments of Dr. Parker, City Temple, in his recent defences of Mr. Beecher, by Senex Rusticus. London : R. Coulcher, 50 Chancery Lane, 1874.

Paxton's Complete and Illustrated Edition ; The Great

BIBLIOGRAPHY

Brooklyn Romance. All the Documents of the Beecher-Tilton Case, unabridged. New York: J. H. Paxton, 1874.

The Great Sensation; History of the Beecher-Tilton-Woodhull Scandal. Chicago, 1873.

Ye Tilt-on Beecher; or, The muddle of ye mutual friends in verse, by the author of Ye Ball. pp. 24. New York, 1874.

The Brooklyn Council of 1874 ; Letter Missive, Statements, and Documents, together with a full stenographical report of the proceedings, and the result of the Council. New York, 1874.

The Romance of Plymouth Church, its Pastor, and his Accusers, by E. P. Doyle. Hartford, Conn., 1874.

Beecher and his Accusers, including Life of H. W. B., by F. P. Williamson. Philadelphia, 1874.

New York Tribune Extra, No. 16. The Brooklyn Congregational Council (complete). New York, 1874.

Wickedness in High Places, by E. B. Fairfield. Mansfield, O., 1874.

Case of E. B. Fairfield, by R. R. Raymond. New York, 1874.

Metropolitan Sermons. New York Tribune Extras, Nos. 19 and 20. Includes sketches of four sermons by H. W. B.

The Story of Henry Ward Beecher and Theo. and Mrs. Tilton, by the Editor of the Anglo-American Times. London: Anglo-American Press, 1874.

History of Plymouth Church, — Manual, Officers, and full list Members. pp. 92. 1874.

Truth Stranger than Fiction. Guelph, Ont., 1874.

The Beecher-Tilton Investigation ; Full and Impartial Account. pp. 126. E. E. Barclay & Co.: Philadelphia, 1874.

Drama of Deceit. (A Satire in Verse on H. W. B.) Worcester, Mass., 1875.

The Little Clincher, being the Great Biblical Defense of Henry Ward Beecher ; Spicy Poems and Pleasing Articles on the Beecher-Tilton Scandal (with scurrilous illustrations). Washington, D. C., 1875.

BIBLIOGRAPHY

Case of Mr. Beecher. Opening address by Benj. F. Tracey. New York, 1875.

Official Report of Trial of Henry Ward Beecher. Notes and References, edited by Austin Abbott. 2 vols. New York, 1874.

The Vail Removed. (A Scurrilous Attack on H. W. B.) New York, 1874.

A Looking-Glass for Henry Ward Beecher. (Similar to above in part.)

H. W. B. vs. Theo. Tilton : Trial Proceedings. New York: McDivitt & Campbell. 2 vols., 1875.

True History of the Brooklyn Scandal, by C. F. Marshall. Philadelphia: National Pub. Co., 1875.

Catholic Sermons, Select Discourses by Eminent Ministers of Various Denominations. Vol. ii., pp. 97–108, Thankfulness, H. W. B. London: F. E. Langley, 29 Warwick ·
Lane, Paternoster Row, E. C., 1875.

The Brooklyn Council of 1876. (Published by Plymouth Church.) New York: A. S. Barnes, 1875.

Non-conformity upon the Henry Ward Beecher Case, — A protest against the action of Joseph Parker, in the City Temple, in sympathy with H. W. B. London, 1875. 2 editions.

Uncontradicted Testimony in the Beecher Case. Preface by Lyman Abbott. New York: D. Appleton & Co., 1875.

The Result of the Brooklyn Advisory Council of 1876, with the Letters of Dr. Leonard Bacon, President Timothy Dwight, D. D., etc., etc. New York : A. S. Barnes & Co.

The Beecher Trial. A Review of the Evidence for the New York Times, July 2, 1875. New York, 1875.

Mr. Beecher's Trial : with Portrait. Harper's Weekly Supplement, June 5, 1875.

An Address on Congregationalism as affected by the declarations of the Advisory Council held in Brooklyn, N. Y., February, 1876. By Richard S. Storrs, D. D. March 13, 1876. No publisher.

References and citations prepared for the convenience of the Brooklyn Council of 1876. With prefatory note by Henry M. Storrs. No publisher.

BIBLIOGRAPHY

Ingersoll, Beecher, and Dogma, by R. S. Dement. Chicago, 1875.

Views and Interviews on Journalism. (Includes address by H. W. B., before State Editorial Reunion at Poughkeepsie.) Chas. F. Wingate, 1875.

The Brooklyn Theatre Fire. Includes address by H. W. B., at Memorial Services, Brooklyn. Daily Times Print, 1876.

The Holocaust at the Brooklyn Theatre. Includes address by H. W.B. Daily Argus, Brooklyn, 1876.

Oratory. An Oration by H. W. B. Philadelphia, 1876, '86, '92, '95, '97, '99.

Centennial Orations. Includes address by H. W. B. Tribune Extra, No. 32, 1876.

The Plymouth Chimes. Devoted to Plymouth Church and its Missions. 1877–1903.

Address to the Army of the Republic, H. W. B. Springfield, Mass., 1878.

Past Perils and the Perils of To-day. A sermon by H. W. B. Christian Union Print, New York, 1878.

The Background of Mystery. A Sermon by H. W. B., December 15, 1877.

The Whole World in Pain. A sermon by H. W. B. Christian Union Print, 1878.

The Strike and its Lessons. A sermon by H. W. B. New York, 1878.

In the West. A sermon by H. W. B., with note by Lyman Abbott. Christian Union Print, 1878.

Christianity Unchanged by Change. Two sermons by H. W. B., under one cover. Christian Union, No. 10, 1878.

An Hour with the American Hebrew. Includes sermon by H. W. B. on Jew and Gentile. 1879, New York.

The Plymouth Triangle. A paper of Plymouth Fair, with article by H. W. B. Brooklyn, March, 1879.

An Account of the Visit of the 13th Regiment, N. G. S., New York to Montreal, Canada. Includes address by H. W. B. Brooklyn, 1879.

Golden Gleams from Henry Ward Beecher's Words and Works, by John T. Lloyd. Newcastle-on-Tyne, England, 1880.

BIBLIOGRAPHY

Plans for Reading. Edited by Lyman Abbott. Includes article by H. W. B. New York, 1880.

Channing Memorial. Address by H. W. B. Brooklyn Academy of Music. Boston, 1880.

Memorable Men of the Nineteenth Century. Life, H. W. B., with portrait. J. T. Lloyd, London, 1881.

Sermons of H. W. B., 1873–74. Fords, Howard & Hulbert, New York, 1882.

New England Society of Brooklyn. Addresses by H. W. B. In Proceedings for 1881, '82, '84, '86.

Henry Ward Beecher's Statement of Belief before the New York and Brooklyn Association. New York: Funk & Wagnalls, 1882 ; The Christian Union, 1882.

O. A. Brownson, Works, vol. xiii. and vol. xix. Beecherism and its Tendency. Detroit, 1882 and 1887.

Progress of Thought in the Church, by H. W. Beecher. North American Review, August, 1882.

In Memoriam: Hobart Schroeder. Portions Mr. Beecher's Friday evening talk. No date.

Funeral Service of Dr. H. B. White. Address of H. W. B. March 28, 1883.

On Free Trade and Congressional Elections. H. W. B. 1883.

A Circuit of the Continent : Account of a tour through the West and South. By Henry Ward Beecher. With portrait. Being his Thanksgiving Day discourse, Nov. 29, 1883. New York: Fords, Howard & Hulbert.

Life of Henry Ward Beecher by Lyman Abbott, assisted by S. B. Halliday. pp. 604. New York: Funk & Wagnalls, 1883; and with additional matter, London, 1887.

Articles of Faith and Principles and Rules of Plymouth Church. Brooklyn, 1884.

Leading Orators of 25 Campaigns, by W. C. Roberts, Portrait and sketch of H. W. B. New York: K. L. Strouse & Co., 1884.

Address at the Brooklyn Rink, by H. W. B. Brooklyn, October, 1884.

Wendell Phillips ; A Commemoration Discourse, by H. W. B. Fords, Howard & Hulbert, 1884.

BIBLIOGRAPHY

Beecher's Cleveland Letters : — Two Letters on the Reconstruction of the Southern States, written by H. W. B., in 1866, with introductory postscript. 1884.

A Circuit of the Continent. A Thanksgiving sermon by H. W. B. New York: Fords, Howard & Hulbert, 1884.

Comforting Thoughts (arranged by Irene Ovington from Beecher's sermons). New York: Fords, Howard & Hulbert, 1884, '90, '93, 1901, with introduction by Newell Dwight Hillis.

A Surrender to Infidelity. A reply to Rev. H. W. Beecher. A sermon preached by Justin D. Fulton, D. D., in the Centennial Baptist Church, Brooklyn. New York: Funk & Wagnalls, 1884.

Fifty Years among Authors, Books and Publishers. Reminiscences by J. C. Derby. Chapter on H. W. B. New York, 1884.

Evolution and Religion. A few sermons by H. W. B., with portrait. New York : Gallison & Hobson, 1885.

Evolution and Religion. Part i. Theoretical. Part ii. Practical. Eight sermons discussing the bearing of the Evolutionary Philosophy on the Fundamental Doctrines of Evangelical Christianity. New York: Fords, Howard & Hulbert, 1885, '86. London: James Clarke & Co.

Dedication Ceremonies of N. Y. Lodge No. 1, B. P. O. Elks, at Evergreen Cemetery. Address of H. W. B. New York, 1885.

H. B. Claflin Memorial Address, by H. W. B., March 14, 1885. New York, 1885.

Funeral Sermon of Mary Carrington Healy, by H. W. B. No date.

The New Theology of Henry Ward Beecher Briefly Reviewed, by Henry Webb. Philadelphia, 1885.

Memorial Volume of City of Boston, of U. S. Grant, including Eulogy of Grant by H. W. B. Boston, 1886.

Beecher Book of Days. Compiled by Eleanor Kirk and C. B. Lerow. New York, 1886.

E. T. Mason's Humorous Masterpieces. Selections from H. W. B. New York, 1886.

Henry Ward Beecher's Last Sermon. Preached in Plymouth Church. London, 1887.

BIBLIOGRAPHY

I am resolved what to do. Last sermon of Henry Ward Beecher, February 27, 1887. New York: Gallager & Hoeffer, 1887.

Sermons in the Brooklyn Magazine, 1886–87.

The Beecher Calendar for 1887. New York, 1887.

Beecher as a Humorist. Selections from the published works of H. W. B. by Eleanor Kirk. New York. Fords, Howard & Hulbert, 1887.

Henry Ward Beecher : A Memorial — Plymouth Church, 1887.

The Christian Union Supplement : March 17, 1887. Illustrated. Containing biographical sketch, tribute, sermon by H. W. B., incidents, and anecdotes. The Christian Union Pub. Co.

Henry Ward Beecher : His Life and Work. Partly reprint of above. Illustrated. The Christian World, London, No date.

Beecher Memorial. Contemporaneous Tributes to His Memory. Edited by Edward W. Bok. New York: 1887. Same, London, James Clarke & Co., 1887.

Memorial of Henry Ward Beecher, by Jos. H. Knight. New York, 1887.

A Tribute to H. W. Beecher, by Rev. Frank Fitch, March 13, 1887. Buffalo, New York, 1887.

Henry Ward Beecher. A Sermon by John W. Chadwick, March 13, 1887. G. H. Ellis, Boston, 1887.

Henry Ward Beecher. A discourse delivered in the Union Park Congregational Church, March 13, 1887, by Rev. F. Noble, D. D. Chicago, 1887.

Sermon in Plymouth Church, by Rev. Thomas Armitage, D. D., March 7, 1887. Brooklyn, 1887.

Joseph Parker's Eulogy on Henry Ward Beecher, with letters by Gladstone and Grover Cleveland, with postscript, James Clarke & Co., London, 1887.

Sermon by Rev. Duncan McGregor, D. D., preached in the Carroll Park M. E. Church on the death of Henry Ward Beecher. Printed by request of the Trustees. Brooklyn, 1887.

Henry Ward Beecher : A sketch of his career : with

analyses of his power as a preacher, lecturer, orator, and journalist; and incidents and reminiscences of his life. By Lyman Abbott, D. D., assisted by Rev. S. B. Halliday. Hartford, Conn.: Am. Pub. Co., 1887.

A Chaplain's Record. Article on H. W. Beecher, by Capt. D. E. Austen, in North American Review, April, 1887. New York, 1887.

Patriotic Addresses in England and America, 1850 to 1885, by John R. Howard, with biographical sketch. New York, 1887 and 1891.

Life of Henry Ward Beecher, by Joseph Howard, Jr. Hubbard Bros.: Philadelphia.

Routledge's World Library — Henry Ward Beecher in the Pulpit, with an introduction by Rev. Hugh Reginald Haweis, M. A. London: Routledge & Son, Ludgate Hall, 1886.

A Summer in England with Henry Ward Beecher, by James B. Pond. New York: Fords, Howard & Hulbert, 1887.

Beecher's Personality. Article in the North American Review, by W. S. Searle, M. D. May, 1887.

Henry Ward Beecher in England in 1886. James Clarke & Co. Addresses, Lectures, Sermons and Prayers, London, 1887. With biographical sketch and portrait.

Beecher : Christian Philosopher, Pulpit Orator, Patriot and Philanthropist. A volume of representative selections, with biographical sketch, by Thos. W. Hanford. Chicago, 1887.

Catalogue of the library, etc., of H. W. B. American Art Association: New York, 1887.

Henry W. Beecher. A Lecture delivered by Felix Adler, for the Society of Ethical Culture at Chickering Hall, New York, 1887.

Annual Cyclopædia, Biography of H. W. B. New York, 1887.

Proverbs from Plymouth Pulpit. By Wm. Drysdale. New York: D. Appleton & Co., 1887.

As above, with introductory note by Joseph Parker, D. D., City Temple, London. Chas. Burnett & Co., 1887.

BIBLIOGRAPHY

The Moral Uses of Luxury and Beauty, by H. W. B. The Christian Union Print, 1887.

The Boyhood of Henry Ward Beecher. A Litchfield Beecher Day, by Frank S. Child, New Creston, Conn. 1887. pp. 32.

Life and Work of Henry Ward Beecher, by Thos. W. Knox. Hartford, Conn., 1887.

Speeches on the American Rebellion (first published in America). Edited by John Anderson, Jr. New York, 1887.

Religion and Duty ; or, Fifty-eight Sunday Readings from Henry Ward Beecher. Selected and arranged by Rev. J. Reeves Brown. London : James Clarke & Co., 1887.

The Apostle Preacher. A sermon preached in Wood St. Congregational Church, High Burnet, on Sunday, March 27, 1887, in memory of the late Henry Ward Beecher, by Rev. J. Matthews, with a preparatory note by Rev. Joseph Parker, D. D. London: G. W. Cowing.

Life of Henry Ward Beecher, by W. C. Griswold. Portrait and illustrations. Centrebrook, Conn., 1887.

Anecdotes of Henry Ward Beecher, by N. A. Shenstone. Chicago : R. R. Donnelly & Son, 1887.

Albany Law Journal, J. D. Parsons, March 19, 1887.

Proposed Memorial to the late Henry Ward Beecher. F. W. Evans, Mt. Lebanon College, New York, 1887.

Biography of Henry Ward Beecher, by W. C. Beecher and Samuel Scoville, assisted by Mrs. H. W. Beecher. New York : Chas. L. Webster & Co., 1888.

The above, London, by Sampson, Low, Marston & Co., 1888.

Current Religious Perils, by Joseph Cook. (Contains remarks on H. W. B.)

Henry Ward Beecher. Memorial Address delivered in Plymouth Church, by R. W. Raymond, March 11, 1888.

A String of Pearls. Selections from H. W. B. New York, 1888.

Beecher, by G. W. Washburn. J. B. Lippincott : Philadelphia, 1888.

Life of Harriet Beecher Stowe, by C. E. Stowe. (Contains letters from H. W. B.) New York, 1889.

BIBLIOGRAPHY

Signs of Promise. Sermons by Lyman Abbott. (Contains Memorial Sermons on H. W. B.) New York, 1889.

Crown of Life. Selections from the writings of H. W. B., by Mary Storrs Haynes, with introduction by R. W. Raymond. Boston : D. Lothrop & Co.

Memorial Service in Plymouth Church, March, 1891, with Memorial Address by Thos. G. Shearman. New York : Fords, Howard & Hulbert, 1891.

Mr. Beecher as I knew him. Mrs. H. W. Beecher, in Ladies' Home Journal, Philadelphia, October, 1895.

Faith. Mr. Beecher's last (morning) sermon. Ellinwood : Brooklyn, 1891, '92.

The Hidden Manna and the White Stone. A sermon by Mr. Beecher, July 6, 1866, with appendix by Mrs. Beecher. Ellinwood : Brooklyn, 1892.

A Book of Prayer, by H. W. Beecher. Compiled by Ellinwood. Fords, Howard & Hulbert, 1892 ; Dickinson : London, 1892.

Addresses. Edited by F. Saunders. (Includes the Advance of a Century by H. W. B.) 1893.

Bible Studies. Readings in the early history of the Old Testament, with familiar comments ; Plymouth Church, 1878–79. Edited by John R. Howard. Fords, Howard & Hulbert, New York, 1893.

Best Thoughts of Henry Ward Beecher, with portrait and biographical sketch, by Lyman Abbott, D. D. H. G. Goodspeed & Co., 1893.

Life of H. W. Beecher, the Shakespeare of the Pulpit. By J. H. Barrows, D. D. New York : Funk & Wagnalls, 1893. London and Toronto.

Other Essays from the Easy Chair. G. W. Curtis. Includes account of Mr. Beecher's preaching on Lincoln's death. New York, 1893.

The Plymouth Hymnal. Edited by Lyman Abbott. (Contains historical introduction on the service rendered to hymnology by H. W. B.) New York : The Outlook Co., 1893.

Donn Piatt : Sunday Meditations. Includes selected sketches by H. W. B. Cincinnati : Robt. Clark, 1893.

BIBLIOGRAPHY

Beecher Exonerated. A poem by Isaac M. Inman. New York : Franklin Press Co., 1893.

History of the 13th Regiment. Chapter on H. W. B. as chaplain, with portrait. Brooklyn, 1894.

Famous Leaders Among Men. Sarah Knowles Bolton. Includes account of H. W. B. New York and Boston, 1894.

Metaphors, Similes, and other Characteristic Sayings from the Discourses of H. W. B. Edited by Ellinwood. Introduction by H. B. Sprague. Andrew Graham : New York, 1895 ; London, 1895.

Specimens of Argumentative Modes. Compiled by George P. Baker, Assistant Professor in English, Harvard University. Henry Holt & Co., 1896. Includes speech delivered by H. W. Beecher in Philharmonic Hall, Liverpool, October 18, 1863, with notes by the editor, as an illustration of persuasive oratory.

Library of the World's Best Literature. Includes portrait of H. W. B., and review of his work, by Lyman Abbott, in vol. iii. New York, 1896.

Men Who Win ; or, Making Things Happen, by Wm. Thayer. Has chapter on H. W. B. T. Nelson & Sons, New York, 1896.

The Literature of America, by W. W. Birdsall and others. Account of H. W. B. Chicago and Philadelphia, 1897.

The New Puritanism. Addresses at the Semi-Centennial of Plymouth Church, by Lyman Abbott, Amory H. Bradford, Charles A. Berry, George A. Gordon, Washington Gladden, and W. J. Tucker. Introduction by R. W. Raymond. New York : Fords, Howard & Hulbert, 1897 ; London : James Clarke & Co., 1897.

Poetical Sermons; Including the Ballad of Plymouth Church, and The Heart of the Republic. (Poems on H. W. B., by W. E. Davenport.) New York: G. P. Putnam's Sons, 1897.

Address on H. W. B., by J. B. Pond, before the Long Island Historical Society. Brooklyn, 1897.

Giants of the Republic, by J. H. Vincent. Chapter on H. W. B. 1898.

BIBLIOGRAPHY

Autobiographical Reminiscences. Edited by T. J. Ellinwood. Selections from talks by H. W. B. New York, 1898.

R. C. Ringwalts. Modern American Oratory. Includes The Sepulchre in the Garden, by H. W. B. New York, 1898.

American Orations. Edited by A. Johnson. Includes H. W. B.'s Liverpool Address. 1898.

The Fruit of the Spirit, by Rev. Alford B. Penniman. Chapter on H. W. B. Adams, Mass., New York, 1898.

Reminiscences, by Justin M'Carthy. Chapter on H. W. B., and Woman's Rights. Harper Bros.: New York, 1899.

Patriotic Nuggets. New York: Fords, Howard & Hulbert, 1899.

The Clergy in American Life and Letters, by D. D. Addison. Includes account of H. W. B. London: Macmillan, 1900.

The World's Best Orations. Edited by David J. Brewer. Includes oration by H. W. B. New York, 1899.

Brooklyn Eagle Library. No. 39, Plymouth Church Annals. February, 1900.

Eccentricities of Genius, by J. B. Pond. Chapter on H. W. B. New York: G. W. Dillingham, 1901.

Henry Ward Beecher. Article in Encyclopædia Britannica, by Lyman Abbott, D. D. 1902.

Henry Ward Beecher Souvenir. (A booklet of quotations.) No date.

Translation into German, by Rossiter W. Raymond, of Life Thoughts, by H. W. B. Berlin. No date.

Translation into German of Royal Truths, with a Sermon on the Slavery Question, by H. W. B. Berlin.

Translation into German of Sermons, by H. W. B., with a biographical introduction by Henri Tollin. Berlin, 1870.

Translation into Welsh of quotations from H. W. B. and others. Crexham, Hughes & Son. No date.

HENRY WARD BEECHER

CHAPTER I

THE MEANING OF MR. BEECHER'S LIFE

THE beginning of Mr. Beecher's real life was a spiritual experience which he himself has graphically described. I can find no exact date for this experience; but the opening sentence of his description implies that it occurred after his graduation from Amherst College; and in his address to the London ministers in 1886 he refers to it as having taken place in the Ohio woods, and "when he had studied theology," evidently therefore during his seminary course.

I was a child of teaching and prayer; I was reared in the household of faith; I knew the Catechism as it was taught; I was instructed in the Scriptures as they were expounded from the pulpit and read by men; and yet, till after I was twenty-one years old, I groped without the knowledge of God in Christ Jesus. I know not what the tablets of eternity have written down, but I think that when I stand in Zion and before God, the brightest thing I shall look back upon will be that blessed morning of May when it pleased God to reveal to my wandering soul the idea that it was his nature to love a man in his sins for the sake of helping him out of them; that he did

not do it out of compliment to Christ, or to a law, or a
plan of salvation, but from the fullness of his great heart;
that he was a Being not made mad by sin, but sorry; that
he was not furious with wrath toward the sinner, but pitied
him — in short that he felt toward me as my mother felt
toward me, to whose eyes my wrong-doing brought tears,
who never pressed me so close to her as when I had done
wrong, and who would fain with her yearning love lift
me out of trouble. And when I found that Jesus Christ
had such a disposition, and that when his disciples did
wrong he drew them closer to him than he did before
— and when pride, and jealousy, and rivalry, and all vul-
gar and worldly feelings rankled in their bosoms, he
opened his heart to them as a medicine to heal these
infirmities; when I found that it was Christ's nature to
lift men out of weakness to strength, out of impurity to
goodness, out of everything low and debasing to superiority, I felt that I had found a God. I shall never forget the feelings with which I walked forth that May
morning. The golden pavements will never feel to my
feet as then the grass felt to them; and the singing of
the birds in the woods — for I roamed in the woods —
was cacophonous to the sweet music of my thoughts; and
there were no forms in the universe which seemed to me
graceful enough to represent the Being, a conception of
whose character had just dawned on my mind. I felt,
when I had with the Psalmist called upon the heavens,
the earth, the mountains, the streams, the floods, the birds,
the beasts, and universal being to praise God, that I had
called upon nothing that could praise him enough for
the revelation of such a nature as that in the Lord Jesus
Christ.

Time went on, and next came the disclosure of a Christ
ever present with me — a Christ that was never far from
me, but was always near me, as a companion and friend,

to uphold and sustain me. This was the last and the best revelation of God's Spirit to my soul. It is what I consider to be the culminating work of God's grace in a man; and no man is a Christian until he has experienced it. I do not mean that a man cannot be a good man until then; but he has not got to Jerusalem till the gate has been opened to him, and he has seen the King sitting in his glory, with love to him individually.

To the interpretation of this vision and the impartation of the life which it begot in him he thenceforth gave himself. Was this vision true? Was this life of value? By the answer to these two questions his character and career must be measured.

Some changes in public sentiment are so radical and so widespread that it is almost impossible for one born in the later time to realize from what they have been delivered or the price which has been paid for their deliverance. It is difficult for readers living in the light and warmth of the twentieth century to realize the conception of religious truth and life which dominated the reason and the conscience in the beginning of the nineteenth century. But some understanding of this conception is absolutely necessary if one would comprehend the life or estimate the public service of Henry Ward Beecher. For that service lies not so much in any definite contribution to theological thought as in a change made in the atmosphere of religious thinking and living.

The nineteenth century opened with very little

of either light or warmth in the Puritan churches
of England and America. Aggressive piety was almost confined to the Methodist churches, which had
not yet lost the enthusiasm of their first great love
and their first surprising successes. The philosophy
of Locke was the dominant philosophy in England,
and was preparing the public mind for the materialism of Maudsley, the agnosticism of Herbert Spencer, and the Utilitarianism of Bentham and of Mill.
In the Church of England worship was a dull routine and faith a cold intellectualism. The orthodox
definition of faith made it synonymous with belief,
the orthodox definition of virtue made it synonymous with happiness. Mental philosophy ignored
the spiritual element in man ; moral philosophy denied the virtues of self-denial and suffering. Already,
as the first quarter of that century drew to its close,
the protest of the unquenchable instincts of the
heart had begun to make itself felt in three distinct
but substantially contemporaneous movements. In
the Oxford Movement earnest men, making quest
for that life which the popular philosophy of the
day either quietly ignored or dogmatically denied,
turned their faces backward, and sought, by reviving the mystical doctrines and the elaborate ritual
of the half-pagan church of the early ages, to revive
the life which had animated both. Under the inspiration of such devout souls as the poet John Keble
and the prophet John Henry Newman, there was
a revival of archæology in religion, the results of
which are still to be seen in a revived Anglo-Ro-

manism, an imitative ritualism, and a vigorous and vital work of Christian beneficence among the poor and the outcast. Simultaneously started, though without organism or acknowledged leader, the Broad Church Movement, in which men, equally dissatisfied with the superficial philosophy of the age, sought for spiritual truth by looking within for the witness to it, a movement whose prophets — Erskine, Maurice, Thomas Arnold, Robertson, Kingsley, Stanley, and Farrar — have made their voices heard across the Atlantic, where their interpretation of life has been caught up and reëchoed by such prophets as our own Munger, Mulford, Brooks, and a score of others. The same dissatisfaction with the ideals of the Church and the universities sent still another school in search of spiritual life to the Scriptures, whose truths found new interpreters in such scholars as Tregelles, Wordsworth, Davidson, Ellicott, Alford, and Conybeare and Howson.

This threefold reaction against a spiritless psychology and a superficial if not an Epicurean moral philosophy must not be forgotten in making any true estimate of the progress of thought in our own churches on this side of the Atlantic. For here, too, the churches had lost their power over the masses of the people, though from other causes. They were manacled by a fatalism which they had inherited from the Reformation. Luther himself declared that man had lost his freedom by the Fall, and that God had in his secret counsels reserved certain of his children to inevitable reprobation. Calvin, equipped with less tender sympathies and with more remorseless logic, had undertaken to drag these counsels out from the secret places where Luther left them in hiding, and to blazon them abroad throughout all Europe. The Methodist revolt against a fatalism as inconsistent with Scripture as it is with personal consciousness had only intensified in the churches of Puritan descent the dangerous dogmas of unconditional election and reprobation. These churches held that God existed for his own glory; that he had eternally elected a few to salvation, and reprobated the many to endless sin and shame; that he had made this choice for them without reference to their character or actions; that the decree was absolutely irrevocable; that the damnation of the many, and the salvation of the few served equally, not only to enhance his majesty and redound to his praise, but also to increase his joy and the holy joy of the blessed. The least of the evils which accompanied the preaching of this travesty on the Scriptures, founded on the misapprehension of a few enigmatical texts taken out of their connection and therefore robbed of their true meaning, was the infidelity which it fostered. It quickened unbelief and deadened vital piety. There were no revivals. The churches did not believe in them. The minister was a winnower whose Gospel was a fan in his hand, with which he selected the eternally chosen grain, while the unalterable chaff was swept away into unquenchable fire.

Theology is at once the cause and the product of the religious life; and the religious life of New England in the first quarter of the nineteenth century was such as this theology might well be expected to indicate. Intemperance was all but universal. It entered not only every village, but every home. Every store was a drinking store. The noisome odors of the bar polluted even the parsonage on the occasion of ordinations and other kindred ministerial gatherings. Slavery not merely held three millions of slaves in bondage, but controlled the nation, and openly formed its plan for making of the republic a great slave empire; denied the right of free speech in both North and South; denied the right of petition in Congress; and so stifled the Church that only in isolated pulpits was the voice of remonstrance raised against it. There was no missionary zeal, and at the beginning of the century no missionary organization, either home or foreign. The American Board, the mother of them all, was organized only three years before Mr. Beecher was born, and then against the open opposition of conservatism in the Church and the still more serious obstacle of an almost universal indifference. Infidelity was common. Thomas Paine was far more popular in his day than Robert Ingersoll has been in ours, and Byron was far more read and admired than is Swinburne now. When Dr. Dwight took the presidency of Yale College, there were in it two Thomas Paine societies and only four or five students known to

be professing Christians; and so popular was
French infidelity that a number of the leading
members of the Senior class had dropped their
own names and taken instead the names of leading French infidels, as Voltaire, Rousseau, and
D'Alembert.   There was, it. is true, a " Moral
Society of Yale College;" but apparently it was
organized only to debate religious and ethical questions, and it is significant that it was a secret society, and any disclosure of its proceedings was punishable by expulsion.[1]   In the churches long creeds
were being substituted for the short and simple
covenants of the earlier Puritans, in a vain hope
thus to turn back the current. The great Unitarian revolt against Puritan theology had already
begun with the settlement of Channing in Boston
in 1803, a revolt which became organic in the
formation of the Unitarian Association in 1825.
There was already impending the battle between
the Old School and the New School in theology,
which subsequently rent the Presbyterian denomination, and would have rent the Congregationalists also if they had been sufficiently organized to
be capable of division.

Such was the legacy which the Puritan theology
of the eighteenth century had left to New England: a fear of God; a reverence for his law; a
strenuous though narrow and conventional con-

---

[1] *Life of Timothy Dwight: Introduction to Dwight's Theology,*
p. 20; *Two Centuries of Christian Activity at Yale College,* p. 55;
Autobiography and Correspondence of Lyman Beecher, i. 43.

science; but also a religion divorced from ethics; a Church silent in the presence of intemperance and slavery; without missionary zeal or missionary organization; threatened by the intellectual revolt which eventually carried from it some of its wisest and noblest men; and surrounded by a community lapsing into indifference and neglect or combining in open and cynical infidelity.

But already conscience was beginning to protest within the Church against these spiritual conditions. Dr. Timothy Dwight in New Haven put the infidelity of Thomas Paine on trial by a restatement of Christian doctrine in more rational forms than those which had created the infidel reaction against Christianity. Dr. Lyman Beecher in Boston restated orthodox doctrine in reply to the criticisms of Dr. Channing, and in such a way as to provoke the criticisms of the conservative in the orthodox churches. Albert Barnes was put on trial in Philadelphia for teaching that God is love and man is free. Drs. Finney and Nettleton emphasized their faith in a new theology by the " new measures" which they inaugurated in revivals of religion. The organization in 1810 of the American Board of Commissioners for Foreign Missions was followed by the organization of the American Home Missionary Society [1] in 1826. The first gun in the long temperance campaign, fired by Dr. Lyman Beecher in 1826, was followed by the

[1] The name has since been changed to The Congregational Home Missionary Society.

organization of the Washingtonian Society and the birth of the Washingtonian Movement in 1840. Into this atmosphere of awakening life Henry Ward Beecher was born, and in it he grew up to manhood. The theological movement which had radically changed the character and spirit of the Church had in America many leaders; chief among them I count Horace Bushnell, Charles G. Finney, and Henry Ward Beecher: the first, the prophet of faith; the second, the prophet of hope; the third, the prophet of love.

Dr. Emmons died in 1840, the last of the merely logical preachers of New England; and with him died the orthodox rationalism which, up to the close of the eighteenth century, dominated the Puritan pulpit. This rationalism assumed that man is a reasonable creature; that the reason is the supreme faculty; that this reason is to be convinced by the truth; and when it is convinced, the will must of necessity obey; and that when this result is reached, the man is a converted man and a new creature. Such was the philosophy which, sometimes avowed, sometimes unrecognized, underlay the earlier Puritan preaching. The whole fabric of the religious life was built *by* logical processes, *with* doctrine, *on* the human reason. But all men are not logical, and all men do not obey the truth even when it is made clear to their logical understanding. Spiritual truth is not mined by picks and beaten out by hammers; it is not to be arrived at by slow processes of demonstration, but to be apprehended and appreciated upon the bare presentation of it. Truth is a form of life; and only as it is received as a life, vitalizing and dominating the soul, is it spiritually efficacious. Of this philosophy, which is more than a philosophy, Horace Bushnell was the chief exponent in the Puritan churches. That the invisible world is immediately and directly seen by the spirit of men ; that God is no mere hypothesis to account for the phenomena of creation, but man's best friend, his Father, and intimate personal companion; that inspiration is no remote phenomenon, once attested by miracles now buried forever in the grave of a dead God, but the universal and eternal communion between living souls and the living God; that the Bible is no infallible record offered as a substitute for such communion, but a prophetical illustration of its reality and an incentive to its continuance; that the forgiveness of sins is infinitely more than any theory of atonement, and that no theory of atonement can comprehend the full meaning of the forgiveness of sins — these were not the theories of a philosopher, but the vital convictions, because the living experiences, of the saint, whose sainthood must be in the heart of the critic of Horace Bushnell before he can criticise, and in the heart of the disciple before he can comprehend.

This progress toward a more spiritual apprehension of truth carried with it a clearer conception of human liberty. All theories of fatalism fall away before the personal test of self-consciousness.

That man is a free moral agent; that he can do
right and is therefore blameworthy for doing
wrong; that he is sinful — not because he was
made so, but because he had made himself so:
the nineteenth century is the century of political
and industrial emancipation, because in the redis-
covery of this truth it has won spiritual emancipation. The Lutherans have long since disowned
Luther's theory of a secret counsel of God. The
Calvinists have abandoned John Calvin's doctrine
that man lost moral freedom by the Fall. The
doctrines of limited atonement and of unconditional election, though they may still be preserved
in fossiliferous creeds, are rarely, if ever, dragged
forth from their archæological retreat, at least by
any son of the Puritan in any Puritan church.
Civilization disowns them absolutely, unanimously,
and with indignation. The power of Charles G.
Finney lay in his vigorous and vehement interpretation of this indignant protest within the orthodox
Church against the spirit of fatalism. His clarion-
like voice, his logical mind, his legal education, his
intensity of conviction, his singularly unaffected
and unconventional piety, his impressive personality, combined with his overmastering sense of
man's liberty and therefore of man's responsibility,
made him the most remarkable revival preacher
of his age. To men paralyzed by the despair
engendered by fatalism, his message was, You can,
therefore you may; to men paralyzed by the indifference engendered by fatalism, his message was,

You can, therefore you must. Liberty and responsibility are always coterminous; hope and duty are different aspects of the same experience. Dr. Finney was the preacher of liberty and responsibility; he was therefore an apostle of duty and of hope.

If Horace Bushnell was the apostle of faith, and Charles G. Finney was the apostle of hope, Mr. Beecher was characteristically the apostle of love. The Puritan did not believe that God is love. His conception of God was represented by the phrase most commonly used to describe him — "The Moral Governor of the Universe." The phrase "Fatherhood of God" is rarely found in the sermons of the older Puritan divines. The dominant doctrine concerning God in the Puritan churches in the first third of the nineteenth century is fairly represented in Dr. Edward Payson's sermon on "Jehovah, a King": "Jehovah is a great king; under obligations to make laws for his subjects; the best and wisest laws possible; and to enforce those laws and inflict the threatened punishment on all who transgress them." The dominant doctrine concerning the Bible is represented by Dr. Lyman Beecher's sermon in 1817 on "The Bible a Code of Laws": "The word of God is a code of law which the Moral Governor of the Universe has given us to set forth his glory."

To Henry Ward Beecher, from that day in May when the vision was afforded to him which he has recounted, Christ was God; not a messenger sent from

God; not a Someone coming between God and the human soul to appease God and admit the human soul to the privileges of a purchased mercy; not a manifestation of the mercy of God, holding back for a little while the wrath of God, as hounds are held back by the leash until it is cut and they are set free; but God manifest in the flesh: no wrath in God that was not in Christ; no justice in God that there was not in Christ; no judgment which God has ever rendered or ever will render that Christ has not typified in his earthly judgments on Publican and Pharisee; no meekness, tenderness, sympathy, patience, long-suffering in Christ that are not in the Father whom he manifested on the earth. This to Mr. Beecher was not a theory: it was a vital experience. He honored Christ as he honored the Father; to him all revelation of God was in Christ, all revelation of duty was in Christ's life, all revelation of truth was in Christ's teaching. Criticised because he lectured in Boston upon Theodore Parker's platform, he thus replied to the intimation that he was at one with Theodore Parker in his religious beliefs: —

Could Theodore Parker worship my God? — Christ Jesus is his name. All that there is of God to me is bound up in that name. A dim and shadowy effluence rises from Christ, and that I am taught to call the Father. A yet more tenuous and invisible film of thought arises, and that is the Holy Spirit. But neither are to me aught tangible, restful, accessible. They are to be revealed to my knowledge hereafter, but now only to my

faith. But Christ stands my *manifest* God. All that
I know is of him, and in him. I put my soul into his
arms, as, when I was born, my father put me into my
mother's arms. I draw all my life from him. I
bear him in my thoughts hourly, as I humbly believe
that he also bears me. For I do truly believe that we
love each other! — I, a speck, a particle, a nothing, only
a mere beginning of something that is gloriously yet to
be when the warmth of God's bosom shall have been
a summer for my growth; — and HE, the Wonderful
Counselor, the Mighty God, the Everlasting Father,
the Prince of Peace!

How this faith grew up in Mr. Beecher, how as
a boy he was prepared for it, what it came to mean
to him, what in theological and ethical instruction
it involved, how far he was faithful to it, and what
effect his preaching of it by pen and voice has produced in the life of the American people, it will
be the purpose of this volume to show. For in
this faith we find the key to the interpretation of
his character and his career, as a preacher, a moral
reformer, an editor, a lecturer, and an author.

CHAPTER II

THE MAKING OF THE MAN

HENRY WARD BEECHER was born in Litchfield, Connecticut, June 24, 1813, the eighth child of Lyman and Roxana Foote Beecher.[1] I make no attempt to trace his genealogy farther back; those who desire to do so will find the material in the "Autobiography and Correspondence of Lyman Beecher."

Lyman Beecher was a Congregational minister, who attained in his day an eminence scarcely less than that which his son later attained. During his active pastorate (1798–1834) the country was smaller; the means of intercommunication less; there were no railroads; steamboats were just coming into use; the telegraph did not exist; newspapers were few and poorly equipped, and rarely gave reports of sermons or religious assemblages; the questions which stirred the public excited neither the passion of enthusiasm nor the passion of rancor which was aroused by the antislavery conflict and the Civil War. For these reasons, if for no other, the reputation of the

[1] The statement in the family *Biography of Rev. Henry Ward Beecher* that he was the ninth child (page 41) is evidently a slip of either pen or type, as appears from a comparison with other statements in the *Biography* and with the *Autobiography and Correspondence of Lyman Beecher.*

father never extended so widely as that of the son. But contemporaries who were familiar with both not infrequently rated the elder preacher as the equal in forcefulness and power of the younger. I recall, as one of the dim memories of my boyhood, a sermon which I heard Lyman Beecher preach in Boston something over half a century ago, probably after his retirement from the active ministry. It was directed against the doctrine that man can be saved by good works. I recall the figure of the preacher, the spectacles upon the nose while he was reading his notes and thrust up upon the forehead or sometimes held in the hand while he was extemporizing, the impassioned gestures, the torrent of words, the vehemence of conviction behind them, and the general outline of the sermon — an imaginary ledger page, with the good deeds put on the credit side, and the failures, the omissions, and the sins on the debit side, and the balance cast up at the foot of the page. More than this I do not recall. But I am sure that no sermon would be remembered by me for fifty years if it had not been one of extraordinary impressiveness. In fact there is only one other sermon, only two addresses of any kind, of that period, that have left any impression on my mind: the first, a sermon by the elder Tyng to young men; the second, the address by Daniel Webster given in 1850, in Niblo's Garden.

Both the theological and the moral issues of 1813 were very different from those of the latter half of

the nineteenth century. In theology the burning
questions were two : one, Is man a free moral agent,
or is he under unalterable decrees of an omnipotent
Creator? the other, Is man so ruined in the Fall
that he can be saved only by divine omnipotent
grace through Jesus Christ, or is he by nature a
child of God, possessing God's nature, needing little
more than the corrections which come through
normal development and healthful education, and
is Jesus Christ only a teacher to direct him and
an example for him to follow?

It seems strange now to read, in a letter of one
of Dr. Lyman Beecher's contemporaries written to
him in 1816, the following sentence : " The doctrines of free agency and sinners' immediate duty
to repent do wonders among my people. I preach
them publicly and privately. I have no fear. My
congregation the first Sabbath I preached after I
got home stared as if I was crazy. 'I am not mad,
most noble Festus.'" It is difficult for us to-day to
imagine a condition in which such preaching should
have aroused opposition, excited enthusiasm, and
produced revivals ; but such was the fact. Dr. Lyman Beecher was an earnest advocate of this, which
was then the " new theology," and he employed
freely what were then known as the " new methods :"
the prayer-meeting, the revival sermon, the inquiry
bench, rising for prayer, and the open confession of
Christ. A little later, when he moved from Litchfield to Boston, he represented the conservative tendencies in opposition to Unitarianism, as before he

had represented the progressive tendencies in opposition to Calvinism, and became by dint of his forcefulness and the earnestness of his convictions and his dramatic and oratorical ability the representative of the Orthodox, as Channing was the representative of the Unitarians. He was by nature a warrior and delighted in battle. Theology was to him no dry and jejune science, but living and practical. Truth was instrumental ; his problem always how so to use it as to stir, quicken, and develop life. He brought his theological controversies into the home circle, and set his boys arguing with him on every kind of question, political, moral, and theological. He thus developed their mental muscle, taught them to do their own thinking, and to stand by their convictions and defend them against strong opposition. He had a delightful, naive, childlike egotism, quite free from self-conceit, yet inspiring him with a kind of self-assurance which is often the precursor of victory. Henry Ward Beecher once said to me : " My father always had the angel of hope looking over his shoulder when he wrote. I have always written with the angel of sorrow perched upon my pen ; success has always come as a surprise to me." Henry Ward Beecher was a man of many moods, and it was not safe to take too seriously such a self-interpretation, but that he rightly interpreted his father I have no doubt. The father's " Autobiography and Correspondence " affords many illustrations of this wholly unconscious egotism ; one instance will suffice to make clear to the sympathetic reader this characteristic. The death of Alexander Hamilton in his duel with Aaron Burr had shocked the whole country. Dr. Lyman Beecher had taken the occasion to write and preach a sermon on dueling, which being published created no little stir. He followed it with a resolution in the synod at Newark, New Jersey, — for at this time he was settled in East Hampton, Long Island, and was in the Presbytery, — recommending the formation of societies against dueling. What ensued he thus describes : —

I anticipated no opposition. Everything seemed going straight. But next morning a strong reaction was developed, led by Dr. ——. The fact was, a class of men in his parish, politically affiliated with men of dueling principles, went to him and said the thing must be stopped. He came into the house and made opposition, and thereupon others joined, and it suddenly raised such a storm as I never was in before nor since. The opposition came up like a squall, sudden and furious, and there I was, the thunder and lightning right in my face; but I did not back out. When my turn came, I rose and knocked away their arguments, and made them ludicrous. Never made an argument so short, strong, and pointed in my life. I shall never forget it. There was a large body; house full; my opponent a D. D.; and I was only thirty, a young man nobody had ever heard of. I shall never forget the looks of Dr. Miller after I began to let off. He put on his spectacles, came round till he got right opposite to where I stood, and there he stared at me with perfect amazement. Oh, I declare! if I did not switch 'em, and scorch 'em, and stamp on 'em! It swept all before it. Dr. —— made no reply. It was the centre of old fogyism, but I mowed it down, and carried the vote of the house.[1]

From this incident the reader will correctly surmise that Dr. Lyman Beecher carried into ethical questions the same intensity of conviction and fiery earnestness which he carried into theological controversies. He was more of a theologian than his son, but he was not less a moral reformer. Drinking in his time was universal; drunkenness was common; alcoholic liquors were always provided at church ordinations, and not infrequently by the church, and charged in as a part of its expenses. It was customary to appoint a committee on temperance at the General Association, and it was customary for the committee to satisfy itself with platitudes. In 1812 a committee of the General Association of Massachusetts brought in a report of this description, the gist of it being, as Lyman Beecher afterwards summarized it, that intemperance had been for some time increasing in a most alarming manner, but that the committee were obliged to confess that they did not perceive that anything could be done. This report of inability was just the thing to stir the blood of Lyman Beecher. He rose instantly and moved the appointment of a new committee; he was necessarily made its chairman; and the next day he brought in a report which he characterizes as " the most important paper that ever I wrote." This was followed

[1] *Autobiography and Correspondence of Lyman Beecher*, vol. i. p. 153.

by a series of resolutions recommending the ministers to preach on the subject of temperance, the churches to discontinue the use of ardent spirits at church meetings, and the people to cease using them as part of hospitable entertainment in social visits, to substitute palatable and nutritious drinks in the place of alcohol in providing for the workingmen on the farm and elsewhere, and to coöperate with the civil magistrates in the execution of the laws. He did not at that time urge total abstinence. Fourteen years later he preached a famous series of sermons on temperance, which was one of the causes that led to the great Washingtonian Movement.

Such was the father of Henry Ward Beecher. The mother was not less remarkable, though in temperament and character singularly different. Roxana Foote came of a Cavalier ancestry, and her family had remained loyal to King George throughout the American Revolution. She was early confirmed in the Episcopal Church, and remained attached to its ceremonial; but the reader must remember that the Episcopal Church at that time was in its religious conceptions, if not in its theological dogmas, as Puritan as the Congregational Church. Her temperament was poetic. She was a lover of polite literature, a great lover of nature, and would surely have been an enthusiastic lover of art and music had she lived under circumstances in which she could have indulged and developed such a love. She wrote and spoke the

French language fluently; sang, accompanying
her voice on the guitar; had considerable skill in
the use of the pencil and the brush; and notable
skill in the various uses of the needle, from plain
sewing to fine embroidery. Her delicate and sensitive nature incapacitated her for certain of the
functions which at that time in New England a
pastor's wife was expected to perform; for she was
so sensitive and of so great natural timidity that
she never spoke in company or before strangers
without blushing, and was absolutely unable to
lead the devotions in the women's prayer-meetings.
Yet with this personal timidity was intermingled
that peculiar strength which comes from close and
intimate communion with God. Gentle and yet
strong, lover of peace yet glorying in her husband's
battles and in his victories, wholly at one with him
in a supreme consecration to God, her piety of
spirit and her placidity of temperament combined
to give to her an equipoise which made her the
trusted counselor of her husband, on whose judgment he depended, and in whose calm his own
more turbulent spirit found rest.

She died when Henry was but three years old,
yet her influence remained a potent factor in the
formation of his character. From her he inherited
his love of nature, of music, and of art; from her
the susceptibility to culture, which his education
never fully developed; from her that femininity
of character, that tenderness and sweetness of
spirit, which endeared him to those who knew him

best, but was almost wholly unrevealed to the
world without, and sometimes assumed by censori-
ous critics to be nothing more than a dramatic assumption. To her also must perhaps be attributed
his affection for the Book of Common Prayer,
which he loved and read, but never, I think, used
in public. I fancy he never could have become an
Episcopal clergyman ; the spontaneity of his
character, his unconventionalism, his serene disregard of traditions of every kind, would have
made it impossible for him to express his devotional spirit in words selected for or imposed upon
him by others. His love and reverence for her he
retained throughout his life. He was accustomed
to say that through his feeling for this almost unknown mother he could understand the feeling of
the devout Roman Catholic for the Virgin Mary.
Do those who die remain as guardian angels to
guide, to guard, and to inspire us ? The question
is one which it is impossible to answer. Certainly
the affirmative cannot be demonstrated, but certainly there is much to warrant the hope, if not to
sustain the hypothesis. Perhaps it is my own half
conscious experience of the influence of a mother
who died in my early childhood which makes me
the more ready to believe that this mother's personal influence over her boy of strange contradictions did not end when God took her from his
sight. About a year after the mother's death the
father married Miss Harriet F. Porter, of Portland, Maine, — " a beautiful lady, very fair, with

bright blue eyes and soft brown hair, bound round with a black velvet bandeau," but " so fair, so delicate, so elegant that we [children] were almost afraid to go near her." [1] Serene, ladylike, polished, never lacking in self-possession, but stately and not easy of approach, she inspired the children with a reverential affection, but even more with awe. It was impossible that Henry should ever have become intimate with her. His nature was too shy, hers too reserved. Yet indirectly she strongly affected his early experience by intensifying his awe of religion as something preternatural, and by cultivating in him a habit of self-inquiry and self-reproach that were quite foreign to the healthful development of so exuberant a nature.

The father, mother, and stepmother were not the only ones who exercised a strong formative influence over Henry Ward. He came into a family of brothers and sisters, each of whom possessed a strongly marked individuality. It would indeed be difficult to name another family in our times in which were so many children who in after life developed character akin to genius. Catharine, as a school-teacher, became one of the pioneers in the movement for giving woman a higher education, a movement whose consummation she did not live to see. Edward, as college president in the West and as pastor in the East, attained no inconsiderable eminence as educator, preacher, and theologian. Harriet became perhaps the most famous

[1] Mrs. Stowe: quoted in *Biography*, p. 54.

of all American novelists. This was not wholly
because a great historical situation gave to her
dramatic ability a rare opportunity of which she
availed herself in writing "Uncle Tom's Cabin."
Had she never written this, her most effective and
striking fiction, "The Minister's Wooing," would
still have made her famous. It takes a place in
the front rank of historical novels as a graphic
and vital picture of a notable epoch. Charles, as
the musical collaborator of his brother Henry in
the preparation of the "Plymouth Collection,"
was one of the earlier contributors to the cause
of congregational singing, and, although his music
no longer survives, and his editorial judgment
does not stand the test of later musical criticism,
the churches of Puritan faith and order owe him
no little debt for the impulse he gave to congregational singing. A half brother, Thomas K.
Beecher, built up in Elmira, New York, an institutional church before the institutional church
had been heard of, and it remains to this day
one of the best conceived, in its equipment, of
any of its class. So unique was the family that
the classification of humanity, suggested by some
American wit, has passed into a proverb: he
divided mankind into " the good, the bad, and the
Beechers."

There were other members of the family, too, of
whose influence in the formation of Henry's character account must be taken. There was Aunt
Esther, Lyman Beecher's half sister, who, after

the death of the mother, became the caretaker and
housekeeper; who was, as Henry Ward Beecher
once said, " so good and modest that she would
spend ages in Heaven wondering how it ever happened, that she ever got there, and that all the
angels will be wondering why she was not there
from all eternity; " in whom with this modesty
and goodness was combined the Puritan conscience
applied in that housekeeping which was her specific sphere; who was anxious, self-exacting, self-
distrustful, but never fault-finding; a close economist, keeping house for Mr. Lyman Beecher, who
was a careless though never a self-indulgent
spender; a thorough believer in the maxim that
order is the first law of Heaven; superintending a
house whose master was too impetuous and eager
to observe that law, .but whose unselfishness of
disposition prevented the friction which otherwise
would have been inevitable. There was Aunt Mary,
the mother's sister, who was a lover of literature
and fiction, and a beautiful reader, and was accustomed to read from Irving and Walter Scott to the
family circle. Although she died a few months
after Henry Ward was born, she left a sacred
memory and a sacred influence behind her. There
was Uncle Samuel, the mother's sea-captain brother,
who made occasional incursions into the family,
bringing all sorts of mementoes from foreign shores,
with exciting stories of his adventures, and whose
humorously combative nature led him to glorify
the virtues of the Turks and the pagans and the

Jews, and arouse the master of the house to long
and heated discussions, semi-theological.

There was the society of the town also to share
in moulding the character of the boy. In the first
quarter of the nineteenth century, manufacturing
was in its infancy; there were no factory towns;
and the concentration of population in great cities
had not yet begun. The English habit of living in
the country was still continued; and the best society
was found in the rural districts. There were excellent schools, which made Litchfield an educational
centre. It was a county town, and there gathered
here from time to time, for days together, leading
members of the bar. Its church was a social centre,
and it was ambitious to have an able and intellectual
preacher, and was proud of the one it had. In the
autobiography of Lyman Beecher it is said that
Count ———, who in youth had spent some years in
Litchfield as a student of the law school, in later
life, though he had in the interim moved in the
highest circles of French society, dwelt with enthusiasm on the society of Litchfield, which he declared
was the most charming in the world. Some allowance must be made for the politeness of a French-
man, and for the imperfection of an old man's
recollections, but the testimony is significant.

In such society and in such a family let the
reader imagine Henry Ward Beecher growing up.
The family government was firm but not rigid;
in general gentle, occasionally severe. Prompt obedience was required. Two or three experiences of

discipline at the father's hand were sufficient to teach this lesson; thereafter a decided word from father or mother was always sufficient. These occasions of discipline did nothing to break the fellowship between the father and the child. The father's chief daily recreations were frolics with his children. "I remember him," says Catharine Beecher, "more as a playmate than in any other character during my childhood. He was fond of playing pranks upon us, and trying the queerest experiments with us, for his amusement as well as ours. I remember once he swung me out of the garret window by the hands, to see if it would frighten me, which it did not in the least." The father was fond of fishing, and took the children often with him on his fishing excursions. He shared, too, the chores and work of the household with the boys; and often lightened the household duties with story-telling, one of the children giving, while the rest worked, the best account he could of incidents in one of Scott's novels, which they had recently read together in the family circle. A Puritan family it certainly was, in the strength of its conscience, in the authority of law, in the exactitude of obedience required. But the picture which in after years remained on the minds of the children was not like the conventional picture of the Puritan home. It is thus portrayed by Mrs Stowe: "One of the most vivid impressions of the family as it was in my childish days was of a great household inspired by the spirit of cheerfulness and hilarity, and of

my father, although pressed and driven with business, always lending an attentive ear to anything
in the way of life and social fellowship."

Outside the family there were none who exercised any very direct influence in moulding the character of the growing boy, unless possibly the very
humble serving-man, whose religion was simply
emotive and untheological, and whom Henry Ward
ever after held in grateful remembrance. I am inclined to believe, however, that Mr. Beecher's gratitude exaggerated the influence which Charles Smith
exerted upon him. There was not much to inspire
in the church services, held twice every Sunday in
the meeting-house, with its turnip-like canopy over
the minister's head, and its large square pews, and
its singers' seat, and its quaint fuguing tunes, or
in the sermons, unintended and unadapted for children; and as little was there to give true education
in the district school, in its square pine building,
blazing in the unshaded sun in summer, with its
box-iron stove red-hot in winter, and under the
rigorous and unsympathetic discipline of its sharp-
eyed school-mistress, "precise, unsympathetic, keen,
untiring."

So the boy grew up with that curious contradictory nature, so often recognized in after life as
belonging to children, so rarely recognized in the
child by those who have his training. To observers
he seemed simply a wild, careless, frolicsome boy,
full of pranks and mischief, bubbling over with
animal spirits; restless in school and in church,

lover of nature, lover of adventure. Later, when the family moved to Boston, he became a master spirit among the schoolboys, carrying into boyish battles the spirit which he had inherited from his father, which made him a leader in many a youthful campaign against the "Prince Streeters" and the "Charlestown Pigs." One incident of this boy life which he records serves as well as a hundred to illustrate his nature. In the game of "Follow Your Leader" he led his fellows a weary and perilous chase, seeing with increasing exhilaration one after another drop off and abandon him, until at length, from the bowsprit of a ship alongside the wharf, he sprang off into the deep water, clothes all on, and rose to the surface sputtering, to look back and see the last two boys standing on the bowsprit, not daring to essay the feat he had achieved.

Yet all this time, within this rough, boisterous, romping, healthy boy was another boy — tender, delicate, sensitive, shy; not so much misunderstood as absolutely not understood. His father was too busy to be his comrade in the quieter experiences of his soul, and, truth to tell, could not have understood them, no matter what leisure he might have had. The stepmother was too saintly to be serviceable to a boy who was often introversive, self-examining, self-torturing; who had only the "natural virtues," which his father's theology counted no evidence of a regenerate nature; who had never experienced conversion; who thought of

his father and his second mother as ready to die,
and of himself as not ready to die, and so of a
great gap between himself and them, growing ever
wider and wider, and certain to issue at last in' the
great gulf which separated Lazarus from Dives.
The younger generation of this age can never
understand the anguish of soul suffered by children brought up in even the more liberal schools
of Puritan theology of the olden time, in which
religion was regarded, not as the transfusion of all
life by the spirit of love and consecration, but as
a separate and preternatural experience, apart from
life, into which one could come only by a spiritual
cataclysm, called regeneration.   It is out of her
own experience that Mrs. Stowe has, in " The
Minister's Wooing," so graphically described the
effects of this theology on simple-hearted natures.

At length the love of adventure and the spirit of
unrest combined provoked in the growing boy a
resolve to go to sea.   His wise father did not oppose
him — rather commended him ; but told him that
for success in this he must have a course in mathematics and navigation, and to the boy's response,
" I am ready," answered by sending him to Mt.
Pleasant, a preparatory school at Amherst, Massachusetts.

Here came a new and potent influence in the
formation of his character. Up to this time he
had been no student, and by his instructors was
counted rather exceptionally dull, though by his
companions in play exceptionally bright.   The

teacher of mathematics at Mt. Pleasant school, W. P. Fitzgerald, taught him to conquer in studying ; the teacher of elocution, John Lovell, inspired him with patience to endure the drudgery of a daily drill. Now for the first time, at the age of fourteen, he began to put into brain activity the force and vigor which up to this time had either gone into sports or had been worse than wasted in desultory wrestling with spiritual problems too great for him. Ever after his experience at Mt. Pleasant he proved himself capable of that hard work which some one has declared to be the essence of genius. It has often been said that Mr. Beecher was not a student. If to be a student is to be patient, persistent, assid-uous in the accumulation of facts and the investi-gation of minute details, it is true Mr. Beecher never was a student. He was accustomed to get the results of such investigations from others for whose ability he always entertained the greatest respect. But if to be a student is to formulate to one's self the problem to be investigated, to gather light from all sources in its investigation, and in that light to wrestle with the problem until a solu-tion is found which one dares defend against all opposers, Mr. Beecher was preëminently a student. He was no mere omnivorous reader, browsing among books for self-indulgence, nor gathering from them simply to pass on to others, as a kind of reporter, what he had read. He both read for a purpose and used to good purpose what he read. For this capacity to study questions, to reach

results, and to defend them against all assailants,
he was indebted first of all to his father, next, so
I judge from his own reminiscences, to the Mt.
Pleasant preparatory school.

He had not yet joined the church, for he had not
been converted; but in a letter to his sister he
quite unconsciously illustrates the kind of religious
life which has grown up in him without conversion:
" I do not like," he says, " to read the Bible as
well as to pray, but I suppose it is the same as it
is with a lover, who loves to talk with his mistress
in person better than to write when she is afar off."
A little later than this there was a revival at Mt.
Pleasant, and a wave of feeling passed over him
which he thought might be conversion. His father
was quite satisfied on the subject, and partly from
a kind of shamefacedness which kept the boy from
saying he did not think he was a Christian, he " let
them take me into the Church." Like a ship built
on the land that on some moment must be launched
into the sea are some souls; like a fish born in the
sea and growing up there are others. Henry Ward
Beecher belonged to the latter class; he never was
launched and needed no launching. The churches
of the Puritans have grown wiser than they were
in his father's time, for which wisdom no little
thanks are due to Dr. Bushnell and his bitterly
criticised book on " Christian Nurture."

This is the boy who in 1830, at seventeen years
of age, entered Amherst College, in a class of forty
members. Out of the evangelical passion in the

New England churches during the early half of
the nineteenth century, of which Dr. Lyman
Beecher was so distinguished a representative, this
college was born, in 1821. It was organized to
promote the interests of evangelical religion by
providing for the education of indigent young men
for the ministry. The story of its birth is one of
persistent and indomitable enthusiasm overcoming
great obstacles. The friends of Williams College
feared the rivalry of a new institution; many of
the friends of Christian education doubted the
wisdom of establishing two colleges in western
Massachusetts; the Unitarian element in the state
saw in this new movement a new attack upon lib-
eralism, and prepared to thwart it at the outset.
It was difficult to secure an agreement among the
advocates of the evangelical faith, difficult, when
the agreement was reached, to raise the fifty thousand dollars which constituted the financial basis
for beginning the work, difficult, when the money
had been secured, and the first building had been
erected, to obtain a charter from the legislature.
But when these obstacles had been overcome, there
was no difficulty in securing students. In 1830,
when Henry Ward Beecher was ready to enter
college, Amherst had its land, two dormitories, a
chapel with recitation rooms annexed, the beginning of a college library, a faculty consisting of a
president, six professors, and one tutor, and about
two hundred pupils. Everything, however, was
on a scale of extreme simplicity. The salaries of

the professors ranged from $600 to $800 a year, the expenses of tuition from $30 to $40, board from $1 to $1.25 a week. The students took care of their rooms, made their own fires, and generally sawed their wood. The entire expenses for a four years' course did not exceed $800. The students assembled for prayers every morning at a quarter before five in the summer, and at a quarter before six in the winter. Their working-day was divided into three nearly equal portions, in each of which two or three hours were set apart for study, and each study period was followed immediately by a recitation. The college discipline was rigorous, the college regulations minute and exact. Obedience was enforced by a system of fines. There were long vacations to enable the students to add to their slender resources by teaching in the district schools.

Such was the college which Henry Ward Beecher entered in the eighteenth year of his age. He carried with him a nature of strange contradictions: a masculine robustness of nature mated to a femininity of spirit; great spontaneity of character coupled with a morbid habit of self-examination; an inborn love for church and for his fellowmen together with a hopeless endeavor to create in himself that preternatural change which was thought to be essential to Christian character; a habit of hard work, but a habit of working according to his own mood, not according to rules prescribed for him by others. His college stand-

ing is indicated by his later remark that he once
stood next to the head of his class; it was when
the class was arranged in a circle. He studied
the lessons allotted him by the college, so far as
was necessary to enable him to get through, but
no farther; but he threw himself with enthusiasm
into courses of reading and study to which his
mood impelled or his judgment guided him. In
accordance with the custom of the time he taught
school during the long winter vacation to add to
his limited means. The missionary spirit which
he had imbibed from his father already began to
ferment within him; and he conducted prayer-
meetings, gave lectures on temperance, and later
on phrenology, and preached in villages what would
be called sermons, except that he was not a minister. Once he earned ten dollars as a lecturer,
and spent it in buying an edition of Burke, the
foundation of his future library. He got no great
standing at college for scholarship, and no appointment at Commencement; but he was regarded as
one of the fine debaters in the college debating
society, and outside of it was recognized by his
classmates as an intellectual leader. He was
profoundly religious, yet perpetually perplexed by
skepticism; was alternately inspired by a great
hope and whelmed in a sort of half despair. At
the end of four years he graduated, leaving behind
him an academic record respectable but not eminent, having carried on throughout the four years
an aggressive though fitful and boyish Christian

and philanthropic work, and carrying with him
the results of a wide though desultory reading;
very much in earnest in his resolve to use his experience and his voice for the service of his fellow
men; very much in uncertainty respecting himself
and the value of his own inner life.

CHAPTER III

IN 1834 Henry Ward Beecher was graduated from Amherst College, at twenty-one years of age. During these twenty-one years America had made rapid growth in size and population, and new and complex problems were arising which the young graduate would in his later years help to solve. In 1813 the little village of Cleveland, Ohio, formed the northwestern outpost of the nation. The frontier line ran thence in a southwesterly direction to the Tennessee River, and thence in a southeasterly direction to the southern border of Georgia. In 1834 the republic had extended far to the west of this line; the Mississippi River formed its western frontier, the southern shores of Lake Erie and Lake Michigan its northern frontier. Michigan, Wisconsin, Minnesota, and Iowa were, however, still practically uninhabited, and all west of the territory now occupied by those states was untrodden wilderness. The population had increased from less than eight million to over twelve million. The increase had been nearly equally divided between North and South, but not between East and West; the centre of population was a little east of Washington. The first steamboat to make its way against the Mississippi current from New Orleans to Cincinnati had given in 1815 a prophecy of the future commercial importance of the latter city which far-seeing business men were not slow to comprehend; it promised to be the metropolis of the West, for Chicago, though an important trading-post on the frontier, was but just incorporated as a town and had a population of less than four thousand. The railroad was yet in its experimental stage. In a race run in 1829 between a locomotive and a horse, the horse outdistanced the locomotive. A year and a half later the first real railroad was operated in the state of South Carolina, and in six months thereafter a second short line of railroad between Albany and Schenectady was in operation; but as yet a railroad to be operated by a steam locomotive was looked upon by most practical business men as wholly impracticable. The "big ditch," as the Erie Canal was contemptuously called, had been dug between Albany and Buffalo, making a completed waterway between the Northwest and the ocean — the foundation of the future commercial greatness of New York City. Baltimore and Philadelphia, which had to depend upon teaming over the Alleghanies, awoke to the necessity of finding some contrivance to compete with the canal, and this necessity gave to the railroad enterprise its first considerable impulse. As yet, however, though many roads were planned, few were constructed, and as late as 1830 there were but thirty-six miles of completed roadbed in the country. When the young graduate went from Amherst College to Cincinnati, whither his father had now removed, he must have gone either by stage to Albany, by canal to Buffalo, by steamboat on Lake Erie, perhaps to Cleveland, and then again by stage across Ohio to the Ohio River, or by stage over the Alleghanies to Pittsburg and thence by boat on the Ohio to Cincinnati.

While Henry Ward Beecher was at Amherst College his father had removed from Boston to Cincinnati, to take the presidency of Lane Theological Seminary. The young metropolis of the West was described by one of the promoters of this enterprise as at the heart of four millions of people, and in twenty years to be at the heart of twelve millions — "the most important point in our nation for a great central theological institution of the first character." For Christian men were as far-seeing as commercial men, and as eager to take advantage of the opportunities which the growing West afforded. They procured a charter in 1829, secured a donation of sixty acres of land, and started the new seminary with one professor and three or four students. What the students did for instruction, when after a few months the professor was sent East to obtain funds, history does not tell. The professor failed in his endeavor and resigned. The enterprise would apparently have been abandoned but for the indomitable enterprise of one man, the Rev. F. Y. Vail, who wisely judged that to get Eastern funds Eastern confidence must first be secured, and for this purpose an Eastern man obtained to

act as president of the yet unborn institution. He
came to Boston and applied to Dr. Lyman Beecher.
" There was not on earth a place but that," said
Dr. Beecher afterwards, " I would have opened my
ears to for a moment, but I had felt, and thought,
and labored a great deal about raising up ministers,
and the idea that I might be called to teach the
best mode of preaching to young ministry of the
broad West flashed through my mind like lightning. I went home and ran in, and found Esther
alone in the sitting-room. I was in such a state of
emotion and excitement I could not speak, and she
was frightened. At last I told her. It was the
greatest thought that ever entered my soul; it filled
it, and displaced everything else." He accepted the
call. His acceptance secured a gift of twenty thousand dollars from Arthur Tappan, of New York,
whose interest in all forward movements was shown
throughout his life, both by his generous benefactions and his active services. It was a matter of
course that Henry Ward Beecher, now fully resolved upon the ministry as his life work, should
go, on graduation, to Lane Theological Seminary,
to complete his preparations under the instructions
of the father whose theological debates in the family, during the son's boyhood, had already familiarized him with theology, both abstract and applied.

Cincinnati was at this time a city of about thirty
thousand inhabitants. The seminary was outside,
in the woods, where the whistle of the quail, the
flight of the turkey, the rush of wild pigeons, were

to be heard. The father did not believe in dissociating theology and religion. He lectured during the week, and preached in the city on Sunday; carried, alternately, his theology into his sermons, and his religion into his lectures. The young student did not, so far as I can learn, get a great deal out of the regular theological course. He began writing a journal " of events, feelings, thoughts, plans, etc., just as they have met me; thus giving in part a transcript of my inner and outer life." His biographers say that they " find very little, almost nothing, concerning the regulation, work, and studies of the theological course, possibly because some other book, which has not come down to us, contains these." I think it far more probable that it was because the work and studies of the theological course, as prescribed by the authorities, did not greatly interest him. This was not because he was idle, but because his temper was such that he was never able — perhaps I should rather say never inclined — to work along lines marked out for him by others. He was an omnivorous reader, and always read to some purpose and for some result. Thus, when he had finished Scott's " Antiquary," he wrote a comparison of " The Antiquary " and " Ivanhoe; " and a little later, a critical comparison between Scott and Shakespeare. Whether his comparison is adequate or even sound is not a matter of consequence; that he wrote it illustrates the fact that his reading was thoughtful and discriminating. His studies, however, constituted by no means the whole, perhaps not even the major part, of his life. He sang in the church choir, and sometimes led it; he conducted a Bible-class, which was practically a lecture on the Bible, and gave, contemporaneously, a course of temperance lectures through the week; and he preached on Sundays, as opportunity offered, throughout the theological course. He began also to accumulate a library, which numbered early in the second year of his theological course a hundred and thirty-five volumes, intelligently selected and carefully read, only about one third of them professional books. The anti-slavery controversy was beginning to assume serious proportions. He was much more interested in it than in the theological controversies in which his father was engaged; at one time added amateur editorship to preaching, lecturing, teaching, and choir leading; at another volunteered as a special constable, and for several nights patrolled the streets of Cincinnati to protect the negroes and their friends from a mob. On the whole the picture of these seminary days, which we gather from his journal and letters, so far as published, are those rather of a zealous man of affairs than of a patient and painstaking student. It must be remembered, however, that in 1834 no such sharp line between the period of preparation and that of action was drawn as is drawn in our day. Engineering schools were practically unknown; the engineer rose from the ranks. Law schools were few and poorly patronized. John

Marshall, perhaps the greatest jurist America has ever seen, went directly from a country academy into a law office, from a law office into politics, and from politics to the bench; a single course of law lectures at William and Mary College was all the academic legal instruction he ever received. Only a minority of the ministers of that day took any theological seminary course, many of them no college course; piety, that kind of familiarity with the Bible which all children obtained through home training, and a very moderate acquaintance with the well-established theology of the time being considered an adequate equipment for preaching the Gospel. It was quite in accordance, therefore, with the spirit of the time that Henry Ward Beecher should divide his energy between academic studies and practical work, giving, I suspect, if not the larger portion of his time, certainly the larger portion of his energy and enthusiasm, to the work. Whether the modern method of keeping the student apart from life in academic pursuits for ten or fifteen years, and then plunging him at once into active life, under such pressure as makes the continuance of systematic study almost impossible, furnishes a better preparation for life than the method of our fathers, in which practice and theory were more intermingled, both in the period of study and in the period of work, may be open to question; I am inclined to think a partial reversion to the older method would be an improvement on the method now pursued.

Throughout the seminary course there were periods in which Henry Ward Beecher was subject to serious skepticism and to serious spiritual depression. At times he thought of abandoning the ministry altogether, on account of his theological doubts, — for they were theological rather than religious; at other times he resolved to preach whether Presbytery approved or not. He would at all events maintain his independence. " I must," he said, " preach the Gospel as it is revealed to me, not as it is laid down in the schools." It was at some time in this seminary course that he had that experience of Christ, as a supreme manifestation of God, which I have recorded in the opening of the first chapter of this volume. From the time of that revelation he seems never to have had a doubt respecting his mission, or a hesitancy about endeavoring to fulfill it, only hesitation about the path to be taken toward its fulfillment.

About twenty miles south of Cincinnati was the little village of Lawrenceburg, Indiana, on the Ohio River. It had at one time hoped to be the metropolis of the West; it is hardly larger to-day than when Henry Ward Beecher settled there, while Cincinnati has become one of America's great cities. Here was a feeble Presbyterian church, consisting of twenty persons. In one of his sermons Mr. Beecher thus graphically describes his early experiences there : —

I remember that the flock which I found gathered in the wilderness consisted of twenty persons. Nineteen of them were women, and the other was nothing. I remember the days of our poverty, our straitness. I was sexton of my own church at that time. There were no lamps there, so I bought some; and I filled them and lit them. I swept the church, and lighted my own fire. I did not ring the bell, because there was none to ring. I opened the church before prayer-meetings and preaching, and locked it when they were over. I took care of everything connected with the building.

His journal contains some definite resolves, on some of which I think he instinctively acted all his life long: " Remember you can gain men easily if you get round their *prejudices* and put truth in their minds; but *never* if you attack prejudices." " My people must be alert to make the church agreeable, to give *seats*, and wait on *strangers*." " Secure *a large congregation;* let this be the *first* thing." His resolution to " visit widely " I do not think he ever fulfilled. What the Methodist contemporary in Lawrenceburg said respecting Mr. Beecher there, Mr. Beecher's subsequent life confirms: " Mr. Beecher could outpreach me, but I could outvisit him." The church voted him a salary of two hundred and fifty dollars, which seems to have dwindled in the payment to one hundred and fifty; the Home Missionary Society added one hundred and fifty more. Three hundred dollars was a small salary, even in those days, on which to marry and begin housekeeping, but Mr. Beecher's courage always overtopped his caution. With characteristic impetuosity, as soon as he had been formally called and before he had been formally ordained, he wrote to Miss Eunice Bullard, to whom he was engaged, suggesting that their marriage be celebrated shortly after his ordination, and then followed and almost overtook his letter with a proposal to have the wedding first and the ordination afterwards. This sort of impetuosity generally succeeds in such cases, and it did in this case. They were married August 3, 1837, left New York a little later, and, traveling day and night, reached Cincinnati the last of August. Four children of this marriage survived Mr. Beecher: Henry Barton; William C.; Herbert F.; and Harriet E.; the latter married the Rev. Samuel Scoville, a Congregational clergyman. The family life of Mr. Beecher has been written by the son, William C., and the son-in-law, Samuel Scoville, assisted by the widow, Mrs. Henry Ward Beecher. To that volume the reader of this is referred for all the domestic side of Mr. Beecher's life. It would not be seemly either to repeat here what they have written, or to supplement it by anything additional.

The ordination of Mr. Beecher was not so simple an affair as he had perhaps anticipated it would be. The battle between the Old School and the New School party in the Presbyterian Church was already in progress. Lyman Beecher represented the New School or progressive element. The Miami Presbytery was largely composed of Scotch-Irish Presbyterians, whose views were what they would call consistently, what their opponents would call extremely, Calvinistic. Henry Ward Beecher was familiar with theological distinctions, little as he cared for them. He had been trained in them from his boyhood. He was always quick-witted, and never quicker than when under mental excitement. His resolve to get round prejudices, not to attack them, was put to the test, and his skill in fulfilling that resolve was demonstrated. In spite of a prolonged and hostile examination, he stood his ground, and, if orthodoxy alone had been in question, would have been ordained in spite of opposition, but when a resolution was introduced requiring the candidate to pledge his adhesion to the Old School Presbyterian General Assembly, and so part company with his father, who was a leader in the New School party, he peremptorily refused, at the hazard of relinquishing his church and the little salary which was pledged to him, and beginning his married life with nothing. But his little church cared more for its minister than for the theological controversy, and promptly declared itself independent of the Presbytery.

The two years of his ministry in Lawrenceburg were years of poverty, but of joyful self-denial. The bride and groom lived in two rooms over a stable at a rental of forty dollars per annum. They furnished the rooms with second-hand furniture — a little of it bought, more of it given. The preacher welcomed gifts of cast-off clothing, and thought himself "sumptuously clothed." His little church was crowded, but his people were better satisfied with his preaching than he was himself. He has not recorded any notable spiritual results from it. The sermon was yet to him an end, not a means to an end. He knew how to make a sermon that would interest, but not how so to use a sermon as to affect character. After two years of ministry in this discouraging field, where he worked hard for little pay and with no considerable results, he accepted a call, thrice repeated, and removed to Indianapolis.

The growth of this country has been so rapid, and the changes in its conditions so kaleidoscopic, that it is impossible for us now to realize the material, social, and moral conditions which existed less than three quarters of a century ago. In 1839, when Mr. Beecher moved to Indianapolis, it was an unkempt village, growing up in the midst of a wilderness. A few houses, clustered together, constituted the centre of the future town. From this centre houses of wood straggled off in every direction. Many of the unoccupied squares were fenced in, so as to constitute paddocks, in each one of which one or more milch cows were kept during the day. The passages between the squares, into which, according to Western fashion, the town was laid out, were overgrown with dog-fennel, save where wagon tracks had made a sinuous road, avoiding a stump on the one side and a mud hole on the other. When these roadways became impassable some enterprising traveler opened a new one through the dog-fennel. In winter these ways were often impassable by reason of mud, in summer insufferable by reason of dust. There was no sewerage; the town was flat; and the water stood in pools, or found its way slowly through open ditches, often choked up with weeds or refuse. Save in the very centre of the town, there were no sidewalks; such as existed were mere strips of gravel, with depths of mud on either side. Pioneers coming hither from the East to make their fortune had foreseen a great future for this embryo capital. They had already planned six railroads to centre in this town, for the travel which did not yet exist, and the legislature, more audacious than private capital, had undertaken to begin their construction. A state bank had been organized, a state-house built, a fire-engine company formed, and a great scheme of public works for the improvement of the anticipated city had been devised and entered upon. The result of this enterprise had shown that, in material as in spiritual things, faith without works is dead. The vigorously engineered boom had collapsed, and in 1839 and for several years thereafter the village was suffering from the consequences of too much misdirected energy.

As a result of the division of the Presbyterian Church into Old School and New School, fifteen members of the First Presbyterian Church had withdrawn to found the Second Presbyterian Church. The rivalry between the two churches was intensified, rather than lessened, by the fact that both possessed the same traditions and the same creed. The new church was worshiping in a hall, but had already projected the construction of a meeting-house. Mr. Beecher's promised salary in Indianapolis was twice his nominal salary in Lawrenceburg. But six hundred dollars a year was not munificent even then; it may be reasonably estimated as about equivalent to twelve hundred dollars in our own time. The first of the Indiana railroads had been built from Madison as far as Vernon, twenty miles on its way to the capital, and it is said that Mr. Beecher and his wife took the first train over this uncompleted railroad, riding this twenty miles in a box-car; the rest of the journey, it is to be presumed, they took over the miry roads, through the untraveled wilderness, in a springless wagon.

From the scanty materials furnished by such books as W. R. Hallaway's "History of Indianapolis," and J. P. Dunn's "History of Indiana," and the letters of Mr. Beecher himself, it is possible to form some conception, though vague and inadequate, of the kind of population in which the next eight years of Mr. Beecher's life were to be spent. The earlier settlers of Indiana were French Catholics, coming up from Louisiana and down from Canada. They possessed both the virtues and the vices characteristic of the French pioneer. They were kindly, humane, easy-going. They brought slavery with them, but it was a form of slavery quite different from that which later prevailed in the Anglo-Saxon portions of the continent. Their laws provided for the education of the slaves in the Roman Catholic faith, and for the protection of marriage relations, and forbade excessive and cruel punishments ; in brief, it was, to quote Mr. Dunn, " as endurable as any slavery could be." The ordinance of 1787, under which the whole Northwest Territory was organized, forbade slavery; but it was strenuously contended, with considerable support from judicial decisions, that this ordinance did not forbid the continuance of slave relations which existed before the ordinance was passed ; and in fact, up to the admission of Indiana to the Union as a state, December 11, 1816, slavery in a mild form still continued throughout the territory. In the judgment of these French settlers there was nothing immoral in drinking, or even in drunkenness, and it must be said, in explanation if not in defense of their position, that drunkenness with them rarely led to the brawls and the violence which it so often inspires in the Celtic and Anglo-Saxon races. Gambling was also looked upon as an entirely innocent recreation, though again it must be said, in explanation if not in defense, that the gambling was generally for sums which the gamblers could afford to lose, was conducted according to the rules of the game, and was inspired, not by greed and covetousness, but by the pleasurable excitements incident to such games of chance.

But into this population had come a new element, bringing with it a much more strenuous life.

Pioneers from the Atlantic seaboard, mostly from the middle states, had come hither, seeking their fortune. They brought an intensity of nature wholly foreign to the French character. They were more thrifty but more greedy of gain; more enterprising but harder and less good-natured. When they gambled, it was to make money; when they drank, they quarreled; and drinking and gambling being both against their conscience, demoralized their character and became gross and flagrant vices. When enterprise gambles, it becomes professional gambling, and professional gambling is rarely if ever honest. The fact that Indianapolis was the capital of the state brought to it a class of politicians whose character was not always above reproach and intensified the tendency toward the twin vices of drunkenness and gambling. Street brawls were frequent, and were sometimes of a ferocious character. "Fighting," says Mr. Hallaway, "in the early days of the capital was quite a feature in its social or unsocial life. No Saturday passed without one, or commonly half a dozen brawls." One incident which Mr. Hallaway narrates serves to illustrate, better than any general description could do, the rude character of the people and the period. A certain bully of the town, often drunken and violent, and when so an unendurable terror to his neighbors, made his appearance at a Methodist camp-meeting. His drunken threats terrified the congregation, and threatened to break up the services. The Methodist preacher once or twice

requested him to go away in peace; finding this
unavailing, he came down from his pulpit, gave the
fellow the first thrashing he had ever had in his
life, and then went back and finished his sermon.
The thrashing seems to have been effectual — perhaps did more good than the sermon; at all events,
as the story goes, with a dramatic fitness quite
worthy of Shakespeare, the bully, humiliated at
being thrashed by a preacher, and unable to with-
stand the jeers of his comrades, reformed, and lived
the rest of his life, and died at last, a temperate
and self-respecting citizen.

It will be a mistake, however, if the reader should
get the impression that Indianapolis was wholly
given over to these influences. If some of the immigrants from the East had left their religion and
their conscience behind them, there were others
who brought into the religious life of the nascent
metropolis the same energy and enterprise which
they brought into its commercial activities. There
were some vigorous and efficient churches, and
some strong and effective preachers, in the place.
Four years before Mr. Beecher's arrival there had
been organized, by the moral leaders in the community, an agricultural society, a benevolent society, and a literary society; all of course undenominational, yet all working in harmony with the
Christian churches of the place, and indirectly
supported by them. Within four years after his
arrival, there was organized a state hospital for
the insane, of which Mr. Beecher was made one of

the trustees, and a female collegiate institute for
the higher education of girls, and musical taste had
been sufficiently developed to call for the opening
of a piano factory. One of the noblest Christian
men I have ever known must have been already
exerting a considerable influence in Indianapolis.
Sympathetic but never sentimental; never conceal-
ing his faith, and never obtruding it; refusing
upon principle to accumulate wealth, though he
had good opportunity to do so; using alike his
money and his time in the service of his Master
and his fellow men — " Uncle Billy Jackson," as he
was affectionately called through all that community, bore a witness to the sweetness and the strength
of a true Christian character, such as transcends
all eloquence of the voice. He illustrated a certain
type of Christian character, careless of creeds,
" zealous of good works," possessing the spirit of
Christianity but not very regardful of its forms,
with the enterprise, the energy, and the unconventionalism of the West directed in spiritual channels and to spiritual ends, such as is rarely seen
except in new communities during their formative
period. Men and women of this type, with others
less original but not less devout, gathered about
Mr. Beecher, and supported him in his work. Of
them he subsequently said : —

My memory of these persons will never grow dim.
My heart goes out to them; and I guess they think of
me. I think they requite all the love I bestow upon
them. When dying, many and many of them have sent

me messages. Many and many of them, as they parted from this shore, bore testimony that the sweetest hours of their life were those passed under my instructions, and sent back messages of encouragement to me. How many times I think of five or six rare, beautiful, sainted ones, who sent me messages from the other side — I think they were halfway across at any rate — that my preaching of Christ was true; that they had gone so far that they felt it to be true! I felt as though they were messages from heaven itself. And shall I have under my own roof spirits that are more sacred to me than these?

From the beginning the new preacher was what men call a success. Notwithstanding malarial attacks, to which, in common with all his neighbors, he was sometimes subject, he was generally over-flowing with health and energy. His vivid imagination, redundant rhetoric, and dramatic personification of every character he wished to portray, his musical voice, capable of every intonation, from thunder of indignation to gentlest and softest note of invitation, and, behind all, his absolute freedom from cant and every suspicion of professionalism, gave him unexampled power in the pulpit. His animal spirits, hopeful temper, humaneness of disposition, which made him unfeignedly interested in everything that interested any of his fellows, attracted to him socially all sorts and conditions of men. His lack of conventionality, illustrated by the fact that he was the first minister to be seen with a felt hat, and that he did not hesitate to take an active part in painting his house, or carrying

home a load of groceries in a wheelbarrow, would
have subjected him to criticism in an older community, but in this heterogeneous population it won
for him additional commendation. The hall which
constituted the temporary meeting-place of his
church was crowded from the first, and at the close
of the first year the church had constructed and
moved into a permanent and more commodious
edifice, which in turn was thronged. From the first
his church was a church of strangers. The members
of the legislature attended it almost in a body.
The rule that he had laid down for himself in Lawrenceburg — "My people must be alert to make
the church agreeable, to give seats, and wait on
strangers" — was carried out in Indianapolis, as
it was subsequently in Brooklyn. He was always
more interested in preaching to sinners than to
saints, to skeptics than to believers, to the world
than to the church. In this respect he was essentially an evangelist, and would not have remained
long in any church whose doors were not hospit-
ably open to all the people. That he had crowded
and attentive congregations never satisfied him.
Years afterwards, in Brooklyn, when, as the result
of some sermon, an unexpected conversion followed,
and some one in prayer-meeting spoke of the arrow
shot at a venture accomplishing its mission, Mr.
Beecher replied: "I never shoot an arrow at a
venture; I always aim at a mark, though I may
not hit the mark I aim at." It was in Indianapolis, if we may trust Mr. Beecher's recollection,

that he first began to recognize this fundamental principle underlying all successful preaching. It is this which distinguishes the sermon from an essay or a literary address. If it be a true sermon, it has a definite object in the preacher's mind. It is not an end, but a means to an end. The subject is to be chosen, the text selected, the line of argument or exposition pursued, the illustrations employed, the rhetoric adapted — all to this one definite end which, from first to last, the preacher has in view. In expounding this truth Mr. Beecher disavows any claim for originality. "Others had learned this," he says. "It was the secret of success in every man who ever was eminent for usefulness in preaching. But no man can inherit experience; it must be born in each man for himself." It was in Indianapolis that this experience was born in him; and without this experience he never would have been the great preacher he became. He labored continuously and zealously for revivals. At one time he preached seventy nights in succession; at another he rode two days through the forests, to Terre Haute, to join with Dr. Jewett, the Congregational preacher there, in revival services. The memory of those services, of that preaching, and of the house-to-house and store-to-store visiting which the two preachers conducted in connection with the services, remained a significant and sacred memory when I went to become the successor of Dr. Jewett in Terre Haute in 1865.

Mr. Beecher's active labors did not prevent industrious study. He continued his accumulation of a library. He went over the four Gospels, compiling them and classifying their incidents and teachings according to a method of his own, and in the process familiarizing himself with their most vital truths. He added editorial to pastoral labors. There were nothing but political papers in the state at the time. At the request of the "Indiana Journal" Mr. Beecher undertook to edit a department in it, to be printed monthly, under the title "Western Farmer and Gardener." Any one who is familiar with Loudon's cyclopedias of horticulture and agriculture, will, I think, agree with me that, however valuable as authorities, they do not appeal to the imagination. Mr. Beecher supplied the imagination. He read and re-read in these cyclopedias, which he found in the state library, and invested them with pictorial character by his own creative mind. "In our little one-story cottage," he says, "after the day's work was done, we pored over these monuments of an almost incredible industry, and read, we suppose, not only every line, but much of it many times over; until at length we had a topographical knowledge of many of the fine English estates quite as intimate, we dare say, as was possessed by many of their truant owners." Only a man who possessed the power of creating a picture, provided he was given pigments and a canvas, could have obtained such a knowledge by such a process. How vivid this

creative work was is illustrated by a curious incident which I had from his own lips. He wrote a
description of some remarkable flower, the name
of which I have now forgotten, which was copied
far and wide as a rare portrait of a rare plant.
Some years afterward the gardener in an Eastern
hothouse showed him a specimen of the flower
which he had so graphically described. Mr.
Beecher asked its name, whereat the astonished
and indignant gardener, thinking his guest was
chaffing, told Mr. Beecher, to his astonishment,
that he was looking on the original of his own
description, and could hardly believe Mr. Beecher's
solemn assertion that he had never set eyes on the
flower before.

The study of men now began to grow with Mr.
Beecher into a habit which was continued throughout his life. As a boy at college he had taken up
phrenology and put into the study of it much more
enthusiasm than he did into scholastic philosophy;
he accepted in the main its craniology; observed
critically the shape of men's heads, their complexion, the color of their eyes and hair; classified
them according to their temperaments, and judged
of them accordingly. This method of study, entered
upon in an amateurish way in college, became now
instinctive. But it was men not phrenology which
interested him, and phrenology only because it was
a means of studying men. His interest in men
was both personal and professional; the two were
so intermingled that it would be as impossible for

his biographer as I doubt not it was for him to
discriminate between them. He mixed with all
sorts of men, partly because all sorts of men interested him dramatically, partly because he wished
to study them as a lawyer studies his jury, or as a
doctor studies his patients. It is said of Christ
that he knew what was in men; Mr. Beecher made
it his business to learn what is in man — the average man, the merchant, the lawyer, the politician,
the man of the street and the shop. He was as
audacious in his disregard of social distinctions as
was his Master; as careless of what people would
say or think. When in his course of "Lectures to
Young Men," of which I shall speak more fully
presently, he wished to depict the perils of gambling, then the popular vice in Indianapolis, he
succeeded, I know not by what method, in getting
one of the gambling fraternity to visit him in his
study, and describe to him the practices of the
profession, as a novelist might have done had he
wished to dramatize the vice. The result was a
description so realistic and vivid as to stir the
whole capital as it had never been stirred on that
subject before. Yet his professional interest in
humanity was only an incident in an interest which
was far wider. All life appealed to him; all
opportunity summoned him; every kind of achievement had attractions for him. Washington Hall
took fire. "Mr. Beecher," Mr. Hallaway tells us
in his "History of Indianapolis," "was one of the
foremost in carrying the hose-pipe right into the

burning portion of the house, and after two hours'
work, came out a mass of soot and dirt and ice
and blood from his cut hands; but with the fire
subdued." Yet these and kindred incidents were
but incidents; his work was that of a preacher,
and to preaching everything else in his life was
subordinated.

Mr. Beecher's preaching at this period of his
life was preëminently revival preaching; but the
reader would misapprehend its nature if he thought,
from this characterization of it, that it was devoted
to producing emotional excitements. Emotional it
certainly was, for the young preacher threw his
heart into everything he said; he believed, to use
Paul's phrase, "with the heart unto righteousness." But with him the one clause was as essential as the other. He was preëminently a practical
preacher. His three sermons on slavery produced,
in their way, as real an impression in Indianapolis
as his father's six sermons on intemperance had
produced nineteen years before in Connecticut,
though the impression was more local and more
temporary. But his most distinctive and most permanent work in his Indianapolis pastorate was his
course of " Lectures to Young Men." These are,
indeed, so far as I know, the only sermons of his
Indianapolis ministry which have been preserved.[1]
They illustrate all the combined characteristics of

[1] One special sermon and one address delivered in the West
were printed, but they are out of print. See Bibliography in end
of this volume.

his power as a preacher : his knowledge of men ; his grasp of moral principles ; his quick detection of hypocrisies and false pretenses with which vices are disguised ; his logical power of orderly arrangement of thought ; his artistic power of graphic portraiture ; his directness of purpose ; his incisiveness of speech ; and, above all, his absolute courage. I wish it were possible to transfer to these pages the whole of his lecture on " Gamblers and Gambling," and ask the reader to consider it as delivered by a soul on fire with an eager purpose to save young men, using voice, face, and gesture, all thoroughly trained instruments of expression, and spoken to a community in which gambling constituted a recognized and profitable profession.

His text is the picture of the soldiers gambling at the foot of the Cross. He begins by describing the vice of gambling ; portrays the first steps — a comparatively innocent wager of a sixpence over a pack of cards ; traces the downward progress, as he has seen it himself, and sets, as in a Rogues' Gallery, the photographic likenesses of the different types of gamblers — the taciturn, quiet gambler ; the jolly, roystering gambler ; the lying, cheating gambler ; the broken-down lawyer or politician, turned gambler. Next he traces the evil of gambling to its source and spring — the passion for excitement ; and describes the evils which it begets — idleness, the overthrow of domesticity, the provocation to other vices, especially drink and dishonesty ; all this given in words which, even now, read in a wholly different atmosphere, and sixty years after they were uttered, are aflame with the speaker's indignation. He ends his sermon with four pictures portraying the successive scenes in a gambler's life. Two of these scenes I transfer to these pages as an illustration of the type of Mr. Beecher's oratory in 1840, though with full consciousness that these paragraphs, wrested from their connection, do his oratory injustice.

Scene the third. Years have passed on. He has seen youth ruined, at first with expostulation, then with only silent regret, then consenting to take part of the spoils; and, finally, he has himself decoyed, and stripped them without mercy. Go with me into that dilapidated house, not far from the landing at New Orleans. Look into that dirty room. Around a broken table, sitting upon boxes, kegs, or rickety chairs, see a filthy crew dealing cards smouched with tobacco, grease, and liquor. One has a pirate-face burnished and burnt with brandy; a shock of grizzly, matted hair, half covering his villain eyes, which glare out like a wild beast's from a thicket. Close by him wheezes a white-faced, dropsical wretch, vermin-covered, and stenchful. A scoundrel Spaniard and a burly negro (the jolliest of the four) complete the group. They have spectators, — drunken sailors, and ogling, thieving, drinking women, who should have died long ago, when all that was womanly died. Here hour draws on hour, sometimes with brutal laughter, sometimes with threat and oath and uproar. The last few stolen dollars lost, and temper too, each charges each with cheating, and high words ensue, and blows; and the whole gang burst out the door, beating, biting, scratching, and rolling over and over in the dirt and dust. The worst,

the fiercest, the drunkest of the four is our friend who
began by making up the game.

Scene the fourth. Upon this bright day stand with
me, if you would be sick of humanity, and look over that
multitude of men kindly gathered to see a murderer
hung. At last a guarded cart drags on a thrice-guarded
wretch. At the gallows' ladder his courage fails. His
coward feet refuse to ascend; dragged up, he is supported by bustling officials; his brain reels, his eye
swims, while the meek minister utters a final prayer by
his leaden ear. The prayer is said, the noose is fixed,
the signal is given; a shudder runs through the crowd
as he swings free. After a moment his convulsed limbs
stretch down and hang heavily and still; and he who
began to gamble to make up a game, and ended with
stabbing an enraged victim whom he had fleeced, has
here played his last game, — himself the stake.

No doubt the modern critic will condemn these
pictures as over-oratorical, as he will condemn
Hogarth's pictures of "The Rake's Progress" as
theatrical; for what the second are in art, the first
are in literature. But oratory is to be measured
by its practical effectiveness. It is an instrument
for producing results, and the instrument must be
adapted to the time, the place, the circumstance;
the orator is himself in some sense a product of
that time and place and circumstance. It is doubtful whether the oratory of Daniel Webster would
hold the United States Senate to-day; it is certain
that the oratory of Rufus Choate would not win
from the juries of to-day the verdicts he was accustomed to win from the juries of his time. Mr.

Beecher's later preaching in a different community possessed a different quality, as we shall see. The one conclusive answer to all criticisms on his oratory in Indianapolis in 1840 is the fact that the year following their delivery, and, as there is good reason to believe, in no small measure as a consequence of their delivery, the professional gamblers were driven out of Indianapolis by a committee organized to carry on a war against them, and threatening them with prosecutions which they thought it best to avoid by flight.

Thus throughout the eight years of Mr. Beecher's pastorate in Indianapolis he was more than a parish minister; he was preacher, editor, moral reformer, public citizen. Throughout those years the popular judgments respecting him were as conflicting as they were in his later life. He was variously regarded with love, with admiration, with distrust, with dread, with bitter hatred. " Woe unto you," said Christ, " when all men speak well of you! " Never in his ministry did Mr. Beecher fall under this condemnation. He paid little heed to the theological discussions which were at that time the subject of heated debate in the Presbyterian Church. To men who regarded religion as identical with theology his indifference to theology seemed to be irreligion. His sense of humor confirmed this impression in the minds of that considerable class who think that a man cannot be serious unless he is always solemn. His disregard of social conventionalism shocked the taste of some, his disre-

gard of religious conventionalism made him seem
irreverent to others. He was by nature a radical
and a reformer. To those who regard social safety
as dependent upon the preservation of the established order he appeared, as Paul did to the same
class of minds in the first century, as one bent on
turning the world upside down ; they dreaded him.
To the lewd fellows of the baser sort he was especially obnoxious. He did not concern himself with
the question of the Fall, or the extent or degree
of Total Depravity, and already foreshadowed, by
his indifference to these doctrines, his later re-
pudiation of them. But if he did not preach
against sin in the abstract, he acquainted himself
with the sins which were current and popular in
the city in which he ministered, and described
them in scathing terms, and condemned them with
a fiery indignation, of which the quotation I have
given above furnishes a single illustration. The
men who profited by drunkenness and gambling
found their traffic interfered with, and felt the
latent moral sense of the community aroused
against them, and they hated him. More than
once he was threatened with assault; but he never
believed in non-resistance ; he was vigorous and
muscular ; and though I do not know that he was
familiar with the art of boxing, it is certain that,
had he been assailed, he would have lacked neither
the will nor the power to make a vigorous defense.
He was absolutely fearless, and this was itself a
protection. On one occasion it is narrated of him

that a would-be assailant met him on the street,
pistol in hand, and demanded of him a retraction
of some utterance of the preceding Sunday. " Take
it back right here," he demanded, with an oath,
" or I will shoot you on the spot." " Shoot away,"
was the preacher's response, as he walked calmly
on. Whether the would-be assassin was cowed
by the preacher's calmness, or whether he only
intended a threat which he did not mean to carry
out, the shooting did not take place.

But if Mr. Beecher was distrusted, dreaded, and
hated by some classes in the community, he was
admired and loved by others. To his dying day
he retained a boyish nature. His love for children,
his unaffected and spontaneous interest in their life
and in all their sports drew the children to him.
" Children and dogs," he once said, " are good
judges of human nature." He stood this test well.
There are some persons whose sympathetic nature
is chiefly receptive — they need sympathy; there
are others whose sympathy enables them to understand the perplexities, the burdens, and the sorrows
of others, and whose strength makes them a tower
of refuge into which the pursued may flee. Such
was Mr. Beecher's nature ; his sympathy was a
door at which any one might knock, through which
any one in any kind of trouble might enter. This
combination of sympathy and strength drew to
him the troubled and distraught. Of pastoral
work, in the conventional sense of that term, he
did very little; but he rendered personal help,

through personal sympathy, to many who were not
in his church or regular attendants upon his ministry. His interest in public questions, his knowledge of actual conditions, his audacity in describing them as they existed, his courage in confronting
them, and in challenging to battle those who lived
by the weaknesses, the follies, and the vices of
mankind, fascinated the strong men of the community, and drew them to hear him; many went
away to criticise, but returned again, attracted in
spite of themselves. His unfeigned love of his fellow men, his indomitable faith in them and hope
for them, inspired similar faith and hope and love
in others; for these are qualities which are always
contagious. His presentation of God as a Father
of infinite compassion, whose character is revealed
in the earthly life of Jesus Christ, was, in that time
and place, extraordinarily novel; men knew not
what to make of it; and curiosity commingled
with higher motives to attract audiences eager to
hear this strange gospel. The sincerity and simplicity of the preacher's faith, and his unmistak-
able access to God in public prayer, with whom he
talked as with a friend in familiar intercourse,
appealed to the truly devout souls, and brought to
him that kind of gratitude and affection which the
soul always feels toward one who has brought him
into a new fellowship with God. His message was
interpreted with a freshness of thought, a vividness
of imagination, a power of impassioned feeling,
and an oratorical skill, which had become to him a

second nature; but these outward qualities would never have given him his influence had they not been instruments for the expression of a gospel of life and love. His reputation extended throughout the state. When men came up to the capital they went as matter of course to hear Henry Ward Beecher, if they remained in the city over Sunday. Saints and sinners alike crowded to hear him. The echoes of his fame extended beyond the boundaries of the state. He began to be heard of on the Atlantic seaboard. Simultaneously he received two invitations — one to become assistant pastor in the old established and famous Park Street Congregational Church, of Boston, then, next to the Old South Church in Boston, the most influential one of the denomination in the United States; the other to the just organized Plymouth Church of Brooklyn. He had expected to spend his life out in the West; but his life in the West proved to be only a preparation for a larger life of national influence and importance.

CHAPTER IV

OPPOSITE the lower end of Manhattan Island, and separated from it by the East River, Long Island rises in a precipitous bluff from sixty to seventy feet above the tidal water at its base. This bluff extends along the river for nearly a mile, and early became a residence district for merchants doing business in the adjoining city. The region still bears the name of Brooklyn Heights, or in local parlance, "The Heights." In 1847 Brooklyn, which had been incorporated thirteen years before, had become a city of sixty thousand inhabitants; New York contained half a million of inhabitants, and extended from the Battery to Fourteenth Street, beyond which was open country. On the northern edge of "The Heights," where the hill slopes down to the river, was a Presbyterian church. The worshipers had found its location unsatisfactory because too far from the centre of the aristocratic section, all of which lay to the south; to the north was, and still is, a population to which a church may minister, but which can do little to build up a church. The church had therefore purchased lots farther south, on "The Heights," and they offered their Orange

Street property for sale. Half a dozen earnest Congregationalists interested, as subsequent history showed, less in Congregationalism than in that theological and civic liberty for which the Puritan churches have historically stood, decided to purchase this property and make it a nesting-place for a second Congregational church in the city of Brooklyn. They purchased the property for twenty thousand dollars, and then looked about for a preacher, a church, and a congregation. At that time the great religious and philanthropic societies were accustomed to hold their annual meetings during one week in May, which was accordingly designated Anniversary Week. Mr. William T. Cutter, one of the men interested in the new enterprise, who had heard Mr. Beecher in the West, secured from one of the missionary societies an invitation to him to deliver the annual address or sermon on this Anniversary Week. Thus brought to New York, it was not difficult to secure his consent to preach in the Orange Street church edifice on Sunday. He afterwards said that he accepted the invitation to deliver the missionary address in order "to urge young men to go West, to show what a good field the West was, and to cast some fiery arrows at men that had worked there and got tired and slunk away and come back. . . . I came East not knowing what I did; it was a trap." The unconscious candidate of the unborn church produced the impression which Mr. Cutter believed he would produce. Early in June a church of twenty-one members was organized, and a call was at once extended to Mr. Beecher to become its pastor. An almost simultaneous call to the Park Street Church in Boston was promptly declined; with more hesitation and after considerable delay the call to Brooklyn was accepted. A few sentences from a private letter, written in the preliminary correspondence before the question was settled, indicate the spirit with which the young preacher entered upon his new field. As the letter expresses with great clearness and evident sincerity the purpose which animated Mr. Beecher throughout his career, it is worth quoting at some length.

But if ever I come to you or go to any other place, although I have no plans as to situations, I have, I hope, an immovable plan in respect to the objects which I shall pursue. So help me God, I do not mean to be a *party man*, nor to head or follow any partisan effort. I desire to aid in a *development of truth* and in the production of goodness by it. I do not care in *whose hands* truth may be found, or in what communion; I will thankfully take it of *any*. Nor do I feel bound in any sort to look upon untruth or mistake with favor because it lies within the sphere of any church to which I may be attached.

I do not have that mawkish charity which seems to arise from regarding all tenets as pretty much alike — the charity, in fact, of indifference — but another sort: a hunger for what is true, an exultation in the sight of it, and such an estimate and glory in the truth as it is in Christ that no distinction of sect or form shall be for one moment worthy to be compared with it. I will overleap anything that stands between me and truth. Whoever loves the Lord Jesus Christ in *sincerity and in truth* is my *brother*. He that doeth God's will was, in Christ's judgment, His mother, His sister, His brother, His friend, His disciple.

On the first Sunday of his public ministry, October 10, 1847, the preacher made his position perfectly clear. His morning sermon was on Jesus Christ as the source of true religion, and the power of personal character; the evening sermon on the relation of the Church to the public ethical problems of the day — specifically, its duty to deal honestly and courageously with intemperance and with slavery. The reader of the present generation cannot easily comprehend what such an utterance as this indicated in the first half of the nineteenth century, in what was practically part of the commercial metropolis of the nation. Not only were the great missionary societies silent on the subject of slavery, not only were the churches, with rare exceptions, equally silent, but this silence was defended and eulogized. Religion was regarded as a purely personal matter; its office to make right the relations of the individual soul with God. This done, it was assumed that the relations between individuals would of themselves become righteous, and the social duties due from man to his fellow men would be performed. Hence the pulpit had little to say respecting the purely temporal and social aspects of life, and, with rare exceptions, nothing concerning its political aspects, except on special occasions, as on fast days and thanksgiving

days, and even then only to a limited extent. The
revolution in preaching, which, as a result has
made the pulpit a powerful force in dealing with
every-day problems, — a revolution in which Mr.
Beecher was a foremost leader, — has been so successful that those who know only the American
pulpit of to-day can hardly imagine what it was in
1847. No doubt the desire for peace, the fear of
disturbing the churches, the consciousness in the
preachers of inability to deal with the complicated
problem of slavery for which they had received no
special training, the spirit of conservatism which
makes any innovation seem difficult if not dangerous, and the strong political and commercial interests banded together in the support of the slavo-
cracy combined to make silence easy and speech
difficult; yet it is but just to recognize the fact
that the Christian religion in that generation was
largely regarded as a means, not for making life
on this earth better and happier, but for preparing, in this life, by theological beliefs or by so-
called religious experiences, for a better and happier life hereafter.

Whether because the doctrines which he presented were obnoxious, or because his Western
unconventionality repelled more than it attracted,
or because there were few or no social influences
to draw men to the new enterprise, or because the
preacher had not yet got himself in hand, did not
understand his surroundings, had not, as the saying is, found himself, or simply because the best

and most effective public teaching does not instantly attract, the new preacher at first drew but moderate congregations. It was not until early in 1848, that is, after six months of preaching, that the church building began to be crowded; but from that time on, it was unable to accommodate the congregations. It was therefore not a disaster but a good fortune that in 1849 the church building was so badly damaged by fire that it became necessary to rebuild. A temporary " tabernacle " of wood was erected to serve as a place of worship until the first Sunday in January, 1850, when the new church was ready for occupancy. This consisted of two buildings — the church auditorium, and the lecture and Sunday-school room; the latter in two stories, the lecture-room below, the Sunday-school room above, with what was then a novelty in church architecture, social parlors,[1] and I believe also a kitchen. The size of the auditorium was, in popular reports, exaggerated; its legitimate seating capacity was 2050. This was subsequently increased by aisle seats so contrived as to be folded, when not in use, against the adjoining pew. Including those occupying these seats, the average congregation during Mr. Beecher's ministry approximated twenty-five hundred; including those who stood in the vacant spaces or on the stairs and in the hallways the auditorium sometimes contained approximately three thousand.

[1] These were subsequently thrown into the Sunday-school room to accommodate the increasing number of pupils. The present parlors were built in 1862.

Bædeker's "United States" characterizes Plymouth Church as "without architectural pretensions." It is, indeed, both in exterior and interior, absolutely unadorned. It contains no stained-glass windows and no ecclesiastical ornaments, and is characterized by no architectural beauty. This was due to no accident but to deliberate design. There are two services which, from the earliest ages, the Church of God has rendered in the community: it has expressed and at the same time cultivated the piety of devout souls; and it has furnished religious instruction and inspiration both to the devout and to the undevout. These services can be conjoined; but they also can be and sometimes have been entirely separated. In the Jewish Church the worship was conducted by the priesthood, who gave no religious instruction in connection with the Temple services; religious instruction was given by the prophets, who conducted no worship in connection with their public teaching. In Christ's conversation with his disciples at the Last Supper, as recorded in the Fourth Gospel, devotion and instruction were intermingled; but no public worship accompanied the Sermon on the Mount as it is recorded by Matthew. Prayer and teaching were combined in the simple services of the Apostolic Church, held in the houses of disciples; but Paul's famous sermon at Athens was unaccompanied with any worship. In the modern church the worship and the instruction are habitually though not always united; but in one class of churches greater provision is made for the worship, in the other for the teaching. The Roman Catholic and Episcopal churches lay emphasis on the ritual and the sacraments, and relegate the sermon to a second place or omit it altogether; the Puritan churches make the sermon predominant and attach less relative importance to prayer and praise. The first construct a cathedral, equip it with all the æsthetic elements, musical and artistic, capable of promoting spiritual delight in the worshiper, and allow this cathedral to be used for no other purpose than that of the worship of God, generally but not always accompanied with public instruction. The second build a "meeting-house," where the people of the community may gather for any legitimate function, where academic exercises may be held, literary, political, and moral reform lectures may be delivered, and on Sunday religious instruction may be afforded, which is almost invariably though not necessarily accompanied with public worship. The best type in America of the first conception of the church building as a house of worship is probably that furnished by Trinity Church, Boston; the best type in America of the second conception of the church building as a house for religious instruction is probably that furnished by Plymouth Church, Brooklyn. It would be difficult to find in church, hall, or theatre a more perfect auditorium. Standing upon the platform, which serves as a pulpit, the speaker is seen by every person in the house — there are no

great pillars to obstruct the view — and heard by
every auditor in the house — there is no vaulted
roof in which the voice is lost, no angles to catch
and to deflect it. A voice of very ordinary carrying power can be heard in a conversational tone
throughout the edifice, and a voice like Mr.
Beecher's, of extraordinary carrying power, can
be heard in tones scarcely raised above a whisper. For nearly forty years Mr. Beecher preached
in this meeting-house. Without adventitious aids,
either musical or æsthetic, by the simple power of
his oratory as some would say, of his personal
character I should prefer to say, he drew to this
meeting-house a congregation which ordinarily
filled every seat, and which often so crowded it
that hundreds were turned away unable to get
admittance.

The congregation was large but not wealthy.
Wealth is conservative, and Mr. Beecher's radical-
ism repelled those who were interested in maintaining the established order. To meet the cost of
the church a scheme was devised of popular subscriptions to stock, the interest of which was payable in pew rents only, the principal being payable
from the surplus revenues of the church. The problem how to pay the current expenses still remained
to be solved. This is always a problem of difficulty,
but in the case of Plymouth Church it was one of
peculiar difficulty ; for almost from the day of the
completion of the new edifice the demand for pews
was in excess of the supply. How to meet this

demand without favoritism, and without excluding by high prices the plain people to whom Mr. Beecher wished to preach, was a question not easily answered. To answer it a rental was attached to the pews lower than that customarily charged in other churches in the city, and for a considerable number of the pews so low that no one need feel himself excluded by reason of the expense; then every year the pews were put up for hire at public auction; and the sums bid in excess of the rent attached were added to the fixed rents in making up the income of the church. Good-natured rivalry among certain of the wealthier or more prominent members of the church often pushed up the price of a few seats in the centre of the church to a high figure; others were bid in at a moderate premium; a large number were always left to be taken without any premium at all. This plan of "auctioning off" the pews, which was discontinued after Mr. Beecher's death, is not free from objection, but the objection is chiefly one of sentiment. While it was in operation it resulted in giving an income which speedily paid off the debt upon the church, and thereafter furnished, over and above all the church expenses, a considerable sum which was wisely used in paying the cost of the city missionary enterprises which the church carried on.

The church was Congregational. Mr. Beecher was radical, the members who gathered about him were radicals, and the church was in its Congregationalism radical. The principles of Congregation-

alism are two. First, the independence of the local
church. Each church is absolutely autonomous,
frames its own organization, adopts its own creed,
arranges its own ritual, administers its own discipline. From its decisions there is no appeal; it
recognizes no superior ecclesiastical body. There
is, it is true, a fellowship of the churches, but it is
simply fellowship. The Conferences of the Congregational churches are social and intellectual
assemblies; the Councils of the Congregational
churches are bodies to give advice, not to enact
law. The relation between Congregational churches
Mr. Beecher has somewhere aptly compared to
the relations between families in a village: if one
family misbehaves itself, the others cease to visit
it; but they have no power over its local administration of its own concerns. The other principle
of Congregationalism is the absolute equality of
all its members. The minister is without any
ecclesiastical authority whatever. Theoretically he
may be, and in England he sometimes is, simply a
layman, selected by the congregation to be their
teacher because he is apt to teach. No doubt in
practice these principles are sometimes materially
modified. The resolutions of Conferences and the
acts of Councils come to have the effect of law;
the withdrawal of fellowship, the effect of penalty.
A church which in its creed, its ritual, or its discipline departs too far from the traditions and
habits of other Congregational churches is liable
to be disfellowshiped and to suffer opprobrium, if

nothing worse, in its isolation. In some Congregational churches also the minister is made *ex officio* moderator of all business meetings, and thus given a power to appoint committees; in others a standing committee is created, through which all business must pass, and from which no appeal to the church is effective, even if it is allowed. As we shall see later, Plymouth Church was determined to maintain its independency, no matter what sacrifice that independency might involve. It was equally determined to maintain the equality of all its members. Its pastor was not *ex officio* moderator of its business meetings, and in fact infrequently presided. It is rare that a pastor possesses as great influence in his church as Mr. Beecher possessed, but he had no ecclesiastical power whatever beyond that of the single vote which he cast in what was a pure democracy.

Theologically, the church was orthodox. It adopted a creed which embodied the doctrines of the Fall of man, the Depravity of the human race, the Trinity in unity of the Godhead, the provision for salvation through the atonement of Jesus Christ, the inspiration and authority of the Bible, the future judgment with its final awards of everlasting punishment and eternal life; in brief, its theology was of the New School Presbyterian Church, and of the New England theology of the orthodox Congregational churches of the middle of the nineteenth century. But from the very initiation of the church its pastor's influence was steadily exerted in

favor of substituting spiritual and ethical standards
for intellectual standards of character. The questions asked in the examination of candidates for
admission were practical rather than doctrinal. In
the pulpit, in the prayer-meeting, and in the administration of the church the question, What do
you believe? was rarely heard; the question, What
is your life? was, in varying forms, constantly reiterated. The creed adopted by the church at its
foundation remains unchanged as the historic creed
of the church; but since 1870 subscription to this
creed has no longer been required; the only condition of admission to the church is assent to and
acceptance of the following covenant: —

Do you now avouch the Lord Jehovah to be your
God, Jesus Christ to be your Saviour, the Holy Spirit
to be your Sanctifier? Renouncing the dominion of this
world over you, do you consecrate your whole soul and
body to the service of God? Do you receive his word
as the rule of your life, and by his grace assisting you,
will you persevere in this consecration unto the end?

If any one thinks this covenant furnishes too
open a door for admission to the Church of Christ,
I reply by saying that one of the most prominent,
influential, and devout members of that church, for
many years one of its deacons, told me that for a
year he remained outside the church before he
could decide that he would pledge himself to consecrate his " whole soul and body to the service of
God." Such a covenant as the above, if it be truly
interpreted and earnestly pressed, constitutes a far

stricter test of membership than can be furnished
by any creed, long or short.

From the first the church was preëminently a
social organization. Circumstances conspired to
make it so. Its original membership was composed
of households of about equal social standing.
Without either the very rich or the very poor,
Brooklyn, though a city of sixty thousand inhabitants, still retained village characteristics, as indeed
to some extent it does to this day.[1] The new pastor therefore had not to create but only to foster
the social life of the church. There were at first
three weekly services: a lecture on Tuesday evening, a social gathering on Thursday evening, and
a prayer-meeting on Friday evening. The first two
were ere long discontinued, and the three were
combined in the Friday evening meeting, which
became lecture, social gathering, and prayer-
meeting. The people were accustomed, however,
to gather in the lecture-room in little groups before the hour of service, and to remain for social
intercourse after the conclusion of the service. Not
infrequently this after social meeting was almost
as long as the more formal meeting which preceded
it. But that meeting itself was informal. Mr.
Beecher sat in his chair upon the platform and
talked to the congregation, as a friend with friends.
The congregation caught the spirit of informality

[1] Chauncey Depew in an after-dinner speech some ten years ago
characterized it as the fourth largest city and quite the largest
village in the United States.

from his spirit; and though the size of the meeting prevented it from ever becoming truly colloquial, and the tact of the pastor prevented its ever degenerating into a debating-society, there was a freedom in the interchange of opinions and experiences which was sometimes startling to those accustomed to the more staid methods of ordinary assemblages for worship. In the latter years the pastor's talks were taken down by a shorthand writer, and many of them were published in the press, and some of them collected in book form as " Lecture-room Talks." To many of his congregation Mr. Beecher seemed at his best in these 'informal meetings, in which he was less the orator than the personal counselor and friend.

But it was not only at occasional meetings organized for social intercourse, nor at informal Friday evening meetings, that the social life of the church was developed. The village church which I attended in my boyhood was on Sunday morning truly a " meeting-house." The farmers drove in from miles about, fastened their horses in the shed, and gossiped with one another over the crops, while their wives talked over family concerns until the church bell tolled. Service over, the social gossip was taken up where it had been dropped, and continued until, little by little, the congregation melted away. This New England method was unconsciously adopted in a modified form in the Plymouth Church services. After the first year the pewholders found it necessary to be at church ten minutes before service began, to make sure of their seats. They did not sit meditatively during these ten minutes; they talked freely, in the vestibule, in the aisles, in the pews, sometimes going from pew to pew. The buzz of conversation did not stop when the organ voluntary began; but when the preacher rose in the pulpit to offer the invocation, there was an instant hush. I always have thought that Mr. Beecher's habit of commencing the invocation in tones hardly audible was caused, not wholly by the wise determination not to imperil his voice, but also by the purpose to add impulse to the desire for silence in order to reverential participation. After the benediction was a second social gathering; friends and strangers streamed up to shake hands with Mr. Beecher, who remained near the pulpit for that purpose, and who thus encouraged them to shake hands with one another, cementing old friendships and making new acquaintances. I am here describing the habit of Plymouth Church neither to commend nor to criticise it. It was partly due to the neighborhood character of the early church, partly to the *quasi* village life of the community, partly to the transference to a city of early habits by the New Englanders who made the great proportion of the congregation, partly to the social necessities of a new and democratic organization in which are so many topics for mutual consideration, partly to the preacher's strong conviction that freedom of social intercourse of man with his fellow man is in no wise incongruous with the spirit of devoutness in man toward his God. If every preacher could by his strong and spiritual personality transfuse the congregation with the spirit of devotion in the first brief prayer of invocation, as Mr. Beecher did, it would be safe for every congregation to maintain the social prelude to religious service which Plymouth Church maintained, — but not otherwise.

Music was from the first a feature of the worship in Plymouth Church, but it was music furnished by, not to, the congregation. Back of the pulpit stood an organ of considerable size and a gallery which furnished accommodation for a considerable chorus choir ; the organ was subsequently replaced by what was, when constructed, I believe, the largest church organ in America. When John Zundel first came to Plymouth Church I do not know, but for many years he was, as its organist, Mr. Beecher's spiritual coadjutor. Nervous, irritable, with genius, but, I suspect, without what in our time would be regarded as adequate training, he loved music as an expression of the spiritual life. " I cannot," he said, " pray with my lips, I pray with my fingers." His music was profoundly devotional. He sympathized heartily in what was regarded in the earlier years of Plymouth Church as one of Mr. Beecher's oddities, — his passionate desire for congregational singing. Artists would probably criticise his accompaniment of the congregation, for he often marked the time with strongly accentuated pedal movement, but the result was that " dragging " was almost unknown in the congregational singing of Plymouth Church. The effect of a melody sung by two thousand out of the three thousand of the congregation — and certainly that proportion sang in Plymouth Church — might not have been musical, but to any one sensitive to human feeling it was intensely devotional. Here, again, allowance must be made for differences of temperament. The cultivated musician might well find his devotional nature more appealed to by the choral singing in a great cathedral, or even by the concealed quartette in a cathedral-like church, but most men are more sensitive to human feeling than to musical chords, and to such the congregational singing of Plymouth Church would be a greater expression and inspiration of devotional life.

This congregational singing did not, however, spring spontaneously into existence. I believe the scientists are generally agreed that, in biology, spontaneous generation has no place; I am sure it has none in social development. There was neither music-book nor hymn-book adapted to congregational singing when Mr. Beecher came to Brooklyn; congregational singing was not common in practice, and those who advocated it were looked upon as impracticable innovators. Yet we can now see that unconsciously the Puritan churches had been preparing for it. The habit of singing sacred music in the home, the singing-schools and the musical institutes common throughout New England, the revival spirit caught from the

Methodists and naturally expressing itself in popular songs, and the pioneer musical work done by Lowell Mason and his two pupils, George F. Root and George James Webb, had done much to create a desire for popular participation in church music, though as yet but little to develop ability for it. Mr. Beecher was no musician, but he loved music. He proposed to the musical conductor in Plymouth Church to prepare a hymn and tunebook for the use of the congregation in church services. " Temple Melodies," almost the first book of its description, was the result. It did not satisfy Mr. Beecher's ideal. Its success inspired him with the ambition for a larger undertaking, and he began the preparation of " Plymouth Collection " with a catholic courage rare in any minister. He laid all poetry under contribution; not only the Calvinistic Watts and the Arminian Wesley, but also such Roman Catholic authors as F. W. Faber, Madame Guion, and Francis Xavier; such Unitarians as Miss Martineau, Henry W. Longfellow, Sarah Adams, and John Pierpont; such secular poets as Mrs. Browning, William Cullen Bryant, John G. Whittier, and James Russell Lowell. There is now scarcely a single collection of any value in use in our churches which does not contain contributions from these sources. But though their use in 1855 was not wholly unprecedented, Mr. Beecher was severely criticised for his boldness. " Even those who applauded him anticipated no great results from the innovation." Said a re-

view of " Plymouth Collection," in the " Brooklyn
Eagle," " We do not look for any great extension
of really congregational singing in the more settled
parts of our country. Refinement (it is so called,
we believe) does not tend in that direction." It
certainly did not. Even chorus singing in the city
churches was rare ; the favorite instrument for
church music was the quartette. When " Plymouth
Collection " was published it is doubtful if there was
a score of congregations in the United States which
were supplied with music-books for congregational
use ; now the use of such books is almost universal in the non-liturgical churches in our cities,
towns, and larger villages. The musical development in England and America which " Plymouth
Collection " has done something to promote has,
during the last half century, called into existence
a great number of new hymns and tunes, and thus
left " Plymouth Collection " wholly inadequate for
present church service. But it was the work of a
pioneer, and in estimating the relation of Mr.
Beecher to the church life of America, what he
did to give impulse to congregational singing, by
showing its possibilities while as yet it was only an
apparently impossible dream of the idealist, ought
never to be forgotten.

In coming to Brooklyn Mr. Beecher brought
with him a definite purpose to make Plymouth
Church a spiritual church. He says : " I had no
theory ; but I had a very strong impression on my
mind that the first five years in the life of a church

would determine the history of that church and give to it its position and genius ; that if the earliest years of a church were controversial or barren it would take scores of years to right it ; but that if a church were consecrated, active, and energetic during the first five years of its life, it would probably go on through generations developing the same features. My supreme anxiety, therefore, in gathering a church, was to have all of its members united in a fervent, loving disposition ; to have them all in sympathy with men ; and to have all of them desirous of bringing to bear the glorious truths of the Gospel upon the hearts and consciences of those about them." From the first and with increasing power this spiritual atmosphere was prevalent in Plymouth Church. Conversions were frequent, additions on confession of faith numerous, and presently, revivals of religion accompanied with great ingathering of members. The first service in the new Plymouth Church was held on the first Sunday in January, 1850. In 1852 one hundred and two were added to the church on confession of faith ; six years later three hundred and sixty-nine. These were the fruits of definitely marked revivals of religion, accompanied by some unusual services ; but in both cases the services were the product of the revival ; the revival was not the product of the services.

The revival of 1857–58 was the last of those spiritual quickenings produced by the theological revolution which I have described in the first chapter. It extended throughout the country; my impression is that it was nowhere more fruitful in spiritual results than in New York, and that in New York no church gave greater evidence of its practical power in the spiritual life than Plymouth Church. I write of it from personal recollection, dimmed but not effaced by the lapse of years.

One Sunday evening in the winter of 1857, Mr. George A. Bell, an active and devoted member of Plymouth Church, invited me to meet with a few other members of the church the next morning on our way to business for an hour of prayer. The morning brought a blocking snowstorm; a little over a score gathered in the lecture-room; the pastor was not present. He was invited but declined; disavowed his belief in manufactured revivals; appeared almost to discourage the meetings; really threw the responsibility for beginning them upon the laity of the church. Reluctantly they took it; for two or three weeks they carried the meetings on, with increasing attendance and interest. Then one Sunday evening Mr. Beecher announced his intention to be present and thereafter he invariably presided. This was the beginning of a remarkable series of prayer-meetings, continued until the early summer of 1857, and resumed again in the winter of 1858. Those who attended those meetings will never forget them; " their freedom of intercourse, their social warmth, their spiritual tenderness; the commingling of humor and pathos, of the intellectual and the emotional, of the practical and the spiritual, in a word their *life*, genuine, free, untrammeled, varied life, gave them a character wholly indescribable." [1] Always at the close those who desired prayer for themselves or others were asked to indicate their desire; such requests were always presented, and a closing prayer was invariably offered by Mr. Beecher, who grouped together these requests in a supplication, in which none of them were forgotten. After the meeting, which was always closed promptly at the end of the hour, Mr. Beecher remained to converse with those who desired personal counsel for themselves or others. He called in assistants, both men and women, in whose tact and judgment he had confidence, to aid him in this personal work, and often to carry it on by visiting inquirers in their homes.

In this revival Mr. Beecher had no help from any professional evangelist and little help from any of his brother ministers. Every spiritually efficient minister was too busy in his own parish to take much part in the work of other parishes. He made no attempt to drive men into the kingdom of God; little or none to make them feel either the present evil or the future peril of an unsaved condition; the burden of his preaching was a presentation of the joy inherent in the life of faith, hope, and love. "I have sat in my own pulpit," he once

[1] *Henry Ward Beecher: A Sketch of His Career*, by Lyman Abbott, assisted by Rev. S. B. Halliday. American Publishing Company.

said to me, " and seen Finney get the sinner down
and pound him until I have wanted to pull Finney
by the coat and cry out, O let him up, let him up."
Dr. Finney drove men to repentance; Mr. Beecher
drew them. The themes of his revival preaching
might almost be summed up in the saying of
Hosea: " I drew them with bands of love." One
evening he read a letter from an unknown young
man, unknown I think to him, certainly to the
congregation, saying that he was going to destruction under temptations which he could neither resist nor escape, and imploring Mr. Beecher " to
preach to me the terror of the law, anything to
arouse me from this fearful lethargy." With this
as his text Mr. Beecher preached the love of God
in Jesus Christ as the only remedy for sin, saying,
" If this love of God will not move you, the fear of
God will not." The incident was characteristic.
Mr. Beecher believed in retribution — at that
time more definitely than he did subsequently.
But he rarely preached it, and when he did so, it
was only as a dark background, that he might
make the love of God revealed in Jesus Christ
more luminous. The most definite declaration of
his faith in this subject at this time is found in
the following paragraph in his sermon on " The
Gentleness of God : " —

Sometimes, in dark caves, men have gone to the edge
of unspeaking precipices, and, wondering what was the
depth, have cast down fragments of rock, and listened
for the report of their fall, that they might judge how

deep that blackness was; and listening — still listening
— no sound returns; no sullen plash, no clinking stroke
as of rock against rock — nothing but silence, utter silence! And so I stand upon the precipice of life. I
sound the depths of the other world with curious in-
quiries. But from it comes no echo and no answer to
my questions. No analogies can grapple and bring up
from the depths of the darkness of the lost world the
probable truths. No philosophy has line and plummet
long enough to sound the depths. There remains for us
only the few authoritative and solemn words of God.
These declare that the bliss of the righteous is everlasting; and with equal directness and simplicity they declare that the doom of the wicked is everlasting.

And therefore it is that I make haste, with an inconceivable ardor, to persuade you to be reconciled to your
God. I hold up before you that God who loves the sinner and abhors the sin; who loves goodness with infinite
fervor, and breathes it upon those who put their trust
in him; who makes all the elements his ministering servants; who sends years, and weeks, and days, and
hours, all radiant with benefaction, and, if we would
but hear their voice, all pleading the goodness of God
as an argument of repentance and of obedience. And
remember that it is this God who yet declares that he
will at last by no means clear the guilty! Make your
peace with him now, or abandon all hopes of peace.[1]

With this persuasive, attracting, enticing characteristic of his revival preaching was another, —
its extreme simplicity. It was without technical
theological terminology; it was without metaphy-
sical refinements; it presented the religious life as
preëminently natural, the sacrifice it required was

[1] *Sermons*, Harper & Brothers' edition, vol. i. p. 109.

a " reasonable sacrifice." Of this characteristic a
notable illustration is afforded by an address delivered in March, 1858, in Burton's old theatre on
Chambers Street, on " How to become a Christian." It was delivered at a week-day meeting;
the theatre was crowded to its utmost capacity; I
had difficulty in getting in. The interested reader
will find it reported in the " New Star Papers." I
can here only quote a few typical sentences; any
condensation would fail to interpret its spirit: —

I do not think that there is a man in this congregation that is not abundantly qualified to-day, before the
sun goes down, to become a true Christian in the spiritual
and experimental sense of the term.

A man who knows enough to take care of his business, to live obediently to the laws of the land, to live
in the affection of the family, knows enough to begin a
Christian life.

It is not needful that you have a great deal of feeling.
. . . The less feeling there is required to effect a moral
revolution, the better.

Do you desire the love of God? Do you desire it
more than you do your pleasure, more than ambition,
more than selfish indulgence? . . . Why do you not
take three minutes of this sovereign power of choice to
become a Christian?

I care for you; not out of my own nature, but because the spirit of my Master makes me thus care for
your soul. He sent me to tell you that He — glorious
as He is — that He cares for you ten thousand times
more than I do.

Such preaching as this was not calculated to

produce excitement. The emotionalism, developing occasionally into hysteria, which has too often accompanied revivals of religion, and which some readers erroneously imagine to be characteristic of all revivals of religion, was noticeably absent from the experience of Plymouth Church. It is not too much to say that it was never seen there, in either Sunday service or weekly prayer-meeting. Feeling there was, often deep feeling; but always natural, moral, rational. "The less feeling there is required to effect a moral revolution, the better," interprets all Mr. Beecher's spiritual endeavor. The sermons were expository, not hortatory, though expository rather of spiritual experience than of either the letter of Scripture or the doctrine of theology. The prayer-meetings were simple, colloquial, unconventional. The spiritual activity of both pastor and people was unmarked by efforts either to coerce or cajole attendants into uniting with the church; it was characterized, on the contrary, with distinct efforts to caution, especially the young, from too sudden action springing from momentary impulse. At the end of ten years, partly as the result of these revivals, the church had grown in membership from twenty-one to twelve hundred and forty-one. Anticipating here for a moment future history, it is legitimate to add that at the semi-centennial of Plymouth Church, celebrated in 1897, it was reported that thirty-six hundred and thirty-three persons had come into the kingdom of God through the doors of the church, an average of little over seventy-two each year, for the most part, without special measures or meetings of any kind. Humanly speaking, these results were due primarily to the intellectual and spiritual power of the pastor. To some account of him and his methods, as I personally knew both at this epoch in his ministry, the next chapter will be devoted.

CHAPTER V

THE PASTOR OF PLYMOUTH CHURCH

IT was seven years after the organization of Plymouth Church that I first began to attend it, and I here speak of Mr. Beecher as I knew him then, but I judge that no great change had been made either in his person, his habits, or his preaching in those seven years, save that perhaps his powers had improved a little, certain roughness due to his Western experiences had been rubbed off by attrition with the East, and the too exuberant rhetoric of his earliest ministry was mastered and pruned. In person he was slightly under six feet; powerfully built; not corpulent, but stocky. His general appearance suggested great physical strength. Mr. Fowler, the phrenologist, said of him that he was a " splendid animal," and no one looking on his magnificent physique could doubt the fact. He had a great brain; a great forehead, bearing witness to his intellect; a domed crown bearing witness to his reverence and his benevolence; a broad back of the head, bearing witness to the strength and force of his will; and heavy eyebrows, indicating power of observation. He had a good digestion and an excellent nervous system. Shortly before his death, in answer to some one who asked him if he was going to Europe for his health, he replied, "I already have more health than I know what to do with." Vigor of health was characteristic of him throughout his life. No doubt nature had endowed him with a fine physique, but he coöperated with nature and took excellent and intelligent care of his body. He used neither tobacco nor alcohol, until the latter years of his life, when he made occasional and rare use of the lighter forms of the latter. He did not use tea or coffee in excess, and in his diet was never self-indulgent. He had studied the relation of different foods to different physiological conditions, and adapted his own diet intelligently to his own needs ; eating, for instance, little beef, because it made blood, and he was too full-blooded by nature. He was an early riser, and usually finished his work in the study in time to allow some out-of-door exercise or excursion before a two-o'clock dinner. The afternoon was given to rest; part of it to sleep, part of it to social calling or out-of-door employment. After a light supper he entered on the work of the evening, which was almost invariably given up to some public engagement. He was always a sound sleeper, and had the gift, somewhat rare I think, of throwing off cares and anxieties, whether they belonged to him or others, when he believed that further carrying them would do no good to him or to them. He early adopted the principle that it is better to rest before one's work as a preparation for it, than after one's work as a recuperation from it. Saturday, therefore, was always given to rest; for he believed that the sabbath commandment was as applicable to ministers as to laymen, and, with rare exceptions, he did his work six days in the week, and rested on the seventh. But Saturday, not Sunday, was his rest-day.

Whatever he may have been before, after I knew him he was not, in any ordinary sense of the term, a pastor. The work of a pastor is twofold: to organize his church as a captain of its spiritual industries, and to visit from house to house, doing personally in the household work somewhat analogous to that done by the Catholic priest in the confessional. Mr. Beecher did neither.

He did not organize his church. He inspired those who gathered about him with generous aspirations, pointed out to them work to be done, incited them to do it, but left them to do it in their own way. Even up to the time of his death, it might be said that Plymouth Church was rather a body of workers than a working body. Many, if not most churches, are over-organized; the machinery is too great for the steam generated to operate it. Plymouth Church was under-organized; the steam generated by the Friday evening meeting and the Sunday morning service was greater than the organism afforded scope for. There were organizations and very effective ones in connection with Plymouth Church, but they were independent of any one central control; and while their efficiency was due to the energizing power of Mr.

Beecher, their form and framework were due to the organizing capacity of others.

Nor did Mr. Beecher, to any considerable extent, do pastoral work from house to house. He did little visiting, except of a restful sort, in the houses of intimate friends. He was not often to be seen at the bed of the sick, or even of the dying; he was not always to be had for either the funerals or the weddings incident to his great parish. When the necessity for this work became apparent, and it also became apparent that the one man could not do the preaching and public speaking in which Mr. Beecher was engaged, and also the personal, pastoral, house-to-house visiting, a pastor's assistant was secured, and on the Rev. S. B. Halliday, for years Mr. Beecher's faithful coadjutor, this form of personal work devolved, and by him it was done with admirable fidelity. Nevertheless, Mr. Beecher did do, in his own way, a personal work much greater and more influential, I am inclined to think, than the average of even notably efficient pastors. For sometimes half an hour after the Friday evening prayer-meeting he held what I may call a religious reception. He sat on or near the platform, to talk with old friends or meet with new acquaintances; he shook hands with any one that offered him a hand; an old friend returning after a long absence was instantly recognized and greeted with the warm cordiality of the love that is without dissimulation; if any one wished to see him privately, he sat down in the pew beside the seeker, heard his experience, divined his need before the narrative was half finished, and went to the heart of the matter in a quick sympathetic or pungent sentence ; if further help was needed, he referred the petitioner to some wise counselor, or made with him an appointment for some further and fuller interview. He expressed to me once his admiration for the tact, skill, and forcefulness of Dr. Nettleton's personal work of this description. I fancy that he had studied Dr. Nettleton's methods, and to good advantage.

But it was as an orator, in the pulpit and on the platform, in church, lecture-hall, and public assembly, that Mr. Beecher exercised his principal influence on the nation, and on his own church. By oratory I mean the art of influencing masses of men by spoken address. Any man who possesses this art, and actually does so influence men, I call an orator, whatever his elocutionary or rhetorical gifts, whatever the methods which he employs. In fact, Mr. Beecher had remarkable elocutionary and rhetorical gifts. He gave me once an account of the methods which he pursued in his boyhood, when under a skilled elocutionist, he spent sometimes an hour at a time simply practicing the use of the vowel *o*, with its varied intonations, or took a posture at a chalk-mark on the floor and went through varied gestures, exercising each movement of the arm under his instructor's direction, as he was told how far the arm should come forward,

where it should start from, how far go back, and
under what circumstances these movements should
be made. Whatever stiffness and artificiality such
drill might have at first produced had entirely disappeared by the time Mr. Beecher came to Brooklyn;
for the effects of this drill made ease, flexibility, and
variety of voice and movement a second nature to
him. His voice, his arms, his whole body, and in
some sense preëminently his face, were the quick
and potent servants of his alert mind. Training had
given his voice great carrying power. His contemporary and friend, Dr. Joseph P. Thompson, once
said to me that the secret of vocal power without
vocal weariness is knowing how to use the bellows. Mr. Beecher knew how to use the bellows.
He never strained his throat in vehemence of
speech; the throat was simply used to determine
the quality of the tone; the forcefulness of it was
given by the abdominal muscles. The reading of
the Scripture lesson in too many Congregational
churches is a piece of perfunctory ritualism. It.
was a lesson in elocution to hear Mr. Beecher read
a Scripture lesson. You might not agree with his
interpretation, but you could not misunderstand it.
I recall once hearing him, in a sermon on the gentleness of Christ, pause and say: "But did not
Christ denounce the Pharisees with bitterest invec-
tive? That depends upon the spirit with which He
uttered and with which we read His words." Then
he took up the New Testament, turned to the
twenty-third chapter of Matthew and read three or

four verses — "Woe unto you, scribes and Pharisees, hypocrites" — with thunder in the tones,
frown upon the brow, wrath in the voice; then,
without note or comment, he read them again as a
lamentation, with infinite pathos, with suppressed
tears in the tones of his voice. Then he closed the
New Testament and went on with his sermon.

With this remarkable elocutionary power was a
sympathetic imagination that made him, for the
moment, enter into and participate in every experience which he described. Coupled with a keen
and quick observation of things, his imagination
made him a graphic painter of scenes, which were
portrayed with a vividness such as made them for
the moment present to the audience. Coupled
with a sympathetic insight, his imagination made
him a dramatic portrayer of characters, who were
introduced upon the platform as though they for
the moment were addressing the audience. Coupled
with his devout spirit, his imagination enabled him
to realize himself and make his congregation realize
the presence of the living God, as really known
through transcending knowledge. Thus variously
working, his imagination made him at once the
most graphic, the most dramatic, and the most
devout of orators. Whether in his pulpit or his
parlor, he enacted with his voice, gesture, and facial
expression the incidents he narrated. His face had
not less flexibility than his voice, nor was it less
obedient to his instant and unconscious volition.
It was this dramatic quality which made men say

of him sometimes that he was a great actor. That he could have made a great actor, in the professional sense of the term, I do not believe; he could not have coerced himself into playing a part; moral enthusiasm was necessary to create the conditions under which face and voice and gesture would serve his purpose.

His rhetoric, no less than his elocution, was always subordinate to moral ends. Both were instruments which he had come by ten years of practical use, unconsciously for the purpose of moving the audience he was addressing. I do not think, after he came to Brooklyn, he ever preached sermons analogous to those "Lectures to Young Men" delivered in Indianapolis, to which I have referred in a previous chapter. His descriptive powers became subordinated to his philosophical thought. It might be too much to say that he was rhetorical and imaginative rather than thoughtful in Indianapolis; but it is certain that he was thoughtful rather than imaginative and rhetorical in Brooklyn. It was because his rhetorical forms were thus instrumental that he almost never verbally repeated himself. He acted on the aphoristic advice which Professor Edwards A. Park is said to have given his students: "There is no objection to preaching an old sermon if it is born again." Mr. Beecher had favorite and familiar lines of thought and he repeated them again and again. But he had no old sermons. I do not recall that he ever repeated a sermon "by request." I do not think he could have done so if

he had tried; any more than he could have repeated a conversation. In a sense, every sermon,
every address was a conversation with his audience.
In the phrasing of it always, in the figures employed
often, in the anatomical structure of it sometimes,
the audience took an unconscious part. It was this
conversational attitude in which Mr. Beecher stood
to his audiences, and as a result of which he received from them impressions while he was impress-
ing himself upon them, that made his sermons
always fresh; this also partly accounted for the
great variableness of his power. That power depended partly on his own mood, but also partly on
the mood of his audience.

His interest was in men, not in theories; in
life, not in philosophy. He saw everything in the
concrete, and his generalizations were, therefore,
always interpreted in concrete forms. His illustrations were not ornaments attached to his discourse,
like fringe upon a garment; they were woven into
it, a part of its web and woof, so that, in general, it
was impossible to remember the illustration without remembering the truth which it illustrated.
At the same time he dealt not with isolated facts
but with broad principles. From the particulars
he evolved the general truth, then returned to the
particulars to illustrate and enforce it. Although
his method changed somewhat afterward, his sermons at this time generally revolved, each one
about one central principle, so that the congregation went away, not dazzled by pyrotechnics, not to

discuss the orator and his methods, but impressed by some vital principle which elocution, oratory, rhetoric, argument had combined to enforce.

Whatever interested men, interested him. He was thus an instinctive student of human affairs; knew about trades, industries, domestic concerns, the affairs of the kitchen, the street, the shop; and they all came into his discourses, not only to illuminate his thought, but also to make connection with the men and women before him whose lives were in these various spheres. It was interesting to sit, as at one time I did, in the choir-gallery, looking upon the great congregation, and see how different references to different phases of life would catch and compel the attention of different hearers. He would capture a merchant with an illustration from the stock exchange, an artist with a reference to a picture, a mother with a reference to a garden or to children, a musician with a reference to a symphony or an oratorio, and they all would bear upon the one central truth which he determined not merely to make clear to the minds but to make potent in the lives of his hearers.

It has been sometimes said that Mr. Beecher was not a scholar. Whether he was or no I will not undertake to say, for the term scholar connotes different ideas to different minds; I will simply describe him as he was. He made no direct use of the Hebrew, and if he had ever known the language, had, I am sure, forgotten it. If he wanted exegetical information on a passage of the Old

Testament, he went to his brother Dr. Edward
Beecher, or to his friend Dr. Thomas J. Conant,
both of whom were expert Hebraists. He was familiar with the Greek, and in his New Testament
studies made constant use of it. When I decided
to go into the ministry I sought his advice as to the
best books for my library ; he said, " Buy Alford's
Greek Testament, whatever you do." It took all
the little money I had, but I was very glad afterwards I had made the expenditure. In his time
this certainly was, if it is not still, the best critical
apparatus for the study of the Greek New Testament. During his anti-slavery campaigns he not
only had in his library " Curtis on the Constitution " and " Kent's Commentaries on Law," but he
carefully studied them. No one would claim for
him that he was a constitutional lawyer, but he
had his own well-considered opinions, formed after
careful study, on the great constitutional questions
involved in the anti-slavery controversy. He was
familiar with the best books of his time on physiology, was a believer in the principles of phrenology, which he acquired at their fountain head, the
works of Gaul and Spurzheim, and he made habitual use of the phrenological nomenclature in his
analyses of human life. He was familiar with certain of the great classics, though that familiarity
rarely appeared in his addresses, partly because he
was not given to quotation, partly because he had
no verbal memory, and could not quote without
breaking in upon the current of his discourse to

read the quotation. He read and re-read such writers as Homer, Dante, Milton, Thackeray, Scott,
— the first two in translations. He not only read,
he studied them. The best discrimination between
Dante and Milton I have ever heard or seen I
heard from his lips in private conversation. He was
familiar, too, with the latest contributions of modern thinkers on subjects co-related to his themes —
Herbert Spencer, John Tyndal, Thomas H. Huxley,
Matthew Arnold, and I believe was instrumental
in securing the republication of their works in this
country, and so introducing them to American
readers. Rarely was I at his house, unless for the
briefest errand, that he did not call my attention
to some noteworthy book, or some specially valuable article in a late review, English or American.
This familiarity with current literature was partly
due to his habit of mousing among the book-stores
and in the libraries, and getting information as to
the things most worth knowing from others whose
business it was to know the whole field of literature
and philosophy. When he went on a lecture tour
he carried with him a black bag; I suppose at
some time it must have been new. In that black
bag was a small library. It usually contained a
book of poetry, one of philosophy, one of history,
one of fiction. Pursuing synchronously courses of
poetry, history, philosophy, and fiction, he took up
his course in either one according to the mood of
the hour. He called himself a slow reader; I rather
think he was, for he read not primarily to acquire

information but to stimulate thought. He chose books of power, and when the thought was stimulated, closed the book, and followed the clue which it had put into his hand; yet he acquired the habit of quickly ascertaining what a book had for him, would turn with a kind of unerring instinct to that portion and pass by the rest. " I never read a book through," he said to me once; "a book is like a fish: you cut off the head, you cut off the tail, you cut off the fins, you take out the backbone, and there is a little piece of meat left." I called on him once at his dinner hour to obtain his opinion on a treatise on phrenology. At the end of the first course he left the table and sat down by the window, took the pages, and ran over them, much in this way: " Yes! no! that is not true." " Ah! that is old." " Yes, that is so." " Well, I don't know about that." In fifteen minutes he had gone through the volume and knew it better than I did after an hour or two of examination. I believe he read Froude's " History of England " between the dinner courses. Such reading is an unsocial habit not to be recommended, but it is one which certainly would not be fallen into by a man who was " no student."

But a book is only the reflection of a man; it only tells what a man has thought about something. Mr. Beecher got directly from men much which most students get indirectly through printed pages. He was preëminently a student of nature, man, and the Bible.

In nature he saw a hieroglyphic language and read the lesson which it had for him. Whether he was familiar with the writings of Wordsworth I do not know; but no man I have ever known possessed a mind so much in this respect like that of Wordsworth as Henry Ward Beecher. He says in one of his lecture-room talks, "Have you ever, as a part of your obedience to Christ, taken time to sit down and think what birds and flowers mean? You have taken flowers and you have enjoyed them — their forms, their colors, their odors — simply as objects which had a relation to a certain sense of beauty in yourself. That is very well, although it is the merest superficial treatment of that profound subject, and does not fulfill the command of God. The command of prayer, of meekness, of humility may rank higher in the moral scale, but they are not one whit more commands than is this passage a command in relation to birds and flowers, and they do not address you one whit more than this does. Consider. It is not *smell*, it is not *admire*, it is not *enjoy*, it is not even *look at;* it is CONSIDER. And to consider is to ponder; it is to take a thing up into your mind and turn it over and over that you may know what it means." In these words he describes his own habits. He *considered*, that is, pondered much. If he read books less than most ministers, he thought more about what he read than most ministers think. If he ate less, he digested more, and it is what we digest, not what we eat, that makes us strong.

He carried the same spirit into his study of
men. He did not visit much from house to house,
nor, so far as I know, did he ever belong to a
club; clubs were not as common then as now.
But he made himself a welcome guest in the shop,
the office, the factory. He did not confine his fellowship to any class or circle in society. He says
somewhere, "There is no man that is not wiser
than I am on some subjects; I can get something
from everybody." In another place he says,
"There is not a deck-hand on the ferry-boats, nor
a man at Fulton Ferry whom I do not know, and
who has not helped me." This was the secret of
his interest in all manner of things. While he
was getting information from men he was getting
insight into men. In his Yale lectures to young
men he tells them how in his pastoral intercourse
he adjusts his ministry to the character of the man,
as their character is interpreted to him by the
structure and organism of the individual before
him. Despite this constant intuitive study, he was
easily cheated. There is a profound truth in the
epigram attributed to Edward Eggleston — "I
never knew a person who knew man so well and
men so ill as Henry Ward Beecher." He studied
men with a "charity which thinketh no evil;"
looked not so much to see what was in the man to-
day as what were the possibilities for the man in
the future. But it was because of this ineradicable
faith in the possibility of goodness in men that he
was the great preacher. "We are saved by hope:"

if the pulpit universally recognized this truth it would possess a much greater saving grace.

In the same spirit in which he studied nature and man, he studied the Bible. A pocket Bible was his constant companion. If by being a Bible preacher is meant a preacher who gathers by concordance a great accumulation of texts and quotes them as demonstration of a proposition which he wishes to establish, Mr. Beecher was not a Bible preacher. If by a Bible preacher is meant a man who is suffused through and through with the spirit, inspiration, and uplifting influence which is in this collection of Hebrew literature, Mr. Beecher was preëminently a Bible preacher. "Under the fossil," says M. Taine, "there was an animal; and behind the document there was a man. Why do you study the shell except to bring before you the animal? So you study the document only to know the man." So Mr. Beecher studied the Bible. "A Bible alone," he says, "is nothing. A Bible is what the man is who stands behind it — a book of hieroglyphics, if he be nothing but a spiritual Champollion; a book of rituals, if he be nothing but a curiosity-monger or an ingenious framer of odds and ends of things; and a valuable guide, full of truth and full of benefit for mankind, if he be a great soul filled with living thought." The Bible is primarily a revelation of the higher spiritual experience of men; it is a revelation of God just in so far as God is in spiritual experience. The study of the Bible as a document, that we may know the

men who produced the document, and so better
understand the spiritual experience in and through
which God is revealed, constitutes the miscalled
" Higher Criticism." It was the recognition of the
man behind the document, and the spiritual experience in the man, which both made famous and
subjected to severe criticism Dean Milman's " History of the Jews" and Dean Stanley's "History
of the Jewish Church." To what extent the same
spirit actuated Mr. Beecher's pulpit use of the Old
Testament, and to what extent the results of the
" Higher Criticism" were anticipated by him, is
indicated by the volume of popular lectures on the
Bible preached during the winter of 1878–79, and
subsequently published under the title " Bible
Studies."

But it was the New Testament which he chiefly
studied. He did not merely read it and re-read it ;
he did not merely study the interpreters of it ; his
study was not mainly nor even largely textual and
verbal ; I doubt whether he ever spent much time
over questions of grammatical construction or verbal translation ; the object of his study was always
to get at the living thought of the writer, to understand and put himself in possession of the writer's
experience. In this study he made use of his pen,
working over the passage under his consideration,
analyzing it and writing down the analysis, either
to clarify it, to fasten it in his own mind, or to
preserve it for future reference. A striking illustration of this his method of study is an analysis

of the seventh chapter of Romans, which he wrote, I believe, some time in the seventies. He subsequently gave it to me, and it was published in " The Christian Union " in 1887, at the time of his death. The analysis is worked out in a manner analogous to that of a lawyer's brief, and with a detail which recalls the method of Dr. Charles G. Finney.[1] While he thus familiarized himself, not only with the writings and the thoughts, but even more with the vital experiences of Paul, he gave, if not a more assiduous, a more constant and comprehensive study to the life and teachings of Jesus Christ. " Christ," says William Arnot, " is the living Seed ; the Bible is the husk that contains the Seed." It was that he might understand and interpret this living Seed that Mr. Beecher studied and used the Four Gospels. I doubt whether any minister ever lived who in a stricter sense preached Jesus Christ. When he died, leaving his life of Christ but half finished, his sons were able to complete it, with scarcely a break, by quotations from his sermons, except that there was no sermon to be found describing the crucifixion. This scene was so sacred to Mr. Beecher that he never ventured to attempt a portrayal of it.

If it is a mistake to suppose that Mr. Beecher was no student, it is equally a mistake to suppose that he was accustomed to speak without preparation. In his early ministry he had made a careful analytical study of the old English divines, not so

[1] See Appendix II.

much for their thought as for their style. He wrote
his early sermons fully and sometimes with considerable care. I think his "Lectures to Young Men,"
given in Indianapolis, were fully written. Rhetoric
had thus become to him, as had elocution, a second
nature. But at the time of which I am writing his
preparation of his theme was chiefly a brooding, a
meditating, a considering. This took no little time;
but the immediate analysis of his theme, its formulation, and the verbal phrasing of it, were accomplished with marvelous rapidity. He told me
once his method; I describe it from memory. "I
have," he says, "half a dozen or more topics lying
loose in my mind through the week; I think of
one or another, as occasion may serve, anywhere,
— at home, in the street, in the horse-car. I
rarely know what theme I shall use until Sunday
morning. Then, after breakfast, I go into my
study, as a man goes into his orchard; I feel among
these themes as he feels among the apples, to find
the ripest and the best; the theme which seems
most ripe I pluck; then I select my text, analyze my
subject, prepare my sermon, and go into the pulpit
to preach it while it is fresh."

In this preparation he wrote the introduction
and the earlier portions of his sermon in full, but
as the time for the church service grew near, the
writing was more abbreviated; then mere heads
were jotted down, in single sentences, or perhaps
single words; and at last, almost as the bell began
to toll, he caught up his unfinished manuscript,

walked with long, rapid strides to the church,
edged his way through the throng, with a greet-
ing here and there to a special friend, dropped
his soft felt hat by the side of his chair, put his
notes on the table beside him, sometimes added
to them with a pencil while the choir was singing the anthem.[1] When the time for the sermon
came, the notes lay on the open Bible before him.
He read in a quiet manner, not always easily audible throughout the church unless it were notably
still, the first and fully written pages, dropped his
manuscript to throw in a thought that flashed
upon him, came back to it again, dropped it again,
presently dropped it altogether, either not to recur
to it at all, or to recur to it only to catch from
some word or sentence a hint as to the next point
in the current of his thought. To the careless it
seemed that Mr. Beecher's preparation of his sermon was left to Sunday morning; in fact, he rarely
if ever in his ordinary preaching treated a theme
until he had given to it weeks of meditation. In
his earlier years there lay on his study table a
little notebook with flexible covers, about the size
of a sheet of commercial note-paper, full of hints,
subjects, themes, sketches of possible sermons,
with an occasional fully articulated skeleton. Later
I think he gave up this notebook, but his pocket
was generally half full of letters, on the back of

---

[1] This was his method during the earlier years of his Brooklyn
ministry; subsequently he often preached from mere notes jotted
down on a sheet of note-paper.

any one of which he would jot down thoughts for
sermons, as they might strike him, wherever he
happened to be. A single illustration may serve
to make clear this excogitation of his sermons.
He was to preach at an ordination in New England. "I think," he said to me, "I shall preach a
sermon on pulpit dynamics; you had better look
for it." I did look for it, and it was nothing but
a description of the incidental advantages of and
happiness in the ministry as a profession. When
I next met him I asked, "Where is that sermon
on pulpit dynamics?" "It was not ripe," he replied; "but I shall get something out of it yet."
What he did get out of it was, ten years later, the
Yale "Lectures on Preaching," one of the best
pieces of work he ever did.

When I turn from some account of Mr. Beecher's
general and specific methods of preparation to an
analysis of the sermons themselves, the difficulty of
furnishing any generic analysis is almost insuperable. This is partly due to the extraordinary variety of elements which entered into them. "The
most myriad-minded man since Shakespeare,"
Charles H. Spurgeon is said to have called Mr.
Beecher. This myriad-mindedness shows itself in
the structure and composition of his sermons. He
advised the young men at Yale Theological Seminary never to preach two sermons alike, if they
could help it — counsel founded upon his own practice. The Harper and Brothers edition of his
"Sermons" containing a selection of forty-six dis-

courses, taken from the preaching of ten years, includes an autobiographical exposition of the spirit and purpose of his ministry in " Thirteen Years in the Gospel Ministry, a Sermon of Ministerial Experience ; " a prose poem in " The Sepulchre in the Garden ; " a theological discourse in " The Divinity of Christ maintained in a Consideration of his Relations to the Soul of Man ; " a spiritual rhapsody in " The Gentleness of God ; " a meditation, the fruit of a spring day spent on his farm, in " The Lilies of the Field, a Study of Spring for the Careworn ; " an interpretation of nature in " The Storm and its Lessons ; " an exposition of the simplest ethical duties in " Faithfulness in Little Things ; " an exposition of an Old Testament story in " Three Eras in Life : God — Love — Grief — as Exemplified in the Experience of Jacob ; " — in truth, there are scarcely two sermons in this collection which in form, structure, and method are alike.

There are, however, certain general characteristics which may be said to belong to all of Mr. Beecher's sermons. He rarely preached a textual or expository sermon.[1] " A text," he has somewhere said, " is like a gate ; some ministers swing back and forth on it ; I push it open and go in." His texts were rarely more than mottoes for, or introductions to his discourse. This was by no accident ; it sprang by necessity out of his methods

[1] His *Bible Studies* may be regarded as an exception, but they were lectures rather than sermons.

of preparation. He first determined the object
that he wished to accomplish by his sermon — some
change in life, practical, spiritual, or intellectual,
in an individual, or in a type, or in a church, or in
the entire community ; then he selected the theme
which would be, in his judgment, most instrumental
to this end ; and lastly the text which would serve
as an introduction to the theme. I do not mean
that his mind always went through these processes
in this order ; I do mean that in the order of importance the object to be accomplished came first,
the theme by which it was to be accomplished second, the text which was to introduce the theme
third. He never forced texts out of their connection, nor imputed to them a fanciful meaning, nor
employed them as mere devices to awaken a guess-
ing curiosity in the minds of the congregation.
Strictly doctrinal sermons were few ; occasionally
he preached one for the purpose of defining his
position and reaffirming his substantial agreement
with the evangelical Protestantism in which he had
been bred. When he essayed an entrance into pure
theology he was not at his best. His argument
for the divinity of Christ derived from his relations to the human soul is effective, not because it
is an exposition of philosophy, but because it is an
interpretation of experience ; but when he attempts
to define this divinity, as in a sermon preached in
1879, and subsequently in the introduction to his
life of Christ, as " simply the Divine Spirit in a
human body," he offers a definition with which it

is impossible to reconcile the spirit of his own preaching. Nowhere in religious literature is the essential humanity of Christ's nature more illustrated and enforced than in Mr. Beecher's preaching; nor anywhere is Christ's essential divinity more emphasized.

In truth, Mr. Beecher was indifferent as to theological theories, ritualistic observances, and church connections; only the realities of life interested him. He was a Congregationalist, partly because he was born in New England, partly because he was independent by nature; but he was quite ready to co-work with ministers of all denominations, and he would have been equally ready to work in any denomination if he could have had in it equal liberty. As we have seen, the creed of his church did not differ from that of New School Presbyterianism; there was a baptistry under the pulpit, and candidates for admission were baptized by immersion or sprinkling, as they preferred; the prayer-meetings had the fervor of Methodist prayer-meetings; Mr. Beecher was by nature too unconventional to adopt a liturgy, but for the liturgy of the Episcopal Church he had a great affection. "Should our own children," he says, "find their religious wants better met in the service of the Episcopal Church than in the Plymouth Congregational Church, we should take them by the hand and lead them to its altars." On the questions at issue between the different denominations I think he rarely if ever preached, unless the preaching of his later years against certain tenets of the severer type of Calvinism affords an exception.

But though he was not a theological preacher, if by that is meant a preacher whose aim it is to expound a certain philosophy of religion, a simple but consistent theology underlay all his ministry from its beginning to its end. Professor William James, in his volume on the " Varieties of Religious Experience," declares that " there is a certain uniform deliverance in which religions all appear to meet. It consists of two parts: 1. An uneasiness; 2. Its solution. — 1. The uneasiness, reduced to its simplest terms, is a sense that there is something wrong about us as we naturally stand. 2. The solution is a sense that we are saved from the wrongness by making proper connection with the higher powers." This is very analogous to Professor Christlieb's declaration that evangelical Christianity is all summed up in the two words " sin " and " salvation." In the evangelical theology as interpreted by Christlieb, in the message of universal religion as interpreted by Professor James, Henry Ward Beecher was a devout and earnest believer. It is true that in his later years he repudiated the doctrine of the Fall of man in Adam, and he always repudiated the idea that the race could justly be held responsible for any such fall. It is true that he repudiated, in vigorous and even vehement terms, the doctrine of Total Depravity. This word, he said, " is an interloper; it is not to be found in the Scriptures; we do not believe that it is even to be found in the catechism and confessions of faith of Protestant or Catholic Christendom; we do not feel called upon to give the mischievous phrase any respect; we do not believe in it, nor in the thing which it obviously signifies; it is an unscrupulous, monstrous, and unredeemable lie." But he did believe, "with continual sorrow of heart and daily overflowing evidence, in the deep sinfulness of universal man;" believed that "no man lives who does not need to repent of sin, and to turn from it;" believed that "turning from sin is work so deep and touches so closely the very springs of being that no man will ever change except by the help of God." This was in him no theoretic conception based either on *a priori* reasoning or on ancient Biblical history; it was a conviction borne in upon him by his own personal experience and by his wide observation of life. Few ministers in the American pulpit have preached more searchingly on human sins, or awakened more vividly in men's consciousness the sense of their wrong-doing; it is doubtful whether any minister has preached more effectively practical ethics — the supreme obligation of love to God and man as the controlling motive of the life, and the various specific obligations which that supreme obligation involves.

But this was not the burden of Mr. Beecher's preaching. His aim was less to convince men "that there is something wrong about us as we naturally stand" than to make available to them

the true solution, namely, "that we are saved from
the wrongness by making proper connection with
the higher powers." He believed that the Gospel
is the "power of God unto salvation," and his
preëminent ambition in the ministry was to make
that Gospel effectual. He affirmed in the strongest terms that success in preaching depends on the
power of the preacher to put before men the Lord
Jesus Christ; that high above all other influences
is Christ, "a living Person who gave himself a
ransom for sinners and now ever lives to make
intercession for them;" that "there can be no
sound and effective method of preaching ethics
even which does not derive its authority from
the Lord Christ;" that "all reformations of evil
in society, all civil and social reformations, should
spring from this vital centre;" that "all philan-
thropies are partial and imperfect that do not grow
out of this same root;" that "all public questions
of justice, of liberty, of equity, of purity, of intelligence should be vitalized by the power which is
in Christ Jesus."[1] In these respects Mr. Beecher's
preaching was the antipodes of naturalistic. He
believed profoundly in the declaration of the Nicene Creed that Jesus Christ "for us men and for
our salvation came down from Heaven." He believed, in other words, that the connection with the
higher powers has been made for us by the life,
sufferings, and death of Jesus Christ; and the aim
of his preaching was to persuade men to accept

[1] *Sermons*, Harper and Brothers' edition, vol. ii. p. 200.

this connection, and so escape from the sinfulness in which they were enmeshed.[1]

As his preaching was non-naturalistic, so it was non-rationalistic. The basis of naturalism in religion is the assumption that men can save themselves from sinfulness without a divine helper; the basis of rationalism in preaching is the doctrine that men are governed by their reason, and if they are persuaded of a truth will follow it. Mr. Beecher did not believe that men are governed by their reason; he believed that they are governed by their motive powers. He therefore appealed directly to their emotions. It was often said in criticism of him that he was an emotional preacher. He would not have denied the assertion. He was an emotional preacher, partly by reason of his emotional temperament, partly by reason of his psychological conception of the forces that determine life. Even more than to show men the right way, he sought to furnish them with power which would impel them in the right way. He believed in enthusiasm, and he imparted enthusiasm to all who came under his dominating influence. He did not confound the sentiments and the emotions; he did not attempt to play upon the sentiments. As little as any man I ever knew was he ambitious to move men either to laughter or to tears, except as through laughter and tears he could inspire men to higher spiritual living. With him oratory was not an end, but a

[1] Compare for a consideration of the substance of his preaching, chapters I. and IV.

means. His aim was not to amuse, excite, or even instruct, but through instruction and inspiration, through humor and pathos, to bring the whole man into vital union with God, and the whole life into conformity with the law of God as it is interpreted by the life and character of Christ.

Thus his preaching was more than emotional, it was spiritual. He believed in the potential divinity in every man; he believed that if this potential divinity were once awakened and given its true place, it would bring all the man into subjection to the law of God, and he sought, by reason, by imagination, by humor, by pathos, by illustration, and by emotion, but yet more than by any or all of these, by direct spiritual contact, to evoke this divine potentiality and make it actual and effective. Mr. Beecher would not have been the preacher that he was if he had not been essentially a mystic. By a mystic I mean a man who possesses the power of seeing immediately and directly the invisible and the eternal. "If I were asked," he told the Yale theological students, "what had been in my own ministry the unseen source of more help and more power than anything else, I should say that my mother gave to me a temperament that enabled me to see the unseeable and to know the unknowable, to realize things not created as if they were, and oftentimes far more than if they were, present to my outward senses." Mr. Beecher's imagination was not a mere faculty for ornamentation, it was a power of immediately perceiving the invisible. His

belief in God was not what Carlyle contemptuously
calls " an hypothetical God." God was to him a
perpetual presence. He knew God and walked with
him. So natural and simple was this faith that it
required for its cultivation no adventitious circumstances ; it was entirely congruous in his mind with
secular activities, domestic enjoyments, ebullient
mirth. He had the faith of a child who never thinks
that he may not be merry in his father's presence.
Merriment and reverence were not to him in the
least incongruous. Men who were repelled by a
faith of a more austere type appreciated a faith
which was so simply and naturally human. The
consciousness of God was awakened in men by one
who recognized God's fellowship in all the common experiences of life. This pervasive faith made
him not merely an orator about religion, but an
imparter of religion, and constituted the secret of
his pulpit power. It interprets at once his real reverence and his seeming irreverence ; his fellowship
with God no less in secular than in sacred hours,
and his disregard for the conventions of religion
the utility of which for less impressionable souls he
sometimes failed to realize. And yet this mystical
power that makes all ideals realities because all
ideals are parts of the Infinite and the Eternal
power was mated in Mr. Beecher to a cool, hard,
practical common sense. He was mystical, but he
was rational. All the visions that were brought to
his mind through his imagination he tested and
measured by the judgment. He was not at times

a rationalist, and at times a mystic; all his mysticism was rationalistic mysticism, and all his rationalism was a mystical rationalism. A great deal of the skepticism of our day I think is due to the fact that men are trying to demonstrate religious truth by the faculties by which it can only be tested; they are trying to build up faith in God by the process by which only faith in God can be measured after it exists. As though men should attempt to make flowers by tearing flowers to pieces; as though men should attempt to make life by dissecting the living body. Mr. Beecher saw and knew the Eternal. Then what he had seen he brought to the judgment bar of reason and conscience, and his pulpit gave the joint testimony of his faith and his reason.

This mystic quality of Mr. Beecher gave to his prayers a spiritual power quite as remarkable as the power of his preaching. The Puritan doctrine that regeneration entirely changes the character was perhaps the cause which led the Puritan churches to assume that any regenerate soul can lead a congregation in prayer, and to impose upon every layman, cultivated and uncultivated, the duty of praying in public in the prayer-meeting. In truth, there is no intellectual exercise so difficult as that of public prayer. He who would conduct the devotions of a congregation must not think of the congregation, otherwise he will instinctively address them; he must think of the congregation, otherwise he will engage in a mere monologue, while the congregation listen to his closet talk with God. Which of these two is the more indecorous and irreverent it is not easy to say. It is because of this inherent difficulty that extemporaneous prayers fall so readily into one of three categories: unrealized ritual, practically a repetition of old-time forms, without the graceful and well-ordered phraseology which belongs to an historic liturgy; a spiritual monologue, with the congregation in the attitude of eavesdroppers; or a public speech, nominally addressed to God, really to the human audience. Mr. Beecher's prayers for many years were taken down by a shorthand writer and were published with his sermons in "The Christian Union," subsequently in pamphlet form, and eventually selections of them in two volumes. Having undertaken some years ago to compile a book of devotions for private and family use, I necessarily made a somewhat large collection, and a somewhat careful study, of the literature of prayer. If there is any collection of prayers which surpasses these published prayers of Mr. Beecher in simple spiritual eloquence, in the self-revelation of childlikeness of heart and familiarity of fellowship with the Everlasting Father, and in understanding and interpretation of the wants, simple and complex, superficial and profound, of the human heart, I have never seen it. Rarely does one of these prayers trench in character upon public address; occasionally it is, in part at least, a monologue; more frequently it is sim-

ply a new phrasing of common and oft reiterated
petitions; but in general it is a gathering up of
the experiences of the varied congregation and
their interpretation to the Father on behalf of his
children. A prophet is one who interprets God to
man; a priest is one who interprets man to God.
Mr. Beecher would have disavowed being a priest;
he would have insisted that every man can carry
his own wants to God without the intervention of
any intermediary. But far more than most ministers he was a true priest, interpreting men's deeper
wants to themselves, and so acting as their interpreter in declaring those deeper wants to him who
alone can provide for them.

No one can understand Mr. Beecher as a social
reformer who does not first understand him as a
pastor and preacher, a minister to the spiritual
life, a prophet and priest, an interpreter of man to
God and of God to man. From this aspect of his
character and life we turn to that aspect presented
by his career as a reformer, a service necessarily
more prominent in the history of his country, but,
as I believe, less profoundly influential in the real
life of his generation.

CHAPTER VI

THE movements of the generation just preceding the existing generation are usually those least comprehended by the existing generation; they are not remote enough to constitute past history, they are not recent enough to constitute current history; but it is impossible to understand correctly the attitude of Mr. Beecher, or to measure intelligently the influence which he exerted, without understanding something of the complicated issues which he confronted when he came to Brooklyn in 1847.

It is therefore necessary to turn aside from the narration of the events of his life in order to trace briefly the growth both of slavery and of the anti-slavery sentiment in the United States, and to describe briefly the conflicting opinions of the abolitionists on the one side, and of the timid, the reactionaries, and the apologists for slavery on the other, as they existed at the time when Mr. Beecher began to take a prominent part in the discussions to which slavery gave rise.

The anti-slavery issue in 1847 was far more complicated than it appears to be to the reader in 1900. Roughly speaking, the community in the North was divided into three parties: there was

an occasional advocate of slavery, a conservative,
who defended it because " whatever is, is right; "
an economist, who thought it essential to the cotton
industry, and the cotton industry essential to the
welfare of the country; a romanticist, entranced by
the patriarchal aspects of domestic slavery, or repelled from the anti-slavery movement by the vituperative spirit of the radical abolitionists; but on
the whole there was no sentiment in the North in
favor of slavery. There was a great deal of apathy;
there were a great many who regarded the issue as
remote, and dreaded its approach; there were men
who cared more for the integrity of the political
party, or of the ecclesiastical organization, than
they did for their fellow men; there were ministers
who did not think that Christianity had to do with
social questions, and who condemned the preaching
of liberty and humanity as the preaching of politics;
there were editors who had never studied the Constitution of the United States, and did not realize
that under the Constitution anything could be done
to limit or restrict what they conceded to be a
serious evil; there were moralists, all of whose
indignation was expended on the abolitionists for
their attacks on the Constitution and the Church,
and who had no indignation left to expend on the
pro-slavery spirit, which denied in the Southern
States, and sought to deny throughout the nation,
free press, free speech, and free schools. These
classes, grouped together, constituted what was
sometimes called the " conservative," sometimes

the " pro-slavery " party, though neither epithet
properly described them. There were, secondly,
the abolitionists, who demanded the immediate
and unconditional abolition of slavery, and as a
means to that end, the dissolution of the Union,
under the mistaken impression that so they would
secure immediate and unconditional abolition. And
there were, thirdly, the anti-slavery men who believed that the Constitution gave to the federal
government ample powers to prevent the extension
of slavery, who wished to exert those powers for
that purpose, and who believed that, if the extension of slavery was thus prevented, it would be
possible to secure eventually the peaceable abolition of slavery even in the slave states. In order
to understand Beecher's share in the ultimate overthrow of slavery, it is necessary to understand these
three parties and something of the history which
produced them.

The year 1620, which saw the Pilgrim Fathers
landing on Plymouth Rock, saw a vessel with
slaves on board landing on the Virginia coast.
Nor was slavery at first confined to any section.
In 1790 — the first term of George Washington —
it existed in every state of the Union, except only
Massachusetts ; it did not finally disappear from
the state of New York until 1827 ; and, as has
been shown in a preceding chapter, was maintained,
in spite of the Ordinance of 1787, in Indiana until
the admission of Indiana as a state into the Union
in the year 1816. From the first it existed under

protest. The abolition sentiment, nurtured in England by the abolition movement under the leadership of Wilberforce and Clarkson, crossed the sea and made itself felt in the American Colonies. The first anti-slavery societies included Southern as well as Northern men. In the original draft of the Declaration of Independence, one of the counts in the indictment against King George was, that he had insisted on maintaining the slave-trade in spite of the protests of the state of Virginia. The first anti-slavery convention, held in 1793 in the city of Philadelphia, was attended alike by Northern and Southern men, and emphasized the issue between slavery and freedom as distinctly as it was emphasized, half a century later, by Henry Ward Beecher, William H. Seward, and Abraham Lincoln. In the address issued by that convention it was distinctly affirmed that liberty and slavery cannot exist together on the same continent. This anti-slavery movement was nurtured and promoted by the churches. The Presbyterian and Methodist churches, especially, were distinctly anti-slavery in their teachings, as well as in their sentiments, and the Friends' Meeting was even more outspoken and vigorous. Nor was this work of the Christian Church and of the philanthropic anti-slavery societies nugatory. The anti-slavery sentiment grew apace. Partly owing to the industrial conditions, partly to political considerations, and partly to humane, philanthropic, and religious teachings, slavery was gradually abolished in the

states north of the so-called Mason and Dixon's
Line — the geographical boundary between Pennsylvania and Maryland. In 1830 it had disappeared
absolutely from the last of the so-called Northern
States. Moreover, under the influence of these
teachings, the slave-trade had been abolished by
Congress in 1808, the earliest date at which such
abolition was permitted by the Constitution, and it
had been practically abolished earlier than that by
statutes enacted in nearly every state in the Union
prohibiting the importation of slaves from abroad.[1]
This abolition of slavery was accomplished by a
gradual and wholly peaceful process, and in most
if not all the states with some measure of compensation to the slave-owners.

If this movement could have gone on unchecked
slavery might have been peacefully abolished
throughout the United States by the end of the
nineteenth century. But it was not allowed to go
on unchecked. Simultaneously with the growth of
anti-slavery sentiment there grew up a pro-slavery
sentiment. The invention of the cotton-gin in 1793,
and its general adoption by the year 1812, had
created a great demand for cotton. Experience
had demonstrated that cotton could be raised only
by negro labor, and it was assumed, without argument, that negro labor must be slave labor. The
South, responding to the demand for negro labor
created by the increased price and value upon cot-

[1] Georgia and South Carolina took no such action; North
Carolina levied a tax on all slaves imported.

ton, began to put a value upon slavery as an industrial condition which they had not earlier done. This demand created a new industry — the rearing of slaves in the Border States, to be shipped and sold as laborers in the Gulf States. The men who engaged in this traffic were universally despised throughout the South; but the traffic went on, and indeed was a necessity of the slave system. These industrial changes not only increased the commercial value of slavery, but also changed its character. Slaves engaged in domestic service as house servants were still kindly treated. They were regarded as in some sense members of the family ; were well fed, well clothed, well cared for, and in general kindly, though not always respectfully, treated. An attachment grew up between them and the master, the mistress, and the children of the home, such as was unknown in the domestic service of the Northern States. But no such relations were possible between master and servant when the master was engaged in rearing slaves for sale, and none such were possible on the great cotton and sugar plantations of the South, where the negroes worked in gangs under overseers, often of their own race.[1] Thus, while from the North slavery disappeared, in the South slavery became the distinguishing characteristic of its industrial system, and at the same time radically changed in its character. Thomas

[1] " Louisiana sugar planters did not hesitate to avow openly that, on the whole, they found it the best economy to work off their stock of negroes about once in seven years and then buy an entire

Jefferson had urged in his later years that all children born in slavery after a certain date should be freed, provided with a home and with some measure of education at public expense, and as soon as they reached competent age sent to some place outside the country, as San Domingo; but he was the last Southern statesman of any note to advocate abolition, either gradual or immediate.

These changes in the economic conditions of the South were accompanied inevitably by others. Wherever labor is servile, labor is disgraced. Labor in the South was disgraced, and the free negro and the poor white occupied positions less respected than those of the slave. The Southern States relapsed into a condition of feudalism far inferior to that of the middle ages. Socially and politically, they became an oligarchy; retaining the form but not the spirit of democracy, ruled by a small body of land-owners and slave-owners. Education is fatal to slavery, and the education of the slave was discouraged in all the Southern States and absolutely prohibited in many of them. The education of the poor white would have inevitably produced discontent among the negroes; therefore there was no adequate provision for their education. The movement for free schools, beginning in New England and moving westward, never crossed into the region dominated by the slave power. Until after

new set of hands." James Ford Rhodes: *History of the U. S.*, vol. i. p. 308. See this entire chapter IV. for a very judicial historical picture of American slavery as it existed in 1850.

the Civil War not a single Southern State possessed any approximation to a free-school system.

The South was a purely agricultural country
and wished to buy its manufactured articles in
the cheapest market; it therefore believed in free
trade. The North was a manufacturing community; it wanted a monopoly for its manufactured
articles, and therefore demanded a protective tariff.
From the formation of the Constitution two parties, representing two political tendencies, divided
the nation: one, led by Thomas Jefferson, dreaded
concentration of political power and emphasized
the value of local self-government; the other, led
by Alexander Hamilton, dreaded the perils arising
from sectional self-interest and emphasized the
importance of a strong national organization. The
Constitution was an endeavor to harmonize these
two forces — the centrifugal and the centripetal.
For reasons which it is not necessary to go into
here, the centrifugal, or Democratic, or Jefferso-
nian, tendencies were greatest in the South; the
centripetal, or national, or Hamiltonian, forces
were greatest in the North. The North prospered,
the South did not. Immigration poured into the
North, and avoided the South. The industry of
the North was diversified; the South gave itself
up to a single industry, and that one dependent on
slave labor. Socially, the South was Cavalier and
aristocratic; the North Puritan and democratic.
Thus, the South and the North, united under the

same Constitution, drifted farther and farther apart, and became at first alien and then hostile to one another — industrially, economically, politically, socially. Mason and Dixon's Line crept westward with the westward growth of the nation : all south of that line became aristocratic, feudal, slave; all north of that line became democratic, modern, free.

When the inclination is strong it can generally discover or invent reasons to justify it. The South wished slavery, and found reasons for its maintenance. The economic advantage was pleaded : We must have slave labor for our cotton, our sugar, and our rice industry. The social argument was pleaded : The blacks must be kept in subjection to the whites or we shall have intermarriage and all the evils that will follow from intermarriage. The religious argument was pleaded : The curse of God upon the descendants of Ham ; the uncondemned existence of slavery in the Old Testament times ; the fact that Jesus Christ did not in explicit terms condemn it in New Testament times. Southern ministers forgot the radical difference between Roman slavery and Hebrew slavery; they forgot that Hebrew legislation surrounded slavery with such conditions that in the time of Christ slavery had almost if not entirely disappeared from Palestine, except as it was imported there by Rome ; they forgot that under the beneficent teachings of Christianity slavery gradually disappeared from Europe; they assumed that a condition of labor,

permitted for a little while in the early barbarism
of Judaism, was the best condition of labor for the
foremost and freest country on the face of the
globe in the nineteenth century.

At the same time with this growth of slavery
in the South and this abolition of slavery in the
North, there grew up in the North an unwonted
prejudice against the African. It would perhaps
be difficult to say why this prejudice was greater
in the North than in the South; but of the fact
there can be no doubt. The negro was no longer a
negro: he was a "nigger." Special sections of the
great cities were, by a kind of common consent, set
apart for the negroes, like the ghettoes for the
Jews in the mediæval cities. In the theatres they
were banished to the upper galleries, which were
called derisively "the nigger heaven." They were
directed to the galleries, or to special, and generally undesirable, pews in the churches. Only the
more servile forms of labor were permitted to them.
In Boston, later the centre of the Abolition Movement, on the great days when the Ancient and
Honorable Artillery paraded on Boston Common,
the negroes were customarily hooted off the public
grounds before the parade began.

Something such was the condition of the country
in the year 1831. In that year two events occurred,
having no apparent connection, but having a certain striking dramatic relation: in Virginia a slave
insurrection broke out, accompanied with deeds of
barbarism and cruelty; in Boston, William Lloyd

Garrison started "The Liberator," pledged to instant and immediate abolition.

William Lloyd Garrison is a type of the radical abolitionist of the North, the antipodes of the proslavery propagandists of the South. Which produced the other has ever been a matter of hot debate between the respective advocates of South and North. The truth is, each produced the other: the fire creates a draught; the draught increases the fire. It was inevitable that the extension of slavery and the change in its character should excite alike assailants and advocates; it was inevitable that every assault should intensify the resolute purpose of the advocate, and every advocacy should intensify the resolute purpose of the assailant. Mr. Garrison contended that slavery was a sin, and, because a sin, should be instantly abandoned. His position is thus defined by Mr. Oliver Johnson, one of his friends and biographers: —

Mr. Garrison had learned the doctrine of immediatism from Dr. Beecher himself. The very keynote of the revivals of that day, in which the Doctor took so prominent a part, was the duty of every sinner to repent instantly and give his heart to Christ; but the men who were most eloquent in urging this doctrine in its application to the sin of unbelief, were prompt to deny it in its application to the sin of slavery. Sin in general was something for which there could be no apology or excuse, but the particular sin of treating men as chattels and compelling them to work without wages could only be put away, if at all, by a process requiring whole generations for its consummation! Such was the moral blindness of the time — a blindness not of the multitude alone, but of the professed expounders of the will of God.[1]

This was not all. If slavery was a sin, so Mr. Garrison argued, the slaveholder is a sinner. The original slaveholder stole the slave from his home in Africa; he was a man-stealer. But the participant is as bad as the thief; therefore the man who took the slave from the slave-dealer is himself a man-stealer. But a thief can give no title to his goods; therefore the slave-owner, who in Georgia or South Carolina had, two centuries after the original theft, inherited a negro, was himself a man-stealer. He ought not, so Mr. Garrison argued, to be admitted to fellowship in any church; he ought, so Mr. Garrison argued, to be treated as a man-stealer, and no more socially recognized than any other thief. The proposition for gradual emancipation Mr. Garrison vehemently condemned: slavery was a sin to be instantly broken off. The proposition for compensation he equally condemned: to compensate the slaveholder, he said, is to pay him for his stolen goods, to acknowledge that his crime is not a crime. But the Constitution of the United States interposed a considerable obstacle to the instant and immediate emancipation of the slave. The Northern States had no more power over slavery in South Carolina

[1] Oliver Johnson: *Life and Times of William Lloyd Garrison*, p. 45.

than over serfdom in Russia. William Lloyd Garrison was quite ready to meet this constitutional argument. He found in the Book of Isaiah a text which he thought appropriate. That prophet had declared that the men in his time who had no faith in God scoffed at the divine warnings because they had made a covenant with death and an agreement with hell, and the prophet scornfully affirmed that such covenant with death and agreement with hell would be annulled, as the people would find to their cost. William Lloyd Garrison applied this phrase to the Constitution of the United States. It was, he said, a covenant with death and an agreement with hell; let us away with it. The Northern States were responsible for the sin of slavery because they allowed themselves to remain in partnership with the slaveholders. He demanded the instant abolition of this partnership with slaveholders by the secession of the Northern States from the Union.

These radical and uncompromising principles were put forth in a radical and uncompromising temper. Whoever did not agree with the abolitionists, both in the end to be sought and in the methods to be pursued, was denounced as a proslavery man. When the time for political action came, Frederick Douglass, himself an emancipated negro, and the foremost representative of his race then, as Booker T. Washington is the foremost representative now, withdrew from the Abolition party, to vote with the Liberty party. He was

instantly scored by the abolitionists as an apostate
and renegade. James G. Birney was nominated
as a candidate by the Liberty party on a platform
demanding that there should be no further extension for slavery. He was instantly denounced as
a political place-hunter. Those in the Church of
Christ who did not agree with the radical principles of the radical abolitionists came in for a
similar denunciation. Said Mr. Garrison : —

" Christianity indignantly rejects the sanctimonious
pretensions of the great mass of the clergy in our land.
It is becoming more and more apparent that they are
nothing better than hirelings, in the bad sense of that
term — that they are blind leaders of the blind, dumb
dogs that cannot bark, spiritual popes — that they love
the fleece better than the flock — that they are mighty
hindrances to the march of human freedom, and to the
enfranchisement of the souls of men." [1]

It is perhaps not astonishing that ministers so
characterized did not find themselves prompted to
march in company with the leader who so characterized them.

Along with these principles and this temper, it
was charged upon the abolitionists that they sought
to bring about the instant and immediate emancipation which they demanded by insurrectionary
and incendiary methods. That charge has been
denied. Whether true or false, it certainly was not
without ground. Abolition tracts were freely cir-

[1] *William Lloyd Garrison: The Story of his Life, Told by his
Children*, vol. ii. p. 140.

culated throughout the Southern States; pictures were printed upon cheap handkerchiefs, such as might be easily circulated among the slaves, and were sent to them — pictures, the only effect of which, whatever may have been their object, must have been to arouse the slaves to insurrection. The notion was currently entertained that the slave population was restless, discontented, ready to revolt, kept in subjection only by a knowledge that the whole resources of the federal government would be employed to put the insurrection down. This notion attributed to the negroes a knowledge which they did not possess and sentiments which belong to a much higher state of moral development than they had attained. John Brown's famous raid assumed a readiness on the part of the slave to rise in revolt if the opportunity was afforded him, which the subsequent history of the Civil War demonstrated beyond all question to be wholly lacking. But the programme as well as the platform of the abolitionists took for granted the existence of such a widespread discontent among the negroes of the South, which only awaited an opportunity to break out in efficacious revolt. It is not the only case in history in which reformers have attributed their own instincts and inclinations to a people wholly incapable of them.

It is never quite fair to cite single paragraphs out of passionate utterances in a time of great excitement, for the purpose of interpreting the views of a party, a faction, or a leader, since in such times all men are apt to say what in cooler blood they would modify. But the careful enunciation of its principles by a party may be justly taken by the historian as a true interpretation both of its purpose and its spirit. The following declaration of principles was kept standing at the head of the columns of "The Liberator," the official organ of the radical abolitionists: —

All men are born free and equal, with certain natural, essential, and unalienable rights — among which are life, liberty, and the pursuit of happiness.

Three millions of the American people are in chains and slavery — held as chattels personal, and bought and sold as marketable commodities.

Seventy thousand infants, the offspring of slave parents, kidnapped as soon as born, and permanently added to the slave population of Christian (!), Republican (!!), Democratic (!!!) America every year.

Immediate, unconditional emancipation.

Slave-holders, slave-traders, and slave-drivers are to be placed on the same level of infamy, and in the same fiendish category, as kidnappers and men-stealers — a race of monsters unparalleled in their assumption of power, and their despotic cruelty.

The existing Constitution of the United States is a covenant with death, and an agreement with hell.

No Union with Slave-holders! [1]

The first three paragraphs state truly enough, though the latter of the three is inflammatory rhetoric, the evils of American slavery as it existed in 1847 ; the other four, which embody the remedy

[1] *The Liberator* of January 1, 1847.

for those evils which the abolitionists proposed, were each one of them false; Mr. Beecher believed each one of them to be false.

No Union with slaveholders was not a sound principle of political action. Secession from the Union was neither right nor expedient. It was not right, because the North as well as the South was responsible for the existence of slavery; the North as well as the South had entertained and maintained it; the importation of slaves was carried on by New England shipping merchants and defended by New England representatives; and when the proposition came before the Constitutional Convention for the prohibition of the slave-trade New England voted for the clause that it should not be abolished until 1808. Thus the North shared with the South in the responsibility for the sin and shame of slavery, and it had no right, Pilate-like, to wash its hands and say, "We are guiltless of this matter." It was under sacred obligation to remain in the partnership and work for the renovation of the nation. As it was not right, so neither was it expedient. There was no time when the Middle States would have thought of withdrawing if the New England states had followed the advice of Garrison and Phillips. If they had followed that advice, slavery would almost certainly have forced itself upon the far West, as it attempted to do upon Kansas, would probably have reëntered Indiana, and not impossibly have won recognition in even Ohio, Pennsylvania, and New York. If the North Atlantic

States had followed the counsels of "The Liberator" and withdrawn from the Union, there is every probability that to-day all the Southern States, and a possibility that a considerable proportion of the Western States, would have been united in a great slave confederacy. The advice of the abolitionists, if followed, would not have abolished slavery; it would have established slavery.

It is not true that the United States Constitution was "a covenant with death and an agreement with hell." It had some serious defects — the most serious, that of compromise with slavery, which later gave birth to the fugitive-slave law; but its excellencies exceeded its defects. It was a noble instrument of freedom, greater than any other that has ever been framed by a single convention or in a single generation. By it there was conferred upon Congress ample power to put such restraint upon slavery as would eventually bring it to an end. Under the Constitution Congress had power to abolish the slave-trade and that power had been exercised. It had power to put restraints upon the interstate slave-trade, if not to abolish it altogether; and such restriction would have crippled slavery, such abolition would have ultimately destroyed it. It had power to refuse the admission of any new slave state into the Union and to prohibit slavery in any territory of the United States, the exercise of which power would have put slavery in the way of ultimate extinction. It had power, conferred by an explicit clause of the Constitution,

to protect a free press and free speech in every
state in the Union, a power which, had it been
wisely and vigorously exercised, would have made
possible a continuance of the agitation for emancipation in the slave states themselves. More than
all this, John Quincy Adams, in the hot debates
in the House of Representatives, had suggested
that, if war ever broke out, slavery could be abolished under the war powers which the Constitution
confers. His utterance was prophetic, and slavery
was so abolished. The Constitution was no covenant with death, no agreement with hell: it had
in it all the vital powers necessary for the immediate restriction and the eventual extinction of
slavery on the American Continent.

The slaveholder was not a man-stealer. The original slave-dealer in Africa was; but the man who
found himself in a slave state, the owner of slaves
bequeathed to him by his ancestors, was as truly
under the domination of the slave system as the
slave himself. What could he do? Emancipate
his slaves? In one state, if he did so, a tax was
laid upon the emancipated slave for the very purpose of sending him back into slavery again; in
another state, if he did so, he must give bonds that
the slave would never become a pauper, or the act
of manumission was illegal; in another state, he
could not emancipate him legally unless he carried
him out of the state. What should this man do,
who had a hundred slaves in his possession, and
no money with which to provide for them? Should

he set his slaves free, run away from responsibility, and leave them to be sold again at the auction block to the highest bidder? This in many cases would have been the result of "immediate, unconditional emancipation," and this would not have been liberation.

It was therefore not true that immediate, unconditional emancipation was the duty of the hour. It certainly was not the duty of the Northern readers of "The Liberator : " they had no more political power to emancipate the slaves in the Southern States than they had to emancipate the slaves in Turkey. It was not necessarily the duty of the individual slaveholder: if he undertook immediate, unconditional emancipation, he would in many cases only pass his slave from one state of servitude to another and a worse state. Whether it was the duty of the individual state must at least be gravely questioned. When a great wrong has been done by a community, and has been wrought into the social fabric of the community, it cannot be abolished by a single act of legislation. When an individual is engaged in wrong-doing, it is his duty immediately to cease wrong-doing; the doctrine of immediatism, applied by Dr. Beecher to the individual, is sound. When a community has become pervaded by a social injustice which has been wrought into its very structure, it is not always its duty, by an immediate act of legislation, to destroy the structure, in order that it may destroy the evil; the duty of immediatism, applied to the community by Mr. Garrison, was unsound. The single-taxer traces land ownership back to robbery: the Romans stole the land from the Europeans, the Normans from the Anglo-Saxons, the Anglo-Saxons from the Indians; therefore the single-taxer proposes to abolish all ownership in land. Even if it be true that all land ownership is a kind of robbery, it does not follow that it ought to be instantly abolished, with the result of overturning in a day the whole fabric of civilization built upon the private ownership of land. No man ought to work twelve hours a day three hundred and sixty-five days in the year, with no opportunity for a Sabbath or a holiday, save as he secures it sometimes by working eighteen hours a day. It does not follow that the iron-master, who finds himself as much under the domination of the present industrial system as the iron-worker, must put on three shifts, while his neighbors are working with two, and bankrupt himself, or must close his mills and turn his hands out to starve. It is true that slavery was founded on man-stealing; it is not true that the best remedy for slavery was immediate and unconditional abolition of the slave system, without preparation of either slave or society for a better industrial condition.

The doctrine of the abolitionists, summarized in the last four clauses of the platform published in " The Liberator," Mr. Beecher never accepted ; he was not an abolitionist. The abolitionist affirmed, " No union with slaveholders; " Mr. Beecher

said, "We shall abide by the Union."[1] The abolitionist denounced the Constitution as "a covenant
with death and an agreement with hell;" Mr.
Beecher affirmed, "We believe that the compromises of the Constitution look to the destruction
of slavery, not to its establishment."[2] Abolitionists
denounced slaveholders "as a race of monsters,
unparalleled in their assumption of power and their
despotic cruelty;" Mr. Beecher affirmed that both
slave and master "are to be treated with Christian wisdom and forbearance: we must seek to
benefit the slave as much as the white man, the
white man as really as the slave."[3] The abolitionists demanded "immediate, unconditional emancipation;" Mr. Beecher said: "We do not ask to
interfere with the internal policy of a single state.
. . . We will not ask to take one guarantee from
the institution."[4] It is true that Mr. Beecher never
fell into the error of some about him who lost the
true perspective. He never imagined that abolitionism was the provoking cause of the pro-slavery
spirit, or fancied that if Garrison and Phillips
could be silenced, slavery would of itself pass out
of existence. He never imagined that abolition
was the permanent and enduring evil to be fought,
and slavery the lesser and temporary evil to be con-
doned. He never turned aside from the work of

[1] *The Independent*, Feb. 21, 1850: *Patriotic Addresses*, p. 177.
[2] *The Independent*, Feb. 21, 1850: *Patriotic Addresses*, p. 171.
[3] Oct. 30, 1859: *Patriotic Addresses*, p. 209.
[4] *Biography:* p. 242.

arousing the public conscience of the North to do its whole duty respecting slavery, in order to enter into a war of words with men who, by erroneous methods and in an unloving spirit, were seeking the same ultimate end as himself — the enfranchisement of the enslaved race. He devoted the strength of his intellect, the power of his passion, the play of his humor, the keenness of his sarcasm, his vivid imagination, his rhetorical and elocutionary power, to the cause of freedom ; but he believed that this cause of freedom was best subserved by remaining in the Union, by sustaining the Constitution, by treating slave and slave-owner alike as brother men, by using the political power of the nation to prevent the extension of slavery into new territory, and by trusting to the moral influence of persuasion to bring about its gradual abolition in the states where it already existed. In his anti-slavery principles Henry Ward Beecher was at one, not with William Lloyd Garrison and Wendell Phillips, but with James G. Birney, William H. Seward, Salmon P. Chase, Abraham Lincoln. He was not what he has sometimes been called — an abolitionist ; he was an anti-slavery reformer, working within the Constitution, under the law, by practical methods. This general definition of his position must be borne in mind by the reader, if he would understand correctly the history of the events in which Mr. Beecher took part, and of his participation in them, as recorded in the next chapter.

CHAPTER VII

THE ANTI-SLAVERY REFORMER

Mr. Beecher's first participation in any public discussion of the slavery question was in Amherst College. He was chosen one of the disputants in the college debating society. The question for discussion was African colonization, a chimerical scheme, then new, for solving the slavery question by transporting the negroes back to Africa. "Fortunately," he says in his sermon upon the death of Wendell Phillips, " I was assigned to the negative side of the question. In preparing to speak I prepared my whole life. I contended against colonization as a condition of emancipation — enforced colonization was little better than enforced slavery — and advocated immediate emancipation on the broad ground of human rights." His next public service in the anti-slavery cause was in Cincinnati, where, while a student at Lane Seminary, he showed his enthusiasm by volunteering as a special constable, and patrolling the streets to protect the negroes and their friends when pro-slavery riots broke out in the city. There is no record of his speaking on this subject at Lawrenceburg.

In Indianapolis his method of dealing with the

topic was characteristic of his combined courage and caution. In a campaign the wise leader, when considering what to do, takes counsel of courage; when considering how to do it, takes counsel of caution. In Indianapolis there was little hostility to slavery, and bitter hostility to abolitionism. Had Mr. Beecher begun his ministry by an attack on slavery, his ministry would have ended on the day on which it began. For some years, apparently, he did not deal with the question directly. His first reference to it was incidental and by way of illustration. He pictured a father ransoming his son from captivity among the Algerines in such a way as to enlist the sympathy of his hearers with the white slave against the negro slaveholders. " They all thought," he afterwards told the Yale theological students, " I was going to apply it [the illustration] to slavery; but I did not. I applied it to my subject, and it passed off: and they all drew a long breath. It was not long before I had another illustration from that quarter. And so, before I had been there a year, I had gone all over the sore spots of slavery, in illustrating the subjects of Christian experience and doctrine. It broke the ice." It was not until toward the close of his Indianapolis ministry that he preached directly on slavery. He did so in compliance with a recommendation by the Presbytery to all Presbyterian clergy to preach at least one sermon during the year on this theme. Mr. Beecher preached three: in the first, discussing ancient slavery, especially

among the Hebrews; in the second, the doctrine
and practice of the New Testament respecting
slavery; in the third, the moral aspects of American slavery and its effects upon the community.
One of these sermons was published in pamphlet
form, but is out of print. We may assume that in
them was embodied his subsequent teaching, in
which he drew sharply the distinction between Roman and Hebraic slavery, and showed that the existence of the latter afforded no justification for the
former, so great was the difference between the two.

When he came to Brooklyn the conditions in
which he found himself were very different from
those which he confronted in Indianapolis. He
was the pastor of a church just organized. Its
character and spirit would depend largely upon
his ministry. The men who had organized this
church were of New England origin, and entertained New England convictions respecting the sin
and shame of slavery. The year after he came
to Brooklyn "The New York Independent" was
founded. Its three editors, Dr. Leonard Bacon,
Dr. Joseph P. Thompson, and Dr. Richard S.
Storrs, were all pronounced anti-slavery men; two
of its founders, Seth B. Hunt and Henry C.
Bowen, were among the founders of Plymouth
Church. How free a platform Mr. Beecher was
to have in Plymouth Church depended, therefore, primarily upon himself. In his first Sunday
evening sermon he declared his intention to apply
the principles of Jesus Christ to intemperance, to

slavery, and to all other great national sins; and it was his custom thereafter each year, before the pew-renting, to preach a vigorous anti-slavery sermon, that not only the members of his church, but his pewholders also, might know what kind of a gospel they were invited to support. Thus, partly by reason of his circumstances, partly by reason of his courage in availing himself of them, Mr. Beecher avoided the peril which confronted so many ministers in that epoch, who could not speak upon the subject of slavery without stirring up, not only hostility to themselves, but possible intestine warfare within the church, and as a probable result either their own expulsion from the pastorate or the departure from their church and congregation of some of their eminent and perhaps necessary supporters. Throughout the campaign of which we are to give some account in this and the succeeding chapter, Mr. Beecher was supported by a substantially unanimous and generally enthusiastic church and congregation.

Nevertheless, for the first two years Mr. Beecher's main work in Brooklyn was that of a parochial pastor and preacher. He gave himself to the work of building up his church by his spiritual ministry to the congregations which were attracted to it. Like a wise general, he organized and inspired his army before he began his campaign. The burning of the original church building, necessitating the erection of the new one, added to the difficulties incident to a new pastorate, and increased his parochial

labors. Six months of illness, during which time
he was forbidden to preach, interposed another and
a serious obstacle to his ministry. Despite these
facts, the church had grown at the close of the
year 1849, that is, in less than two years and a
half, from twenty-one members to three hundred
and twenty-seven. The church was stronger than
the number of its membership would indicate, for
it was thoroughly loyal to its leader, and was full
of enthusiasm for its work.

During these two years and a half the act which
most distinctly identified Mr. Beecher in the public
mind with the anti-slavery cause was the dramatic
conduct of an auction sale of two negro girls, purchased, as the result of the sale, for freedom. These
two young women, of light complexion, but born of
a slave mother, finding themselves about to be sold
from Washington for exportation to New Orleans,
and probably for a fate more dreadful than death,
endeavored to escape, were captured, and brought
back to Washington. The story of their attempted
flight reached Northern ears; a meeting was held
in the Broadway Tabernacle for the purpose of
raising the necessary funds for their emancipation;
the young preacher from the West was one of the
speakers; he extemporized on the platform a slave
auction and called for bids; the necessary amount
was secured; and the girls were pronounced freed
before the meeting adjourned. This was the first
of a series of similar purchases of slaves, through
Mr. Beecher's instrumentality, during a period of

ten or twelve years. He was criticised by radical
abolitionists for wasting his energies in the emancipation of a few individuals, while the great slave
empire was left undisturbed ; by others, for his
recognition of the right of the owner to his slaves
by paying money to the owner for their manumission ; and by still others, more anxious that all
things should be done decorously and in order than
that anything should be done at all, for sensation-
alism in his methods. But Mr. Beecher's object
was not merely the manumission of a few individual slaves : he believed in the humanity of his fellow men ; he believed that thousands of his fellow
citizens, who would regard with apathy if not with
complacency the slave system at a distance, would
regard with abhorrence the return of an individual
slave girl to a life of enforced sin and shame. At
a later period he said : " The very men who give
their counsel and zeal and money against the unseen
slave *of the South* irresistibly pity the particular
fugitive whom they may *see* running through the
North. They give the Union Committee money to
catch the slave, and give the slave money to escape
from the Committee." He judged that in no way
could he so successfully arouse the dormant feeling
of the North against the slave system as by inviting the coöperation of Northern men and women
to secure the emancipation of individual slaves.
Had he been inclined to defend his method from
those who criticised it as sensational, he might
have referred them to the method of the Hebrew

prophets, who taught so often and so effectually
by dramatic object-lessons.

But such utterances as his first Sunday evening
sermon, in 1847, and such acts as the purchase of
the Edmondson girls, in 1848, were but like the
tuning of the instruments before the symphony, or
the testing of the arms before the beginning of the
battle. In the best sense of the term Mr. Beecher
was an opportunist. He spoke, not like Ralph
Waldo Emerson, merely to declare himself, — he
spoke always for a purpose; his speech was always
addressed to an audience, and always for the purpose of convincing it. He watched, therefore, for
his opportunity, seized it when it came, adjusted
his address to the occasion, and thus enhanced
its effectiveness. His opportunity came with the
introduction of the compromise measures into Congress by Henry Clay, in January, 1850, the same
month in which Plymouth Church entered into
its new building.   The object of these compromise
measures was to readjust the relations between the
North and the South; to put an end to the growing separation between them and heal the breach
which already existed; and to do this on the basis
of the Constitution of the United States by a series
of mutual concessions. The sincerity of Henry
Clay's patriotic purpose will not be doubted by
the impartial student of history. He was seventy-
three years of age; he had recently embraced the
Christian religion; the beginnings of his speech
on the compromise resolutions indicated not only

the seriousness of his mind but the religious spirit
which animated him.

The compromise resolutions included eight propositions, part of them concessions to the North,
part of them to the South: The admission of California with her free constitution, a concession to
the North; no restriction as to slavery in the terri-
torial governments to be established by Congress
in the territory acquired from Mexico, a concession to the South. A declaration that it is inexpedient to abolish slavery in the District of Columbia
without compensation and without the consent of
the state of Maryland and the people of the District, a concession to the South; prohibition of the
slave-trade in the District of Columbia, a concession to the North. More effectual provision for the
rendition of fugitive slaves, a concession to the
South; a declaration that Congress has no power
to interfere with the slave-trade between the states,
a concession to the South. On the whole, the
North had a right to think that the concessions
to the South not only were greater in number but
greater in importance than the concessions to the
North; nevertheless, if the issue between North
and South was one to be adjusted by mutual concessions, the compromise measures were in the
main well conceived.

The ablest argument for these measures, from
the Northern side, is that presented by Daniel
Webster in his famous speech of the 7th of March,
1850. It is not necessary here to pass upon his

motives; they were probably mixed, as the motives
of most men are; in my judgment, there is no just
ground for saying, with Von Holst, that it " was a
candidate's speech, and that its chief object was to
win favor of the South." The Union and the Constitution were Daniel Webster's idol. He knew no
higher end in life than to maintain the Union,
no higher law for political action than the Constitution. With prescience greater than that of his
critics, he foresaw the terrible results to the country if the growing antagonism between North and
South was not allayed and the growing breach was
not healed. There must be either a reëstablishment of the Union or war between North and
South. Events proved him to be wiser in this prophetic judgment than his assailants. The argument
for the compromise measures, from the point of
view of one who feared civil war between the sections, and who recognized no higher law than that
of the Constitution, and no higher ideal than the
preservation of the Union, can be easily summarized in a few words. The Constitution was itself a
succession of compromises. Political life is possible
only on the basis of a succession of compromises.
The objections of the North to the compromise measures were not well considered. The absence of restriction as to slavery in New Mexico would do no
harm, since slavery could never be maintained in a
territory where tobacco, corn, cotton, and rice could
not be raised, and where the land could be made
fertile only by irrigation. To prohibit slavery in

New Mexico was only "to reënact the will of God."
Mr. Webster declared himself ready to assert the
principle of the exclusion of slavery whenever necessary, but he would not do a thing unnecessarily
that wounds the feelings of others. He contended
that it was the duty of the North, under the Constitution, not only to allow but to provide the
means for the rendition of fugitive slaves, and that
the South justly complained that the constitutional
duty of the North in this respect had not been fulfilled.

The speech was received with an outburst of
bitter wrath by the anti-slavery reformers of New
England. Webster was called "a recreant son of
Massachusetts," "a fallen star — Lucifer descend-
ing from Heaven;" his speech, "a blow struck at
freedom and the constitutional rights of the free
states which no Southern arm could have given;"
comparable to no deed in American history done
by a son of New England "but the act of Bene-
dict Arnold;" to be estimated only "as a bid for
the presidency." What was then regarded as the
sober second thought of New England did not sustain these reproaches; his old friends came to his
rescue; and presently the 7th of March speech
came to be recognized as the representative utterance of the overwhelming majority in the North,
who, with Webster, reverenced the Union, recognized the Constitution as the supreme standard for
political action, dreaded a civil war, which they regarded as among the possibilities of a near future,

and believed that the issues between North and
South could be adjusted by mutual concessions.

In estimating the public sentiment of the time,
the reader must recall, not merely the definite argument of a Clay and a Webster in favor of the
compromise measures, but the indefinite feelings of
the community which lay below all such arguments.
The slave was property. It might indeed be argued
that he ought not to be, but in fact he was; emancipation would mean the financial ruin of unnumbered thousands who had invested their all in this
property, which was impliedly secured to them by
the Constitution and explicitly secured to them
by law. The Constitution was the noblest document
struck off by the mind of man in a single epoch,
the basis of the national organization, the secret of
their growth, the hope of their future; abolitionism
condemned the Constitution as "a covenant with
death and an agreement with hell." The union of
the states had given peace and prosperity to millions, and if it were preserved would give peace and
prosperity to millions more; if it were dissolved
the hope of democracy would perish from the earth.
No one could estimate the world's loss in such a
catastrophe; no one could be sure that it would
bring any real gain even to the negro. The sacred
rights of property, the sacred Constitution, the
sacred Union which that Constitution created and
conserved were all in peril; abolitionism threatened them all; compromise alone could save them:
such was the argument, and it carried conviction

to the hearts of the great majority of patriotic citizens, and made many who loved both liberty and their fellow men hesitate at action the issue of which in its effects on both no man could foresee.

Such were the political conditions, although the 7th of March speech had not then been delivered, when Mr. Beecher wrote and published in " The Independent " an editorial whose title indicated his denial of the fundamental principle underlying the compromise measures. The article was entitled "Shall we compromise?" In this article the impossibility of compromise is affirmed with eloquent fervor. " Slavery is right, and slavery is wrong; slavery shall live, slavery shall die; slavery shall extend, slavery shall not extend: are these conflicts to be settled by any mode of parceling out certain territories? Now the battle rages at one point. By and by it will rage at another. These oppugnant elements, slavery and liberty, inherent in our political system, animating our Constitution, checkering our public policy, breeding in statesmen opposite principles of government, and making our whole wisdom of public legislation on many of the greatest questions cross-eyed and contradictory, — these elements are seeking each other's life. One or the other must die." Thus, denying at the outset the fundamental postulate of Mr. Clay and Mr. Webster, Mr. Beecher proceeded to contrast the two theories, the Northern, or democratic, the Southern, or aristocratic, their birth, their growth, their inevitable results. The North puts honor

upon its laborers, who become reading and reflecting men; the South makes labor a disgraceful necessity, denying it education and compelling it by
the lash. "Liberty is a universal right — it belongs to *men*, on the one side; it is a privilege, and
belongs to a *class*, on the other side." "The North
compacts, the South stratifies." He recognized the
fact that the possibilities of both systems were in
the Constitution, but they were there only in the
seed. The compromises of the Constitution were
adopted in the expectation that slavery would be
eradicated by the superior vitality of liberty. Those
compromises "looked to the destruction of slavery,
and not to its establishment." But slavery had acquired a new growth and a new power. The agita-
tions which disturbed the community were not due
to the abolitionists; they were due to the existence of these two irreconcilable systems. The South
has "found out that slavery cannot live and stand
still." It therefore demands room for extension;
"for every Free state a state for Slavery; one dark
orb must be swung into its orbit, to grow and tra-
vail in pain, for every new orb of liberty over
which the morning stars shall sing for joy." "No
compromises can help us which dodge the question; certainly none which settle it for slavery."
It is the duty of the North "openly, firmly, and
forever to refuse to slavery another inch of territory, and to see that it never gets any by fraud."
"It is her duty to declare that she will under no
considerations be a party to any further inhumanity

and injustice." Mr. Clay's resolutions demanded
better provision for the recovery of fugitive slaves.
Mr. Beecher did not deny that such provisions are
called for by the compromises of the Constitution,
but he declared that there is a higher law than the
Constitution. "Not even the Constitution shall
make me unjust." "I put constitution against
constitution — God's against man's. Where they
agree, they are doubly sacred; where they differ,
my reply to all questioners, but especially to all
timid Christian scruples, is in the language of
Peter: 'Whether it be right in the sight of God
to hearken unto you more than unto God, judge
ye.'" As there is a higher law than the Constitution, so there is a higher ideal than the Union.
"The very value of our Union is to be found in
those principles of justice, liberty, and humanity
which inspire it." If "these principles must be
yielded up to preserve the Union, then a corpse
only will be left in our arms, deflowered, lifeless,
worthless." "Religion and humanity are a price
too dear to pay even for the Union;" and religion
and humanity are set at naught by slavery, which
takes liberty from those to whom God gave it, forbids food for the understanding or the heart, takes
honesty from the conscience, and defense from virtue, "gives authority into the hands of lustful or
pecuniary cupidity, scorns the family, and invades
it whenever desire or the want of money prevails,
with the same coolness with which a drover singles
out a heifer, or a butcher strikes down a bullock.

These are not the accidents of slavery; they are its
legitimate fruits, they are its vitality. If you stop
these evils you will destroy the system." The article closes with a declaration of war against slavery.
" We shall study to circumscribe slavery where it
now exists. We shall oppose every party that se-
cretly or openly connives at it. We shall be hostile
to every measure which consults its interests. . . .
We will compromise any measures tending to prevent the extension of slavery. We will compromise
as to the particulars of its death, laying out, and
burial. But every compromise must include the
advantage of liberty and the disadvantage of
slavery." " We shall abide by the Union. . . .
If there be those who cannot abide the Union, because it is pure and religious, just and humane, let
them beware of that tumultuous scene into which
they purpose to leap." But he does not believe
that any such issue will result. " Firmness is the
remedy for threats. If good men, having good
representatives, are but firm, the storm will beat
the stout oak and rage like a demon through its
twisted branches, but pass on and spend itself in
the wilderness; meanwhile the returning sun shall
find the noble tree unwrecked and fast-rooted."

It is said that this article was read to John C.
Calhoun, then on his death-bed, that he asked the
name of the author, and said: " That man under-
stands the thing; he has gone to the bottom of it;
he will be heard from again." It is because in this
article Mr. Beecher did go to the bottom of the

questions involved in the compromise measures that we have given its substance at so great length. In it he anticipated by three weeks William H. Seward's declaration that there is a higher law than the Constitution, and by nearly ten years Abraham Lincoln's declaration that there is an irreconcilable conflict between slavery and liberty; in it the fundamental principles of the Republican party were asserted six years before the Republican party was organized, and ten years before it elected Abraham Lincoln upon a platform embodying those principles. In it were contained in compact statement substantially all for which its author was to contend through the ten years of incessant campaigning which preceded the Civil War.

There is no advantage in treating Mr. Beecher's views on the subject of slavery, from this time forward, in any chronological order, because there was in those views no chronological development. He did not speak on the subject of slavery until he had studied it in its various relations, well considered its various aspects, and determined what his message should be concerning the whole subject, and all the questions that would be likely to grow out of it. In this respect he set an example which ministers in haste to speak on the social questions of our time would do well to follow. His position on the complicated questions involved will be better interpreted by giving them topically than by giving them chronologically. In doing this I depend largely upon the volume of " Patriotic

Addresses," in which John R. Howard has brought
together the most important of Mr. Beecher's public speeches on slavery, the Civil War, and reconstruction.

I. The apologists for and defenders of American slavery Mr. Beecher met with a clear definition
of the American system and a scholarly discrimination of it from Hebrew slavery. The American
slave was a chattel; he was the property of his
master. The end of the system was judicially declared to be " the profit of the master, his security,
and the public peace." The slave was judicially
defined to be " one doomed in his own person
and in his posterity to live without knowledge, and
without capacity to make anything his own, and to
toil that others may reap the fruits." The system forbade marriage and legalized and promoted
lust. " A wedding among this unhappy people is
but a name, — a mere form to content their conscience or their love of imitating their superiors.
Every auctioneer in the community has the power
to put asunder whom God has joined. The degeneracy of their owner is the degeneracy of the
marriage relation in half the slaves on his plantation." Such a system as this Mr. Beecher declared
to be incapable of reformation. " To say to three
million men made by God, ' Ye are not men, but
like oxen and horses, like dogs and hogs, ye are
things, property, chattels,' — why, to talk of the
abuse of a system which has this for its elementary
principle is as wild as it would be to talk of the

abuse of robbery, the abuse of murder, the abuse of adultery.' " There was nothing in the Hebrew system of slavery to afford justification for the American system. Among the Hebrews there were three forms of servitude. First, that into which the Hebrews themselves might come — a kind of apprenticeship. Secondly, a public slavery; that of the Gibeonites, who did service for the commonwealth. Thirdly, the Hebrew bond-service, which was slavery proper. This slavery was not enacted by Moses. He found it and he regulated it and limited it. Only a heathen could be made a slave. As a condition of his enslavement he must be circumcised, that is, introduced into the privilege of the Church, and the master was obliged to give him a religious education; if he was wronged, he could apply to the courts for redress; if he was maimed, he immediately became free; if he ran away, he could not be forcibly returned. " All the laws of Moses were in favor of the slave — for his advantage, his benefit, his encouragement, his defense."

The Hebrews legislated for their slaves as men, but we make them property — chattels. They are not men but brutes. Four thousand years ago the slave enjoyed the privileges of the Church — the Temple worship; now we give him no religion. Four thousand years ago the slave enjoyed the rights and privileges of the family state; now the chastity of man and woman is no more regarded than that of a dog. Four thousand years ago the laws were made for the slave; now they are made for the master. Four thousand years ago a slave could

seek redress in court; now there is not a court from
Mason and Dixon's Line through to Texas where a slave
can open his mouth as a witness and be believed. Ah!
if you will only bring American slavery on the platform
of Hebrew slavery — if you will give the slave the Bible,
and send him to school, and open the doors of the courts
to him, then we will let it alone — it will take care of
itself. In old times slaves were treated as children of a
family, trained, nurtured, educated. Let the Southern
slaveholder do like this. Then would slavery soon cease,
for the care and expense would be greater than any one
could bear.[1]

II. Between this slave system of the South and
the free system of the North compromise was impossible. The policy of the South was not one of
vexatious haughtiness; it sprang from the irresist-
ible nature of their industrial system. If their
aggressive temper were due to violence provoked by
agitation, it would be reasonable to expect " that
forbearance, conciliation, and compromise will restore good temper, and with returning temper that
things will grow peaceable." But the aggressive
demands of the South came from a law stronger
than the volition — from a law which underlies
society and compels its movements. The South
could not endure free speech; it was fatal to the
slave system. " One spark may explode a magazine, and one word touch off a servile insurrection
fatal alike to master and slave. To keep fetters on
their servants they must keep fetters on their own
tongues. Their mouth is a prison, their tongue is

[1] *Patriotic Addresses*, 183, 184.

a prisoner. Liberty of the speech and of the press, liberty of political action, in the slave states, but especially the more southern ones, would break them up." If American slavery was to continue, therefore, free speech must be abolished, for "free speech is wrong if slavery is right." And it was as impossible to allow free speech in Congress or in the North as in the South. "There is no theoretic disposition to abridge liberty of speech in Congress, but our country is now so sympathetically connected, the transmission of news is so marvelously easy and quick, that Congress has become a speaking-trumpet. The whole nation hears its speeches. . . . The Southern man says: 'With you it is not a necessity to speak, with us it is a matter of necessity to have silence. . . . It is only a theoretic sentiment that impels you, it is self-existence that drives us.' As a matter of fact this is true. A system of slavery is imperiled by the natural contact of a system of liberty." The same necessity compels the South to demand the extension of slavery. Free states increase in wealth and population, slave states remain stationary or deteriorate. "Virginia cannot grow — Pennsylvania cannot stand still. The Carolinas are sinking by the nature of their industry, New York is advancing prodigiously. Georgia has no chance in a match with Ohio. If the slave states stand as they are and depend upon the inherent energies of their own system, they are doomed, inevitably, to become the last and least. That which they lack, therefore, in intrinsic force, they are compelled to seek by extension. Arkansas supplements Virginia. When New York weighs down the Carolinas, Texas is thrown in to bring up the scale." But uncompromising adherence to principle does not involve war upon the South. "If by compromise is only meant forbearance, kindness, well-wishing, conciliation, fidelity to agreements, a concession in things, not principles, why, then, we believe in compromise; — only that is not compromise, interpreted by the facts of our past history." The anti-slavery Northerner wishes no harm to the South or to its people, covets not their territory, is not jealous of their honors, does not ask to molest the South in her own institutions, does not even deny them liberty to retake their fugitive slaves where they can find them. "But we will not be made constables to slavery, to run and catch, to serve writs and return prisoners. . . . We will, and with growing earnestness to the end, fulfill every just duty, every honorable agreement, and every generous act, within the limits of truth and honor; all this and no more, — no more though the heavens fall, — no more, if states unclasp their hands, — no more, if they raise up violence against us, — no more." Compromise was a sham. The promise of peace through compromise was a deceitful promise. "The only way to peace is that way which shall chain slavery to the place it now has, and say to the dragon, ' In thy den thou must dwell, and lie down in thine own slime, but thou shalt not go forth to

ravage free territory or leave thy trail upon un-
spotted soil.'"

III. The duty of the North was in his view perfectly simple and perfectly plain. It was to use
the power conferred upon it under the Constitution
to confine slavery within its then existing limits.
That it possessed such power had been conceded in
Congress by the foremost statesman of the Southern States, John C. Calhoun. It was not until it
became clear that the consent of the North to the
extension of slavery into free territory would be
difficult if not impossible to obtain, that the doctrine was developed that Congress could not prohibit slavery in the territories, — that slavery was
national, not local. Mr. Beecher did not argue the
constitutional question. He assumed the correct-
ness of the view held alike by North and South in
the earlier days of the republic. The North had
no right to interfere with slavery in the states; but
it had the right to prohibit the extension of slavery
in free territory; and it was under a sacred obligation to exercise this right. That exercise exhausted its powers under the Constitution, and
therefore fulfilled its political obligations. Such
restriction effected, the North must trust to time,
patience, and kindly influence, for the ultimate
extinction of slavery. This principle of political
action was so fundamental to Mr. Beecher's whole
course during the decade of anti-slavery agitation
from 1850 to 1860, and it so differentiates him
from the abolitionists, on the one hand, and the

so-called conservatives, on the other, that we quote at considerable length from his own statement in " The Independent." [1]

Our policy for the future is plain. All the natural laws of God are warring upon slavery. We have only to let the process go on. Let slavery alone. Let it go to seed. Hold it to its own natural fruit. Cause it to abide by itself. Cut off every branch that hangs beyond the wall, every root that spreads. Shut it up to itself and let it alone. We do not ask to interfere with the internal policy of a single state by congressional enactments: we will not ask to take one guarantee from the institution. We only ask that a line be drawn about it; that an insuperable bank be cast up; that it be fixed and forever settled that slavery must find no new sources, new fields, new prerogatives, but that it must abide in its place, subject to all the legitimate changes which will be brought upon it by the spirit of a nation essentially democratic, by schools taught by enlightened men, by colleges sending annually into every profession thousands bred to justice and hating its reverse, by churches preaching a gospel that has always heralded civil liberty, by manufactories that always thrive best when the masses are free and refined and therefore have their wants multiplied, by free agriculture and free commerce.

When slavery begins, under such treatment, to flag, we demand that she be denied political favoritism to regain her loss; we demand that no laws be enacted to give health to her paralysis and strength to her relaxing grasp. She boldly and honestly demanded a right to equality with the North, and prophetically spoke by Calhoun that the North would preponderate and crush her. It is true.

---

[1] Quoted in the *Biography*, 242, 243.

Time is her enemy. Liberty will, if let alone, always be a match for oppression. Now, it is because statesmen propose stepping in between slavery and the appointed bourne, to which she goes, scourged by God and Nature, that we resent these statesmen and refuse to follow them. If her wounds can be stanched, if she may have adventitious aid in new privileges, slavery will renew her strength and stave off the final day. But if it be forbidden one additional favor, and be obliged to stand up by the side of free labor, free schools, free churches, free institutions; if it be obliged to live in a land of free books, free papers, and free Bibles, it will either die or else it ought to live.

Was Mr. Beecher right? Would the restriction of slavery have resulted in the ultimate extinction of slavery? History does not answer that question, for slavery was overthrown by a very different process. But it is clear that the slave power believed with Mr. Beecher, that the extension of slavery was necessary to its continued existence. Senator Toombs, of Georgia, wished to see the South American states annexed in order to make room for slavery; Pierre Soulé, of Louisiana, sought the annexation of Cuba for the same purpose; Barringer, of North Carolina, speaking in 1861, for the secessionists, declared that no compromise could be considered which did not concede new territory to the slave states. " They know," he said, " that when slavery is gathered into a *cul de sac* and surrounded by a wall of free states, it is destroyed. Slavery must have expansion. It must expand by the acquisition of territory which now we do not

own." It was because the leaders of the slave power
were convinced of this truth that when, by the election of Abraham Lincoln, the North declared that
there should be no more extension of slavery in the
Union, they resolved to destroy the Union and seek
extension elsewhere. The abolitionists who sought
to destroy the Union in order to destroy slavery
enlisted on behalf of slavery the sentiments of
national patriotism and national pride; the anti-
slavery reformers, among whom Mr. Beecher was
a leader, by insisting on the maintenance of the
Union and the restriction of slavery, at last saw
the sentiments of national patriotism and national
pride enlisted in the destruction of slavery that the
nation might be preserved.

IV. What was the duty of the North respecting
the Fugitive-Slave Law? The answer to this question in 1850–60 was not so clear as it now seems
to the unconsidering reader. The Constitution of
the United States (Art. IV., sec. ii., 3) provided
that persons lawfully bound in any state to service
or labor, who fled into another state, should be
delivered up on demand. This clause had been
unanimously adopted, and without debate, by the
Constitutional Convention. In point of fact, the
fugitive slaves were not delivered up on demand.
They escaped in considerable number to the North,
and the Northern States made no provision for
their return. On the contrary, many of the states,
by "personal liberty laws," encouraged the escape
of the slave and discouraged their capture and

return.[1]   State officers who assisted slave-hunters
were fined; lawyers who conducted the cases of
alleged owners were disbarred; the confinement
of fugitive slaves in state prison was prohibited;
state prosecuting attorneys were charged with the
duty of defending and if possible securing the dis-
charge of every arrested fugitive slave. Voluntary
organizations were formed in different parts of the
North to aid the escape of fugitive slaves. They
were sent from one trusted member of this organization to another, until they found safety in Canada.
In an official report the secretary of one anti-slavery
society announced that four hundred fugitive slaves
had thus been aided to escape by that one organization. The South, believing that the slave was
property and that the North was bound in honor
by the clause of the Constitution to return the
slave, was indignant; the North, believing the slave
was a man, that the return of a fugitive slave to
bondage was inhuman, and that humanity was of
higher authority than the Constitution, continued
to disregard the clause of the Constitution and to
aid in the escape of the slave.

Among the laws which, combined, constituted
the compromise measures of 1850, was a fugitive-
slave law, which intrusted to federal officers the
execution and enforcement of the provision of
the Constitution of the United States providing for

---

[1] Some, if not most of these laws, were subsequent in date to
the Fugitive-Slave Law; but they illustrate the feeling against
returning fugitive slaves prior to that law.

the return of fugitive slaves. This law provided
for certain commissioners, to be appointed by the
circuit courts of the United States, who were to
take cognizance of fugitive-slave cases. The testimony of two witnesses to the escape of a slave, and
the identification of the arrested fugitive by the
oath of one person, was declared to be satisfactory
proof on which to base his return to his master.
The proceedings were summary; no jury trial was
allowed; the testimony of the accused was not
admitted; all good citizens were required to aid
in the execution of the law; and any attempt to
harbor or conceal a fugitive slave was punishable
with fine and imprisonment.

Few in the North approved the spirit of this
law; none in the North liked it; but many defended it. It was claimed that it simply fulfilled
the constitutional obligation which the North was
in duty bound to fulfill; that the return of a fugitive slave could not be wrong, since Paul returned
Onesimus to slavery; that it was enacted by the
law-making power and that obedience to law was
the duty of the citizen, whether he liked it or not.
Mr. Beecher, I do not think, ever raised any question as to the constitutionality of the law. That it
was constitutional cannot now be questioned by any
impartial historian. No provision had been made
by the states for carrying into effect the clause of
the Constitution requiring the return of persons
held to service or labor when they escaped from
one state to another state. The fact that the

clause was in the Constitution was sufficient to authorize Congress to make provision for carrying it into effect by federal machinery and through the federal courts. The commissioners provided for by the law might properly be regarded as special judges created by statute, with special judicial functions conferred upon them. Jury trial in the state in which the fugitive was arrested was not his constitutional right, since it was assumed that the trial would take place in the state from which he had fled, as it does in the case of an accused fleeing from one state and carried back to it under extradition proceedings for trial. But Mr. Beecher denied that the clause in the Constitution providing for the return of fugitive slaves created a moral obligation to return them. He affirmed that the requirements of humanity were of superior authority to those of the Constitution. That there could be no higher law than the Constitution he condemned as subversive alike of the fundamental postulate of ethics and of the foundations of a free state.

Human nature is a poor affair — man is but a pithy, porous, flabby substance, till you put conscience into him ; and as for building a republic on men who do not hold to the rights of private conscience, who will not follow their own consciences rather than that of any priest or public, you might as well build your custom-house in Wall Street on a foundation of cotton-wool. But the nation that regards conscience more than anything else, above all customs and all laws, is like New England with its granite hills, immovable and invincible ; and the nation that does not regard conscience is a mere base of sand, and quicksand too, at that.[1]

That any ministers should cite the return of Onesimus to his master by Paul as an argument for the return of a fugitive slave in America under the Fugitive-Slave Law, would seem extraordinary, were not such unintelligent use of Scripture common whenever external authority is substituted for moral sense as the final test of conduct. Mr. Beecher did not question the authority, but he denied the analogy : —

There are two ways of sending fugitives back into slavery. Paul gives us an account of one way, — the way he sent back the slave Onesimus. Now, if people will adopt Paul's way, I would not object. In the first place, he instructed him in Christianity and led him to become a Christian. Then he wrote a letter and sent it by Onesimus. The slave was not sent off under the charge of officers, but he went back alone, of his own free will, with a letter and recommendation as a brother beloved.[2]

But he spent little time in replying to half-hearted apologies for the law. He appealed against it to the moral sense of the North. He condemned it on the ground that it violated the law of God ; in eloquent terms and repeatedly he defied it.

The law is bad enough in obliging the officers to execute it, but when it comes down among the citizens, when it forbids us helping a man to liberty, I say, "God do so to me and more also, if I do not help him freedomward."

[1] *Patriotic Addresses*, p. 194.   [2] *Ibid.* p. 189.

He indicted the law not as unconstitutional, but as inhuman in what it undertook to do — send back a man to bondage, and a woman to the shambles of lust; immoral in what it required the citizen to do, in requiring him to coöperate in such active inhumanity; impolitic, because it excited in the North an indignation against the law which gave the fugitive many friends where he before had few, and so practically promoted the escape of fugitive slaves, which it was the object of the law to prevent; injurious to the nation, because it stirred up ill blood between North and South; irreligious, because it led men and even ministers to scout at " the higher law," — the law of conscience, the law of God, the law upon which obedience to all law is based; unpatriotic, because more than anything of recent occurrence it had promoted a disregard of authority and a contempt for all law. To the argument that law when enacted must be obeyed, and that there is an end of all liberty based on law if each individual in a free community may decide for himself whether he will obey the law or not, and discard it at his option, — an argument which perplexed many conscientious citizens, — he replied by drawing sharply the distinction between endurance of wrong when inflicted and the commission of wrong when required.

Every citizen must obey a law which inflicts injury upon his person, estate, and civil privilege, until legally redressed; but no citizen is bound to obey a law which commands *him* to *inflict* injury upon another. We must

endure but never *commit* wrong. We must be patient
when sinned against, but must never sin against others.
The law may heap injustice upon me, but no law can
authorize me to pour injustice upon another. When the
law commanded Daniel not to pray, he disobeyed it;
when it commanded him to be cast into the lion's den,
he submitted.[1]

This principle he summed up in the following
aphoristic sentence: "Obedience to laws, even
though they sin against me : disobedience to every
law that commands me to sin."

V. The duty of the North was not merely negative; it was not merely political; it was not fulfilled by refusing obedience to the Fugitive-Slave
Law and refusing to acquiesce in the extension of
slavery. The North had other and affirmative
duties to perform; it had a transcendent duty of
maintaining in all its anti-slavery campaign a spirit
of brotherly kindness toward master as well as slave.
In an address delivered before the American and
Foreign Anti-Slavery Society in May, 1851, Mr.
Beecher said : —

The first business is to limit slavery within its present
bounds; there is nothing in the Constitution against this,
at any rate; then, secondly, to see to it that the South
has not factitious help from us in the support of slavery;
and thirdly, not to interfere directly with slavery where
it is. We are to do what the sun does when it comes up
over the eastern hills; it looks at a mountain of ice and
melts it. If our missionaries want to convert the Arabs,
they cannot preach to them when they are on horseback,

[1] Quoted in *Biography*, p. 241.

for they will run away; they must make the Arabs sit down and be fixed in one spot. And so must we do with slavery; we must hitch her and anchor her, and then begin with brotherly affection to kill her. And then with our hearts warm and kind, and with no hasty or hard remarks, we must preach the Bible to them, and preach till we make slavery a burden to their consciences, and a burden to their pockets, as it is now a burden on God's forbearance.[1]

This spirit pervaded all his anti-slavery addresses. The North was not to treat the citizens of the South with acrimony and bitterness because they were involved in a system of wrong-doing. It was not to breed discontent among the bondmen. "Whatever gloomy thoughts the slave's own mind may brood, we are not to carry disquiet to him from without." The North ought not to encourage any organized plan to carry the slaves off or to incite them to abscond; still less should it promote or tolerate anything like insurrection and servile war. "By all the conscience of a man, by all the faith of a Christian, and by all the zeal and warmth of a philanthropist, I protest against any counsels that lead to insurrection, servile war, and bloodshed. It is bad for the master, and bad for the slave, bad for all that are neighbors to them, bad for the whole land, — bad from beginning to end."[2]

---

[1] *Patriotic Addresses*, p. 187.

[2] This explicit condemnation of John Brown's method, coupled with appreciation of John Brown's fanatical courage, was uttered in a sermon preached October 30, 1859, while John Brown was in prison awaiting trial.

The North should begin reform at the North. There the free colored people were refused the common rights of citizenship, could not ride in the city cars, were shut out from the common industrial employments, were taxed for the schools and the schools closed against their children, were barely tolerated in the churches. All this ought to be reformed. "What can the North do for the South unless her own heart is purified and ennobled! The North must maintain sympathy and kindness toward the South. We are brethren, and I pray that no fratricidal influences be permitted to sunder this Union." "If I might speak for the North, I would say to the South: ' We love you and hate your slavery. We shall leave no fraternal effort untried to deliver you, and ourselves with you, from the degradation, wickedness, and danger of this system, and for this we cling to the Union. There is health in it.'" The North must be in earnest to rid itself of all complicity with the sin of slavery. "You and I are guilty of the spread of slavery unless we have exerted, normally and legitimately, every influence in our power against it." If we acquiesce in slavery, " we clothe ourselves with the cotton which the slave tills. Is he scorched, is he lashed, does he water the crop with his sweat and tears, it is you and I that wear the shirt and consume the luxury. Our looms and our factories are largely built on the slave's bones; we live on his labor." I think one would search Mr. Beecher's speeches and writings in vain for a single instance in which his condemnation of the sin of slavery was tainted with the Pharisaic tone of " I am holier than thou." His condemnation of slavery was also a confession; he took, as it were, upon himself the sin and shame, against which he summoned all his energies in a long and what at times seemed a hopeless campaign.

VI. What had the Church to do with slavery?

In a Democratic procession in Brooklyn in 1856 a transparency was borne bearing the legend, " Henry Ward Beecher had better stick to the pulpit." That any one should have thought that preaching respecting a system which denied the right of the laborer to his wages, the right of the husband to his wife and the wife to her husband, of the parents to the children and the children to the parents, and of all to education and to freedom in religion, was a violation of this legend, and that to deal with such a system was to depart from the legitimate function of a Christian teacher, seems to us in this twentieth century wholly incredible. But the Democratic legend expressed what was a common and, in the beginning of the decade of which we are writing, an almost universal belief in the churches and among the clergy. It is not true that the churches of the North in 1850 were pro-slavery; but it is true that they did not think it the function of the Church to deal with slavery. Nor was the saying, " Let the minister preach the Gospel," a mere cowardly evasion of a difficult and dangerous duty; genuine conviction lay behind this utterance. I think it was in 1875 that Dwight L. Moody came to Mr. Beecher, asking him to resign his pulpit and go into an evangelical campaign for the conversion of the world. " We two working together," he said, in urging this plan upon Mr. Beecher, " could shake the Continent as it never has been shaken before." Mr. Beecher, in telling me this incident afterwards, said, in substance, — of course I do not pretend at this late date to remember and quote his exact words, — " This proposition of Mr. Moody's was very attractive to me. I should like to go up and down the land preaching the gospel of the love of God in Christ Jesus. But Mr. Moody and I could not possibly work together in such a mission : he believes that the world is lost, and he is seeking to save from the wreck as many individuals as he can ; I believe that this world is to be saved, and I am seeking to bring about the Kingdom of God on this earth." These two conceptions of the Christian religion, one of which regards as its end a world redemption and the creation of a new social order founded on righteousness and inspired by love, the other of which regards the end of the Christian religion the preparation of few or many in this life of probation for a heaven beyond the grave, are not necessarily inconsistent — each may include the other ; in point of fact, however, each has generally been held exclusively of the other. The doctrine of a lost world from which a few are to be saved for a future heaven was inherited by the churches from a mediæval theology, and, though somewhat modified, was still dominant in 1850. The Home Missionary Society, the Foreign Missionary Society, the American Tract Society, all maintained a policy of silence respecting slavery; not merely because speech would imperil the organization, but because slavery belonged to the present social order, — and they maintained that it was not their function to deal with the present social order. Whether in 1850 Mr. Beecher had formulated his theology respecting what has since been called " social salvation " as clearly as he had in 1875, I do not know; I rather think not. It was characteristic of Mr. Beecher, as it is of most men of action, to act on his instincts first and formulate his philosophy afterwards. His theory of life grew out of his living; and it was impossible for such a man as he, inspired by the spirit of humanity which animated him, to live in a country in which slavery was spreading its baleful influences over the whole nation, and have the opportunity to speak, and still keep silence. " I do not know," he said in 1886, in an address before the London Congregational Board, " what it is in me — whether it is my father or my mother or both of them — but the moment that you tell me that a thing that should be done is unpopular, I am right there every time. I fed on the privilege of making men hear things that they did not want to hear because I was a public speaker. I gloried in my gifts, not because they brought praise, for they brought the other thing continually; but men would come and would hear, and I rejoiced in it." It was quite

impossible that a man with this fire in his bones,
with men coming to hear what he had to say, could
be silent on slavery, when slavery was the upper-
most moral issue in the community.

Mr. Beecher was not a preacher *and* an anti-
slavery reformer; he was an anti-slavery reformer
because he was a preacher. Slavery was an obstacle to the Kingdom of God. It was the opposite of
that kingdom which is righteousness and peace and
joy. It involved wrongness and war and misery.
It destroyed men, and Jesus Christ came to build
men up. Mr. Beecher could not preach this Gospel of Christ and work for this Kingdom of God
without coming in conflict with the system which
antagonized the one and destroyed the other. In
his " Review of Thirteen Years in the Ministry " he
states this principle broadly without making special application of it to slavery.

When I hear men say they are ordained to preach
the Gospel, and that they are consequently not to meddle with public questions which disturb the peace, I
always ask myself what Gospel it is that man is ordained to preach which forbids him to meddle with
public questions that disturb the peace; for it is explicitly declared that the Gospel of Christ should cause
disturbance. . . . I hold that it is a Christian minister's
duty not only to preach the Gospel of the New Testament without reservation, but to apply its truths to
every question which relates to the welfare of men;
and, as far as I am concerned, I am willing to do this
and take the consequences, whatever they may be.[1]

[1] *Sermons*, Harper's Edition, vol. i. pp. 28, 29.

In an address delivered before the Anti-Slavery Society, and in a subsequent letter to the "New York Tribune," both of which are quoted from in the "Biography of Henry Ward Beecher," by his son and son-in-law, he states this principle more fully in its specific application to slavery. "My earnest desire is that slavery may be destroyed by the manifest power of Christianity. If it were given me to choose whether it should be destroyed in fifty years by selfish commercial influences, or, standing for seventy-five years, be then the spirit and trophy of Christ, I would rather let it linger twenty-five years more, that God may be honored, and not mammon, in the destruction of it." In response to the "Tribune's" criticism of this sentiment, he reaffirmed and reinforced it.

Our highest and strongest reason for seeking justice among men is *not* the benefit to men themselves, exceedingly strong as that motive is and ought to be. We do not join the movement party of our times simply because we are inspired by an inward and constitutional benevolence. We are conscious of both these motives and of many other collateral ones; but we are earnestly conscious of another feeling stronger than either, that lives unimpaired when these faint, yea, that gives vigor and persistence to these feelings when they are discouraged; and that is a strong, personal, enthusiastic love for Christ Jesus. I regard the movement of the world toward justice and rectitude to be of His inspirations. I believe my own aspirations, having a base in my natural faculties, to be influenced and directed by Christ's spirit. The mingled affection and adoration which I feel for Him is the strongest feeling that I know. Whether I will or not, whether it be a phantasy or a sober sentiment, the fact is the same nevertheless, that that which will give pleasure to Christ's heart and bring to my consciousness a smile of gladness on His face in behalf of my endeavor, is incalculably more to me than any other motive. I would work for the slave for his own sake, but I am sure that I would work ten times as earnestly for the slave for Christ's sake.[1]

If this spirit distinguished Mr. Beecher from the merely anti-slavery reformers on the one hand, and from the theological and ecclesiastical preachers on the other, it distinguished him also from certain anti-slavery preachers who were rather reformers than preachers of the Gospel, and whose churches suffered in consequence from the diversion of their interests and enthusiasms from a spiritual to a merely ethical work. It was this recognition of the anti-slavery movement as a Gospel movement, and of humanity and liberty as essential elements in the Kingdom of God of which the Christian minister is a herald, that enabled him to carry on his church work, and with extraordinary spiritual results, and accompanied by a remarkable revival, in the midst of an anti-slavery campaign from which he never suffered himself to be diverted, and in which he never relaxed his efforts.

[1] Quoted in *Biography*, p. 269.

CHAPTER VIII

THE ANTI-SLAVERY CAMPAIGN

FOR the ten years 1850–60, Mr. Beecher devoted himself to the propagation of the principles stated in the preceding chapter: the fundamental truth — that slavery is inherently and essentially wrong; the ultimate end to be constantly kept in view — the abolition of slavery; the means for the accomplishment of that end — the restriction of slavery within the then existing limits of slave territory; the underlying principle — no participation by the North in the sin of slavery, and therefore no return by the North of fugitive slaves; the spirit — one of good will alike to black and white, to slave and master; a chief instrument in the working out of this reform — the Church of Jesus Christ; the dominant, animating motive — love for Christ and loyalty to Him and His kingdom. He emphasized now one of these principles, now another, according to the exigency of the time, the nature of the audience he addressed, his own mood; but he never retracted, never modified, never added to these fundamental principles. With one exception, hereinafter to be mentioned, all his teaching relating to the slavery question was a development and application of his article in " The New York Inde-

pendent" of February 21, 1850, entitled "Shall
we compromise?"[1]

The compromise measures were enacted in July,
1850. Idaho and New Mexico were organized as
territories, with no reference to slavery. California
was admitted as a free state. Slave-trade was abolished in the District of Columbia. The Fugitive-
Slave Law was enacted and its machinery set in
operation. Wherever a fugitive slave was arrested
popular excitement was aroused, popular hostility
to slavery was intensified, and converts to the anti-
slavery cause were made. Men who assented to
slavery as a patriarchal institution in the remote
South were aroused to indignation when they were
asked to aid or even acquiesce in the return to
slavery of a fugitive who had made his escape from
it. Prominent men took part in stirring up the
public to open, though fruitless, resistance to this
law; others, with greater wisdom, aided in evad-
ing it. This was done not only by radical abolitionists — not only such men as Samuel J. May
and Theodore Parker, but practical politicians like
Thurlow Weed, United States officials like George
S. Hilliard, anti-slavery editors like Horace Greeley, aided and abetted the operation of the "under-
ground railroad." Sometimes these evasions took
on a whimsical turn. The story is told of a United
States marshal in Boston under a Democratic
administration, who, when he was applied to for
aid in arresting a fugitive slave, was accustomed

[1] See page 167 ff.

to reply, "I will see if I can find him;" then always went to William Lloyd Garrison's office and said, "I want to find such and such a negro; tell me where he is." "The next thing I knew," he said afterwards, "the fellow was in Canada." After nearly three years, it is said that not fifty slaves had been recovered under the Fugitive-Slave Law.

But the excitements occasioned by the spasmodic attempts to recover fugitive slaves in the North were both local and short-lived. The general impression was that the compromise measures were a success. The country had a respite from the anti-slavery agitation, and rejoiced in its peace. Whoever attempted to disturb that peace by reopening the question aroused against himself the hostility of the community. Strange as it may appear to us now, to the great mass of the men in the North the slavery question appeared to be settled. So marked was this effect of the compromise measures that President Fillmore, who had succeeded to the office on the death of Zachary Taylor, was able to declare that "the agitation which for a time threatened to disturb the fraternal relations which make us one people is fast subsiding," and to congratulate the country "upon the general acquiescence in these measures of peace which has been accepted in all parts of the Republic." New issues arose to divert public interest to other topics of public discussion. The long dispute between the United States and Great Britain respecting an isthmian canal connect-

ing the Atlantic and the Pacific oceans was settled
by the famous Clayton-Bulwer treaty, and this
achievement turned public attention from national
to international problems. No one then realized that
half a century would pass and the canal would still
be uncompleted and, indeed, scarcely begun. The
dramatic revolution in Hungary aroused public
interest; with the arrival of Kossuth on our shores,
it became a brief but passionate excitement. The
famous letter of Daniel Webster to Mr. Hulsemann,
the Austrian chargé, affirming the interest of the
United States in this revolution, and its right and
intention to recognize, in its own discretion, any *de
facto* revolutionary government, aroused the enthusiasm of American lovers of liberty, and turned
their thoughts for the moment away from the violation of liberty within their own country. A new
native American party, with a secret oath-bound
organization, bearing the popular title of " Know-
Nothing," partly religious, partly political, which
aimed at the exclusion of foreigners from control,
and therefore from office, widened and intensified
the popular impression that the slavery issue was a
past issue, and that other and more immediately important questions had taken its place. This belief
found at once expression and confirmation in the
election of the Democratic candidate for the presidency — Franklin Pierce — by an overwhelming
majority, two hundred and fifty-four electoral votes
against forty-two for the Whig candidate, Winfield
Scott, with a popular majority of more than two

hundred thousand, the largest which had ever been received since any record was made of the popular vote. Says James Ford Rhodes in his "History of the United States:" "The reason of Democratic success was because that party unreservedly indorsed the compromise, and in its approval neither platform nor candidate halted. . . . The people were convinced that the status of every foot of territory in the United States, with regard to slavery, was fixed; that it had ceased to be a political question."

From this pleasing illusion the North was suddenly aroused by the introduction into Congress of the Kansas-Nebraska bill by Senator Stephen A. Douglas, of Illinois. In 1820 Missouri had been admitted to the Union on the conditions — first, that no restriction as to slavery be imposed upon Missouri in framing a state constitution, and, second, that in all the rest of the country ceded by France to the United States north of the southern boundary line of Missouri, there should be neither slavery nor involuntary servitude. This famous Missouri Compromise Senator Douglas proposed to repeal by an act providing for the organization of Kansas and Nebraska as territories, with liberty to the people of those territories to determine for themselves whether they would allow slavery or not. Senator Douglas's enemies, at the time, asserted that his sole motive for this legislation, and for the consequent reopening of the slavery question, was his ambition to secure the Southern vote for the

presidency in a future presidential campaign. The
historian has to do with the public acts, not with
the private motives, of men; but the historian,
whatever his judgment of Senator Douglas's act,
must recognize the truth that better motives than
that of personal ambition might have actuated him.
For ten years he had been urging the organization
of the Nebraska territory upon Congress, but in
vain. His avowed object was to open the line of
communication between the Missouri Valley and
our possessions on the Pacific Ocean, and prevent
the latter from coming under the domination of
Great Britain through the industrial activity of the
Hudson's Bay Fur Company. Three forces had
operated thus far successfully to resist this necessary
measure for the public welfare. The territory west
of the Mississippi and Missouri rivers had been
reserved to the Indians, with a guarantee that it
should never be open to white settlement "so long
as grass should grow and water should run." Mistaken humanitarians resisted any disregard of the
supposed rights and interests of the Indians guar-
anteed under these treaties. The Atlantic States
were jealous of the growth and expansion of the
Mississippi Valley, and resisted any policy which
might tend to promote that growth and expansion.
The South dreaded the political domination of the
North, and was jealous of the industrial growth of
free territory, and therefore it resisted any scheme
for opening the territory west of the Missouri River
subject to the restrictions of the Missouri Com-

promise. Senator Douglas may have believed that the opening of this immense territory to settlement and civilization would far outbalance any disadvantages which might grow out of a temporary reopening of the slavery question; he may have believed that slavery would not enter this territory, that, to quote the words of Daniel Webster, it was not necessary to reënact the laws of God; he may have believed that, since slavery was a state institution and could not be interfered with in the state, it was a legitimate extension of that principle to allow the people of the territory, which was but an inchoate state, to determine for themselves whether they would or would not allow it. Whatever his motive, the passage of the Kansas-Nebraska bill, by a vote of one hundred thirteen to one hundred in the House, and by a vote of thirty-five to thirteen in the Senate, in May, 1854, aroused the indignation of the North as it never had been aroused before. This was not merely, perhaps not mainly, because territory before consecrated to freedom was now thrown open to slavery; it was rather because a sacred compact had been rudely set aside. The North had fulfilled its part in the contract: Missouri was a slave state. The South now nullified its part in the contract and opened the territory north of the southern boundary of Missouri also to slavery. The contention of the anti-slavery advocates that the slavery question could never be settled by compromise was justified. The North began to realize that compromises and compacts were in vain. Much of the hostility which before had been directed against the abolitionists, because they persisted in agitating the slavery question, was now directed against the doctrine of popular sovereignty, because it reopened that agitation.

The Kansas-Nebraska bill was introduced into Congress on the 23d of January, 1854. On the 11th of February Mr. Beecher entered the campaign against this measure. " The Nebraska bill," said he in a speech in Boston, " is the death-struggle of slavery for expansion, seeing that she must have more room to breathe or suffocate. All question as to whether slavery shall be agitated is now at an end. The South says it shall be agitated, and she cannot help it. The mask is off, and all disguises are thrown to the winds, and the slave power stands out in its true character, making its last and most infamous demands upon the North. All we have to do is to say No." Two weeks later he writes to " The New York Independent," expressing the deep religious motive which inspired his opposition to the Kansas-Nebraska bill. " Everywhere I find the Nebraska question to be a theme of anxious interest. But there is little outward expression of strong feeling. I fear that Christian men do not look upon it as a *religious* question. The responsibility which God has placed upon the religious-minded North to hold that vast territory open to the Gospel, to institutions which spring from a religious feeling and will corroborate all religious endeavors, is but little felt. Yet to me that seems a very urgent view, the deepest." He urges upon the people instant and immediate activity; recommends that petitions be circulated in every school district; that documents be distributed among the people, especially the speeches of Chase, Seward, and Sumner; that every man of influence write to his representative; that public meetings be held all through the North; that the women coöperate in this movement; that no one wait for his neighbor, but " the poor men, uncultured men, mechanics and laborers, in short, the great industrial class, move with spontaneousness." He finds at last a people ready to respond. A hundred and fifty-one ministers of New York and vicinity memorialize Congress against the Nebraska bill; three thousand ministers of New England unite in a petition against it. But to Mr. Beecher the popular excitement seems like apathy. He declares that by the bill " it is proposed to doom a territory large enough to make ten states as large as New York to slavery." At times he apprehends the dissolution of the Union. To his own people he says, in a prayer-meeting: " Things have come nearly to the worst in this nation; but with the consciousness of Divine Providence, I will not despair. If God sees fit to destroy this government He will raise up another to carry out His purpose." This is on the 19th of May, 1854; seven days later the Kansas-Nebraska bill is signed and becomes the law of the land.

There were two ways of meeting this movement

for the extension of slavery: one by federal, the other by local action. Both methods were simultaneously adopted by anti-slavery leaders.

There had been for twelve years a Liberty party in the United States, insignificant in numbers, but at least on one occasion influential. The vote for James G. Birney in 1844 had drawn off votes enough from Henry Clay to secure the election of James K. Polk. In that election, the Liberty party had been, or at least at the time appeared to be, however unconsciously, an ally of the slave power. But after the Kansas-Nebraska bill was passed, it began to be clear to those who regarded the slavery question as the most important question before the nation, that there was no longer hope from either the Democratic or the Whig party for even moderate anti-slavery action. The demands of slavery were sustained alike by the Whig Millard Fillmore and the Democratic Franklin Pierce. Nevertheless, shrewd politicians, whose anti-slavery principles could not be questioned, doubted the advisability of attempting the formation of a new party. Chase, Sumner, and Wade approved it, but Sumner had always been an independent, and Chase was a Democrat; Thurlow Weed and William H. Seward at first discouraged it. The latter did not believe that the various opponents of the Nebraska bill were yet ready to work together in a common organization for a common end. I do not know that Mr. Beecher ever took part in the councils of those who were framing the political machinery to resist the extension of slavery. He was never, in any sense of the term, a politician. But when, in 1856, the heterogeneous political elements, which were agreed in nothing but their hostility to further extension of slavery, united in the nomination of John C. Fremont for President of the United States, Mr. Beecher at once entered heartily into the canvass for his election. The week after the nomination he writes from New Hampshire: —

Everywhere I find people aroused to the great question of the times, and it seems as if at last the North were determined to fulfill her mission and restore to the land the principles which she first planted. I find in every quarter that Fremont is gaining friends and bids fair to carry every state in New England.

Two months later, at the end of the summer's vacation, when he would naturally be beginning the fall work with Plymouth Church, at the request of a number of eminent clergymen and others, he was given a leave of absence by the trustees to devote himself to the political campaign "in behalf of the cause of liberty, then felt to be in peril." This was in September, 1856. Upon this campaign he entered with characteristic energy, speaking twice and often three times a week, generally making a two to three hours' speech, often in the open air, to audiences of from eight to ten thousand people. The burden of his campaign speeches was a reiteration of the principles we have already reported as urged by him on the platform and in the press. When the opponents of Mr. Fremont tried to con-

fuse the issue by making a new one, Mr. Beecher
did not follow their lead, and, by turning the laugh
on them, effectually prevented them from diverting
public attention from the real question at issue.
Certain astute politicians had endeavored to secure
the coöperation of the native American party with
the new Republican party, though wiser counsels
had prevailed and had prevented any open alliance
between the two. The opponents of the Republican
party endeavored to set this native American sentiment against John C. Fremont, because in his
runaway match he had been married by a Roman
Catholic priest. His political enemies insisted that
he was a Roman Catholic and concealed the fact
for political ends. The charge, though refuted, was
repeated again and again. Serious argument serves
little purpose in such a case. Mr. Beecher's story
of the dog named " Noble-at-the-empty-hole " over-
whelmed the accusation with ridicule. " Having on
one occasion seen a red squirrel run into a hole in
a stone wall, he could not be persuaded that he was
not there forever. . . . When all other occupations
failed, this hole remained to him. When there were
no chickens to harry, no pigs to bite, no cattle to
chase, no children to romp with, no expeditions to
make with the grown folks, and when he had slept
all that his dog skin would hold, he would walk out
of the yard, yawn and stretch himself, and then look
wistfully at the hole, as if thinking to himself:
' Well, as there is nothing else to do, I may as well
try that hole again.' We had almost forgotten this

little trait until the attack of the 'New York Express' in respect to Colonel Fremont's religion brought it ridiculously to mind again. . . . The 'Express,' like Noble, has opened on this hole in the wall, and can never be done barking at it. Day after day it resorts to this empty hole. When everything else fails, this resource remains. There they are indefatigably, — 'Express' and Noble, — a church without a Fremont, and a hole without a squirrel in it. . . . We never read the 'Express' nowadays without thinking involuntarily, 'Goodness! the dog is letting off at that hole again.'" The story was caught up by the press and went the rounds of the country. "The dog Noble and the empty hole" turned into ridicule the attempt to make political capital out of the marriage of Fremont by a Roman Catholic priest. It is doubtful whether the incident lost General Fremont a vote; it is quite certain that it did not lose him so many as were gained for him by the romance of the runaway match.

Simultaneously with this national movement to prevent the further extension of slavery was a local movement, which eventually proved successful, to secure Kansas and Nebraska for freedom by planting in them a population determined to make of them free states. For this purpose an Emigrant Aid Company was organized in New England in 1854 by Eli Thayer. He was an ardent believer in popular sovereignty. He felt sure, and events proved him right, that under popular sovereignty

freedom would win. A charter was granted by
Massachusetts, capital was secured, emigrants were
invited. Its object was to plant capital in the new
territory in advance of population, and thus furnish the incoming immigrant with the advantage
of mills, schools, and churches. It was not an
abolition society. Financial and patriotic motives
commingled in the intentions of its founders. Its
aim was to build up a prosperous community in
the prosperity of which the immigrant would share.
Its methods were peaceable: its first immigrants
went without any implements of war. " The Emigrant Aid Company," says Mr. Spring in his
history of Kansas, " never bought a firelock or
furnished its patrons with warlike equipments of
any sort."

From the outset this scheme of securing Kansas
and Nebraska for freedom met with opposition
from very different quarters. The men who loved
peace rather than liberty opposed it, because they
foresaw in it only a new phase of the interminable
strife which they abhorred. They anticipated the
incursion of armed forces from Missouri, and as a
result either civil war or the forcible overthrow of
the free-state settlers by their more warlike and less
scrupulous neighbors. Conservative anti-slavery
men regarded it as wholly impracticable. They
believed that these New England immigrants, who
had to travel fifteen hundred miles to the battle-
ground, would be no match for the slave population from the adjoining state of Missouri, who

could in one day blot out all that the free-soilers could do in a year. The abolitionists condemned it as commercial in its spirit and impracticable in its methods. " The Liberator " denounced the Emigrant Aid Company as " a great hindrance to the cause of freedom and a mighty curse to the territory." Wendell Phillips declared that " the fate of Nebraska and Kansas was sealed the first hour Stephen Arnold Douglas consented to play his perfidious part," for so his abolition of the Missouri Compromise was regarded by the anti-slavery sentiment of the North. To take possession of the country by industry, by roads, by mills, by churches, would take, he said, two centuries. Thomas Wentworth Higginson maintained that even if the Emigrant Aid Society were successful, success would achieve nothing ; Nebraska would be only a transplanted Massachusetts, and the original Massachusetts had been tried and found wanting.[1]

From the first Mr. Beecher threw himself heart and soul into this movement, as did many of the New England clergy. The anticipations of the peace-lovers were presently realized. When election day came, over seventeen hundred Missourians came over into Kansas, and swelled the pro-slavery vote. When the next election day came, five thousand Missourians marched into Kansas to assist in the election of the legislature. Judges of election were awed into submission or driven away by threats. Protests against the result of the election

[1] Eli Thayer : *The Kansas Crusade*, p. 101.

were signed at the hazard of life. Election returns were canvassed by the governor, in a room filled with men armed to the teeth. But these Missourians came into Kansas only to vote. Southern presses urged Southern men to carry their slaves with them into the new territory. " Two thousand slaves," said Mr. Stringfellow, a leader of the Missourians, " actually lodged in Kansas will make a slave state out of it. Once fairly there, nobody will disturb them." But no slave-owner was willing to act on this advice. Slaves carried into a state surrounded by freemen, might become discontented and run away, and if they did, their capture would certainly be difficult.

What should the New England settlers do? Should they practice non-resistance and submit to be overawed by incursions from Missouri, or should they arm for self-protection? Many of the supporters of the free-soil cause hesitated: some simply dreaded bloodshed; some on principle were opposed to all use of force; some insisted that Christ taught the doctrine of non-resistance. But the free-soilers on the ground prepared to meet force with force. Mr. Beecher defended their right so to do. He said : —

The New Testament declares that malign revenge or hatred are not to be felt toward an enemy. We do not think it touches at all the question of what kind of instruments men may employ. It simply teaches what is the state of mind which is to direct either kind of instrument, moral or physical. If we reason and argue, love, not malignity, is to animate us. If we are in extremities and defend our lives with weapons, it is not to be in hatred, but calmly, deliberately, and with Christian firmness. We know that there are those who will scoff at the idea of holding a sword or a rifle in a Christian state of mind. I think it just as easy as to hold an argument in a Christian state of mind. The right to use physical force we regard as a very important one. We do not see how it may be right to use a little, but wrong to use a great deal of force, when self-defense is the end, and when the feelings are not malignant, but simply a calm, conscientious standing for right.

He urged the emigrants to go to Kansas; urged those who had sons in Kansas to send them arms; urged parents to pray that their sons "may not have occasion to use them, but if they must be used, that the sons may so wield them that the mother be not ashamed of the son she loves." He practiced what he preached : aided in taking up contributions to arm the free-soilers; pledged twenty-five rifles from Plymouth Church; called for subscriptions in the lecture-room of the church, for their purchase. As the result of these and similar subscriptions in various parts of the country by the friends of the free-soilers, rifles were sent out to Kansas in considerable numbers. One or more consignments were sent in boxes labeled "books." It is said' that one consignment was labeled "Bibles." In one address Mr. Beecher defended the use of rifles, which, he said, would be more useful than Bibles in an argument with wolves. For one or the other of these reasons, Sharpe's

rifles sent to the free-soilers were dubbed
"Beecher's Bibles." In fact, the possession of the
rifles by the free-soilers sufficed to win a blood-
less victory. "We do not know," he subsequently
said, "that a single man has ever been injured
with them. They are guiltless of blood." Nevertheless they won a victory where otherwise defeat
would have been certain. The famous Wakarusa
War did not come to actual hostilities. The Mis-
sourian invaders, twelve to fifteen hundred armed
men, encamped on the Wakarusa River in the
vicinity of Lawrence. It must be said for their
courage that they probably did not fear Sharpe's
rifles in the hands of the free-soil men; but they
did fear the popular sentiment of the country if
they should open the first battle of what might be
a civil war. When they found that there was a
resolute party in Kansas determined to fight for
freedom, they withdrew without firing a shot. The
battle for liberty was won, and, so far as events
can justify moral principles, the moral principle
which Mr. Beecher had advocated was justified by
the peaceful victory achieved by the possession of
Sharpe's rifles.

So passes ten years of constant, though inter-
mittent agitation, probably the most politically
stormy in the history of the American nation.
Cowards are silent, cautious men seek for compromise, belligerent men inflame popular passion
and arouse popular prejudice, honest men are sorely
perplexed. The issue remains always the same;

but the aspect of the issue constantly changes. The slave power grows more and more aggressive. It first asks to be let alone; then it demands new territory by a compromise; then it repudiates the compromise it formerly demanded and seeks new territory through popular sovereignty; then it repudiates popular sovereignty and wishes the nationalization of slavery. Simultaneously the anti-slavery sentiment of the North grows more definite, more resolute, more wide-spread. In all these changes Mr. Beecher never departs from the principles avowed in his first public utterance. When in May, 1856, Charles Sumner is struck down by Preston Brooks and beaten almost to death, Mr. Beecher seeks not to inflame the passion of the North against the assailant, but against the power which that assailant too well represents. "The nature of slavery," he says, in a public meeting in Brooklyn, "has been for a long time to make encroachment. But the time has come when it has walked into the government. It takes possession of the Senate Chamber." John Brown, erroneously assuming that the slaves were eager for their liberty, and if provided with a leader will arise, throw off the yoke of slavery, and win freedom for themselves, undertakes his fatuous raid into Virginia. Mr. Beecher believes neither in the paroxysm of indignation nor in the passion of enthusiasm. His prayer for John Brown and the other imprisoned raiders indicates a principle which history confirms. "Remember these that are in prison — Thy servants

who in Thy providence have been permitted to lift
up their hands in a mistaken way, but out of which
Thou wilt yet induce good." When a public hall
is denied Wendell Phillips for a lecture, because
of his unpopularity, Mr. Beecher, radically as he
differs from Mr. Phillips in both spirit and methods,
secures from the trustees the use of Plymouth
Church for the obnoxious lecturer. Issuing a call
to battle against the compromise measures, Mr.
Beecher gives Mr. Clay sincere praise for desiring peace. But when Daniel Webster, born and
bred in the atmosphere of New England, becomes
the advocate of this same measure, he denounces
the son of Massachusetts for his apostasy.

Nor is he, during these ten years, a man of one
idea. He is not merely an anti-slavery reformer.
Every event which concerns the liberty of his
fellow men concerns him. When Louis Kossuth
comes to America, Plymouth Church is put at his
disposal, and Mr. Beecher in introducing him calls
on the audience to " bear witness to me how often
from this place prayers have been offered and tears
shed when we have heard of the struggles of
Hungary." When the advent of Father Matthew
has revived interest in the temperance cause, Mr.
Beecher avails himself of the opportunity, and
speaks on the same platform with P. T. Barnum,
Dr. George B. Cheever, and Dr. Theodore F. Cuyler, for temperance. When the electric cable to
unite the old world and the new is to be laid, Mr.
Beecher is among the early visitors to the frigate

Niagara, which is charged with the duty of laying it, and writes of the coming event as one which will " bind two continents together, and be a road for the business of the world." The Church and amusements had always been thought to belong in different fields, and the duty of the Church as discharged in warning the young against tabooed amusements. In 1857 we find Mr. Beecher preaching on social amusements, and recommending gymnastics, wrestling, bowling, boating, and field sports generally. Three weeks later he is pleading the cause of the American Indian in a public meeting in New York City. The corner-stone of a new city armory is laid. He is there to speak, on broad lines, of municipal and national patriotism. The centenary of Robert Burns is to be celebrated. Mr. Beecher gives the memorial address: " The nation which reads Robert Burns in the nursery will never have tyrants in the parliament house. In all his weakness, sorrows, joys, and fears, he is universal in his sympathies. . . . Dead, he has made the world rich. His life was a failure until he died; and ever since it has been a marvelous success." A reading-room and a coffee-house are to be opened in the Bowery — one of the first of the now numerous attempts to improve men through other than conventionally religious means. Mr. Beecher is there to indorse it. Italy is engaged in her finally successful effort to throw off the yoke of foreign bondage and become a free and united nation. Mr. Beecher joins in a call for a public meeting, addresses it, and helps to raise a fund for Garibaldi's aid. He speaks on the same platform with Lucy Stone Blackwell for the emancipation of woman : urges the enlargement of her influence because it will involve an enlargement of her character ; insists that " she is better fitted for home when she is fitted for something else." If he believed that the ballot for every one is necessary both as a symbol and as a defense of liberty, he shared with his contemporaries an opinion which experience on a large scale has modified in the minds of many who are devoted to human freedom.

There lies before me as I write a journal kept by a member of Plymouth Church, during a period extending from 1850 to 1869. I am amazed as I turn its pages over at the mere physical endurance of this man. For the ten years with which in this chapter I have to do, he was engaged almost daily in public service. The first four evenings of the week he was generally speaking on some public platform. As if moral reforms were not enough to keep his brain busy, he engaged in the work of lecturing. The lyceum lecture was then one of the great instruments for public education, and Mr. Beecher was in constant demand as a lyceum lecturer, especially after the Fremont campaign. Commerce, art, life, literature, everything but theology, furnished him topics. Among his themes are " The Ministry of the Beautiful," " Character," " Amusements," " Success in Life," " Wit and

Humor," "Mirthfulness," "The Commonwealth."
Beside all this he contributed to the press frequent
articles, grave and gay, long and short, sometimes
serious discussions of public themes, sometimes
chatty sketches of personal experiences or observa-
tions.

This more public ministry did not divert him
from his ministry to and in his own church. He
was almost invariably back from his campaigning
and lecturing in time to be at the Friday evening
meeting. At this meeting, which was always
crowded, he gave what he called a "lecture-room
talk," which was really a brief lecture. In these
lecture-room talks Mr. Beecher rarely dealt with
the topics of his weekly campaigning. His themes
were largely those of personal religious experience.
Religion has to do both with man's relation to his
fellow man and with his personal relation to his
God. In his weekly campaigns Mr. Beecher dealt
wholly with the former. In his lecture-room
talks he generally dealt with the latter. His
themes were such as "Communion," "Tears,"
"Groping after God," "Praise and Prayer,"
"Christian Joyousness," "The Spontaneous Goodness of God." Following the lecture was almost
always an after-meeting which was sometimes social,
sometimes pastoral, sometimes executive; in which
inquirers were met, guidance given, plans of church
work briefly discussed. Saturday was a holiday;
only the most pressing exigency was allowed to
break in upon this rest-day of the preacher. After

he moved to Peekskill from Lenox, where he at first
had his summer retreat, he often went up for the
day to his country home in the spring and fall
when weather invited to outdoor occupations. On
Sunday he was rarely absent from his pulpit. His
people were generous; they made no demands for
pastoral service, and he rendered very little; but
they were always disappointed when he was absent
from his pulpit, and he knew it. Exchanges were
no relief to him, for he had no old sermons. So he
almost invariably preached, and habitually twice on
Sunday, and always to crowded congregations. The
pews and aisles were always full; more often than
not, all standing-room was taken; the pulpit-stairs
were regularly used for seats by the young men and
children of the congregation; often hundreds were
turned away unable to gain entrance to the church.
In the congregation were many Western and Southern merchants, coming to the city, according to the
fashion of those days, to buy goods; and many men
of note in all the ranks of life. Ralph Waldo
Emerson, A. Bronson Alcott, Henry D. Thoreau,
Walt Whitman, Louis Kossuth, Abraham Lincoln
were a few among the notabilities. And it was not
chiefly curiosity to hear the reformer on public
themes that drew this congregation. Sermons on
the topic of the hour were occasional and excep-
tional. His sermons, as his lecture-room talks, were
largely on topics of personal life, — individual
rather than sociological.

During all this time Plymouth Church was not

merely a great congregation, attracted by the fame
of a great preacher. It was a living church, composed of men and women actively engaged in Christian and philanthropic work, under the inspiration
which the preacher furnished. The Sunday-school
was so large as to fill the Sunday-school room full
to overflowing; at times the lecture-room had to be
used to accommodate the overflow. The spiritual
efficiency of a church is indicated by the additions
to its membership upon confession of faith. During these ten years seven hundred and seventy-
three united with Plymouth Church on confession
of their faith. Its spiritual life is indicated by the
response it makes to a general awakening in the
community. It was in the midst of these stirring
events that the church experienced the revival of
which I have spoken in a previous chapter. During this revival Mr. Beecher's attention was concentrated on the spiritual work in his church, for
to this he always gave the first place, and from the
daily morning prayer-meetings held during that
revival he was rarely absent. In addition to his
platform work, his contributions to the press, his
preaching, and the special ministry involved in two
successive revivals, Mr. Beecher also found or made
time to prepare the " Plymouth Collection," of
which I have already spoken, and which was finished and published in 1855.

It is true that Mr. Beecher concentrated his energies on his public teaching, now by his pen, now
on the platform, now in the pulpit. He did little

or no personal pastoral work from house to house, little executive work in administration of church activities. He inspired the church, and left it to direct its own activities. But they were not confined to those which are customary to church life in a great city; and something of the responsibility for them must have fallen upon him. For the Plymouth Church edifice was not idle throughout the week. It was the best auditorium in Brooklyn for public lectures, and was in frequent use. It served as a lecture-hall as well as meeting-house. Among the lecturers who were heard here were Thackeray on the "Four Georges," Professor Youmans on "Alcohol and its Uses," John B. Gough on temperance, Professor Mitchell on astronomy, Charles Sumner, Joshua R. Giddings, George W. Curtis on aspects of the slavery question, and Schuyler Colfax and Thomas Corwin, on I know not what. Abraham Lincoln, it is said, was to have lectured in Plymouth Church on coming East in 1860, but was transferred to Cooper Union in order the more effectually to reach a New York audience.

Yet it would be a mistake were the reader to suppose that either Mr. Beecher or Plymouth Church was what is ordinarily called popular. If he was the most admired orator and the most beloved preacher of his time, he was also the most bitterly hated, excepting only Theodore Parker. No language was too bitter, no epithets too stinging to be applied to him. It was declared that "his pulpit has been turned into a political engine to overthrow the institutions of the Southern States, to dissolve the Union, and to foment civil war;" he was characterized as one of the clergy "who attack not those sinners who hear them, but those who are a thousand miles away;" he was classed with Garrison and Wendell Phillips, and all three were warned that "a trip to Europe just now would prove very beneficial to their health;" that "their ease and comfort will be anything but safe in this country in six months from this time" (December, 1860). These unambiguous hints came from a metropolitan journal of no insignificant reputation. Jewish rabbis and Christian preachers added their voice of condemnation against "all our notorious abolition preachers, who have resorted to the most violent processes of interpretation to avoid the meaning of plain Scripture texts," and "who make that to be sin which in the Bible is not declared to be sin." This hostility reached its climax after the election of Abraham Lincoln. That fall Plymouth Church was threatened with a mob. One evening the services were interrupted by a stone thrown from outside which came crashing through the window. But the congregation fell into no panic; after the sermon an extemporized bodyguard followed the preacher to his home; no further violence was attempted; and Mr. Beecher, in bidding his friends good-night, made a reassuring speech from the steps of his house: "I do not think there is any occasion for alarm, nor do I imagine that I really need your protection. If there had been, and I had fallen, it would have been the best thing that could have happened for the cause; but nothing will happen to me or to my house. I have not lived in this city for thirteen years for nothing." The friendly crowd responded with cheers and cries of "That's so," and separated, and so the incident came to an end.

Abraham Lincoln's speech in Cooper Union, February 27, 1860, won for him the nomination to the presidency by the Republican party. His speech became the platform of the party. In its principles and in its spirit it represented what Mr. Beecher had for ten years urged his fellow citizens to incorporate in a national resolve and embody in national action. It therefore made Abraham Lincoln Mr. Beecher's candidate for the presidency. In the triumph of the Republican party upon this platform, and with this man as its leader, the epoch of anti-slavery agitation came to an end; the epoch of civil war began. For from the day when the election of Abraham Lincoln was announced, the issue before the people of the North regarding slavery was changed. It was no longer, Would they consent to the extension of slavery? That question was answered. It was, Would they respond to Abraham Lincoln's appeal: "Let us have faith that right makes might; and in that faith let us, to the end, dare to do our duty as we understand it"?

*Specimens of Posters displayed in Cities in England
where Mr. Beecher spoke in 1863.*

REV. H. W. BEECHER'S

MISSION TO LIVERPOOL.

THE TRENT AFFAIR.

[Rev. H. W. BEECHER in the *New York Independent*.]

"Should the President quietly yield to the present necessity (viz.: the delivering up of Messrs. Mason and Slidell) as the lesser of two evils and bide our time with England, there will be a

SENSE of WRONG, of NATIONAL HUMILIATION

SO PROFOUND, AND A

HORROR OF THE UNFEELING SELFISHNESS OF THE ENGLISH GOVERNMENT

in the great emergency of our affairs, such as will inevitably break out by and by in flames, and which will only be extinguished by a deluge of blood! We are not living the whole of our life to-day. There is a future to the United States in which the nation will right any injustice of the present hour."

The Rev. Henry Ward Beecher, at a meeting held in New York, at the time when the Confederate Envoys, Messrs. Slidell and Mason, had been surrendered by President Lincoln to the British Government, from whose vessel (the Royal Mail Steamer *Trent*) they were taken, said

"That the Best Blood of England must flow for the outrage England had perpetrated on America."

This opinion of a Christian (?) minister, wishing to obtain a welcome in Liverpool, whose operatives are suffering almost unprecedented hardships, caused by the suicidal war raging in the States of North America, and urged on by the fanatical Statesmen and Preachers of the North, is worthy of consideration.

REV. H. W. BEECHER'S

IDEA OF SLAVERY.

In Plymouth Church, in Brooklyn, N. Y., January 25, 1860, the Rev. Henry Ward Beecher announced his creed on Slavery in six Points:

1. That a man may hold a slave and do no wrong.
2. That immediate Emancipation is impossible.
3. That a Slave-holder may be a good Christian.
4. That the influence of Slavery is not always evil.
5. That some actual Slave-holders are doing more for the cause of Freedom than some violent Reformers.
6 That Anti-slavery Bigotry is worse than the Papacy.

[2d poster ; size, 20x29 inches.]

THE
WAR CHRISTIANS!
THEIR DOCTRINES.

At a Jubilee Demonstration in New York, in January last,

REV. JOHN J. RAYMOND,

The appointed Chaplain of the meeting, in his opening prayer, said: "We thank thee, O God, that thou hast seen fit to raise up one, ABRAHAM, surnamed Lincoln. . . . He is a man whom GOD SHOULD bless, and the people delight to honor."

UNITED STATES SENATOR LANE,

In his Address to the Great Union Meeting at Washington, said : " I would like to live long enough to see every white man now in South Carolina in Hell."

REV. H. WARD BEECHER,

In his Address in Glasgow, last Monday, said : " They (alluding to the NORTH rose like ONE MAN, and with a voice that reverberated throughout the whole world, cried—LET IT (alluding to the South), with all its attendant horrors, GO TO HELL."

FROM THE *Manchester Guardian's* CORRESPONDENCE:

Is this the same Reverend Mr. Beecher who, at a meeting in America, during the discussion of the " *Trent* Affair," said : " That the best blood of England must flow as atonement for the outrage England committed on America"?

[3d poster ; size, 25x38 inches.]

WHO IS
HY. WARD BEECHER?

He is the man who said the best blood of England must be shed to atone for the *Trent* affair.

He is the man who advocates a War of Extermination with the South,—says it is incapable of " re-generation," but proposes to re-people it from the North by " generation."—See " Times."

He is the friend of that inhuman monster, General BUTLER. He is the friend of that so-called Gospel Preacher, CHEEVER, who said in one of his sermons—"Fight against the South till *Hell* Freezes, and then continue the battle on the ice."

He is the friend and supporter of a most debased Female, who uttered at a public meeting in America the most indecent and cruel language that ever polluted female lips.—See " Times."

MEN OF MANCHESTER, ENGLISHMEN!

What reception can you give this wretch, save unmitigated disgust and contempt ? His impudence in coming here is only equalled by his cruelty and impiety. Should he, however, venture to appear, it behooves all right-minded men to render as futile as the first this second attempt to get up a public demonstration in favor of the North, which is now waging War against the South with a vindictive and revengeful cruelty unparalleled in the history of any Christian land.

Cave & Send Printers by Steam Power, Palatine Building, Manchester.

Peekskill Oct 24 67

My dear Mr Abbott
          Harvard is done –
Summer is done, autumn
is most done –

The birds are flown, leaves
are flying & I fly too – So
hereafter send to Brooklyn.

          Truly yours
          HW Beecher

CHAPTER IX

MR. LINCOLN was elected in November, 1860; his inauguration did not take place until March 4, 1861; this *quasi* interregnum of four months between the election and the inauguration of the President of the United States cost the nation unnumbered thousands of dollars and unnumbered thousands of lives. That the Civil War could have been absolutely prevented is not probable; that its duration would have been greatly lessened if Mr. Lincoln had taken the reins of government within four weeks after his election cannot be doubted, for during the four months of interregnum the nation was without a leader. Mr. Lincoln could not lead because he was not President; Mr. Buchanan could not lead because he had not capacity. The nation was confronting a great crisis, and Mr. Buchanan was not the man for a crisis. A skillful diplomat, a shrewd politician, skillful in the evasion of difficult questions, but without a statesman's ability to understand or a brave man's courage to meet them, incapable of comprehending a great situation or grasping a great principle, Mr. Buchanan was exactly *not* the man for the place.

There were in the country two conceptions of

the nature of the federal government. The United States of America is confessedly a union of sovereign states. Ought it to be regarded as a partnership from which any partner may withdraw at will, or a marriage which once consummated is indissoluble? The South held the first view, the North the second. The sovereignty resides in the people. Was the supreme expression of this sovereignty in the State or in the Nation? in an issue between the two which was the final arbiter? The South answered, The State; the North answered, The Nation. Either view was self-consistent; for either view rational argument was possible. Mr. Buchanan, versed in the art of compromising by the simple method of conceding something in every controversy to each disputant, attempted to solve this controversy by such a compromise. He said in effect to the North: "You are right — this is a nation; the union of the states is a marriage; no state has a right to secede." He said in effect to the South: "You are right — the sovereignty of the state is supreme; the sovereignty of the federal government is subordinate, and although no state has a right to secede, the federal government has no right to coerce it into submission if it does secede." Such a compromise, pronounced by the chief executive of the federal government, was entirely satisfactory to the secessionists; they did not in the least care what theory Mr. Buchanan held respecting the right of a state to secede, so long as he refused to use or allow to be used the forces of the federal government in preventing secession. Under his administration seven states were permitted to hold conventions and proclaim their withdrawal from the Union; the Secretary of War was allowed to retain his post and use his power to equip the seceding states for the impending conflict; the United States brigadier-general commanding the Department of Texas was allowed to turn over his entire army, with all the posts and fortifications, arms, munitions of war, horses and equipments, to the Confederate authorities. Before Mr. Lincoln's inauguration, and under Mr. Buchanan's administration, the Confederate States had taken possession of every fort, arsenal, dockyard, mint, custom-house, and court-house in their territory except three — Fort Sumter, Fort Pickens, and Key West. This was not accomplished without strong opposition in the South. In South Carolina, when the minister first dropped from the service the prayer for the President of the United States, James L. Pettigrew, the foremost lawyer of the state, rose in his pew, and slowly and with distinct voice repeated, " Most humbly and heartily we beseech Thee with Thy favor to uphold and bless Thy servant the President of these United States ; " then, placing his prayer-book in the rack, withdrew, with his wife, from the church, which he never reëntered. In Georgia, Alexander H. Stephens, easily the foremost statesman in the South, argued earnestly against secession ; pointed out the fact that the Republican President faced a

Democratic majority, both in the House of Representatives and in the Senate, — could carry no
legislation, could appoint no officer, could not even
form a cabinet hostile to the interests of the country, as the Democratic majority interpreted those
interests. It may fairly be doubted whether the
ordinance of secession would have commanded a
popular vote in any state in the South except
South Carolina if the vote could have been preceded by a full and free discussion, if it could have
been unattended with threatening or violence, and
if the Unionists could have had the moral support
of the federal administration.

But it must be said, in apology for Mr. Buchanan,
if not in defense of him, that if public sentiment
was divided in the South, it was also divided in the
North. The radical abolitionists were opposed to
coercion and welcomed secession. They had themselves been secessionists from the first. Not a few
of those who voted for Mr. Lincoln, when they
found themselves confronting the peril of war,
would have been almost ready to cancel their vote,
and were quite ready to draw back from the principles to which he was committed and from which
he never swerved. The commercial disasters which
war would involve appalled some, the terrible
tragedy of war appalled others, and an honest conviction of the impracticability of coercion convinced still others. Three days after the election
the " New York Tribune," the most influential
journal of the Republican party, in a leading ar-

ticle said: "If the cotton states decide that they can do better out of the Union than in it, we insist on letting them go in peace. . . . We hope never to live in a republic whereof one section is pinned to the residue by bayonets." Most extraordinary compromises were proposed to avoid the peril of war. It was proposed that the Constitution should be amended so as to provide for slave territory south of a given line and free territory north of a given line, each inviolate from interference; that slavery should never be interfered with in the territories; that a clause should be inserted in the Constitution recognizing the doctrine of states rights and denying the power of coercion to the general government; that Mr. Lincoln should resign and another president be elected less objectionable to the South; that the office of president should be abolished and a council of three substituted, each of whom should have a veto on every public act. Those who were most loyal, not only to the government, but to the fundamental principles of the Republican party, were divided in their opinion respecting the best policy to be pursued. It soon became plain that secession of the cotton states could not be prevented by compromise. But it was not so clear that it was impossible to dissuade the border states from casting in their lot with the Confederacy. To prevent them from so doing became the first object of leading men whose loyalty to the nation and to liberty could not be questioned. So clear-headed and loyal a statesman as Charles Francis Adams advocated the appointment of committees and summoning of conferences and shaping of a compromise to secure this result. That during such a time of intellectual confusion a man of Mr. Buchanan's mould, temper, and education should have been perplexed, irresolute, and vacillating is not to be wondered at.

In all this time of confused counsels there were some men, the strongest, as we can now see, who never for a moment lost sight of the one guiding principle that concession should never more be made to the slave power under any pretext whatever, be the consequences what they might. Among these were the silent man at Springfield, and the eloquent man in Brooklyn, neither of whom for an instant hesitated. In December Abraham Lincoln wrote to Mr. Washburne: " Prevent as far as possible any of our friends from demoralizing themselves and their cause by entertaining propositions for compromise of any sort on slavery extension. There is no possible compromise upon it but what puts us under again, and all our work to do over again." There is no reason to suppose that at this time Mr. Lincoln and Mr. Beecher had any understanding or any correspondence with each other; but what Mr. Lincoln said in occasional private letters Mr. Beecher said with vigor from the pulpit, on the platform, and from the press. Mr. Beecher was not a diplomat; he had no skill in political arts; he did not know how to propose a scheme to blind the eyes of his opponents and to tide over a difficulty, — a scheme to be abandoned as soon as the crisis was passed. Despite rumors and reports that he subsequently became a political adviser of Mr. Lincoln, and a still more influential adviser of President Grant, I am not able to find any historical evidence that he ever was the adviser of either. He is a wise man who knows his own powers and his own limitations, exercises the first, and keeps within the second. It was Mr. Beecher's genius to create that public sentiment which underlies and gives force to political action in a democracy, and to give effective and eloquent expression to that sentiment when it had been created. To this work he gave himself with singleness of purpose, for he understood the mission to which he had been called better than any of his critics, better than some of his eulogists.

During this period of interregnum there were two services which could be rendered by a man who had access to the public mind and conscience. He could do something to persuade the Union men in the South that their constitutional rights and liberties were not in danger. They were not wholly without ground for their apprehension, certainly not without excuse for it, for the vehement and inflammatory writings and speeches of the abolitionists had been circulated far and wide. But it was even more important to inform the mind, sustain the courage, and strengthen the resolution of the anti-slavery majority in the North,

to make all the men who had voted for Abraham
Lincoln realize what Abraham Lincoln realized —
that no compromise of any sort concerning the
extension of slavery was possible. To this double
purpose Mr. Beecher gave himself.

At first, in common with the great leaders of
the Republican party, he did not believe that there
was serious peril of war. The Union-savers had
cried " Wolf! Wolf! " so often when there was no
wolf that the anti-slavery reformers had come to
believe that the beast did not exist. They discredited the courage of the South, as the Southerners discredited the courage of the North; they
thought the threat of disunion was uttered only for
political purposes, and had been uttered much too
often; that, to quote Charles Francis Adams's
summary of his father's opinion, " The South was
not in earnest, that its threats were mere brag-
gadocio, that its interests and safety combined to
keep it in the Union." Asked in March, 1860,
to speak on how to save the Union, Mr. Beecher
began his speech by saying, " It is somewhat em-
barrassing to speak on this subject, because I consider that the Union is in no danger. . . . The
Union was never so firm as it is now." In November following the election of Mr. Lincoln he expressed again the same confidence in even stronger
terms: " It is absurd to suppose that the South
with all her interest in the Union will leave it, and
therefore I say the South will never leave the Union.
There is a man now at the helm of the ship of state

who will guide her safely through the perils which
encompass her, a man who knows not what it is to
be scared." Mr. Beecher did not then realize the
far-reaching plan of the Confederate leaders, which
involved the establishment of a great semi-tropical
republic, founded on an African slave-trade, and
including Mexico, Central America, and the West
Indies, united with the slave-holding states of
North America; nor did he realize the power
of popular passion, in a democratic community,
when inflamed, to disregard all considerations of
self-interest.

But, as time went on, and the peril of civil war
became more imminent, the result was to make Mr.
Beecher's insistence on uncompromising adherence
to principle more vigorous. On the 29th of November, 1860, he preached a Thanksgiving sermon, the
character of which is indicated by its title, "Against
a Compromise of Principle." In this sermon he said
that there were three courses possible : — (1) To
go over to the South. (2) To compromise principle.
(3) To maintain principle on just and constitutional
grounds, and abide the issue. The first was not to
be thought of. Compromise was made impossible
by the inherent nature of the issue. "To be of
any use compromise must make the slaves contented, slavery economical, slave states as prosperous as free states. Compromise must shut the
mouth of free speech, . . . must cure the intolerance of the plantation, . . . must make evil as
prosperous as good, enforced slavery as fruitful

as free labor." The North ought to have nothing
to do with halfway measures or halfway men. To
the demands of the Southern secession leaders this
should be its answer : —

The North loves liberty, and will have it. We will
not aggress on you. Keep your institutions within your
own bounds; we will not hinder you. We will not take
advantage to destroy, or one whit to abate, your fair
political prerogatives. You have already gained advantages of us. These we will allow you to hold. You
shall have the Constitution intact, and its full benefit.
The full might and power of public sentiment in the
North shall guarantee to you everything that history
and the Constitution give you. But if you ask us to
augment the area of slavery; to coöperate with you in
cursing new territory; if you ask us to make the air of
the North favorable for a slave's breath, we will not do
it! We love liberty as much as you love slavery, and
we shall stand by our rights with all the vigor with
which we mean to stand by justice toward you.[1]

In reading these words the reader should remember that they were uttered when the Northern pulpits and Northern press were clamoring for some
impossible compromise, when Congress was debating halfway measures, when halfway men were
endeavoring to contrive some platform of concession to slavery and secession that would postpone
the inevitable conflict, when abolitionists were ad-
vising to let the erring sisters depart in peace.

Six weeks later, on a fast-day appointed by the
President, speaking on " Our Blameworthiness,"

[1] *Patriotic Addresses*, p. 242.

Mr. Beecher again indicted slavery as " the most alarming and most fertile cause of national sin. . . . Not only a sin but a fountain from which have flowed many sins." Commonplace as this utterance may seem now, it did not seem so then. On the same day on which Mr. Beecher was declaring that slavery was the great national sin, a neighboring Brooklyn preacher was arguing that slavery was indorsed by the Bible, and was urging the then familiar argument that the blameworthiness of the nation consisted in the fanaticism which denounced slavery. I remember on that same fastday attending a union service in a Western city at which several addresses urging to repentance were made, and only one of the speakers referred to slavery. By the others not the most distant allusion was made to it, while every other sin in the calendar, from Sabbath-breaking to covetousness, came in for a safe and harmless denunciation.

As might be expected, when by the bombardment of Fort Sumter the Confederacy threw down the challenge of war to the federal government, Mr. Beecher was prompt to respond. He was absent lecturing when the news of the bombardment was flashed over the wires. Returning to his home, he gave on Sunday morning his message for the hour to his congregation. The commercial fears which counseled a new attempt at compromise he sought to counteract by arousing a passionate enthusiasm for nationality, liberty, humanity. The fire that even now, more than forty years after the

delivery of the sermon, flashes from the printed
page, it is as impossible to reproduce, in an analysis of the argument, as it is to reproduce in the
heaped up ashes from a camp-fire the pile of logs
aflame, its light illumining the darkness of the
night, and its glow warming the bystanders. The
spirit of his message was conveyed by its text,
" Speak unto the children of Israel that they go
forward." In this sermon Mr. Beecher presented
clearly the demand of the Republican party, the
demand of the South, and the impossibility of any
compromise between the demands. " We ask no
advantages, no new prerogatives, no privileges
whatsoever; we merely say, Let there be no intestine revolution in our institutions, but let them
stand as they were made and for the purposes for
which they were created." On the other hand, the
Confederates " have expunged the doctrine of universal liberty and put in its place the doctrine of
liberty for the strong and servitude for the weak."
The new constitution of the so-called Confederate
States " holds that there is appointed of God a
governing class and a class to be governed, —
a class that were born governors because they are
strong and smart and well-to-do, and a class that
were born servants because they are poor and weak
and unable to take care of themselves." Men in
the North were proposing to secure peace between
liberty and slavery by ignoring the distinction between them. These Northerners he scourged with
unsparing ridicule : —

You can have your American eagle as you want it. If, with the South, you will strike out his eyes, then you shall stand well with Mr. Davis and Mr. Stephens of the Confederate States; if, with the Christians of the South, you will pluck off his wings, you shall stand well with the Southern churches; and if, with the new peace-makers that have risen up in the North, you will pull out his tail-feathers, you shall stand well with the society for the promotion of national unity. But when you have stricken out his eyes so that he can no longer see, when you have plucked off his wings so that he can no longer fly, and when you have pulled out his guiding tail-feathers so that he can no longer steer himself, but rolls in the dirt a mere buzzard, then will he be worth preserving? Such an eagle it is that they mean to depict upon the banner of America!

But he did not merely ridicule; he did not merely denounce — he argued: On what conditions could the North retreat from the war? on what conditions have peace? "On condition that two thirds of the nation shall implicitly yield up to the dictation of one third;" on condition that " we will legalize and establish the right of any discontented community to rebel and set up intestine governments within the government of the United States;" on condition that " we will agree fundamentally to change our Constitution, and instead of maintaining a charter of universal freedom, to write it out as a deliberate charter of oppression;" on condition that we " become partners in slavery, and consent, for the sake of peace, to ratify this gigantic evil;" on condition that "we shall no

longer have any right of discussion, of debate, of
criticism, — shall no longer have any right of *agitation*, as it is called." Against these demands
of the South he placed the duties which the hour
devolved upon the North. " While the air of the
South is full of the pestilent doctrines of slavery,
accursed be our communities if we will not be as
zealous and enthusiastic for liberty as they are
against it." Every man should declare himself.
" We must draw the lines. A great many men
have been on both sides. A great many men have
been thrown backward and forward, like a shuttle,
from one side to the other. It is now time for
every man to choose one side or the other." Commercial interests must not be permitted to interfere. " We must not stop to measure costs — especially the cost of going forward — on any basis so
mean and narrow as that of pecuniary prosperity."
An ultimate and enduring settlement must be kept
ever in mind. " We must aim at a peace built on
foundations so solid of God's immutable truth, that
nothing can reach to unsettle it. Let this conflict
between liberty and slavery never come up again."
And the controversy must be entered into without
wrath or bitterness. " Let not our feeling be
savage or vengeful. We can go into this conflict
with a spirit just as truly Christian as any that ever
inspired us in the performance of a Christian duty.
. . . Let the spirit of fury be far from us; but
the spirit of earnestness, of willingness to do, to
suffer, and to die, if need be, for our land and our

principles, — that may be a religious spirit. We
may consecrate it with prayer."

In this sermon occurred an incident which illustrates both the quickness of the orator to seize the
advantage of the unexpected, and the wisdom of
the Christian to direct the sudden excitement of an
audience to a noble issue. I can best give this
incident by quoting it from the sermon itself: —

Since I came into this desk I have received a dis-
patch from one of our most illustrious citizens, saying
that Sumter is reinforced, and Moultrie is the fort that
has been destroyed. [*Tremendous and prolonged applause, expressed by enthusiastic cheers, clapping of
hands, and waving of handkerchiefs.*] But what if the
rising of the sun to-morrow should reverse the message?
What if the tidings that greet you in the morning should
be but the echo of the old tidings of disaster? You
live in hours in which you are to suffer suspense. Now
lifted up, you will be prematurely cheering, and now
cast down, you will be prematurely desponding. Look
forward, then, past the individual steps, the various vicissitudes of experience, to the glorious end that is coming!
Look beyond the present to that assured victory which
awaits us in the future.

The incident is characteristic of Mr. Beecher.
He often raised his audiences to the highest pitch
of excitement, but never for the mere pleasure of
exciting them. He always endeavored to utilize
the excitement which he had created by giving to
it a practical turn, and making it minister to a
higher life in future conduct.

From the hour in which war began, Plymouth Church became a centre in the war excitement, as it had been an educational centre in the anti-slavery campaign which had preceded. It was continuously used as a means, not only for strengthening courage and stimulating patriotic enthusiasm, but also practically for raising and equipping soldiers. The American flag floated from the roof of the building. At times daily meetings were held for the purpose of making up articles necessary for volunteers. A news express was organized, called the " Plymouth Mail," to forward papers to the enlisted representatives in Plymouth Church. At one service three thousand dollars were raised to aid in equipping one of the regiments. At another a fine outfit of Colt's revolvers were presented by the young men of Plymouth Church to a company. Mr. Beecher equipped one regiment at his own expense. One of his sons volunteered with the father's heartiest approval. Sermons were frequent to companies of soldiers coming to Plymouth Church for the purpose of receiving instruction and inspiration. One of these sermons entitled " The National Flag," delivered to the Brooklyn Fourteenth in May, 1861, was little more than an eloquent incitement to courage and patriotism; another, on " The Camp, Its Dangers and Duties," pointed out the moral dangers incident to camp life, and contained counsel to soldiers how to avoid them, and to friends at home how to strengthen the young men no longer safeguarded by the influences of the home.

From the first Mr. Beecher believed that the war would end in the emancipation of the slave. "That we see," he said, "the beginning of national emancipation we firmly believe. And we would have you firmly believe it, lest, fearing the loss of such an opportunity, you should over-eagerly grasp at accidental advantages, and seek to press forward the consummation by methods and measures which, freeing you from one evil, shall open the door for innumerable others and fill our future with conflicts and immedicable trouble." But he was not in haste to anticipate the course of events; he did not demand an emancipation proclamation immediately. "How far our government, by a just use of its legitimate powers under the Constitution, can avail itself of this war to limit or even to bring slavery to an end, is matter for the wisest deliberation of the wisest men." Even emancipation could not, in his opinion, justify a course which would so centralize the national government as to destroy the state governments. The nation must still maintain "unimpaired in all its beneficence the American doctrine of the sovereignty of local government, except in those elements which have been clearly and undeniably transferred to the federal government." But when the President issued, in September, 1862, the preliminary emancipation proclamation Mr. Beecher heartily indorsed it, while he commended the President for not anticipating in his action the public sentiment of the North. On December 28, four days before the final emancipation proclamation, he took the approaching event as text for a sermon on "Liberty under Laws," which he defined to be "the liberty [of every man] to use himself, in all his powers, according to the laws which God has imposed on those powers;" this he declared was the divine prerogative of every man under the sun.

During all this time Mr. Beecher's work in the pulpit and on the platform was supplemented, as it had been in the previous years, by his work with the pen. In December, 1861, he became editor-in-chief of "The Independent," and for the brief time during which he held that position, its editorials were largely devoted to the one issue before the nation; not so much to the discussion of questions — for the time for discussion had passed — as to the inflaming of zeal, the stimulating of patriotism, the encouraging of devotion, the strengthening of resolution.

When James M. Mason and John Slidell, representatives from the Confederate States to the governments of France and England, were taken from an English mail steamer by Captain Wilkes, of the United States Navy, and the whole country was in a blaze of excitement, and war with England was imminent, Mr. Beecher assumed no wisdom on the question of international law involved and urged no special policy on the administration; he contented himself with declaring, "If we have, to the width of a hair, passed beyond the line of our own proper duty and right, we shall, upon suitable showing, need no menace to make suitable reparation. . . . But if we have done right, all the threatenings in the world will not move this people from their steadfastness." When the question of finance pressed upon the government, he did not discuss the proper method of raising revenue, but he urged the fearless imposition of taxes sufficient for the necessities of the country: " Every honest man in America ought to send to Washington one message in two words, *Fight, Tax.*" When slaves began to come into our lines, he did not discuss the legal or military question raised as to their status, but he insisted that they were to be treated as men, not as slaves: " Let us forget that these blacks were ever *Slaves*, and remember only that they are *Men*. With this as our first principle we cannot go far wrong." When McClellan was halting and hesitating on the Potomac, Mr. Beecher did not, like some of his contemporaries, propose military methods or suggest a form of military campaign ; but he demanded of the army " courage and enterprise " in an editorial bearing those two words as its title. " Since war is upon us, let us have courage to make war." Two months before President Lincoln's first emancipation proclamation he began to urge upon the nation emancipation as a necessity. Mr. Beecher was a great friend of Edwin M. Stanton. In these editorials of the summer of 1862 something of Mr. Stanton's impatience with McClellan's military policy appears in criticism of Mr. Lincoln's administration. We now know better than

Mr. Beecher then could know the difficulties which surrounded Mr. Lincoln, and the necessities which made him cautious not to move more rapidly than he could move with the united force of the loyal North supporting him. But the intensity of these editorials helped to arouse the very public sentiment for which Mr. Lincoln was waiting, and which made Mr. Lincoln's action, when it came, practical and efficient.

We should misinterpret Mr. Beecher if we should leave our readers with the impression that during these exciting months he was simply or even chiefly a reformer. His sermons on the one political subject which agitated the nation were frequent, but they were the exception. As during the previous anti-slavery campaign, his chief message was a personal gospel. On May 30, 1863, he sailed for Europe for what was intended to be a well-earned vacation — but came to be the occasion of the most important single service he ever rendered to his country. The Sunday evening before his departure he took for reaffirmation of the fundamental purpose of his ministry. I think that all those who were familiar with that ministry during the sixteen critical years which he had spent in Brooklyn would bear testimony that in this familiar discourse he not inaptly described it.

Among the earliest, the deepest, and the strongest purposes of my ministry was the determination that it should be a ministry of Christ. Nothing could be further from my heart than to make this pulpit the clustering point of a number of reforms. I never would have consented to serve in a church that was merely what is called a reformatory church. I felt in my soul that all power in moral reforms must spring from a yet deeper power; and for that I struck. And I remember how, in the very beginning, night and day without varying, through all the early months of my ministry here, I had but one feeling — to preach Christ for the awakening of men, for their conversion. My desire was that this should be a revival church — a church in which the Gospel should be preached primarily and mainly for the re-creation of man's moral nature, for the bringing of Christ as a living power upon the living souls of men. My profound conviction of the fruitlessness of man without God was such that it seemed to me gardening in the great Sahara to attempt to make moral reformation in a church which was not profoundly impressed with the great spiritual truths of Christ Jesus. I have no doubt that there are many in this land who would think it an extravagant thing to hear it said that the keynote of my ministry among you had been the evangelization of the soul, or the awakening of men from their sinfulness and their conversion to the Lord Jesus Christ. It has been; and if you had taken that out of my thought and feelings you would have taken away the very central principle of my ministry. By far the largest number of my sermons and the most of my preaching has been aimed at the conviction and the conversion of men.

CHAPTER X

THE CAMPAIGN IN ENGLAND

WHEN the secession movement first assumed serious proportions the sympathy of England was with the secessionists. There were many reasons for this. The political control of England was in the hands of the English aristocracy. Feudal England had always looked with both suspicion and aversion on her democratic daughter. The strongest argument against feudalism was the unparalleled growth of democratic America. Commercial England saw in the republic across the sea a rival who would soon contest with the mother country her claim to commercial supremacy, and she was not unwilling to see that rival dismembered, and her own commercial supremacy thus secured to her. For more than a quarter of a century England had seen the South aggressive and successful, the North timid and retreating. It was not strange that she believed the South brave, the North timid; and England admires pluck and despises cowardice. During the four months between the election and the inauguration of President Lincoln she had seen the secessionists united, purposeful, aggressive; she had seen the North divided, vacillating, frightened. Even Charles Sumner and Salmon P. Chase had intimated willingness to allow the Southern States to go out with slavery if they so desired it; even Mr. Seward, the Secretary of State in the new administration, had repudiated both the right and the desire to use armed force in subjugating the Southern States against the will of a majority of the people. No wonder that under these circumstances the English people, in increasing numbers, shared in the conviction a little later expressed by Mr. Gladstone: " We may anticipate with certainty the success of the Southern States so far as regards their separation from the North. I cannot but believe that that event is as certain as any event yet future and contingent can be." In politics preeminently is it true that " Nothing succeeds like success;" and the anticipated success of the Confederacy won for it many sympathizers in Great Britain who might otherwise have hesitated. In political circles in Great Britain Mr. Lincoln was unknown, and Mr. Seward, his Secretary of State, who was known, and who was erroneously supposed to be the controlling spirit in the new administration, was viewed with great distrust. We now know that this distrust was well grounded, and that if Mr. Seward had been the controlling spirit in the new administration he would have provoked a war with Great Britain for the purpose of arousing the national sentiment in South and North and uniting both sections against a common foe. The Southern States were the great cotton producing states of the world; England was the great cotton

manufacturing community of the world : the prosperity of England, almost the life of many of her
people, was dependent upon the cotton supply furnished by the Southern States, and therefore dependent upon breaking the blockade and opening the
Southern ports to commerce. As the result of the
Civil War the cotton supply had shrunk by May 1,
1862, from 1,500,000 bales to 500,000 bales, of
which less than 12,000 bales had been received
from America; over one half of the spindles of
Lancashire were idle, and in two towns, Blackburn
and Preston, alone, over 20,000 persons were dependent on parochial aid. On the pressure produced by this cotton famine, and anticipated by
the Confederate leaders, they had relied to compel
England's intervention in their behalf. Agents of
the Confederate States, official and unofficial, were
busy in England, quietly working through press
and public men to create public opinion favorable
to their cause. America has never fully realized
the debt it owes to the one brave, loyal, and lonely
American, Charles Francis Adams, our American
Minister to England during the period of the Civil
War, whose courage was equaled by his sagacity,
and to whose diplomacy we primarily owe the fact
that English intervention in behalf of the Confederate States was prevented.

If the question between North and South had
been, in the early years of the war, clearly seen to
be the question whether slavery should dominate
the continent or be destroyed, the anti-slavery con-

science of Great Britain might have been relied upon to counteract, to a considerable extent, the forces in England working on behalf of the Confederate cause; but even to Americans the issue between the two sections was obscured, and it is not strange that Englishmen did not correctly apprehend it. Isolated men of prophetic nature, like James Martineau, saw that if slavery was confined within a limited territory it must perish through the action of economic causes, but the great English public saw nothing but the issue as it was defined by public speech; and repeated, and even official declarations in America, in the early history of the war, distinctly denied that slavery was other than incidentally involved. Even as late as the summer of 1862, Mr. Lincoln had written to Mr. Greeley that ever memorable letter in which he declared that his paramount object in this struggle "is to save the Union, and is not either to save or to destroy slavery. If I could save the Union without freeing any slaves, I would do it; and if I could save it by freeing all the slaves, I would do it; and if I could do it by freeing some and leaving others alone, I would also do that." It is not strange that the English public generally did not discriminate between the *object* of public action and the *effect* of public action; did not see that, while the object of the government must be simply the reëstablishment of the federal authority throughout the nation, the effect of that reëstablishment must inevitably be the eventual overthrow of slavery. When at last, in

January, 1863, the President's proclamation of
emancipation was issued, it did something, but not
much, to clear the atmosphere. It was regarded by
the English journals generally, not as history has
regarded it, the greatest blow ever struck for human
freedom by a single hand, but, to quote one English critic, "the most unparalleled last card ever
played by a reckless gambler." The English people
were invited to recognize it as either a futile bid
for negro support, or, if effective, as a summons to
an insurrection which would be accompanied by
"a carnage so bloody that even the horrors of the
Jacquerie and the massacres of Cawnpore would
wax pale in comparison."

America was not without friends in England,
chiefly to be found among the laboring-class, who
were without a vote, and for the most part without
a voice, yet curiously not wholly without political
influence. As in many another crisis in history,
their instincts were wiser than the sagacity of the
statesmen and the leader-writers; they felt what
they could not have defined — that the cause of free
labor the world over was being fought out on American soil. They could not answer the arguments
adduced on platform and in press on behalf of the
Confederate States, but their sympathies were with
the preservation of the republic, their hopes were
for the overthrow of slavery. The emancipation
proclamation gave a reasonable and historic basis
for those hopes. And in January, 1863, a public
meeting was held in Exeter Hall against interven-

tion in behalf of the Confederate States, the first considerable expression of the before silent conscience of the common people of the land.

Such, briefly described, was the public sentiment in England, when, after " two or three months " of rest upon the Continent, Mr. Beecher reached London in the early fall of 1863.

Dr. John Raymond, Mr. Beecher's friend and companion in his European travels, had returned to America when Mr. Beecher left the Continent of Europe, and Mr. Beecher remained alone in England.[1] At first he refused the requests urged upon him to speak. There were special reasons why he should refuse. He was there simply as a private citizen, without any connection with the government or any authority to speak in its behalf. The rumor, afterward circulated, that he had been informally and unofficially deputed by the administration to go to England, and endeavor to create a sentiment favorable to the North, he explicitly denied. He went wholly on his own responsibility, with no supporter except his own church. Roving

---

[1] The best history of this English episode in Mr. Beecher's life, including Oliver Wendell Holmes's description of it in *The Atlantic Monthly*, Mr. Beecher's autobiographical account, and stenographic reports of the principal addresses, will be found in *Patriotic Addresses*, edited by John R. Howard. The account of his experiences as here given is largely based on Mr. Beecher's own account, given to a group of about twenty friends in his parlors, sometime in the seventies. This account was taken down in shorthand, and with some slight revision is printed in full in *Henry Ward Beecher: A Sketch of his Career*, by Lyman Abbott and S. B. Halliday.

diplomats, sent to England from time to time by
Mr. Seward, acted independently of Mr. Charles
Francis Adams, the American Minister, and thus
discredited Mr. Adams, and enhanced the difficulties of a delicate position. Unappointed volunteers
were also complicating affairs by private intermed-
dling, and by their letter-writing to the London
"Times," were not conducing to the friendly
relations between Great Britain and the United
States.   Mr. Beecher did not wish to be identified
in the public mind with either of these classes of
mischief-makers.   Bitter feeling against America
was sedulously cultivated by some eminent journals and by not a few reputable men. To speak for
America was sure to invite every species of insult
and indignity from Confederate sympathizers, and
was not sure to receive encouragement or support
from the few sympathizers with the North. It was
not even certain that the speaker's efforts would not
be condemned by the administration as possibly well-
meaning but practically injurious efforts. Mr.
Beecher was unfamiliar with the conditions of the
public mind, and by no means confident of his ability to meet them. He was conscious that, added to
the prejudice against him as a representative American, there was personal prejudice, theological and
other, which had been diligently excited against
him as an individual. The strength of these combined prejudices is illustrated by the defensatory
and almost apologetic character of the introductions with which, when he came to speak, he was

on more than one occasion presented to his audiences.

But Mr. Beecher's friends urged him to reconsider his declination. They presented two grounds, one private, one public, why he should accede to their request. They pleaded with him that they had defended the North, and suffered on its behalf, and they affirmed that if he went home refusing his help, his enemies and theirs would declare that the North itself despised them. They assured him that the commercial and aristocratic circles of Great Britain were eager to have Great Britain intervene; that it was of the utmost importance, in order to prevent the danger of intervention, to arouse and instruct the anti-slavery sentiment of England upon the issues of the war; that a movement was on foot to win to the Confederate cause the sympathies of the non-voting English laborers by a series of public meetings; and that in their judgment Mr. Beecher could do more than any other man to forestall and counteract this movement. The recent victories at Vicksburg and at Gettysburg had done something to stem the current of popular feeling in favor of the Confederate cause, and so to make this time opportune for securing a hearing for a representative of the North. The argument prevailed; Mr. Beecher's refusal was changed to consent, and arrangements were made for successive speeches at Manchester, Glasgow, Edinburgh, Liverpool, and London.[1]

[1] The success which attended these meetings led subsequently

There seems to be a kind of unacknowledged
public sentiment in England, which an American
finds it difficult to comprehend, that it is perfectly
fair play to prevent a speaker from being heard if
his opponents can do so by vociferous interruption,
or to capture a meeting organized for one purpose
and turn it to a diametrically opposite purpose if
there is force enough in the opposition to accomplish the result. So long as physical violence is
not resorted to, this sort of tactics seems to be
treated in England as a legitimate part of the
game. It was quite in accordance with English
traditions, therefore, that no sooner were the arrangements for giving Mr. Beecher a hearing
made and announced than counter arrangements
were made to prevent Mr. Beecher from being
heard. Blood-red placards were posted in the
streets of the cities where he was to speak. They
summoned the mob to prevent his speaking. The
audacity of the lies contained in these placards
almost surpasses belief. They charged him with
demanding that " the best blood of England must
flow for the outrage England had perpetrated in
America; " with recommending that London be
sacked; with calling for the extermination of the
people of the South and repeopling it from the
North; and they called on Englishmen to see that
he gets " the welcome he deserves." The only
effect of these posters was to arouse in him the

to three farewell breakfasts at, respectively, London, Manchester, and Liverpool.

resolve, "I won't leave England until I have been heard." But as the time came near for his first address, he began to doubt whether his first resolve had not been wise. That strange foreboding which sometimes comes upon an orator, that sense of intellectual helplessness, that premonition of utter failure, which is often really the precursor of great success, settled upon him. Mr. Hamilton W. Mabie, to whom he at one time narrated his experiences, has kindly written out his recollection of the narrative for me as follows: —

I remember very distinctly my talk with Mr. Beecher, although some things may have become a little blurred in the flight of time. He told me that nothing could describe the weight of antagonistic English opinion which rested on his spirit the moment he arrived in England; he felt as if he were surrounded by an almost impenetrable wall of prejudice and antagonism; he seemed to have the animosity of the entire country on his shoulders. On the day on which he was to make his first speech, he was in an agony of depression all the morning, feeling quite unable to bear up under the awful burden of the concentrated animosity of a nation: he felt something as he imagined Christ might have felt on the road to Calvary; he had never been so depressed before, and was never again under such a burden. He spent most of the morning on his knees, without any help; but finally arrived at a point where his prayer took the form of an offer to surrender everything and even to fail if that was God's will. Gradually, the depression wore off, and was succeeded by a great sense of repose. When he finally drove to the hall his peace was like that of a mountain lake, which nothing could have disturbed. When he entered the hall he found it packed with an audience collected for the express purpose of silencing him. Every time he opened his mouth his voice was drowned by the clamor of the hostile crowd. This went on so long that he began to fear that he should not get a chance to say anything. In the mean time he had studied his audience carefully, and it had photographed itself on his mind. The green baize doors reaching from the circle of chairs on the side, which ran around the outside of what we should call the orchestra, were fastened together. Seats had been brought in and placed around the side walls, and in some cases against these doors. In one of these seats a large, burly, red-haired, red-whiskered man was sitting, who was particularly vociferous, shouting, clapping his hands, pounding his feet, and throwing himself back in his chair. After about twenty minutes of attempted talk, in one of these paroxysms of racket, Mr. Beecher happened to be looking at this man, when he threw himself back with great violence, broke the fastenings of the door, and went head over heels in his chair down the stairs on the outside. The whole thing was so instantaneous and so funny that Mr. Beecher burst into a roar of laughter. The audience were astonished; turned around, following his glance, took in what had happened, and began to laugh themselves. That moment of relaxation he caught, made a witty remark which made them laugh still more, then told them a story which caught their attention, and from that moment held them without a break, as long as he chose to speak.

This last sentence must be taken relatively. It is evident from the published reports that to the end Mr. Beecher had to contend against constant interruption. His own account, as I heard it, confirms the accuracy of these reports. In that account he said : —

As soon as I began to speak the great audience began to show its teeth, and I had not gone on fifteen minutes before an unparalleled scene of confusion and interruption occurred. No American that has not seen an English mob can form any conception of one. I have seen all sorts of camp-meetings and experienced all kinds of public speaking on the stump; I have seen the most disturbed meetings in New York City, and they were all of them as twilight to midnight compared with an English hostile audience. For in England the meeting does not belong to the parties that call it, but to whoever chooses to go, and if they can take it out of your hands it is considered fair play. This meeting had a very large multitude of men in it who came there for the purpose of destroying the meeting and carrying it the other way when it came to the vote. I took the measure of the audience, and said to myself, "About one fourth of this audience are opposed to me, and about one fourth will be rather in sympathy, and my business now is not to appeal to that portion that is opposed to me, nor to those that are already on my side, but to bring over the middle section." How to do this was a problem. The question was, who could hold out longest. There were five or six storm centres, boiling and whirling at the same time; here some one pounding on a group with his umbrella and shouting, "Sit down there;" over yonder a row between two or three combatants; somewhere else a group all yelling together at the top of their voices. It was like talking to a storm at sea. But there were the newspaper reporters just in front, and I said to them, "Now, gentlemen, be kind enough to take down what I say. It will be in sections, but I will have it connected by-and-by." I threw my notes away, and entered on a discussion of the value of freedom as opposed to slavery in the manufacturing interest, arguing that freedom everywhere increases a man's necessities, and what he needs he buys, and that it was, therefore, to the interest of the manufacturing community to stand by the side of labor through the country. I never was more self-possessed and never in more perfect good temper; and I never was more determined that my hearers should feel the curb before I got through with them.

In Liverpool the conditions were even worse than in Manchester. "Liverpool," says Mr. Beecher, "was worse than all the rest put together. My life was threatened, and I had communications to the effect that I had better not venture there. The streets were placarded with the most scurrilous and abusive cards." Here there was threatening of actual violence; but some of Mr. Beecher's friends got warning of the danger, went armed to the meeting, and prevented violence by being prepared for it. For an hour and a half Mr. Beecher fought the mob before he got control, and then spoke an hour and a half afterwards; even then amid continual interruption. "I sometimes felt," he says, "like a shipmaster attempting to preach on board of a ship through a speaking-trumpet, with a tornado on the sea and a mutiny among the men."

As one turns to these speeches, and endeavors in imagination to reproduce the stormy scenes which accompanied them, he is impressed with the quickness of the speaker in turning every adverse incident to his own advantage, the emotional eloquence

of certain evidently extemporaneous passages, the
knowledge of history and of constitutional principles which underlies them, the philosophical unity
which makes of them all, to quote Oliver Wendell
Holmes, "a single speech . . . delivered piece-
meal in different places," and the peculiar adaptation of each address to the special audience to
which it was delivered.

One or two examples may serve to illustrate the
first characteristic : —

Great Britain has thrown her arms of love around
the Southerners, and turns from the Northerners.
("No.") She don't? I have only to say that she
has been caught in very suspicious circumstances.
(Laughter.)

If the South should be rendered independent — (At
this juncture mingled cheering and hissing became immense ; half the audience rose to their feet, waving hats
and handkerchiefs, and in every part of the hall there
was the greatest commotion and uproar.) You have
had your turn now; let me have mine again. (Loud
applause and laughter.) If this present struggle shall
eventuate in the separation of America, and making the
South — [loud applause, hisses, hooting, and cries of
"Bravo!"] — *a slave territory exclusively* — [Cries
of "No! No!" and laughter].

(Interruption and uproar.) My friends, I saw a
man once who was a little late at a railway station chase
an express train. He did n't catch it. (Laughter.)
If you are going to stop this meeting you have got to
stop it before I speak; for after I have got the things
out you may chase as long as you please, you will not
catch them. (Laughter and interruption.)

It is said that when Russia is now engaged in suppressing the liberty of Poland it is an indecent thing for America to flirt with her. I think so too. (Loud cheers.) Now you know what we felt when you were flirting with Mr. Mason at your Lord Mayor's banquet.

I am tempted to draw my pencil through these sentences, conscious how utterly inadequate their reproduction here is to suggest the alertness of the speaker in the circumstances under which they were first produced, — the quickness of resource, the facility of expression, the imperturbable good humor, the control of himself, and therefore the control of his hostile audience. It would be quite useless to take out of their connection the passages of supreme eloquence, which are scattered through these addresses, with their passionate patriotism, their love of liberty, their courageous faith in the power of divine principles, their perception of the essential unity of the Anglo-Saxon race, their comprehensive and catholic inclusion of all struggling humanity everywhere, whose battle the North was engaged in fighting.

These more brilliant qualities in his English speeches have concealed from the public their more sterling and permanent value. I am surprised, intimate as my acquaintance with Mr. Beecher was, at the accuracy of historical information, the statistical knowledge, the detailed acquaintance with economic and industrial aspects of the slavery question, which could not have been crammed up in special preparation for these addresses, separated as he was from his library, and from all access to American sources of information. His clear apprehension of the constitutional issues involved does not surprise me, for I knew him as a careful constitutional student. But his ability to make our complicated federal constitution clear to an English audience would have been remarkable, even if he had been giving an academic lecture to a quiet and note-taking class of Oxford students, instead of a public address to popular and hostile audiences, and subject to perpetual interruption. Could these five speeches be denuded of all their dramatic incidents, — the quick repartee, the sparkling humor, the fervid eloquence, — and reconstructed as one review article, discussing the issues of the hour in their bearing on English people and English politics, the article would be a notable contribution for the clearness of its insight, the breadth of its view, and the unanswerable logic of its argument.

In Manchester, where the spirit of individualism had its birth, where the freedom of labor was recognized, and where the interests of the laboring-man were predominant, Mr. Beecher traced the history of the anti-slavery conflict, showed that it was a conflict between free and slave labor, that the Civil War had grown out of it, and that the result of Northern victory would eventually be "the emancipation of every living being on the continent of America." At Glasgow, the great labor city of the border line between England and Scotland,

emphasizing the same truth, he showed that slavery
brings labor into contempt, that freedom honors
it; that free labor promotes virtue and intelligence,
and that virtue and intelligence compel leniency
of government; that slave labor promotes ignorance and vice, and ignorance and vice compel
tyranny in government; that thus " the American
question is the workingman's question all over the
world. The slave master's doctrine is that capital
should own labor — that the employer should own
the employed. This is Southern doctrine and Southern practice. Northern doctrine and Northern practice is that the laborer should be free, intelligent,
clothed with full citizen's rights, with a share of
the political duties and honors." In Edinburgh he
traced the rise and development of the American
Union, explained the nature of its Constitution,
traced the progress of the anti-slavery conflict, and
showed how the Civil War was the inevitable out-
come of that conflict, and how the victory of the
North inevitably involved the victory of representative government and universal liberty. In Liverpool, whose commercial interests were supposed to
be favorable to the recognition of the Southern
Confederacy and the breaking of the blockade, he
showed that slavery is hostile to commerce and to
manufactures; that Great Britain wanted chiefly,
not cotton, but consumers; that a slave nation must
be a poor customer, buying the fewest and the poorest goods; that a free nation must be a good customer, buying the largest and the best goods; an

economic argument which he supported by vital statistics, convincing and unanswerable. At Exeter Hall, in London, he briefly rehearsed his previous speeches, showed their relation to each other as parts of a consecutive series, and then proceeded to give his audience the American point of view of the issues involved. It was in this speech that he explained so clearly the nature of the American Constitution, which is to the Englishman ordinarily so insoluble a problem. In this speech, too, occurs as eloquent and genuine an expression of the love of liberty, imperishable in the Anglo-Saxon heart, as can be found in Anglo-Saxon literature.

Standing by my cradle, standing by my hearth, standing by the altar of the church, standing by all the places that mark the name and memory of heroic men who poured their blood and lives for principle, I declare that in ten or twenty years of war we will sacrifice everything we have for principle. If the love of popular liberty is dead in Great Britain, you will not understand us; but if the love of liberty lives as it once lived, and has worthy successors of those renowned men that were our ancestors as much as yours, and whose examples and principles we inherit to make fruitful as so much seed-corn in a new and fertile land, then you will understand our firm, invincible determination — deep as the sea, firm as the mountains, but calm as the heavens above us — to fight this war through at all hazards and at every cost.

If by oratory we mean power to produce a real and enduring effect on a great audience, and if the greatest test of oratory is conquering a hostile audi-

ence and producing a permanent effect upon the
hearers in spite of their hostility, then Mr. Beecher's
five orations in England take deserved place among
the great forensic triumphs of the world, — by the
side of the orations of Demosthenes against the
Crown, and Cicero's orations against Catiline. The
orators of the American Revolution spoke to sym-
pathizing audiences, those of the anti-slavery orators in the American anti-slavery campaign produced far less immediate effect, the orations of the
great orators in the British House of Commons —
Chatham, Fox, and Burke — rarely changed the
vote of the House, and the victories which Lord
Erskine won over juries, in spite of the threats of
the judges and the influence of the government,
were not won under circumstances so hostile, nor
were they so far-reaching in their effects. What
effect Mr. Beecher's speeches had on English public sentiment, and on English and American history, it is not possible accurately to estimate. But
this much at least I believe it is safe to say: by
them he enlisted democratic England against feudal
England, the England of the Puritan against the
England of the Cavalier, the England of the plain
people against the England of the aristocracy; by
them he did much to counteract the deliberate and
persistent efforts to misrepresent the American
problem and the American public; did even more
to clear away unintentional and natural misunderstanding ; made English intervention in the American conflict impossible ; aided to make possible the

subsequent arbitration of the international difficulties between England and America, growing out of the Alabama claims; and foresaw, foretold, and prepared for that impalpable and unofficial alliance between England and America which promises in the future to give justice, order, and stability to the whole world.

CHAPTER XI

RECONSTRUCTION

IN November, 1863, Mr. Beecher returned from England, to find himself suddenly popular, in unexpected quarters in his own land. He had fought in Great Britain crowds hostile to America, he had conquered for his native land at least a hearing, and the pride and patriotism of Americans of all classes were gratified and ready to express gratification. In his own city of Brooklyn he was given what was tantamount to an ovation lasting several days. Three successive meetings of welcome were given to him: two by his church on Tuesday and Wednesday evenings; another by the citizens of Brooklyn on Thursday evening in the Academy of Music; on Friday evening an immense war meeting, at the same place, gave him spontaneously another ovation; four days later, still another was given to him at a public meeting in the city of New York. From this time he was brought into more direct personal relations with the administration. And to his English service has been not unnaturally attributed the fact that, when Charleston was surrendered, Mr. Beecher was selected by the President to deliver the address on the occasion of the raising of the flag over the recaptured Fort Sumter.

It was characteristic of Mr. Beecher to turn his own thoughts, and those of the audiences he was privileged to address, from past victories to present and future problems. The question of the reconstruction of the South was already coming to the front. President Lincoln's amnesty proclamation, issued in December, 1863, provided a basis on which government might be organized in any of the Southern States. This proclamation provided that in any states in which there were voters who availed themselves of this proclamation, equal in numbers to ten per cent. of the voters of 1860, they might proceed to organize a state government, and that any provision which might be adopted by such state government in relation to the freed people of such state, which should recognize and declare their permanent freedom, provide for their education, and yet be consistent as a temporary arrangement with their present condition as a laboring, landless, and homeless class, would not be objected to by the national executive. On January 4, 1864, a free-state convention was held at New Orleans under this proclamation, and the first steps were taken for the organization of a reconstructed state government in accordance with its terms. The President's proclamation, and the prompt response of the state of Louisiana, acting under that proclamation, brought the question of reconstruction to the front, although the war was not yet ended.

Mr. Beecher, in public addresses, at once foreshadowed the general principles which he expected to maintain, and which in fact he did maintain during all the reconstruction period. On the 10th of February, 1864, he introduced an ex-Confederate brigadier-general in Plymouth Church, who spoke in favor of the complete abolition of slavery. In introducing him Mr. Beecher said: "I wish to say to the people of the South and Southwest, through the speaker, that there never was a community so large which had so little animosity toward the South — and if slavery were taken away there would be nothing between us but the heart-beat." A year later he declared himself in favor of granting suffrage to the negroes; two months thereafter he took the occasion furnished by the news of the capture of Richmond, telegraphed to him from Secretary Stanton, to rebuke the spirit of revenge and the spirit of exultation over a fallen foe, which was common throughout the North, and to advocate the reëstablishment of fraternal feeling between the two sections which had been at war. Three days later, at a public meeting for the expression of gratulation over recent victories, he repeated these remarks of peace and good will. And to his own church, on the occasion of his departure to deliver his memorable address at Fort Sumter, he said, "I go down to say to them (the people of the South) the day dawns and the darkness of the night is past, and as brethren to brethren I come to say to you, good tidings of great joy. The day on which the old flag is to be raised is Good

Friday ; and as Christ was raised to bring life and liberty into the world, so will the flag carry renewed life and liberty to the South. And as Plymouth Church has been known as an anti-slavery church, let your word be hereafter national fraternity and national benevolence, as I know it will be." The church officially indorsed these principles by a minute passed, I believe, without a dissenting vote. In this minute, the church, aiming to reflect the better sentiment of the North, disavowed in explicit terms all feeling of revenge, and all desire for special privilege,· and urged the Christian men of the South " to hasten on the reconciliation which we and all Christians at the North desire, and to take the lead in restoring peace to a country which can never be divided."

In all the mutations of public feeling and all the strife of parties which followed, and which made the reconstruction period one of such great perplexity, because of such tangled policies and vacillating purposes, Mr. Beecher maintained the spirit of confidence in the South and of good will toward it, expressed by him in this address and by his church in its official response. He believed and taught that a sound reconstruction policy involved a very few fundamental principles, and he emphasized now one, now the other, as necessity seemed to require, but he never departed from them or modified them in any particular. It will therefore be more convenient, in interpreting his attitude, not to follow a strictly chronological order. For his principles remained the same under Andrew Johnson as under Abraham Lincoln, in 1868 as in 1863.

The problem of reconstruction, as it presented itself at the close of the Civil War to the people of the North, was a very difficult and perplexing one. It is not strange that the best minds differed respecting the method of its solution. The great majority of the best citizens in the South believed as firmly as ever in the right of secession, and in the political and industrial subordination of the African race. The loyalty of the masses, and of most of the leaders, consisted in submission to necessity. Emancipation was endured because it could not be avoided. Although the freedman was no longer considered the chattel of the individual master, plans were rife to make him a serf attached to the soil, or, if this were impracticable, to keep him in industrial and political subjection in the state. There was believed to be, not without apparent reason, a real danger that if the South were left free to frame its own institutions, it would build up a new form of feudalism, scarcely less oppugnant to the democratic idea than the old form of feudalism had been. General Grant, whose generous sentiments toward the South are now universally recognized, declared, as the result of a tour of inspection in some of the Southern States during the months of November and December, 1865, that it was not then safe to withdraw the military from the South; that the whites and

blacks each required the protection of the general
government. This was not wholly due to perils
from a turbulent white population. " The late
slave," he said, " seems to be imbued with the idea
that the property of his late master should by right
belong to him, or at least should have no protection from the colored soldier." He added that in
some instances " the freedman's mind does not
seem to be disabused of the idea that a freedman
has the right to live without care or provision for
the future."

A great variety of plans for treating the states
lately in revolt were proposed. Some would regard
the whole Confederate territory as a conquered
province, and govern it under military law, read-
mitting states and territories from time to time,
as the conditions seemed favorable. Some would
readmit the states as they were, excluding from
the suffrage all those persons who had taken an
active part in the war of rebellion, thus leaving
the suffrage in the hands of the loyal whites, who
in all the states would have constituted a limited,
and in some of them a not very intelligent, minority.
Some would establish universal suffrage, except for
the exclusion of a small number of secession leaders,
but including the whole body of the negroes, re-
gardless of their intellectual or moral qualifications. Some, maintaining the somewhat doctrinaire
ground that the state had not been in revolt, but
that a mob had been in possession of the state,
proposed to consider the mob dissolved, and the

state as of right entitled to its old place in the
Union and its old representation in Congress.
There were serious objections to each one of these
plans. To the military plan — because it would
create a centralized power in Washington which
might easily become despotic in the South, and
perilous to the whole nation. To the organization
of the states by giving all the political power to
the loyal whites — because it would create in all
the Southern States government by minority, and
in some of them by a minority very narrow and
not very intelligent. To the plan of universal suffrage — because it would place the prosperity of
the South in the hands of an ignorant democracy,
and would be liable to create a war between the
races. To the restoration of the Southern States
as they were before the war — because it would
reëstablish the slave-holding oligarchy, unchanged
in spirit, though placed under new conditions.

The difficulty of the situation was enhanced by
the strife of parties. Many of the Republican
leaders desired universal suffrage, because they
counted on the negro vote to secure for the Republican party supremacy in the Southern States;
many of the Democratic leaders desired the re-
establishment of the Southern States on the old
basis, because it would restore the Democratic
party to its old supremacy in national affairs. The
ineradicable distrust of the Southern leaders by the
North, and the passionate hate engendered by the
war, were enormously increased by the assassina-

tion of Abraham Lincoln. Finally, the fact that President Johnson, who succeeded Mr. Lincoln, and was himself a Southerner, took, as time went on, more and more of the Southern and Democratic side of the question, developed a bitter hostility between himself and the Republican majority in Congress and throughout the North. All these conditions combined to keep alive sectional feeling, to create a solid North on one side, and a solid South on the other, and to make impossible that harmony of feeling which is essential to harmony of political action. It is easy now to criticise the reconstruction measures which the radical majority in Congress finally adopted and the radical majority in the North ratified, but it is not so easy to point out any better policy which could have been taken. The truth is, after three centuries of slavery, followed by four years of terrible civil war, no policy of reconstruction was possible which would not be accompanied with many and great political, social, and industrial evils. The nation has not yet paid the full penalty of its violation of its fundamental principles of justice and liberty.

Mr. Beecher's views on reconstruction are mainly to be found in three documents: his address at the raising of the Union flag over Fort Sumter, April 14, 1865; his sermon on the "Conditions of a Restored Union," preached in Plymouth Church, October 29, 1865, during the early stages of the debates over the reconstruction of the Southern States; and his two letters, written respectively

August 30 and September 8, 1866, known as the Cleveland letters.[1]

In the address at Fort Sumter, his formulation of the conditions of reconstruction is very simple. These conditions, as he states them, are three in number : —

First. That these United States shall be one and indivisible.

Second. That states are not absolute sovereigns, and have no right to dismember the republic.

Third. That universal liberty is indispensable to republican government, and that slavery shall be utterly and forever abolished.

These conditions, which now seem axiomatic, did not seem so then, not even to all the people of the North, still less to the people of the South. To the emphatic elucidation of these conditions he devotes the first part of this address. To an interpretation of the benefits conferred alike upon North and South by the war he devotes the second part of it. A few sentences must suffice to indicate its general spirit.

We exult, not for passion gratified, but for a sentiment victorious ; not for a temper, but for a conscience ; not as we devoutly believe, that *our* will has been done, but that God's will hath been done.

Let no man misread the meaning of this unfolding flag! It says, " GOVERNMENT hath returned hither." — It proclaims, in the name of vindicated government, peace and protection to loyalty ; humiliation and pain

---

[1] All three documents will be found in *Patriotic Addresses*.

to traitors. This is the flag of sovereignty. The Nation, not the States, is sovereign. Restored to authority this flag commands, not supplicates.

One Nation under one government, without slavery, has been ordained and shall stand. There can be peace on no other basis. On this basis reconstruction is easy, and needs neither architect nor engineer. Without this basis no engineer or architect shall ever reconstruct these rebellious states.

Emerging from such a prolonged rebellion, he is blind who tells you that the State, by a mere amnesty and benevolence of Government, can be put again, by a mere decree, in its old place. It would not be honest, it would not be kind or fraternal, for me to pretend that the Southern revolution against the Union has not reacted, and wrought revolution in the Southern States themselves, and inaugurated a new dispensation. Society is like a broken loom, and the piece which rebellion was weaving, has been cut, and every thread broken. You must put in new warp and new woof, — and weaving anew, as the fabric slowly unwinds, we shall see in it no gorgon figures, no hideous grotesques of the old barbarism, but the figures of vines and golden grains framing in the heads of Justice, Love and Liberty!

Is it feared that the rights of the States will be withheld? The South is not more jealous of their state rights than the North. State rights, from the earliest colonial days have been the peculiar pride and jealousy of New England. In every stage of national formation it was peculiarly Northern, and not Southern, statesmen that guarded State rights as we were forming the Constitution. But, once united, the loyal States gave up forever that which had been delegated to the National Government. And now in the hour of victory, the loyal States

do not mean to trench upon Southern States' rights.
They will not do it or suffer it to be done. There is
not to be one rule for high latitudes and another for
low. We take nothing from Southern States that has
not already been taken from Northern. The South shall
have just those rights that every Eastern, every Middle,
every Western State has, — no more, no less.

In this address Mr. Beecher did not discuss the
question of negro suffrage. In his sermon on the
" Conditions of a Restored Union " [1] he enters more
fully into the question what these conditions should
be. He urges that " the South should be restored
at the earliest practicable moment to a participation in our common government. It is best for us ;
it is best for them." The North should not wait
for their conversion from secession. " Let men say
that secession *ought* to have been allowed — if
they accept the fact that it is *forever disallowed*
by the people of this Continent." The North should
not wait for guarantees for the future. " What
guarantees? How are we to secure them? I think
that the best guarantee that can be given is the
utter destruction of slavery." The North should
not demand that the South be further humbled.
" I think it to be the great need of this Nation to
save the self-respect of the South." But certain
precedent conditions should be imposed. " It is

[1] This sermon was preached in October, 1865, six months after
the assassination of Abraham Lincoln, and before the introduction
of the reconstruction measures into Congress, and the famous speech
of Thaddeus Stevens urging the measures which were subsequently
adopted.

right that state conventions should be required to abolish slavery, and to assist in the amendment of the Constitution of the United States in that regard, so that any state that might try to rejuvenate slavery should under the Constitution be unable to do it." " Before the States of the South are reinstated these conventions should have ascertained, and presented, and established the condition of the freedman. They should have established, first, his right to labor, and to hold property, with all its concomitants. They should have established his right to labor as he pleases, where he pleases, and for whom he pleases, and to have sole and undivided the proceeds of his own earnings, with the liberty to do with them as he pleases just as any other citizen does. They should also have made him to be the equal of all other men before the courts and in the eye of the law. He should be just as much qualified to be a witness as the man that assaults him." Mr. Beecher's statement as to negro suffrage must be given more fully because it involves an explanation of his radical view on the suffrage question in its various aspects : —

I hold that it would have been wise, also, for these conventions to have given him the right of suffrage — for it is always inexpedient and foolish to deny a man his natural rights. And I yet stand on the ground that suffrage in our community is not a privilege, or a prerogative, but a natural right. That is to say, if there is any such thing as a natural right, a man has a natural right to determine the laws that involve his life, and liberty, and property. He has a right to have a voice in the election of those magistrates who have to do with his whole civil prosperity. If the right to determine the laws and magistracies under which one exists is not a natural right, I know not what a natural right is. It is not giving the colored man a privilege to allow him to vote : it is developing a long dormant natural right.

It may be proper to say here that Mr. Beecher accepted, with possibly one reservation, to be presently noted, all the logical deductions from his premise that suffrage is a natural right.[1] He demanded suffrage for the immigrant no less than for the negro. In an address delivered February 20, 1860, he said : " I am for universal suffrage. Would you allow the shiploads of foreigners emptied on these shores to vote at once? I would. Don't you consider it a great evil? I consider it an evil, but less than not having them vote. Although it may be a great inconvenience to teach them, I hold that all foreigners should vote. Then will you go a step farther and admit women to vote? Even so I would. It is my settled conviction, for opinion is not strong enough, that women are not in the way of duty when they do not give consideration to the duty which God in his providence is waiting to put upon them ; for when woman feels that she has a duty to perform in this

[1] From both the premise and the deductions I dissent. The practical effects of universal suffrage afford the final argument against it.

matter and demands the ballot, she will have it."
A year later he reaffirms the same principle, apply-
ing it more fully to woman suffrage, and insisting
that " the individual is the unit of society, and not
the family. And there can be no greater blunder in
philosophical statement than to hold anything else
in our day." A year and a half later, in a speech
for General Grant, October 9, 1868, he consistently
puts voting before education. " It has been said
that a man has been educated to vote, but I declare
that voting educates a man. As to the blacks, how
long would it have been before any one would have
taken the trouble to explain to them about political
affairs if they had not the right of suffrage."

Mr. Beecher's consent that negro suffrage should
be limited in the first instance to negroes who bore
arms is hardly consistent, philosophically, with his
position that suffrage is a natural right : for it may
well be claimed that if government has the power to
protect the natural rights of its citizens, it has the
duty of protecting them. But Mr. Beecher was
never a doctrinaire. Idealist he was in the *ends* he
sought, but he was always practical in his choice of
the means to be employed. As in the preceding
decade he had kept steadily in view the ultimate
abolition of slavery, but had been ready to accomplish it by the restriction of slavery within prescribed limits, so now he sought as the final result
universal suffrage, but was willing to accept a limited suffrage as the first step toward that result.
He believed in universal suffrage, but he did not

believe in forcing his belief upon the South against
the opposition of the Southern whites. " The best
intentions of the government," he said, " will be
defeated, if the laws that are made touching this
matter [the general treatment of the negro] are
such as are calculated to excite the animosity and
hatred of the white people in the South toward the
black people there. I except the single decree of
emancipation. That must stand, though men dis-
like it." The reason why any coercive measures
would be unwise was that they would excite such
race animosity. " All measures," he said, " instituted under the act of emancipation for the blacks,
in order to be permanently useful must have the
cordial consent of the wise and good citizens of
the South. . . . These men [the negroes] are scattered in fifteen States; they are living contiguous
to their old masters; the kindness of the white man
in the South is more important to them than all the
policies of the nation put together." He was therefore willing to let the claim for suffrage wait upon
processes of education. " I am satisfied that, while
we ought to claim for the colored man the right to
the elective franchise, you never will be able to
secure it and maintain it for him, except by making
him so intelligent that men cannot deny it to him.
You cannot long in this country deny to a man
any civil right for which he is manifestly qualified.
And if the colored man is industrious and accu-
mulates property, and makes a wise use of that
property, you cannot long withhold from him his

civil rights. We ought to demand universal suffrage, which is the foundation element of our
American doctrine; yet I demand many things in
theory which I do not at once expect to see realized in practice. I do not expect to see universal
suffrage in the South; but if the Southern people will not agree to universal suffrage, let it
be understood that there shall be a property and
educational qualification. Let it be understood
that men who have acquired a certain amount of
property, and can read and write, shall be allowed
to vote. I do not think that the possession of
property is a true condition on which to found
the right to vote; but as a transition step I will
accept it, when I would not accept it as a final
measure. It is a good initial, though not a good
final." [1]

He was willing to accept even less than this, as
a compromise: —

We want a beginning; and I would be willing, not as
a finality, but as a stepping-stone to what I hope to get
by and by, to take the suffrage for those colored men
who bore arms in our late war for the salvation of this

[1] It is interesting to note that this conditional suffrage has now
been adopted (1902), though as a finality, by the voluntary action
of six of the Southern States, Virginia, North and South Carolina,
Alabama, Mississippi, and Louisiana, in all of which any negro
paying taxes on three hundred dollars' worth of property, and
able to read and write, is entitled by the recently amended consti-
tutions to register and vote. If Mr. Beecher's plan had been
adopted in 1865, a long and bitter experience of race antagonism
in the South, and sectional antagonism in the nation, would apparently have been avoided.

government.[1] Now, I would like to see the man that professes to be a Democrat, who is opposed to a soldier's voting. Where is the man who can look in the face of that black hero who has risked his life in the thunder of battle to preserve this country, and say, You do not deserve to vote? The man who could do that is not himself fit to vote. He lacks the very first element of good citizenship.

Recognizing the fact that universal suffrage to be safe must be accompanied with universal intelligence, Mr. Beecher urged a vigorous prosecution of education in the South.

We are to educate the negroes and to Christianly educate them. We are to raise them in intelligence more and more, until they shall be able to prove themselves worthy of citizenship. For I tell you all the laws in the world cannot bolster a man up so as to place him any higher than his own moral worth and natural forces put him. You may pass laws declaring that black men are men, and that they are our equals in social position; but unless you can make them thoughtful, industrious, self-respecting, and intelligent; unless, in short, you can make them what you say they have a right to be, those laws will be in vain.[2]

[1] This was also Mr. Lincoln's suggestion, in his famous letter to Governor Hahn of Louisiana.

[2] It is interesting to compare this declaration of principles by Mr. Beecher in 1865 with Dr. Booker T. Washington's declaration in 1899: "I believe the past and present teach but one lesson, — to the Negro's friends and to the Negro himself, — that there is but one hope of solution; and that is for the Negro in every part of America to resolve from henceforth that he will throw aside every non-essential, and cling only to essential, — that this pillar of fire by night and pillar of cloud by day shall be property, economy, education, and Christian character." — *The Future of the American Negro*, p. 132.

But this work of education in the Southern States Mr. Beecher would not carry on exclusively for the negro. He would ignore all distinctions of race and color in benefactions, as he would ignore them in the law. He would not treat the South as a pagan land, to which missionaries must be sent, but as a part of a common country to which aid must be given by the richer and more prosperous section. "We are," he said, "as far as in us lies, to prepare the black man for his present condition and for his future, in the same way that we prepare the white man for his. And I think it should be a joint work. I do not think it would be wise for the North to pour ministers, colporters, and school-masters into the South, making a too marked distinction between the black people and the white. We ought to carry the Gospel and education to the whites and blacks alike. Our heart should be set toward our country and all its people, without distinction of caste, class, or color." It is safe to say that if the North had been animated by this spirit, and had acted in this temper, its missionary and educational efforts among the negroes in the South would have lessened instead of intensifying Southern race prejudices, as in many localities it has done.

While Mr. Beecher insisted on a policy of protection for the colored race, he also insisted on a policy of trust and confidence toward the Southern whites. He believed that these two policies were not only reconcilable, but that the protection for

the negroes would best be secured by confidence
in the whites. He therefore agreed with President
Johnson and the Democratic party in desiring the
immediate admission of the Southern States to the
privileges and prerogatives of statehood ; while, at
the same time, he agreed with the Republican party
in desiring adequate protection for the rights and
adequate promotion of the education of the colored
people. It would not be correct to say that he
occupied a position midway between the two con-
tending forces. But he saw the truth, or what he
regarded as the truth, in the position of each of
them. It was this desire of his for the prompt re-
establishment of fraternal relations between North
and South, the quick cessation of military government, the earliest possible reëstablishment of civil
authority, that led him to write the once famous
Cleveland letter. A convention of soldiers and
sailors was called at Cleveland, Ohio. Its object
was to promote the policy of immediate restoration
of the Southern States. Mr. Beecher was invited
to act as its chaplain. He declined the invitation, but in so doing he wrote giving his views at
length, the gist and purpose of his letter being
expressed in its opening sentence : " I heartily
wish it and all other conventions, of what party
soever, success, whose object is the restoration of
all the States late in rebellion to their Federal
relation."

It is difficult to understand now why this letter
should have subjected Mr. Beecher to the vehement

and vituperative abuse to which he was subjected. I suspect that the obnoxious element in the letter was comprised in the phrase "all other conventions, of what party soever." The party feeling between President Johnson and the Republican majority, which a year and a half later led to the impeachment of President Johnson, was already very intense. The Cleveland Convention was supposed to be a convention in President Johnson's interests. Mr. Beecher's letter was supposed to separate the writer from the Republican party, with which he had before coöperated, and to furnish ammunition for the Democratic party, with which President Johnson was beginning to coöperate. It undoubtedly did separate him from the radical wing of the Republican party.

In a letter, written nine days subsequently, to a parishioner, explaining but not retracting his Cleveland letter, he distinctly declares his separation from the radicals. And this frank declaration was the more significant, and to a large section of the Republican party the more obnoxious, because uttered just as the autumn congressional elections were coming on. In this letter he not only defines his former letter, but interprets and reaffirms the political speeches which for a year past he had been delivering in various important cities. "For a year past," he says, "I have been advocating the very principles of the Cleveland letter in all the chief Eastern cities — in Boston, Portland, Springfield, Albany, Utica, Rochester, Buffalo,

Philadelphia, Harrisburg, Pittsburg, and Brooklyn." And what these principles are he makes very clear: —

Deeming the speedy admission of the Southern States as necessary to their own health, as indirectly the best policy for the freedmen, as peculiarly needful for the safety of our Government, which, for the sake of accomplishing a good end, incautious men are in danger of perverting, I favored, and do still favor, the election to Congress of Republicans who will seek the early admission of the recusant states. Having urged it for a year past, I was more than ready to urge it again upon the Representatives to Congress this fall.

The hostility to Mr. Beecher was undoubtedly enhanced by the fact that in previous discussions he had strongly — too strongly as subsequent history shows — indorsed Andrew Johnson, as a wise and statesmanlike president. But for this very reason it should have aroused the less excitement, certainly the less surprise. He was not a Johnson man; he distinctly and in terms disavowed being a Johnson man. But he was not an anti-Johnson man, and in the then state of public feeling in the Republican party — a year and a half later culminating in the impeachment of President Johnson — not to be a political enemy of President Johnson was, in the eyes of the radical faction of the Republican party, nothing less than a capital offense.

There are a great many people who cannot understand loyalty to principle, who do understand loyalty to party. Principle seems to them vague, indefinite, intangible; the party is a visible organism, and whoever leaves it seems to them a deserter. The party is their standard; if the party vacillates and the individual does not vacillate with it, it is he, not the organization, which seems to be unstable. Mr. Beecher adhered to the principles enunciated by Abraham Lincoln in his amnesty proclamation. President Johnson departed from them in the one direction, the radicals in another, and all the efforts of moderate men, of whom Mr. Beecher was a distinguished representative, to secure unity of counsels and of action proved in vain. History looking back now clearly sees what Mr. Beecher not less clearly foresaw. He thus states it in his own words: —

Upon Mr. Johnson's accession I was supremely impressed with the conviction that the whole problem of reconstruction would pivot on the harmony of Mr. Johnson and Congress. With that we could have secured every guaranty and every amendment of the Constitution. Had a united Government said to the South, promptly backed up as it would have been by the united North, "With slavery we must take out of the Constitution whatever slavery put in, and put in whatever slavery for its own support left out," there can scarcely be a doubt that long before this the question would have been settled, the basis of representation in the South conformed to that in the North, and the principle, the most fundamental and important of all, might have been established in the Constitution, viz. that manhood and full citizenship are identical.

Mr. Beecher's independent refusal to follow the leadership of the radical Republicans, more than his maintenance of the policy of immediate restoration of the Southern States, constituted the real cause of objection to his position. At the same time, the candid historian must doubt Mr. Beecher's proposition that "refusing to admit loyal Senators and Representatives from the South to Congress will not help the freedmen, it will not secure for them the vote, it will not protect them, it will not secure any amendment of our Constitution, however just and wise." In point of fact, the exclusion of the Southern States from participation in the government until they had ratified Article XIV. of the Constitution, did secure that important constitutional amendment, and prepared the way for a still more important amendment in the adoption of the Fifteenth Article. But this consent to the necessary amendment of the Constitution was coerced from a reluctant South, when that consent might certainly have been won from a willing South if the promptness and unity of counsel which Mr. Beecher urged could have been secured. And that such willing assent to the industrial freedom of the negro and to a qualified and limited suffrage would have saved the South years of political disaster and industrial distress, and the nation a long sectional strife, transferred from the field of battle to the field of politics, is to an increasing number of people both North and South a demonstrated fact. Rereading in the light of subsequent history the account of the reconstruction period, and in that period, Mr. Beecher's speeches and letters, it appears even more clearly than it did then that his counsels were as wise as his spirit was fraternal, and that in the period of reconstruction he showed the spirit of a statesman as truly as in the period which preceded he had shown the spirit of a prophet and a reformer.

CHAPTER XII

UNDER ACCUSATION

In its immediate effect on national politics the
Cleveland letter was not of great importance.
Party strife was too high to permit either faction
to listen to counsels of conciliation and modera-
tion. But it led to an episode in the life of Mr.
Beecher, which for a time threatened permanently
to becloud his before unsullied reputation. To the
narrative of that episode it is now necessary to
turn.

For the first thirteen years of its existence "The
New York Independent" had been under the editorial control of three editors, Doctors Leonard
Bacon, R. S. Storrs, and Joseph Thompson, all
Congregational ministers of national eminence.
At the expiration of that time, December, 1861,
they resigned, and Mr. Beecher, who had been a
frequent contributor, and whose sermons for the
three years preceding had been published in "The
Independent," became its sole editor. At his request, Mr. Theodore Tilton, a young protégé of Mr.
Beecher and a member of Plymouth Church, for
whom he had almost the affection of a father, was
called in to be the assistant editor. The office work
of an editor was never congenial to Mr. Beecher.

He was in constant demand during the Civil War for public addresses, in addition to his church work. He was neither able nor inclined to give much time to the editorial work beyond writing an occasional "Star Paper" and editorials. When he went to England, he left "The Independent" in the charge of Mr. Tilton, and shortly after his return, in the fall of 1863, he withdrew from the active duties of editor, leaving his name for a time at the head of the columns, although practically Mr. Tilton took his place. At the same time Mr. Beecher entered into a contract with Mr. Bowen, the proprietor of "The Independent," by which he agreed to contribute to the paper and it agreed to publish weekly his sermon or "Lecture-Room Talk." This contract could be dissolved by either party on three months' notice. This was in February, 1864; a year later Mr. Tilton became editor in name as well as in fact.

When in September, 1866, the Cleveland letter appeared, there appeared simultaneously a caustic criticism of it in the columns of "The Independent;" and at the same time the publication of the weekly sermon was suspended, without explanation or notice to Mr. Beecher. He was forthwith deluged with protests from subscribers who assumed that he had withdrawn his sermons from the paper because the paper had criticised him. He endured this misinterpretation for a little while; then he gave the notice required to close the contract between him and "The Independent" and when urged

by the proprietor to reconsider his decision declined
to do so. Three years later, on the first of January,
1870, "The Christian Union" was started by J. B.
Ford & Co., and he became its editor-in-chief.
In twelve months thereafter the circulation of the
new journal had grown to 30,000, while that of
"The Independent" had sensibly decreased. For
Mr. Tilton had proved to be more brilliant as a
newspaper writer than sagacious as a newspaper
leader. His utterances on religious questions were
increasingly distasteful to the orthodox churches;
and the orthodox churches were the constituency
to which in the past "The Independent" had appealed. His utterances on the subject of marriage
and divorce, though possibly no more radical in
theory than those of John Milton, whom he quoted
in support of them, were identified in the public
mind with American theories of socialism and free
love. The religious heresy might have been tolerated; the social heresy was far more obnoxious;
protests poured in upon Mr. Bowen from every
quarter; he was finally forced to the conclusion, to
which he apparently came with reluctance, that a
change of editorial control was indispensable to the
future success of his journal; and Mr. Tilton was
summarily dismissed from his editorial position.

Meanwhile, Mr. Tilton's domestic life was neither
peaceful nor pleasant. The change which had taken
place in his views was an occasion of great anxiety
and pain to his wife, and his mode of expressing
them would have given pain and anxiety to a

woman less sensitive than Mrs. Tilton. She was anxious to know her duty with reference to the religious education of her children, and consulted her pastor. He advised patience. There were other difficulties of a more personal nature, and at length, her patience exhausted, she left her husband, sought refuge at her mother's house, and sent her pastor a request that he would advise her as to her duty. He consulted with one of the deacons of his church and with his wife, and the three united in counseling a permanent separation, which, however, did not at that time take place. Such, briefly stated, were the causes which led Mr. Tilton to the resolve — I quote his own words — " to strike Mr. Beecher to the heart; " such the origin of the charge preferred by Mr. Tilton, and forming the basis of the persecution to which Mr. Beecher was subjected for five years, which began with the resolve of Mr. Tilton in December, 1870, and may be said to have ended with the findings of the advisory council in February, 1876.

As to the charge itself, it is difficult for the judicial historian to state it. First, Mr. Tilton affirmed that Mr. Beecher had made improper proposals to his wife, but accompanied the statement with the most solemn declaration of his wife's absolute innocence and purity, — " as pure as an angel in heaven " were his words; subsequently he converted the charge into one of criminal conduct. Mr. Beecher's Puritan conscience, New England training, and great sensitiveness combined to make

him a purist as regards all relations between
the sexes. On the trial that subsequently took
place, nothing of a suspicious character was proved
against him, except certain letters written by him.
Persuaded by a friend of Mr. Tilton that he had
acted upon misinformation in counseling the permanent separation between Mr. and Mrs. Tilton,
and that his counsel had directly aggravated Mr.
Tilton's domestic difficulties, and indirectly led to
his dismissal by Mr. Bowen, and so to his social
and financial ruin, Mr. Beecher gave both verbal
and written expression to the poignancy of his regret, in language which was subsequently distorted
into a confession of crime. To one familiar with
Mr. Beecher's readiness to excuse his neighbor and
accuse himself, these letters were not ambiguous;
to others they might have been so. That he kept
silence concerning these charges, until they were
given to the public in a form which made silence
no longer possible, was in accordance with Mr.
Beecher's lifelong principle, to pay no attention to
slanders against his name. If he had been more
suspicious and less unworldly, he would not have
accepted without questioning the assertions of
Mr. Tilton's friend, which led him groundlessly to
accuse himself. If he had early taken counsel of
other men more suspicious and less unworldly, he
would probably not have been caught in the net
which was spread for him. But much as his friends
may wish that he could have taken such counsel,
they must recognize the sentiment of honor which

forbade him both as a gentleman and as a minister
to disclose to any one secrets affecting the peace
and good name of a member of his own church.
That he kept silence so long will not be counted as
other than a fact to his honor by any one who con-
siders that the strong incentive to speak was only
counteracted by the stronger obligation of silence.

Not until June, 1874, did Mr. Tilton make any
public charge against Mr. Beecher, and then in
terms wholly vague. Mr. Beecher instantly replied to it by a demand for a full and thorough
investigation. Then ensued a curious conflict, Mr.
Tilton and his friend employing all their resources
to impede, thwart, and prevent an investigation,
Mr. Beecher insisting that it should be absolute,
thorough, and complete. It was not until after
this investigation was begun that the charge
against Mr. Beecher was altered from one of improper proposals to one of criminal conduct. The
change was necessary in order to lay a foundation
for the proceedings at law which Mr. Tilton finally
brought:

I have here stated, though with necessary brevity,
all the facts essential to an understanding of this
case. It only remains to state with equal brevity
the results of the three investigations — one by
Plymouth Church, one by the civil courts, and
one by a council of Congregational churches.

The investigation on behalf of Plymouth Church
was conducted by a special committee of six gentlemen well known in their community, and some

possessing a more than local reputation. Among them were Mr. Henry W. Sage, since known by his benefactions to Cornell University and his services as one of its trustees; Horace B. Claflin, one of the most prominent and influential of the great merchants of New York City; and John Winslow, a well-known Brooklyn lawyer, who brought to the committee a recognized ability in the examination and cross-examination of witnesses and the weighing of evidence. The committee were appointed on the 27th of June, 1874; they presented their report on the 27th of August; and after recounting their endeavors to ascertain the facts, and exhaustively reviewing the evidence which they had been able to obtain, they reported that " we find nothing whatever in the evidence that should impair the perfect confidence of Plymouth Church or the world in the Christian character and integrity of Henry Ward Beecher." This report, with the evidence on which it was based, was reviewed and unanimously approved by the examining committee, and the reports of both committees were laid before the church, after full public notice, and unanimously adopted by fifteen hundred members, substantially the entire resident membership of the church. This action of the church took place on the 28th of August, 1874.

The second investigation was the trial before a civil court of an action brought by Mr. Tilton against Mr. Beecher for alienating the affections of his wife. The trial dragged on for six months and ended in a disagreement of the jury, nine of whom, comprising all who were men of Christian belief, affirming their belief in Mr. Beecher's innocence. Before the trial ended, however, the chief lawyer for the prosecution was with difficulty prevented from abandoning the case, and subsequently publicly avowed his belief in Mr. Beecher's innocence ; and the judge who presided at the trial testified to his convictions, by presiding, eight years later, at the meeting held in the Brooklyn Academy of Music in honor of Mr. Beecher's seventieth birthday, and joining in the resolutions declaring that " by the integrity of his life and the purity of his character he has vanquished misrepresentation and abuse." [1]

A year and a half after this trial the largest and most representative council of Congregational churches ever known in the history of the denomination was called by Plymouth Church to counsel it respecting its action, which had been subjected to severe criticism by the critics of Mr. Beecher. The roll of members actually in attendance was two hundred and forty-four ; they were summoned from all parts of the country and from all schools of thought in the Congregational denomination, and included not a few whose political or theological prepossessions would have made them naturally suspicious of Mr. Beecher. Its sessions were presided over by the Rev. Leonard Bacon, D. D., of New Haven, as moderator, and the Hon. Nelson Dingley, Jr., of Maine, and General Erastus N. Bates of

[1] See chapter XIII. p. 326.

Illinois as assistant moderators. At the opening of
this council Mr. Beecher appeared before it, declaring on behalf of the church that the council was
desired to make whatever investigation it might
wish to make, by whatever plan of investigation it
deemed wise, and on his own behalf that an adequate and just investigation of all the circumstances
in the case was what he most coveted. After the
investigation was completed, he reappeared before
the council, and was questioned at great length,
answering without reserve any question which any
delegate chose to ask; and among the delegates
were not only eminent clergymen, but laymen of
national reputation, and among the latter lawyers
skilled in the art of cross-examination. Being
without power to subpœna witnesses or administer
oaths, the council could not properly try the case
which had been already tried, but it conducted a
public inquiry with a freedom which is impossible
in a court of law, and by its formal resolutions
declared that " we hold the pastor of this church,
as we and all others are bound to hold him, innocent of the charges reported against him, until sub-
stantiated by proof." The closing addresses of
Dr. J. W. Wellman of Massachusetts, Dr. J. M.
Sturtevant, the president of Illinois College, and
Dr. Noah Porter, the president of Yale College,
assured him and the church of the unabated confidence of the council, and of the churches which it
represented. This judgment has since been affirmed
by the spontaneous expressions of Mr. Beecher's

fellow citizens in the city which he made his home
for forty years; and by the verdict of the larger
community at home and abroad, to whose spontaneous expressions of confidence and esteem I shall
presently have occasion to refer.

To those who believe in Christ's declaration that
the religious teacher is to be known by the fruits
of his work, the spiritual results of Mr. Beecher's
ministry during the years in which his enemies were
continuing their frankly avowed endeavors to drive
him in disgrace from his pulpit, his city, and the
editorial chair, will serve as an even more conclusive evidence of Mr. Beecher's character than the
judgment of his church, the churches of his denomination, and the spontaneous and unofficial
verdict of his fellow citizens. The statistics of
Plymouth Church during this time show in the
number of dismissions no indication of suspicion,
distrust, or dissatisfaction in Plymouth Church;
in the number of admissions by letter no indication
of lessened confidence on the part of other Christian churches; and in the number of those received
on confession of their faith no diminution in the
number of those converted to Christ through the
ministry of the church and of its pastor.[1] Num-

---

[1] The following table shows admissions and dismissions for the
four years prior: —

| Years | Admissions | | Dismissions |
	By Letter	On Confession	
1872	62	135	60
1873	126	82	59
1874	53	121	34
1875	70	106	49

bers alone are not significant of spiritual values. That during these four years, 1872–75, Mr. Beecher's congregation remained undiminished and the membership of the church was sensibly increased, might perhaps be attributed to his oratorical gifts; that his church sustained him with almost absolute unanimity might be, and by his critics was, attributed to his magnetic personality. But neither Mr. Beecher's oratorical gifts nor his magnetic personality can account for the fact that the entire work of the church proceeded with unabated spiritual vigor as witnessed by its Sunday-schools, its prayer-meetings, its varied philanthropic and Christian work, the character and life of its members, and the permanence and efficiency of the church which survived him.

To this plain statement of the wholly uncontradicted and unquestioned facts in this case, it may not be improper for me to add an expression of my own personal opinion. I had some special advantages for forming one. I was intimately acquainted with both Mr. Tilton and Mr. Beecher. More than a year before the Cleveland letter I had ventured to warn Mr. Beecher that Mr. Tilton was not the friend Mr. Beecher thought him to be. I was personally acquainted with the incidents which led to his withdrawal from " The Independent " and his subsequent founding of " The Christian Union." My brother, Austin Abbott, was one of Mr. Beecher's counsel in the trial, and I had special facilities for a careful study of the evidence in the case, and certain editorial duties made such study a necessity. In the advisory council subsequently held I was an active member, and my duties as chairman of its business committee made my constant attendance at all its sessions, both public and private, my duty. There was no proof at any time of any act of impropriety on Mr. Beecher's part toward Mrs. Tilton or toward any other woman, — nothing that could be called even an "indiscretion." His only indiscretion was in allowing himself to be on terms of comparative intimacy with men who were unworthy of his confidence, and in accepting as true, without inquiry or investigation, statements which a man of more practical wisdom would certainly have doubted, if he did not instantly recognize their falsehood. After no inconsiderable hesitation I have given to this story larger space than its real importance deserves, only because I feared lest passing it by with mere scant attention would be misconstrued by some reader. Personally I believe that future history will attach as little emphasis to this episode in the life of Mr. Beecher as history now attaches to analogous imputations, with far more to give them color, brought against John Wesley in his lifetime.

CHAPTER XIII

LATER MINISTRY

IN order to give a connected account of this episode in the life of Mr. Beecher, it has been necessary to interrupt the historical continuity of the narrative. To that narrative I now return.

The Cleveland letter written August 30, 1866, recommended that middle way which was the path alike of national honor and of national safety, but in what was then the condition of the nation, neither of the two political parties was willing to take this middle way. For the time being the counsels of such men as Mr. Beecher — for he by no means stood alone — were discarded. The nation could learn only by experience the political lessons which its men of prophetic mind perceived intuitively. Mr. Beecher, therefore, wisely withdrew for a time from the more active participation in public affairs, and gave himself to other and more quiet labors. During the decade 1866–76, he wrote both "Norwood" and the first volume, with part of the second volume, of the "Life of Christ." These were the only volumes he ever wrote; his other books were composed of casual contributions written originally for the periodicals. During these ten years he founded "The Christian Union," and in 1872–74 delivered the famous "Yale Lectures on Preaching" at Yale Theological Seminary.[1] This editorial and literary work was carried on in addition to his regular preaching, his frequent lecturing, and his addresses on various public occasions.

In the fall of 1872 the twenty-fifth anniversary of the organization of Plymouth Church and Mr. Beecher's installation were recognized in a series of meetings, lasting for five days, and known in the history of the church as the "Silver Wedding." These exercises were characterized by the simplicity which under Mr. Beecher's administration had become a second nature to Plymouth Church. Flowers constituted the only decoration; the music was chiefly congregational; only one address that could be called an oration was delivered; this was the only eulogy; the other speeches, if speeches they could be called, were informal, conversational, reminiscent, — nearly all of them by lay members of the church. The week might be described in a word as a home week.

Many absent members returned; others sent letters of affectionate remembrance; others, who had found inspiration in Plymouth Church, though they had never belonged to it, came to testify their affection and receive new gift of life. If the admission had not been rigidly confined to the holders of tickets, even Plymouth Church could not have

[1] See chapters xiv., " Mr. Beecher as Editor and Author," and xv., " The Yale Lectures on Preaching."

contained the crowd which would have thronged it.
Except for a short storm on Thursday night, the
weather was fine. The keynote of the week was
struck at the first meeting by Mr. George A. Bell,
the successive superintendent of its three Sabbath-
schools, in the sentence, "I thank Mr. Beecher
because he has made me to know my God and my
Saviour." The programme of the week was so
arranged as to include the whole life of the church.
Monday night was given up to the children. Tuesday was given to a reunion of all that had worked
in either of the Plymouth Sunday-schools from
their organization. Wednesday was the laymen's
day, when the founders of the church made statements concerning its origin, its history, and its progress. Thursday evening the church was crowded
to its utmost capacity, to hear two addresses — one
of reminiscences and personal experience, by Mr.
Beecher, reciting the history of this church " as it
looks to me from my own standpoint; " the second,
an address by Dr. R. S. Storrs on " Mr. Beecher
as a Preacher." The printed page preserves the
sympathetic insight, the wise analysis, the pictorial
imagination, the iridescent humor, and the finished
literary form of Dr. Storrs's eulogy ; but it cannot
indicate the powerful personality which stood behind the words and uttered itself through them. Dr.
Storrs's simile illustrating Mr. Beecher's oratory
is equally applicable to his own on this occasion :
" I do not know," said he, " very much about Mr.
Beecher's preaching, for I have only heard him

three or four times; but I know enough to recognize the difference between the sermon as he preaches it, and the sermon as it is printed and published to be read afterward : the one is like the fireworks as they appear at night in all their brilliance and glory, the other is like the blackened, smoking framework which the boys stare at the next morning."

But more sacred and moving than any oratory were the morning prayer-meetings, and the Friday evening communion service, conducted as nearly as possible in the spirit of a Friday evening prayer-meeting. The church was thronged with communicants — the body, the side aisles, the galleries. Throughout the week Mr. Beecher contended against an inclination, which he feared rather than perceived, toward hero-worship. His introduction to the communion service emphasized his desire. " In the presence," said he, " of these memorials, let no name be mentioned except that one which is above every name ; " and with a touch almost of sadness, he enforced his request : " If I have taught you to look to any other one, my teaching has been worse than useless." Then followed brief words of Christian experience from laymen, on whom he called — generous, sincere, glowing; after which the communion was administered to twenty-five hundred communicants ; and by a few brief words from Mr. Beecher the thoughts of the church were turned from the past to the future, and the services of the week were brought to a close.

Despite the generous contribution of a hundred thousand dollars by Plymouth Church, presented in the form of an increase of salary during the year of the trial, the enormous expenses involved left Mr. Beecher indebted. Careless as he was in the use of money, he was never careless about his pecuniary obligations. As soon, therefore, as the trial was over he set himself to work to raise the funds necessary to meet obligations which he had incurred, and the easiest and simplest way to do this was by lecturing throughout the country. Doubtless another cause combined to impel him to this course. He believed that the best remedy for worry was effective work; he held with Dr. Chalmers to " the expulsive power of a new affection." The best possible way to erase from his own mind and from that of the public, who had been fed for six months with newspaper reports of the trial, was to give himself to a national ministry through the lecture platform. His lecture tours, under Major J. B. Pond's direction, and for the most part in companionship with him, extended as far west as the Pacific coast and as far south as Memphis. These annual lecture tours under Major Pond's direction began April 18, 1875. From that time until February, 1887, three weeks before his death, Mr. Beecher is said by Major Pond to have traveled with him nearly three hundred thousand miles, and to have lectured under his supervision twelve hundred and sixty-one times. On a single one of these tours Mr. Beecher delivered seventy-five lectures, preached sixteen sermons, and traveled seventeen thousand miles. These lecture tours gave opportunity for the expression of public confidence in him, and of this opportunity the public, East and West, North and South, availed itself. He was rarely in any town over Sunday that he was not invited to preach, and he invariably accepted the invitation, irrespective of the denomination which invited him, and always without compensation. If he was in a college town, he was customarily invited to address the students, and, if other engagements permitted, he accepted the invitation. The warmth of the reception given to him was in some places as unexpected as it was gratifying. In Memphis he was received, when he arrived in the city, with a salute of twenty-one guns, and, as there was no lecture-room large enough to hold the people, Agricultural Hall was taken, and four thousand seats put into it.

It was not always so, however. Political, theological, and personal prejudices combined sometimes in bitter opposition to him, — opposition which I believe he never failed to overcome. One dramatic instance illustrates both facts. On board the sleeper at Baltimore en route to Richmond, a telegram was put into Mr. Pond's hands which read as follows : —

RICHMOND, VA., January 22, 1877.

To J. B. POND, Baltimore, Md.

No use coming. Beecher will not be allowed to speak in Richmond. No tickets sold.

Mr. Pond put the telegram into his pocket and said nothing to Mr. Beecher. On arriving in Richmond the warning was repeated. The local agent abandoned the lecture. Mr. Pond rented the theatre, and issued bills and dodgers announcing that the lecture would be delivered. When the evening came, the theatre was crowded with men ; no women were present. Mr. Pond was advised that " the gallery is full of eggs." When Mr. Beecher rose to speak, he was greeted with yells from the hostile audience. He met them with a good-humored jest at the members of the Virginia legislature, who were present in large numbers. The rest of the audience joined in the laugh at the legislature. In a few minutes Mr. Beecher had the crowd under his control. At the close an informal reception was given him in the hotel, and he was earnestly urged to remain and lecture a second night, that the women might come to hear him.

I rarely heard Mr. Beecher lecture ; I often heard him preach. He was at his best in the pulpit, next on the rostrum, last on the lecture platform. He generally wrote his lectures, but rarely read them, and never memorized them. Mr. Pond is my authority for saying that he never delivered the same lecture twice in the same way. The form and structure of the lecture depended largely upon the audience to which it was to be addressed, and while the substance of it remained unchanged, the illustrations were frequently varied from evening to evening. Local incidents and occasions inspired sometimes his most eloquent passages, as in his peroration in the Richmond lecture, — a tribute to the Commonwealth of Virginia, the mother of Presidents, and his forecast of the noble future which lay before her. Mr. Beecher could not speak without imparting some information, nor without some flash of humor, but he never lectured merely for the purpose of entertaining or instructing his audience. His lectures were all ethical discourses: any one of them might have been a sermon; some of them were. One of the most famous of his lectures, that on " Evolution and Religion," grew out of a sermon, and in turn was elaborated into a course of eight sermons on that subject, subsequently published in book form. On the whole, it may be truly said that his lecture tours constituted a form of religious ministry, ethical and social, rather than spiritual and individual. Not less than his sermons, however, were his lectures inspired by the purpose to interpret and apply the principles and precepts of Jesus Christ, and inspire men with the Christian spirit. In popularity Mr. Beecher as lecturer stood second only to John B. Gough, in inspirational effect second to no one.

Though during this decade the political questions before the country did not compare in either dramatic interest or public influence with those growing out of slavery, Mr. Beecher continued, though in lesser measure, to discuss before the public the questions which from time to time arose. He was a continuous student of social questions, and continued to speak upon them. He advocated unsectarian public schools, and strenuously opposed the division of the public funds between the Roman Catholics and the Protestants, or any use of public funds for sectarian schools of any description. He advocated the Irish cause, speaking on the same platform with John Dillon and Charles Stewart Parnell, and urging the policy, now at last adopted by the English government, of making the tenant population of Ireland land-owners. He vigorously antagonized the exclusion of the Chinese from our coasts, saying, whimsically, that when the camel eats palm, the camel does not become palm, but the palm becomes camel. He opposed prohibition as " an absolute impossibility," and advocated high license. I do not know that either local option or the dispensary system had become a public question in his time, or, if so, that he ever expressed himself definitely upon them. He urged civil-service reform, and opposed the free coinage of silver. He faced with his usual courage anti-Jewish prejudice, of which there was in 1881 a special ebullition, and preached a sermon on the subject of such interest that the substance of it was cabled across the Atlantic, and the " Pall Mall Gazette " declared of it that it would excite, especially in Germany, " much more interest than a presidential message." He spoke and wrote, in presidential elections, for Grant, for Hayes, and for Cleveland ; and on different occasions for the redemption of the ballot-box, for the Sunday opening of libraries, for woman suffrage, for popular amusements, for the enforcement of excise legislation, at public dinners to Professor Tyndall and to Herbert Spencer, and in public tributes to Dr. Livingstone and to Matthew Arnold.

His advocacy, by pen and on the forum, of the election of President Cleveland caused a surprise which the historian cannot but declare to have been extraordinarily unreasonable. Mr. Beecher was always and by nature an independent; he belonged to no party, and was the advocate of none. He spoke on abolition platforms against some of the fundamental principles of the abolitionists; he spoke on Republican platforms against some of the fundamental principles of the Republicans; he preached an evangelical faith to Unitarian congregations; and he would have been glad to preach a Christian faith in a Jewish pulpit, or a Protestant faith in a Roman Catholic pulpit, if the opportunity had been offered to him. Politically, he was an individualist, if not by inheritance, certainly by training. His ten years of anti-slavery campaigning had emphasized his belief in the liberty of the individual, his desire to promote that liberty, and his belief that the individual should be left unhandicapped, to pursue in his own way his own chosen path in life. Economically, he belonged with the Manchester school, though, morally, he repudiated the idea that social order can ever emerge from a mere conflict of selfish interests. Protection is essentially socialistic in its

nature. It assumes that the nation is not merely
a collection of individuals; that it has an interest
apart from the interests of the individuals who
compose it; that it may rightfully adopt a policy
which will promote the interests of the whole,
although it may interfere with the liberties or impair the interests of some. What measure of truth
there is in this socialistic philosophy, toward which
in many ways American society is now turning, it
is not necessary for me here to inquire. Mr. Beecher
did not believe in it. He was, therefore, necessarily
and on principle, a free-trader. He had avowed
himself so, explicitly and emphatically, in his English speeches; he had repeated that avowal, again
and again, on Republican platforms; he had resisted within the Republican party the growth of
the high protective principle. When, as candidate
for governor of the state, Mr. Cleveland ran
against Governor Folger, Mr. Beecher supported
Mr. Cleveland. When, therefore, in 1884, the issue was clearly and sharply made in the first Blaine
and Cleveland campaign, Mr. Beecher had no option
but either to keep silent or to advocate the election
of Mr. Cleveland. Mr. Cleveland stood for civil-
service reform, Mr. Blaine for machine politics;
Mr. Cleveland stood for a tariff for revenue only,
Mr. Blaine for a high protective system. Any one
who knew Mr. Beecher should have known that, if
he had to choose between the party he had associated with and the principles which he held sacred,
he would always leave the party for the sake of the

principles. This he did. His doing so cost him
some warm friendships. All this he foresaw. He
hesitated for weeks before he formed the final decision. I speak in this matter of what I know, for
at his request I went up to Peekskill to counsel
with him on the subject. He made careful inqui-
ries respecting the rumors prejudicial to Mr. Cleveland's character before he espoused Mr. Cleveland's election, and he satisfied himself that, whatever color of truth they might have had in the past,
they were absolutely untrue as respected Mr. Cleveland's character in 1884. The unwise recommen-
dations of some friends, who ought to have known
him better, and who urged him not to become an
advocate of Mr. Cleveland's election because he
could not afford to do so, were perhaps the final
determining element in the formation of his decision. Nothing was more likely to lead Mr.
Beecher into battle than such a warning, that it
would be perilous to himself. It is not necessary
here to rehearse the arguments which Mr. Beecher
presented in support of free trade; it must suffice
to say that they were mainly moral, not economic.
He held that whatever seeming prosperity the protective tariff conferred on one class involved the
real detriment of another class, that it was essentially a selfish policy, and he opposed it " as not
only impolitic, but unjust and morally wrong."

In the decade which we are considering Mr.
Beecher's first work was, as it had been in the
past, as a preacher and in his own church. But

his preaching underwent a noticeable change. It became more intellectual and philosophical. It was addressed less to the will and more to the reason. Mr. Beecher's preaching may be approximately divided into three epochs. In the first it is largely pictorial, imaginative, emotional. This preaching is typified by the " Lectures to Young Men." In the second epoch, the emotions and the imagination have been brought into subjection; the style is less exuberant; the pictures are not less vivid, but they are less numerous; they do not follow one another in such kaleidoscopic succession; the emotion is spiritualized, — it is deeper, devouter, stronger, — not less impassioned, but under better control; the whole sermon converges on one truth; preaching has become a battle, in which all the resources of the commanding general are brought to bear upon the one pivotal point in the field, and reason, imagination, emotion combine to carry away the hearer, capturing his will, and bringing him into subjection to a new purpose, and obedient to a new law of life. Of this epoch the Harpers' edition of sermons selected from those preached in the years 1860–68 afford the best illustration. In the third epoch Mr. Beecher is a teacher. The sermons are expositions; he is an interpreter of faith; he is attempting to show men that the spiritual experience, into which he has before been endeavoring to carry them by all the forces of his nature, is an experience consistent with the highest exercise of the reason; he preaches less for conversion, and more for instruction and edification. Of this type of preaching his eight sermons on "Evolution and Religion" are the most striking illustration.[1] The later change was intentioned; it was a deliberate adaptation of his preaching to new conditions. In the second of his sermons on "Evolution and Religion" he thus defines his purpose: —

The last years of my life I dedicate to this work of religion, to this purpose of God, to this development, on a grander scale, of my Lord and Master Jesus Christ. I believe in God. I believe in immortality. I believe in Jesus Christ as the incarnated representative of the spirit of God. I believe in all the essential truths that go to make up morality and spiritual religion. I am neither an infidel, nor an agnostic, nor an atheist; but if I am anything, by the grace of God I am a lover of Jesus Christ, as the manifestation of God under the limitations of space and matter; and in no part of my life has my ministry seemed to me so solemn, so earnest, so fruitful, as this last decade will seem, if I shall succeed in uncovering to the faith of this people the great truths of the two revelations — God's building revelation of the material globe, and God's building revelation in the unfolding of the human mind. May God direct me in your instruction!

To understand the significance of this decision

[1] *Evolution and Religion:* Part i. Eight sermons discussing the bearings of the evolutionary philosophy on the fundamental doctrines of evangelical Christianity. Part ii. Eighteen sermons discussing the application of the evolutionary principles and theories to the practical aspects of religious life. Fords, Howard & Hulbert. 1885.

and the value of his service in its execution, the reader must conceive the conditions out of which it grew. Darwin's " Origin of Species " was published in 1859, Herbert Spencer's " First Principles," in sections, in 1860–62. Translated into common language for the common people, through innumerable editorials and magazine articles, and rapidly finding their way into academic instruction in all the higher institutions of learning, they began to give currency to the notion of evolution in many circles where its fundamental principle was not in the least comprehended. From the first this doctrine of evolution was generally regarded by the churches as an attack on religion ; and not unnaturally, since it denied two fundamental articles of the Puritan, if not of the Protestant creed, — the Fall of Adam and the inerrancy of the Bible.

The whole Puritan system of theology had been built upon the Fall of Adam. Its first article was the Total Depravity of the human race. On this was supposed to be founded the necessity for revelation, as a divine disclosure to fallen man of truths required for his salvation, which, owing to his Fall, he could not otherwise know ; for redemption by a sacrificial atonement, rendered necessary to purge away his sins and succor him from the deserved wrath of God, on account of the Fall ; and for a new birth, necessary to recover man from the death in which he was involved by the sin of Adam, and from which he could be recovered only by a new creative act. The doctrine of evolution affirmed

that man had come from a lower animal order; it
denied that man was made perfect and had fallen
from a higher to a lower estate; it therefore seemed
to deny the doctrines of revelation, redemption,
and regeneration. It was regarded by substantially
the whole Christian Church as subversive of the
entire system of evangelical faith. At the same
time, and as a necessary consequence, evolution
denied a second fundamental doctrine of the Puritan and later Protestant creed, — that the Bible is
infallible and inerrant. Protestants, refusing the
authority of the Church, had, partly for polemical
reasons, substituted therefor the authority of the
Bible. Evolution treated the Genesis story of the
Fall as a fable; it therefore denied the inerrancy
of the Bible, denied its absolute and binding
authority, and seemed to destroy the foundation
on which the whole Protestant superstructure was
reared. We can now see clearly, what our fathers
did not see, that evangelical faith is not dependent on the doctrine of the Fall of Adam, and
that Protestantism is not dependent on the inerrancy of the Bible. The Fall of Adam is narrated
in the third chapter of Genesis. It is not again
referred to in the Old Testament, nor in the New
Testament, except parenthetically by the Apostle
Paul. In the one chapter where the Apostle Paul
treats of the nature and origin of sin, the seventh
chapter of Romans, he represents it as an emergence of the flesh against the spirit, a representation quite in harmony with the scientific doctrine

of evolution. The doctrine of Adam's Fall occupies
no such fundamental position in the Bible as it occupies in the Puritan creeds. It is equally clear
that the later Protestantism had claimed for the
Bible an authority which the Bible never claims for
itself and which the earlier Reformers did not claim
for it, much as Roman Catholicism had claimed
for the Church an authority which neither the Jewish Church nor the primitive Christian Church
ever claimed for itself. We can see that the frank
recognition of the Bible as the record of a progressive revelation — a book in its successive stages issuing from the spiritual experience of the epoch and
adapted to that experience — recommends it to rational faith and removes insuperable difficulties presented by the conception of it as an inerrant and
infallible record of truth divinely dictated to human amanuenses. But it is not strange that, when
the doctrine of evolution was first expounded,
mainly by men of unecclesiastical, if not anti-eccle-
siastical sympathies, it was regarded as subversive
both of evangelical faith and of regard for the
Bible as a revelation of truth. It is not strange
that it should even now be so regarded by those
who have never studied evolution, and do not know
what it really means, and who have never gone behind the creeds of Christendom to the Bible, from
which those creeds are supposed to have been
drawn, to ascertain whether the creeds state the
truths of religion as the Bible states them, and in
the relations in which the Bible states them.

Mr. Beecher was one of the first ministers in the Christian Church, if not the very first in this country, to advocate the doctrine of evolution as a doctrine which, so far from being inimical to the cause of Christ, was certain to prove its friend and supporter. The first reference in Mr. Beecher's public teaching which I have been able to find, that indicates an acceptance or an inclination to accept the doctrine of evolution, was an incidental reference in a Sunday morning sermon, March 11, 1860: " What word did Adam ever speak or what manly thing did he ever perform, before or after the Fall, that was thought worthy of record? He has a name in the Bible; that is all. The world has come uphill every single step from the day of Adam to this." But it was not until nearly twenty years after that he began the systematic advocacy of evolution as an interpretation of the divine order which is consistent with and helpful to evangelical faith. To understand what this advocacy meant, the reader must also understand what evangelical faith, as Mr. Beecher apprehended it, means.

All religion recognizes man's obligation to God. It was a distinctive characteristic of the Hebrew religion that it also recognized God's obligation to man. The obligation was seen by the Prophets to be mutual: that of subjects to their King, but also that of the King to his subjects; that of the children to their Father, also that of the Father to his children. God was therefore represented in the

Old Testament as a covenant-keeping God. Covenant is mutual and involves mutual obligations. This doctrine of the obligation of God to men reappears in the New Testament as a gospel. Law represents what men owe to God ; the Gospel represents what God will do for men. The first declares what he requires of them; the second, what service he will render to them. An evangelical preacher is one who lays stress on this service which God renders to man, and on man's consequent hope in God. Mr. Beecher was throughout his life, in this sense, an evangelical preacher. He laid stress on duty and righteousness, but he laid far more stress on faith and hope and love — faith as a personal consciousness of God ; hope as an assurance of the future because of God ; and love as an inspiration to life because of the soul's recognition of God's love. The object of Mr. Beecher in the sermons on " Evolution and Religion," and largely in the preaching of the later years of his life, of which these sermons furnish an illustration, was to show that evolution, as an interpretation of God's way of working in the world, is not only consistent with this gospel of God's helpfulness but gives to it a richer and better interpretation.

Do you suppose that now, after fifty years in the Christian ministry, I could attend the funeral of religion cheerfully and joyfully, with every hereditary necessity on me, with the whole education of my youth, with all my associations, all the endearments of my past life in my memory, and with vivid and living sympathy with men, — do you suppose that I could stand here to advocate any truth that would destroy the substance, or in any degree materially injure even the forms of religion? I would die sooner! Do you suppose, from my nature and my whole example, I could go into the course of sermons that I have preached, and into the course of sermons that, God willing, I will preach yet, for any other reason than that I believe that the new view is to give to religion a power and a scope and a character such as has never yet been taken and known in the world at large? Better men than some have been, I suppose, will never be born; better lives than certain single lives will never appear over the horizon of time; but that which I look for is the change of the human race. I am not thinking of *men*, but of *mankind*. I am not in sympathy alone with *the Church*, but with *the whole human family*. And my longing, as it has been for years, is for such teaching and such philosophies as shall lead the whole human race to a higher and a nobler condition.

This paragraph interprets the object and illustrates the spirit of the entire series: that spirit is a broader and profounder faith because Mr. Beecher has come to understand evolution; that purpose is to give this broader and profounder faith to others. He frankly admits that evolution has " revolutionized my educational beliefs, but it has revolutionized those beliefs only to make them more spiritual, more hopeful, more full of the divine life." He has no tendency to rationalism: he reaffirms his belief in the miracles, and in the doctrine of divine design and of a superintending

and personal Providence. He is not a Universalist : he repudiates with intense abhorrence the
doctrine of endless punishment, but he does not
affirm the doctrine of universal restoration ; " analogy would suggest that unfit men have run their
career and perished." He is not a Unitarian : he
reaffirms his acceptance of the Trinity, as the best
hypothetical explanation to account for the teachings of Christian Church history and human experience, and his undiminished faith in Christ as
" the one fit manifestation of God, so far as he
could be made known to human intelligence." He
repudiates the doctrine of the Fall, but reaffirms
in the strongest language his belief in the reality
and universality of sinfulness, and in the necessity
of repentance and that new birth which is the beginning of the new spiritual life. In his lectures
on " Bible Studies," given on Sunday evenings
during the autumn, winter, and spring of 1878–
79, he had anticipated much of the modern criticism, though he had done so, not in a scholastic
discussion of theories, but in a practical use of
the Old Testament narratives. In his sermons on
" Evolution and Religion " he repudiates the doctrine of the plenary and verbal inspiration of the
Bible, and with it the doctrine that the Bible is
inerrant and infallible, and substitutes therefor
the doctrine of the Bible as " the record of the
gradual and progressive unfolding of human knowledge in respect to social and spiritual things
through vast periods of time." At the same time

he declares his reverence for the Bible as "the book which has reached the highest conception of God yet attained by human consciousness;" a book which "gives the only grand ideal of manhood known to literature;" a "living book" with "power of inspiring men with the noblest desires;" a "book that creates life."

There is nothing in these views which to the modern reader will seem radical or revolutionary. In the score of years which have elapsed since these sermons were preached, evolution has won for itself universal recognition. Practically all scientists are now evolutionists; all collegiate instruction in every department is based on the assumption of the fundamental truth of evolution as the law of life and progress; and the great majority of ministers and theologians either frankly accept it or silently acquiesce in it. It is not necessary here to revive the bitterness of those years and repeat the vilification and abuse to which Mr. Beecher was subjected for the crime of being in advance of the churches of his time. This abuse, however, led to one significant act on his part which has sometimes been misinterpreted. Criticism of his theological views, coming from some of his brethren in the Congregational ministry, and especially in the local association to which he belonged, led him in October, 1882, to withdraw from its membership, solely because he did not wish that other members should be embarrassed by any supposition that they indorsed or were responsible

for his at that time unpopular opinions. He did
not, however, become an independent. He remained to the day of his death a Congregationalist
in good standing, always continuing his membership in the state association, and always retaining his fellowship with the ministers and churches
of the Congregational faith and order. He took
the occasion of his withdrawal from the local association to restate his evangelical faith. This statement, made with his customary frankness, to his
own brethren in the ministry, was taken down by
a shorthand reporter.[1]   It is the fullest as it is the
latest statement of Mr. Beecher's theological views,
nor do I know any reason to think that he subsequently departed in any important respect from
these views.

Neither the Sunday evening lectures on the Old
Testament nor the Sunday morning sermons on
" Evolution and Religion " are a mere exposition
of critical and philosophical theories. In both series
Mr. Beecher is still a preacher, not a lecturer.
Other volumes of a later date by other authors will
give to the reader a better intellectual conception
of modern criticism as applied to the Old Testament, and of the philosophy of evolution as applied
in theological science; but any preacher who' desires to know how to use the Old Testament for
spiritual ends, while holding it to be not an infallible standard, but the record of a progressive revelation, will find few books more serviceable to his

[1] See Appendix.

purpose than Mr. Beecher's " Bible Studies ; " and
any preacher who desires to know how to use the
doctrine of evolution, as an instrument for the unfolding of spiritual truth in our time for practical
and spiritual ends, will find few if any volumes
more serviceable for his purpose than the one
containing Mr. Beecher's first eight sermons on
" Evolution and Religion."

If any one asks what was the spiritual effect of
this teaching as compared with that of the preceding epoch, the answer must be twofold : First, that
Mr. Beecher did not suddenly become an evolutionist. " Slowly," he says, " and through a whole
fifty years I have been under the influence, first
obscurely, indirectly, of the great doctrine of evolution." The doctrine that the kingdom of God is
a growth, and comes not with observation, underlay all his preaching ; and I do not know of any
pastor of the last half of the last century whose
preaching was accompanied with greater apparent
spiritual results in accessions to the church on profession of faith than that of Mr. Beecher. In the
second place, although in the later decade there
were no such great revivals as that of 1858, when
three hundred and sixty-nine were added to the
church on confession of their faith, most of them
at a single communion, the average additions to
the church on confession of faith were, with that
exception, about the same during the last decade
as during the earlier years, though they were unaccompanied by any such emotional conditions as

accompanied the two special revivals which occurred during the first ten years of his ministry.

In 1881 Mr. Beecher severed his connection with " The Christian Union." Writing had grown increasingly distasteful to him. Confinement to the desk he avoided. His editorial relations to " The Christian Union " had been indeed throughout all my connection with it, that is, since 1876, somewhat slight and constantly lessening. I had hoped, through the services of a shorthand writer, to get from him, in conversation, material which would serve for editorial purpose; but I did not to any considerable extent succeed. He was always expecting to write editorials, but almost never did. Occasionally he would send me a letter while on his lecture tours, but they were infrequent. He left the supervision of the paper wholly in my hands, although on great questions I constantly consulted with him. His ideas found their way to its columns through the inspiration which he afforded both to me and to others of the staff, but not in the inimitable form in which he would have put them. His name and mine stood at the head of the paper as joint editors. He came to feel, as I did, that this put both him and the paper in a false position, giving the public an impression that it was getting what really he was not furnishing. So at length, in 1881, he sold his interest in the paper, and laid down his editorial work.

His lecturing, public speaking, and preaching he continued with unabated vigor to the end. Few were the public occasions at which he was not an honored guest. He was invited to speak at four of the six New England dinners in the city of Brooklyn between 1880 and 1886, an honor accorded to no other man. On the 25th of January, 1883, a public meeting was tendered to him on the occasion of his seventieth birthday. The Academy of Music was crowded to its utmost capacity; and half an hour before the exercises commenced the doors had to be closed. A great throng remained outside, to whom, before the exercises within began, Mr. Beecher spoke briefly. Upon the stage within were many of the most eminent clergymen of Brooklyn and New York; indeed, it would be easier to make a list of those who were absent than of those who were present, either in person or by letter. The meeting was presided over by Judge Joseph Neilson, who had presided at the trial of Mr. Beecher in the same city eight years before. Addresses of eulogy were delivered by Dr. Armitage on "Mr. Beecher as a Man," Dr. Robert Collyer on "Mr. Beecher's English Campaign," Dr. Fulton on "Mr. Beecher as a Christian," and by the Hon. Seth Low, then the mayor of Brooklyn, on "Mr. Beecher as a Citizen;" and letters expressive of confidence and esteem were read from Oliver Wendell Holmes, John G. Whittier, George William Curtis, Wendell Phillips, Andrew D. White, Mark Hopkins, Senator Henry L. Dawes of Massachusetts, General W. T. Sherman, Whitelaw Reid, Professor J. D. Dana, ex-President

Hayes, and others. A resolution was passed by a rising vote expressing the appreciation, by his fellow citizens of Brooklyn, of Mr. Beecher " as a religious teacher, a public citizen, a generous neighbor and friend, and a man who by the integrity of his life and the purity of his character has vanquished misrepresentation and abuse, corrected and counteracted misunderstanding, and converted public alienation into personal affection."

So passed his closing years. His campaigning days were over. To the end there were those who were alienated from him for various reasons: some, because in the battles through which he had passed he had dealt blows which left scars; some, for ecclesiastical reasons which will seem to posterity, and indeed seem even now, wholly insignificant; some, because his theological positions subjected him to undeserved religious suspicion; some, because his political independence could not be understood by those who can see no difference between loyalty to party and loyalty to principles. But all these combined made but an insignificant minority. He was in Brooklyn easily its most distinguished and its most honored citizen, respected by all, revered by many, loved by those who knew him best, his church devotedly attached to him. To the end he retained his physical and his intellectual force. His preaching was less imaginative and less impassioned than in the earlier years, but it was never more vigorous. Never did it appeal so effectively to men of large minds. His winters were given to work with a vigor which few men who have passed seventy could parallel; his summers were spent in the new home which he had built in Peekskill, and in which, as he once said to me, he had desired to express himself by showing in material form what a country home should be. Before, however, I come to speak of the last scene in this great life, I must devote two chapters to certain phases of his life work, necessarily passed by in this history, in order to maintain unbroken the continuity of the narrative.

CHAPTER XIV

EDITOR AND AUTHOR

In this chapter I propose to bring together some facts illustrating Mr. Beecher's character and work in the sphere of journalism and authorship, such as could not well be inserted in their chronological order, except in brief reference, without interfering with the continuity of the historical narrative.

Mr. Beecher began editorial work before he was ordained to the ministry. He acted for four or five months as editor of "The Cincinnati Journal," while he was still a student in Lane Seminary. His editorials produced such an impression that they were copied with approval by "The Cincinnati Gazette," at that time regarded as the ablest journal west of the Alleghanies. In Indianapolis he edited an agricultural department in "The Indiana Journal," as a sort of recreation from the more serious labors of his ministry. During his editorship "The Western Farmer and Gardener," under which title the agricultural department of "The Indiana Journal" was published in monthly numbers, gained a national reputation.

This editing was recreative; real writing as a serious business of life, he did not enter upon to any extent until after he came to Brooklyn in 1847. "The Independent," which was started the following year, was a Congregational newspaper, established for the maintenance of Puritan doctrines and principles and their fearless application to social problems, especially that presented by slavery. Of its three editors, the Rev. Joseph P. Thompson, pastor of the Broadway Tabernacle in New York City, had especial administrative capacity,[1] and was practically the managing editor of the journal. Mr. Beecher's genius was soon recognized by his Congregational associates, and he was engaged as a regular contributor. He was too independent to work well in harness; his associates preferred that he should alone be responsible for his utterances, and he preferred the freedom which such independence conferred. His methods of preparation and composition were peculiar, and were in striking contrast to those of his associate, Dr. Thompson. Dr. Thompson had his regular day at the office, was always punctual, calculated the amount of matter required, rarely if ever gave too much or too little, and his copy was the delight of compositors. Mr. Beecher came into the office about the time his manuscript was expected, sometimes boiling over with excitement, sometimes bubbling over with humor, talked of anything and everything but the business before him, finally caught up his pen, turned to the nearest desk, shut himself up in his shell, impenetrable as if he were a turtle, drove his pen across the

[1] See chapter XII. p. 288.

paper as if it were a printing-machine and he an
electric battery, threw off the pages as he wrote
them, left them to be gathered up and carried by
the boy to the compositors' room, and trusted a
subordinate to read proof, correct errors, and supply omissions. But what he wrote was caught
up and quoted from one end of the land to the
other. In effectiveness of utterance Mr. Beecher's
leaders in "The Independent" have never been
surpassed in American journalism. Comparisons
are perilous, but I think it is safe to say that no
Northern journal, except perhaps "The New York
Tribune" and "The New York Evening Post,"
exerted so powerful an influence in creating and
guiding public opinion during the ten years which
preceded the Civil War as did "The New York
Independent."

At the close of this epoch, and just on the eve
of the outbreak of the Civil War, the Congregational triumvirate resigned and Mr. Beecher became editor-in-chief of "The Independent." In the
issue of December 19, 1861, appears his salutatory.
It is brief. In it he declares that the change of
editorship does not involve any change in the principles, purpose, or general spirit of the paper,
which will continue "firmly to hold and to teach
those great cardinal doctrines of religion that are
substantially held in common by the Congregational
orthodox churches of New England and by the
Presbyterian churches of our whole land. But as
heretofore, this will be done for the promotion of

vital godliness rather than for sectarianism," and
it " will not forget that there is an ethical as well
as an emotive life in true religion," and therefore
will assume " the liberty of meddling with every
question which agitates the civil or Christian community." During the brief term of Mr. Beecher's
active control as editor-in-chief of " The Independent " the influence of the paper was maintained, if
it was not enhanced. Its efficient service in sustaining the courage of the people, urging aggressive,
patient, and persistent heroism, chiding the delays
which McClellan's dilatory policy imposed upon the
administration, preparing the way for the emancipation proclamation, and urging the issuing of one,
has already been referred to in a previous chapter.
What Mr. Beecher could have made of " The Independent " if he had been adequately supported is
matter for surmise, not for history. He was not
adequately supported. Mr. Tilton was as lacking
in administrative ability as Mr. Beecher ; he was
not more systematic by temperament, he was not
steadied by great faith in great principles, and he
was always ambitious to be editor-in-chief himself ;
and at the end of two years Mr. Beecher resigned
the editorship, to leave his friend and protégé in his
place.

In January, 1870, the publishing firm of J. B.
Ford & Company having bought a small and un-

---

[1] The effect of this resignation and his ultimate entire withdrawal from the paper, and the reasons that led to it, have been
stated in a preceding chapter. Chapter XII.

successful religious weekly entitled "The Church Union," started for the purpose of securing the organic unity of all Protestant Evangelical churches, changed its name to "The Christian Union," and Mr. Beecher assumed its editorship. At the same time with its change of name, its character and purpose were changed. Mr. Beecher signalized his advent by insisting from the first that the paper which preached religion should also practice it. "He shut down at once and forever," says Mr. John R. Howard, his publisher, "upon a large class of profitable business, in excluding medical advertisements, and in ordering a strict censorship upon whatever might offend the taste or impose upon the credulity of readers." Those who remember the class of advertising on which religious journals of that period, with few exceptions, largely depended for their income, will perhaps realize what so radical action involved in this starting of a new journal. Mr. Beecher's salutatory was much more elaborate than that issued when he took the editorial charge of "The Independent," and indicates the enlarged conception of religious journalism which had grown out of his meditation on the enterprise during the four or five preceding years. This salutatory defines also his conception of religion. Simple as these definitions now seem, they subjected him to severe criticism then. "Religion is but the expression of man's deepest and noblest nature. Although the development of religion has a relation to time and history, religion itself is a life and

not a philosophy, nor an organization. Its place is
in the human soul. Its elements existed before a
tenet was held or an act performed. Not until
human nature perishes will religion cease. It does
not depend for existence upon historic testimony.
Although illustrated by miracles, it may exist without miracles ; although enforced by arguments, it
may exist without arguments, as the inevitable
outworking of a divine and constitutional element
in man." This is but saying in another form what
Sabatier has said in the epigrammatic expression,
" Man is incurably religious." To Mr. Beecher
the religious nature was " as much a part of creation as the globe itself and its physical properties,
and far more important." Religion is, therefore,
more than Christianity, but " Christianity is the
best exposition of that [religious] nature, its relations, duties, and aspirations." These aspirations
of the religious nature, fed by Christianity, are
common to all Christian denominations ; and it is to
the interpretation of these common elements in the
Christian life Mr. Beecher consecrated " The Christian Union." " This paper will not identify itself
with that which is special to the organization of any
of the great Christian denominations, but rather
with that interior religious life which in all sects
witnesses to the indwelling of the Holy Spirit." It
was therefore to be the purpose of the paper to represent, not Church union, but Christian union. " We
distinguish between oneness of Church and oneness
of Christian sympathy. Not only shall we not

labor for an external and ecclesiastical unity, but
we should regard it as a step backward. . . .
There will never be moral unity among Christians
until the phantasy of Corporate Unity is expelled
from the imagination." For this reason "'The
Christian Union' will devote no time to inveigh-
ing against sects, but it will spare no pains to
persuade Christians of every sect to treat one another with Christian charity, love, and sympathy."
"Above all and hardest of all, it will be our
endeavor to breathe, through the columns of 'The
Christian Union,' such Christian love, courage,
equity, and gentleness as shall exemplify the doctrine which it unfolds, and shall bring it into sympathy with the mind and will of the Lord Jesus
Christ."

If the reader thinks these quotations are the
utterances of truisms, he might be induced to
change his mind if he were to turn over the pages
of the first issues of "The Christian Union," and
see how severely Mr. Beecher was assailed because
of them. He is attacked for recognizing the right
of denominations to exist, and not demanding a
union which shall obliterate them; for proposing
to lay emphasis on the practical, rather than on the
ethical aspects of religion; for affirming the indestructible religious nature of man, in the face of
Paul's declaration that none of the princes of this
world knew the wisdom of God; and his ability
to act as a guide to Protestantism is denied because "he is too impulsive;" "he is too senti-

mental;" "he is too loose;" "he is too ready to surrender truth." To this latter accusation Mr. Beecher replies : " We shall take it to heart, and strive henceforth to be slower, drier, tighter, and more obstinate."

At the time when " The Christian Union " was organized, undenominational religious journalism was unknown, if not unthought of. It was supposed to be necessary to have a church constituency behind each church organ. The religious journals were, I think without an exception, denominational in their character ; most of them were organs of an ecclesiastical system ; and it was their primary function to represent, maintain, and defend the ecclesiastical organization, its creeds, its rituals, its methods, its personnel. These denominational organs were ecclesiastical, theological, controversial ; as partisan in the realm of religion as the party press in the realm of public affairs. The notion that, underlying all the sects, there is a great indestructible religious sentiment, that this indestructible religious sentiment is more than the creeds which interpret it in dogmatic forms, more than the rituals which interpret it in worship, and more than the organizations which interpret it in aggressive action, though it is the commonplace of popular opinion to-day, was an incredible novelty when Mr. Beecher propounded it as the basis of a religious journal in 1870. He had always appealed from the ecclesiastics to the people in his pulpit: he now made the same appeal to a wider constitu-

ency in the press. Along with this conception of
Christian life and this belief in a Christian constituency, was a conception of religion as a vitalizing force, to be applied to every department of
human activity. He determined to make a paper,
not for church people merely, but for the plain
people of every creed and no creed, and therefore
a paper which should " seek to interpret the Bible
rather as a religion of life than as a book of
doctrine." In my notebook is one sentence which
he threw out in a subsequent discussion concerning the " Farm and Garden " department of the
paper : " It is the aim of ' The Christian Union,' "
said he, " to gospelize all the industrial functions
of life."

But both these aims — to represent what is common rather than what is denominational, and to
represent what is practical rather than what is
scientific, in the religious life — were subordinate
to his purpose to maintain in the pages of " The
Christian Union " a Christian spirit, one in " sympathy with the mind and will of the Lord Jesus
Christ." How fully he carried out this purpose no
one who was not with him in the times of great
trial and provocation can ever fully know. He often
reiterated this sentiment in our editorial conferences
after I became associated with him on the paper.
" If you are good-natured," he said once, " there is
nothing which you cannot say ; if you are not good-
natured, you cannot say anything." Never in the
five years in which we were associated do I recall a

single instance in which he manifested an acerb or
irritated spirit, a desire to hit back, a wish to get
even with an antagonist, or even an ambition for a
victory over him. He would not allow the journal
to be used in his own defense. He would defend
Plymouth Church, if the church were attacked; he
would restate and explain his own statements of
doctrine, if they had been misinterpreted or misunderstood; but he would never use the editorial
columns, as he never used his pulpit, for purposes
of personal defense. He was quick and keen in repartee, but it was always good-natured repartee. He
never wrote, and rarely uttered, a sentence which
had a sting in it: not because he could not, but
because he would not. He would not even allow
himself to be defended in the columns of the paper
by his associates. After I became co-editor, it was
not my custom to send to him the proofs of the
editorial pages for his examination: he trusted
them to me absolutely from the first; but on one
occasion a daily paper had attacked him so venom-
ously, and with such gross misrepresentation of
what he had said, that I resolved to depart from the
standing rule of our journal, and reply. I sent my
reply, in proof, to him, unwilling to set at naught,
without his consent, the rule which he had established, and he returned the reply to me with the
request, which, of course, was tantamount to a
command, to suppress the editorial. I think now,
as I thought then, that he carried this principle too
far. The journal suffered from the silence which

he imposed upon it, during the time in which he was subjected to vituperation and abuse, because there were many who could not understand the chivalric cause for such silence, and counted it as giving a *quasi* consent to the rumors which were rife concerning him.

In my judgment Mr. Beecher was a great editorial writer, and he would be universally counted so were it not that his eminence as a writer has been dimmed by his greater eminence as an orator. An editorial writer must be interested in current events, acquainted with current opinion, have a grasp of great fundamental principles, an accurate, though not necessarily a detailed knowledge of facts, must be able to concentrate on one theme, in one article, all his powers, must have an imagination which presents principles in concrete forms, an emotion which vivifies his teaching with life, must write a vigorous, terse English, must waste no words in rhetorical amplifications, and must possess power to create, not merely reflect, public opinion. All these powers Mr. Beecher had in an eminent degree, and, superadded to them, an iridescent humor and a self-controlled emotion, which prevented his editorials from ever being afflicted with dullness : they now flashed fire and now were rich with color, like his own favorite opal. Re-reading the pages of the first volume of " The Christian Union," to which he contributed more largely than to any subsequent issues, I am impressed with these qualities manifesting themselves in different proportions in different contributions, — now in a strong discussion of some great public question; now in a succession of paragraphs, like an after-dinner table-talk.

The phenomenal success into which " The Christian Union " leaped from its birth was due partly to the conception which Mr. Beecher had of what a religious journal should be, and to the spirit which he infused into it through others. But it was not less due to the loyal seconding and support of Mr. George S. Merriam, Mr. Beecher's associate in the editorship, and the boundless energy and sagacity of the publishers, Fords, Howard & Hulbert. What as editor Mr. Beecher did in those first years of " The Christian Union," in it, and for it, and through it, Mr. George S. Merriam, who was its real editor from May, 1870, to December, 1875, tells in the following letter, which, written to me, at my request for information, he permits me to incorporate here : —

I went to the paper in May, 1870, almost immediately after it started, and remained, for the most part as managing editor, until December, 1875, when I left on account of a difference with Mr. Beecher over a business question. During that period Mr. Beecher wrote very little and edited still less. The exact amount of his writing could be learned, if it were worth while, from the record of all contributions to the paper which I kept in the big editorial book, which I suppose is still in your archives. He was so absorbed by other occupations, and so distracted by cares, that we could get from him little work and usually little attention — and I think the tongue rather than the pen was his natural weapon. Brilliantly though he often wrote, it seemed to require a special occasion and considerable pressure to induce him to write. But *talk*, — why, when he was in good mood, and that was much of the time, an audience of two or three, and a congenial theme, would move him to speech as eloquent as if he were in Plymouth pulpit. He would sit on the table (if so it chanced in an office), and hold forth so brilliantly that Edward Ford, most enterprising of publishers, once had a scheme for keeping a stenographer in ambush, and getting articles from him unawares.

Of editing as a practical business he knew almost nothing. But he had the great merit of giving his subordinates free rein, when he knew he could trust them. He never interfered needlessly, never nagged, rarely censured (he hated to give pain, in that as in all ways), and, to say truth, seldom praised. He pretty much let the paper run itself, making us glad once in a while by a trenchant editorial on public affairs, or a charming "Star Paper;" hastily reading the editorial proofs at his house Monday morning, curbing now and then his too eager and outspoken lieutenant by blue pencil lines through his effusions, but for the most part tolerant and uncritical; in emergencies selecting the business or editorial conductors — not always with the soundest judgment; coming into the occasional stockholders' meetings, sanguine and optimistic, and feeling when he had said a thing as if he had done it.

Yet the paper was deeply indebted to him for its character and for its life. It was begun, not at his initiative, but by young men who devotedly believed in him, and who aimed to gain for him a larger audience. The best of its capital was the popularity of his name. Its financial support came from business men who not only admired but loved him — men of the type of Henry W—— and my father — who put in their money quite as much in a missionary as a commercial spirit. Its leading editorial writers were inspired by his religious ideas, and guided by his methods of imparting those ideas. Its most valuable feature, in my judgment, was the reports by Mr. Ellinwood of his "Lecture-Room Talks," in some ways better than his sermons, and through the paper far more widely distributed, with a character of their own, less philosophical and eloquent than the sermons, familiar, colloquial, and winning; rich in inspiration, suggestion, comfort. His name drew the paper's first constituency, and attracted writers. The enterprise of his publishers (I must name Mr. John R. Howard, the sympathetic and skillful editor of Mr. Beecher's and Mrs. Stowe's writings, and Mr. Edward D. Ford, whose unresting energy consumed his life too soon) greatly widened that constituency. The paper shared Mr. Beecher's fortunes, and when his reputation tottered, it came to the verge of ruin. It was rescued by his loyal business friends, who again backed their faith with their substance. Its later history you knew better than I. Its survival as "The Outlook," modified in character, but eminent in strength and influence, is in a sense a monument of Mr. Beecher's power to inspire and to lead, and the faith and loyalty with which his followers responded.

What Mr. Merriam says of Mr. Beecher as editor during those early years of "The Christian Union" is equally true of the later years when I was associated with Mr. Beecher (1876–81), except that he did probably even less practical editing. He liked to talk, but work with the pen grew increasingly distasteful to him. His contributions became more and more rare. He never read the editorial proof after I became his associate. He rarely counseled me as to the position which the paper should take on any specific question. At first I would sometimes go to him for counsel; occasionally he would give it to me; more frequently he would say that he had not yet studied the question under consideration, and when I urged that the subscribers to a weekly paper could not wait indefinitely for the editor to form his opinion on an issue of current interest, he would reply that then I must decide, — he would not speak on any subject until he had studied it. Under the by-laws of the paper the absolute control of all its contents was vested in the editor-in-chief, and in his absence, in his first assistant; and as Mr. Beecher was practically always absent, the control passed naturally into my hands, where he seemed willing to intrust it.

And yet, though Mr. Beecher did no practical editing, I call him a great editor, in the sense in which Mr. Fletcher Harper was a great editor. I do not think Mr. Harper ever wrote a line for publication; I doubt whether he ever read a manuscript; but he created " Harper's Magazine," " Harper's Weekly," and " Harper's Bazaar," and pervaded them with his own informing spirit. If to be the editor of a paper is to sit at its desk, examine its manuscripts, determine its weekly contents, and read and revise its proofs, Mr. Beecher never was an editor. Nor did he do the larger executive work — the determination of the structure of each weekly issue, the selection of contributors, the adjustment of themes, that a due proportion may be preserved in the weekly issues or in the journal as a whole — in short, the architectural building work which belongs to the editorial conduct of a great paper. He was not fitted either by temperament or by inclination for such duties. An editor must take his theme from current events. He must write not concerning the thing which preëminently interests himself, but concerning the things which interest the public. He must not only feel the pulse of his constituency, but to some extent must reflect their sentiments. He may do this deliberately and consciously, as the editor of " The London Times " did in its most influential days; or he may belong by his thought and feeling to a school of thinkers, and by representing them, build up a supporting constituency, as Horace Greeley did in " The Tribune," and William Lloyd Garrison did in " The Liberator." Mr. Beecher was by temperament and training too independent, his critics would say too idiosyncratic, to do either. Routine was always distasteful to him; and editorial work involves a certain subjection to routine.

But he created a new school of journalism, and gave to it impulse and inspiration by his own pen. To the journal which he founded he gave its form, its aim, its purpose, its policy, and he inspired it with his life, and — I may quote here the words

which I wrote when, in 1881, he withdrew from it —
" He leaves it now with the affection and esteem
of all who are connected with it, because he sees it
so fully realizing the dream of fifteen years ago."
The journal which he founded has changed its
name ; it has many features not of his designing ; its
function and purpose have undergone great modifications, — I think great enlargement, — but I hope
its essential spirit remains unaltered : the spirit
which believes in the indestructible religious nature
of man, in Evangelical Christianity as the most spiritual expression of that divine life, and in the application of the precepts and principles of Jesus
Christ, and, still more, of his essential spirit of
faith and hope and love, to the solution of all problems, organic and individual, of our complicated
modern social life. Whatever changes it may
undergo in the future, so long as it continues
to represent the unity of the faith in that love
which is the bond of perfectness, it will continue, to
quote Mr. Merriam's words, " a monument of Mr.
Beecher's power to inspire and to lead."

As an author, Mr. Beecher will be known to
posterity chiefly by his " Life of Christ." His
" Star Papers," recreative writings, written at a
sitting, sometimes as colloquial as his conversation,
sometimes as exalted in diction as the noblest passages in his sermons, covering every conceivable
theme, from " Trouting " or " Building a House "
to " The Liberty of Prayer " or " The Fullness

of God," and written in every variety of mood, from the most boyish and frolicsome to the most serious and spiritual, illustrate the many-sidedness of his nature — the multiplicity of his interests, the catholicity of his tastes, and the versatility of his genius. But the very variety of theme and mood and treatment, and the rapidity of utterance, which sometimes fires his writings with a splendid emotion, and sometimes mars them with crudities of style, will prevent them from taking that place in literature, by the side of the collections of the great essayists, to which their genius, had it been more carefully trained, would have entitled them. "Norwood" furnishes many pictures of New England life, some idyllic, some satirical, all colored by a vivid imagination and transfused with great tenderness of feeling; but "Norwood" can hardly be called a story, certainly not a novel. His own explanation in the preface of the way in which it came to be written, and of his preparation, or, rather, literary unpreparedness, for writing it, sufficiently indicate the reason. At the close of the Civil War Mr. Bonner asked him to write a story for "The Ledger." "Had it been a request to carve a statue or build a man-of-war, the task would hardly have seemed less likely of accomplishment. A very moderate reader even of fictions, I had never studied the mystery of their construction. Plot and counter-plot, the due proportion of parts, the whole machinery of a novel seemed hopelessly outside of my studies."

But he was not unwilling to seek relaxation from the exhausting excitement of public affairs by turning his mind into new channels of thought and interest, and, reflecting that any real human experience was intrinsically interesting, and that the life of a humble family for a single day could hardly fail to serve some purpose, he undertook this story, or rather, we might say, these pictures of New England life.

But his " Life of Christ" was written with enthusiasm. It is true that it was carried on under continual difficulties. By the varied incidents of his busy life the work was frequently interrupted; at one time it was intermitted for several years. The quietude of mind and the continuity of composition which would seem to have been almost indispensable to the highest and best literary result, he was never able to secure. These difficulties were such as finally prevented him from finishing the work. He had but just set himself to its completion when his sudden death brought his work to a close with the second volume unfinished. As a result, we have not his portrayal and interpretation of the Passion Week. Two circumstances noted by the editors, his son and son-in-law, who completed the volume after his death, are very significant of his character as a preacher : one, that there was found in Mr. Beecher's sermons the material for the completion of the work, from and including the resurrection of Lazarus, with one important exception; the other, that this exception was the crucifixion. "We cannot find," say the editors, "after an examination of many hundreds of sermons, published and unpublished, that Mr. Beecher ever preached directly on that subject; on the contrary, he often said that it was impossible; the subject was too awful and sublime." With this exception, Mr. Beecher was, in the strictest and most primitive sense of the term, a preacher of Christ. I do not doubt that, with this exception, practically the whole story of Christ's life, as it is gathered from the four Gospels, would be found retold in effective narrative form in the forty years of Mr. Beecher's ministry in Brooklyn.

An extraordinary number of lives of Christ have been published in the English language, to say nothing of those not translated, and the variety of treatment is extraordinary: the Scholar's life — bringing to bear upon the Gospels, for their illumination, all that painstaking research can discover in Jewish, Greek, and Latin literature; the Philosopher's life — making the simple and artless narrative a text on which to hang elaborate discussions, theological, or critical, or chronological, or literary; the Skeptic's life — written for the purpose of proving that there was in the life no story worth the telling, or that all was beautiful but fabulous, the outgrowth of a superstitious and childish imagination, or a series of exaggerations in which the pen of imaginative and credulous writers has turned simple events into wonder-awakening

miracles, as Christ is thought to have turned the
water into wine; the Hortatory life — in which the
biography is naught, and the moralizing wearisome;
the Imaginative life — in which adjectives are
summoned to furnish a chromo-like color to the
narrative; the Humanistic life — in which Jesus
is portrayed as an enthusiast, and in which the central figure is as feeble as sometimes the subordinate figures are dramatically conceived and graphically portrayed; the Jewish life — in which the
rabbinical legends are gathered together, and the
bitter hostility of the ecclesiasticism of Caiaphas
is reproduced in a modern story. Mr. Beecher's
life I should characterize, in a word, as interpreta-
tive. Few authorities are cited; there is no indication of that familiarity with Jewish law which
characterizes Edersheim's "Life of Christ," or of
that familiarity with classical life which makes
Geikie's "Life of Christ," though less encyclo-
pædic, even more valuable to the lay reader. Mr.
Beecher enters into no philosophical disquisitions,
except in the one chapter in the first volume on
the nature of Christ as a divine spirit in a human
body, — a chapter which might be omitted from
the work without impairing its value, and which
propounds a philosophy with which the rest of
the work can hardly be reconciled. He does not
discuss the skeptic, mythical, legendary, and naturalistic interpretations of the miraculous element
in the Gospels; he simply lives in the first century, breathes its atmosphere, thinks its thoughts,

interprets its life. He enters into the character of the central figure, and portrays a Christ who is at once wholly human and wholly divine. The theology is as simple as that of the Apostles; the faith as childlike and unquestioning; the literary pictures of scenes and events are as unecclesiastical, unconventional, naturally human as the best water-colors in Tissot's remarkable collection; the insight into the character and the teaching of Jesus is certainly unsurpassed, and to my thought unequaled, by any analogous work. As an interpretation of the life, character, and teachings of Jesus Christ, it occupies a unique place in that library of " Lives of Christ " which the nineteenth century produced.

The writer is known by his style even more than the wearer by his clothes. The defects and the excellencies of Mr. Beecher are those of an extreme naturalness: he wrote as he spoke — extemporaneously. His preparations were general, not specific. He rarely revised or polished or perfected; still more rarely did he rewrite. He talked with his pen, and writing was wearisome to him because he could not drive his pen fast enough to keep pace with his thinking. But he never learned to write by dictation; even his letters were autographic. By training and temperament a preacher, he carried the didactic spirit into all his serious writing. Artistic he certainly was, but not continuously, and never did he write merely for art's sake. In one of his sermons he says, " The figures of the

Bible are not mere graceful ornaments — arabesques to grace a border, or fancy frescoes that give mere beauty to a chamber or saloon. They are language." In this sentence he interprets his own use of the imagination. Sometimes in his lighter writing it is an end; he indulges in the play of the imagination for the mere enjoyment of so doing; but generally, his imagination is illuminating; it is called into the service of an earnest purpose. His humor is instinctive and irrepressible. He perceives incongruous relations, and his perception of them flashes out on all occasions, giving a spontaneous and unpremeditated sparkle to his most serious discourses. His style is very varied, depending more than in almost any writer I am familiar with, upon the mood of the moment; but in all its variations, it preserves the qualities of clearness, vigor, and sympathy. The singleness of his purpose made his style clear, for he never considered what was prudent to say, but only how he could make his auditors or readers understand him. His courage, the directness of his aim, and the marshaling of his thoughts, which often march in serried ranks, rank after rank, overwhelming, not only by their number, but by their disciplined array, combined to give to his style great vigor. His sympathy gave to his style a quality which I can compare only to timbre in the voice, — penetrating, inviting, winning, subduing. He was a student of many authors, — not only for their ideas but for their style,—but he was an imitator of none. He formed himself on no mould,—indeed, I am inclined to think that he did not consciously mould himself at all,—he grew. But he lived in intellectual companionship with great authors. Neither in public address nor in private conversation did he indicate a lover's familiarity with Shakespeare among the older authors, or with Browning, Emerson, or Carlyle among the later writers. But he had read and studied Ruskin's "Modern Painters," which he heartily commends as an interpretation of nature; he was familiar with Milton, some of whose prose essays he had read and reread many times; and with Homer and Dante, though only through translations.

Critics treat literature by different and even inconsistent standards. To some literature is an art, to be tested, as a picture, by its beauty of form and color, or as music, by its rhythmic structure. To such Mr. Beecher's writings and addresses will never take a high place in literature. They are too uneven, pass too quickly from the written to the spoken style, from the eloquence of the orator to the effectiveness of the talker — are, in a word, too unfinished. Some regard literature as an expression of life, and count that the best literature which best expresses the highest and most varied life. To such Mr. Beecher's writings will always take a high place. For they express always with effectiveness, generally with vigor, often with real eloquence, frequently with consummate artistic beauty, a life of almost infinite variety.

Before taking up the closing days of Mr. Beecher's life, a chapter must be given to the work which contains his own interpretation of himself as a preacher — "The Yale Lectures on Preaching."

CHAPTER XV

IN 1871 Mr. Henry W. Sage, of Brooklyn, a prominent member of Plymouth Church and a warm friend of Henry Ward Beecher, contributed the necessary funds for the establishment of a lectureship on preaching in the Divinity School at Yale College. In honor of Mr. Beecher's father it was named the Lyman Beecher Lectureship on Preaching; its object was to secure for young men in the seminary a course of lectures on the art of preaching from those actively engaged in the practice of it. It was generally understood that Mr. Sage desired especially to secure such counsels for the benefit of young ministers from his own pastor; and accordingly the first three courses were given by Henry Ward Beecher: the first specifically on preaching, the second on church administration, the third on the use of Christian doctrines, or what might be called applied theology.

In his preface to the first series of these lectures Mr. Beecher indicates what is both their strength and their weakness. "The discourses here given," he says, "were wholly unwritten and were familiar conversational addresses, rather than elaborate speeches. I have not been able to revise the report-

er's notes, or to correct the proofs of the printer."
To such work of revision Mr. Beecher was always
averse. If he had undertaken it in this case the
lectures would probably have lost in familiarity of
tone more than they would have gained in homo-
geneity of structure. As usual in his spoken addresses, he had in mind the audience immediately
before him, not the larger audience he would subsequently reach through the printed page. The lectures are throughout autobiographical in spirit, and
often in form. They possess a literary character
analogous to that of the "Table-Talk" of Luther
or of Coleridge. They are not symmetrically philosophical, but they are, what is better, personal
and vital. It is in this personality that their chief
charm and perhaps their chief value lie. They
not only state the philosophy which Mr. Beecher
had formulated as to the ministerial functions, but
they reveal the secret of his own power, and are
the product of his own life; a self-revelation of
his own inmost spirit, an interpretation of himself
to his audience. As through a window we look in
and see the intellectual and spiritual processes by
which the sermons and addresses which produced
such results were prepared. In here reporting the
substance of these conversational addresses it is
impossible to preserve this charm of personality.
The aphoristic wisdom, the genial humor, the ef-
fervescent spirits, the unconventional piety, the
warmth of human sympathy, the autobiographical
reminiscences, the personal self-revelation, cannot

be preserved, can scarcely be even intimated in such an abstract as is here prescribed. Nor can the largeness of resource, the intellectual readiness, the human sympathy, and the genial humor that characterized his answers to the questions which the students were incited to propound to him at the close of each lecture, be portrayed.

"Pulpit dynamics" is the phrase which Mr. Beecher, in personal conversation with me, used to designate the first volume. It was a felicitous designation. The entire volume is devoted to a consideration of the secret of pulpit power. In it he deals with the minister exclusively as a preacher. "The preacher is a teacher; but he is more." "He looks beyond mere knowledge to a character which that knowledge is to form. It is not enough that men shall *know*. They must *be*." Therefore the preacher must not merely know; he must be. "The truth must exist in him as a living experience, a glowing enthusiasm, an intense reality." The divine truth must be "a part of his own experience, so that when he speaks to men it shall not be he alone that speaks, but God in him." This living force of the human soul brought to bear upon the living souls for the sake of their transformation is the fundamental conception underlying all successful preaching. This emphasis on the personal power of the preacher emphasizes the difference between the evangelical and the hierarchical churches. "Both hold to the indispensableness of divine power; but one believes that power to work

chiefly through church *ordinances*, the other believes that it works through living men." "The
man that preaches with power is an artist. He is
a living creature. But the man who merely comes
to administer ordinances on Sundays or Saints'
Days, who goes through a regular routine, is nothing but the engineer who runs the machine." He
also does good, but not the highest good. That is
wrought by the sermon; and among sermons, that
which is highest is the one preached "for divine
power on men's minds and hearts;" in which the
preacher has "a definite reason why he selected one
subject rather than another, and why he put it in
one form rather than another." "The highest conception of a sermon is, that it is a prescription
which a man has made, either for a certain individual, or for a certain class, or for a certain state of
things that he knows to exist in the congregation."

Next to the character of the preacher and a
definite object in his sermon comes style, — the
avoidance of "scholastic, artificial style;" the formation of a natural style, such as a man in earnest
uses in conversation. In addition to these qualifications for the ministry are fruitfulness in moral ideas,
a genius for them, such as a mathematician has for
mathematics, or a musician for musical ideas; interest in men, sympathy with them, power to move
them; "living by faith, the sense of the infinite
and the invisible, the sense of something else besides what we see with the physical eyes, the sense
of God, of eternity, of heaven;" humility, willing-

ness to be the least of all God's servants and to labor in the humblest sphere.

Entering into this ministry with these qualifications, the preacher must study how to bring his personality to bear on all sorts and conditions of men, by all varieties of approach. " If a man can be saved by pure intellectual preaching, let him have it. If others require a predominance of emotion, provide that for them. If by others the truth is taken more easily through the imagination, give it to them by forms attractive to the imagination. If there are still others who demand it in the form of facts and rules, see that they have it in that form." " Preachers are too apt to set the truth before their congregations in one way only, . . . whereas, preaching should be directed to every element of human nature that God has implanted in us." If the preacher has not the necessary versatility of character he must set himself to develop it : he must learn to be all things to all men. To succeed in such a ministry as this he must make preaching his whole business. Or if he engage in other pursuits, he must so do it that they shall add to his force in preaching, not detract from it. Gardening, lecturing, journeying, æsthetic studies, public affairs, society recreations, may be taken just in so far as they minister to the preacher's power, and no farther. There are material hindrances to this impartation of personality which the preacher should endeavor to avoid or remove. Such a hindrance is the separation of the pews from the

pulpit by a great space between the two. Great
Gothic pillars are another, behind which "the
people can sit and look at the columns during
the whole of the sermon time." The barrel pulpit
is another. "I think the matter so important, that
I tell the truth and lie not, when I say that I
would not accept a settlement in a very advan-
tageous place, if I was obliged to preach out of one
of those old-fashioned swallows' nests on the wall."

In preparing for preaching a first condition is
the study of human nature. There are three schools
of preachers : the Ecclesiastical, the Dogmatic, and
the Life School. The first "regard the Church on
earth as something to be administered, and themselves as channels, in some sense, of Divine Grace,
to direct the flow of that divine institution." The
second are "those who have relied upon a preëxist-
ing system of truth . . . and who apparently proceed upon the supposition that their whole duty is
discharged when they have made a regular and
repetitious statement of all the great points of
doctrine from time to time." The third proceeds
"upon the necessity for all teachers, first, to study
the strengths and weaknesses of human nature
minutely; and then to make use of such portions
of the truth as are required by the special needs
of man, and for the development of the spiritual
nature over the animal or lower side — the preparation of man in his higher nature for a nobler existence hereafter." The live preacher must study
human nature. First, "because it illustrates the

divine nature, which we are to interpret to men."
" The only part of the divine nature which we can
understand is that part which corresponds to ourselves." Therefore, practically, the study of God is
but a higher form of human mental philosophy.
Second, the minister is to cure men. Therefore he
must know what is the disease of which they are
to be cured, and what is normal or healthful human nature, from which sin is a departure. Third,
he must know man in order to know how to approach him, as a surgeon called to amputate a leg
must know anatomy as well as the surgeon's tools.
Every type of human nature, every phase of human
experience, is, therefore, a proper subject for the
preacher's study. He ought to know physiology,
and the psychology which is founded upon it. He
ought to study society and he ought to study the
individual. For such study phrenology is " a convenient basis." " Not only is its nomenclature convenient, but what it teaches concerning craniology
and physiology furnishes valuable indications of
individual character." " I see a man with a small
brow and big in the lower part of his head like a
bull, and I know that that man is not likely to be
a saint." " If I see a man whose forehead is very
high and large, but who is thin in the back of the
head, and with a small neck and trunk, I say to myself . . . he is a man who has great organs, but
nothing to drive them with. He is like a splendid
locomotive without a boiler." And this study of
human nature should be conducted for the purpose

of regenerating it. Therefore the minister must be
familiar with men, not merely generically with
human nature, but specifically with individuals. He
" should take kindly to individual men for the very
purpose of studying them." The minister " must be
a man among men. . . . Books alone are not enough.
Studying is not enough."

As to specific methods of preaching no universal
law can be laid down : the preacher must understand his own temperament and adapt his preaching to it. " That is the best cat that catches the
most rats. And in your case it will be the best
form of sermon that does the work of the sermon
the best. If you can do best by writing, write
your sermons ; and if you can do better by not
writing, do not write them." So as to length of
sermon : that must depend upon the community ;
upon the church ; upon its other services ; and
upon the previous habits of the people. There are
four psychological elements that enter into the successful sermon, — imagination, emotion, enthusiasm, and conviction. Imagination is indispensable
to clearness. It is the true germ of faith. It includes " the power of the minister himself to realize the invisible God as present, and to present him
to the people." Emotion is indispensable to power.
" A minister without feeling is no better than a
book. You might just as well put a book, printed
in large type, on the desk where all could read it,
and have a man turn over the leaves as you read,
as to have a man stand up, and clearly and coldly

recite the prosaic truth through which he has gone by a logical course of reasoning." To imagination and emotion must be added enthusiasm and conviction : the first to give outburst and glow; the second to carry conviction to others. "Do not *prove* things too much." "Preach truth to the *consciousness* of men."

For the most effective work in preaching, physical equipment is necessary. This includes careful drill in the use of the voice and of the whole body. This drill must be so thorough that the right use of both becomes a second nature. "No knowledge is really *knowledge* until you can use it without knowing it." This training should include gesture and bodily carriage, as well as voice. It ought to take place early and be incorporated in the character of the minister. Other training is not less necessary. It should include thorough familiarity with the Bible ; not so much a knowledge of philosophy, as a habit of thinking philosophically, the "habit of looking at truth, not in isolated and fragmentary forms, but in all its relations ; " and skill in the use of illustration, not for ornament, but for producing conviction ; a use based on the principle that " substantially the mode in which we learn a new thing is by its being likened to something that we already know." Illustrations rightly used assist argument, help the hearers to remember, stimulate the imagination, rest the audience by changing the faculties employed in listening, reach through different avenues different hearers, and bridge difficult places by teaching parabolically truth to which men would refuse to listen if presented directly. To be effective they must be various, often homely, accurate, and apt and prompt.

The minister ought to have health, and cultivate health. " What I mean by ' health' is such a feeling or tone in every part of a man's body that he has a natural language of health." " It is buoyancy. It is the insatiable desire of play and of exertion." " A man in health is a fountain, and he flows over at the eye, the lip, and all the time, by every species of action and demonstration." Health, thus defined, is almost indispensable to oratorical power. " The speakers that move a crowd . . . are almost always men of very large physical development, men of very strong digestive powers, and whose lungs have great orating capacity. They are men who, while they have a sufficient thought-power to create all the material needed, have pre-eminently the explosive power by which they can thrust their material out at men." Preaching " means the hardest kind of work," and therefore requires health. Without health " it is impossible to sustain a cheerful and hopeful ministry." Health helps the preacher to give healthful views of Christianity as that which " aims only at a nobler style of manhood and at a better and happier style of living. Health is a sweetener of work and gives a joyous relish for it. To have health one must know how to eat, how to sleep, how to exercise, and how to adjust his eating, his sleep, his exercise, not according to hard and fast rules given to him by another, but according to his own nature and its needs. How Mr. Beecher regulated his own habits he told the students, and from this lecture I have drawn in an earlier chapter, in my description of his personal habits.

In his ninth lecture Mr. Beecher discusses sermon-making: the relative advantages of the written and unwritten discourse, urging neither, only urging that " the essential necessity is that every preacher should be able to *speak* without notes," because there are many occasions in which nothing will answer but the unwritten discourse. But extemporaneous preaching does not mean extemporaneous preparation. " There must be incessant work." Sermons should be variable in style and quality. " If it be possible, never have two plans alike." " If you have preached to-day to the heart through the imagination, to-morrow you are to preach to the heart through the reason." " When you have finished your sermon, not a man of your congregation should be unable to tell you what you have done; but when you begin a sermon, no man in the congregation ought to be able to tell you what you are going to do." The sermon should be suggestive, not exhaustive. " That sermon has been overwrought and overdone which leaves nothing for the mind of the hearer to do." " A much larger use should be made of expository preaching than has been customary in our churches," because of the wealth and diversity of topics which will come up for illustration by means of expository preaching. The preacher should avoid the temptation to preach " great sermons " — " Nebuchadnezzar sermons, over which the vain preacher stands, saying, ' Is not this great Babylon that I have builded for the house of the kingdom, by the might of my power and for the honor of my majesty.' " " Sermons that are truly great come of themselves. They spring from sources deeper than vanity or ambition." As to length of sermons, " that should never be determined by the clock, but upon broader considerations — short sermons for small subjects, and long sermons for large subjects."

In all the preacher's ministry, love must be the central element and the secret of power — to the elucidation of this truth, the tenth and last lecture of the first series is devoted. Love " is not so much a faculty or power, as it is a certain condition of the whole spirit, made up of the contribution of several different elements of the mind, having relations to things superior and to things inferior." " It is the going-out of thought, of feeling, and of sympathy towards others, and towards whatever can receive benefit from us." " It is the wish that whatever we are thinking of, or saying, or doing, may make some one better and happier." It is not lazy, smiling good nature. It has fire and snap, and may be terribly angry. It is not the absence of any power, but it gives quality and direction to all the powers. It is central and fundamental to the minister; it inspires in him joy in

his work, makes it spontaneous and healthful, gives
to it power and abundance, gives catholicity to sympathy and therefore approach to all sorts of men,
sustains in discouragement, gives freedom and tact
and skill and courage. "You can discuss any topic
if you only love men enough; your heart will tell
you how to approach."

Doubtless some of Mr. Beecher's positions in
this series of lectures will be criticised. I am
doubtful whether craniological and physiological
aspects are as sure indications of character as he
seems to think; they did not, as we have seen,
prevent him from falling a prey to designing men.
He does not seem to me, in his criticism of cere-
monialism, to allow sufficiently for the power in the
people of the imagination which he lauds in the
preacher. Who has seen a Roman Catholic congregation bowing at the elevation of the Host, and
not realized their imaginative power to clothe the
Host with an impalpable and invisible personality?
Who can doubt that worshipers, in their use of a
liturgy, are enabled, by their imagination, to see
in it the expression of the penitence, the petitions,
and the gratitude of those whose use of it through
centuries of devotion has impregnated it with a
spiritual life? The administrator of such a liturgy
is more than an "engineer who runs the machine."
A part, too, of these counsels will possibly appear
to the modern reader commonplace. He will say
to them "of course." But they were not common-

place thirty years ago. They were radical then. It
is illustrative of the power of Mr. Beecher's spirit
that the methods of the preacher and the spirit of
the pulpit have undergone so great a change in the
last half century. It is less ecclesiastical and more
practical; it is less theological and more human;
it is less devoted to building up a system and more
devoted to building up men; there is, to use Mr.
Beecher's classification, less ecclesiastical and dogmatic preaching, and more that is vital. And yet
there is certainly abundant occasion for still further improvement. Whatever preachers may think,
most laymen will agree in the opinion that preaching would receive a vast accession of power if
preachers generally realized that sermons are only
means to an end, that every sermon should be
aimed at a definite result, and that all use of doctrine, argument, and illustration, all questions concerning rhetoric and style, and all employment of
voice and gesture should be determined by the
consideration how best to produce on the auditor
a definite ethical and spiritual result, carefully
planned beforehand by the preacher as the sole
object of his sermon, to which all is directed, and
by which all is shaped and patterned.

It is more difficult to give, by analysis, any conception of the second series of lectures, because,
even more than the first, their value lies not so
much in principles expounded, or practical counsels given, as in spiritual life imparted. A certain
unreserve was one of the elements of Mr. Beecher's

power. Like Paul, he gave frank and free expression to his own personal experiences, whenever he believed their disclosure would be spiritually helpful to those who were looking to him for life. This spiritual freedom is a marked characteristic of the second series of his lectures on preaching. A single quotation may serve at once to illustrate this characteristic, and to indicate to the reader one of the hidden sources, perhaps the chief source, of his extraordinary power in the pulpit: —

I can bear this witness, that never in the study, in the most absorbed moments; never on the street, in those chance inspirations that everybody is subject to, when I am lifted up highest; never in any company, where friends are the sweetest and dearest, — never in any circumstances in life is there anything that is to me so touching as when I stand, in ordinary good health, before my great congregation to pray for them. Hundreds and hundreds of times, as I rose to pray and glanced at the congregation, I could not keep back the tears. There came to my mind such a sense of their wants, there were so many hidden sorrows, there were so many weights and burdens, there were so many doubts, there were so many states of weakness, there were so many dangers, so many perils, there were such histories, — not world histories, but eternal world histories, — I had such a sense of compassion for them, my soul so longed for them, that it seemed to me as if I could scarcely open my mouth to speak for them. And when I take my people and carry them before God to plead for them, I never plead for myself as I do for them, — I never could. Indeed, I sometimes, as I have said, hardly feel as if I had anything to ask; but oh, when I know what is going on in the heart of my people, and I am permitted to stand to lead them, to inspire their thought and feeling, and go into the presence of God, there is no time that Jesus is so crowned with glory as then! There is no time that I ever get so far into heaven. I can see my mother there; I see again my little children; I walk again, arm in arm with those who have been my companions and co-workers. I forget the body, I live in the spirit; and it seems as if God permitted me to lay my hand on the very Tree of Life, and to shake down from it both leaves and fruit for the healing of my people!

This personal experience, this combination of spiritual vision and human sympathy, transfuses in an eminent degree the second volume of Mr. Beecher's lectures on preaching. It cannot be interpreted in an analysis; and yet without it the analysis is to the original lectures what a pressed and dried flower, its fragrance gone and its colors dimmed, is to the original living flower as it grows in the garden. The central principle of the volume, from the application of which all its counsels proceed, is that the object of the ministry is the production of Christlikeness of character in man. In choosing the field, therefore, the minister is to go where he is most needed. If there be no church, he is to create one by bringing together men in the religious life that they may help themselves, and help one another spiritually through their social relations. His work in the community is to be primarily spiritual; it is to bring upon them the inspiration of the Holy Ghost. If he is to do this, his ministry must be a prayerful ministry. If he is to lift others up into the presence of the Invisible Father, he must walk in that presence himself: — and this is prayer. He must promote the spirit of prayer in the church, and through this the prayer-meeting, which is a family meeting of a spiritual household in spiritual fellowship. To the conduct of the prayer-meeting Mr. Beecher devotes two lectures, urging its value and giving practical counsels how to conduct it. The same spiritual quality should inhere in the church music; from the opening voluntary to the end it should be worshipful. In this music the whole church ought to take part, because the whole church ought to worship, and in the non-liturgical churches no other congregational worship is provided but that through music.

The same spirit should animate the preacher in his pastoral work. " When people won't come to hear you preach, do you go and talk to them; and when they do come to hear you, and you have hardly anything to preach about, then go to them all the more." But the object of this personal visitation, of the social gatherings of the church, and of all its social life, should not be mere social fellowship; it should be the development in men, by the social life, of the spiritual qualities of faith and hope and love. This spirit is to be carried into the Sunday-schools and missions, and is to inspire all the various forms of lay activity. The world will never be converted to Christ by ministers alone; the

whole church must become a working church. In
this work of the church revivals are not only to be
desired, but to be planned for. The highest experiences rarely come to men singly. The reviving
of the entire community through the reviving of
the church is not only as legitimate as the reviving
of the individual, but often the best way of securing
the individual revival. Such revivals are subject to
law. The conditions necessary to it, the methods of
promoting it, the proper way to conduct it so as to
avoid incidental evils, all are to be matter of careful study. For a consideration of Mr. Beecher's
specific counsels respecting the conduct of prayer-
meetings and the promotion of revivals, the reader
must be referred to the volume. Some of these
counsels are inapplicable to the pastors of liturgical
churches ; some of them would be difficult to apply
in our time. I think Mr. Beecher himself would
have laid, in his later life, more stress on the promotion of normal and unconscious spiritual development and less on specific methods for arousing the
spiritual nature through social coöperation. But
the fundamental principles elucidated in this volume, and still more the spiritual life which pervades
it, are valuable in all churches, in all times, and in
all communities.

The third series in the "Yale Lectures on Preaching" deals with Christian doctrine, or what may
be called applied theology. This volume seems
to me the least distinctive and characteristic of
the three. It deals less with the methods of the

preacher; it is less personal and vital; there is much less autobiographical element in it. He hints at, without expounding, the modern evolutionary conception of the Bible as a progressive revelation through spiritual experience. He bases its authority upon the fact that "it has been so long in the world, and so much taught, that it is an authority now among the common people, certainly throughout Christendom." He lays stress on the fact that the object of the preacher is to bring man into personal relations with God; for this purpose he must first establish God's personality, second, illustrate his disposition, third, develop a sense of his presence. He shows how this is to be done — psychologically through the use of the spiritual imagination, historically through the revelation of God in Jesus Christ. His analysis of Jesus Christ as "the Divine Life in human conditions" is suggestive, inspiring, and in places full of spiritual beauty, but does not compare for completeness of analysis with Dr. Bushnell's famous chapter in "Nature and the Supernatural" on the character of Jesus. He lays stress on the reality of sinfulness, as something more than a mere multitude of individual sins, and on Christian life as a growth embodying three stages, — repentance, conversion, and sanctification; and he sums up the whole teaching of the three courses in one sentence: "Our high mission, our noble calling, is to build up souls, to perfect the Christian life, and to make manhood acceptable to God, and radiant in the sight of all men."

Of all the volumes which Mr. Beecher has left as
his bequest to the world, I regard the " Yale Lectures on Preaching" as the most important, and
likely to be the most permanent in their direct influence upon the Church of Christ. He left no political
writings save the editorials in " The Independent."
The admirable collection of addresses on political
subjects, gathered by Mr. J. R. Howard, are chiefly
valuable as a contribution to the history of a great
moral reform, to the accomplishment of which Mr.
Beecher contributed so largely. His " Life of
Christ" he did not complete. It is beautiful in its
expression, and spiritually suggestive in its thoughts,
but Mr. Beecher will not be known to the future
as a great historian. " Norwood" contains graphic,
vivid pictures of New England life, but no one
would think of calling Mr. Beecher a great novelist.
His " Lectures to Young Men" belong to the earlier epoch in his ministry, and though wonderfully
effective then, would not be equally effective now.
His sermons, preached for immediate effect, are, as
he intended they should be, sermons, not literature,
still less theology. His " Star Papers" and his
" Pleasant Talks about Fruits, Flowers, and Farming" are literary recreations. Not as an author,
historian, or reformer will he be known to history,
but as the great preacher of the nineteenth century,
— certainly without a superior, if not without a
peer. In the " Yale Lectures on Preaching" he
formulates the principles which guided him in his
ministry, and, what is more important, reveals with

modest, unconscious candor the spirit which animated him. Some of his counsels may have become inapplicable, with the change of conditions;
his unconventionalism will repel those who are sensitive to conventional proprieties; and I cannot but
wish that it had been consistent with his temperament to give to these volumes, before his death, a
thorough and painstaking revision; but I do not
know in the whole range of homiletical literature
any other volumes as well worth careful study by
any man of our time who wishes to understand the
secret of pulpit power, and who is sufficiently catholic in his disposition, whatever his denomination
may be, to take that secret from one whom history
will regard as perhaps the most powerful preacher
in American history, if not also in the history of
the Anglo-Saxon people.

CHAPTER XVI

HE FINISHES HIS COURSE

In the spring of 1886 Mr. Beecher yielded to the urgency of Major Pond, and consented to revisit England on a lecture tour. The twenty-three years which had elapsed since his first campaign had converted distrust into confidence and aversion into enthusiasm. When the steamer reached Queenstown, the mail brought hosts of requests from all parts of the country for sermons and lectures. When Mr. Beecher landed at Liverpool delegates from Bradford, Leeds, York, Carnarvon, Manchester, Edinburgh, Belfast, and Dublin were there to welcome the speaker who had found so much difficulty in winning a hearing in 1863. In the fifteen and a half weeks between the 24th of July and the 1st of October Mr. Beecher preached seventeen times, delivered fifty-eight lectures and nine public addresses: his entire visit was a series of public ovations. Of his addresses probably the most important were, one delivered in the City Temple on Friday morning, October 15, to the theological students in the city of London, about six hundred students and about as many clergymen of different denominations being present, in which he declared his convictions concerning the

secret of pulpit power; one delivered before the
Freedman's Aid Society Mission at Westminster
Chapel on October 16, in which he presented with
characteristic hopefulness his views concerning the
character, progress, and future of the negroes; and
one delivered on October 18 before the Congregationalists at Liverpool, which was largely a confession of his religious faith, in which he reaffirmed,
in the strongest terms, his faith in the divinity of
Jesus Christ as the central truth in his theology.

From this European trip Mr. Beecher returned
in the fall of 1886, refreshed and reinvigorated by
his summer's experience of lecturing, preaching,
and visiting. Landing on Sunday morning too
late to preach, he visited, in the afternoon, each one
of the three Sunday-schools connected with Plymouth Church. Early in December his wife was
taken seriously ill, and for six weeks he sedulously
tended her as nurse, accepting from other members
of the family only such assistance as was indispensable. With her returning health, he began to
make preparations for completing the unfinished
"Life of Christ," and promised when this was
done to undertake his autobiography. To Dr.
Joseph Parker, of London, he wrote: "I have my
snug room upstairs, and am working cosily and
every day on my 'Life of Christ,' which, like
the buds of spring, is beginning to swell, like
the returning birds, is beginning to sing, like the
grass, is beginning to grow, and is already very
green! But I am hopeful." He refused all lecture

engagements, that he might devote himself to the completion of this literary task. But it was not to be completed.

Sunday evening, February 27, 1887, was the last service Mr. Beecher ever attended in Plymouth Church. It was remembered afterwards that he lingered for a few moments at the close of the service listening to the choir as they practiced a new musical setting by Mr. H. R. Shelley, the organist of the church, to Faber's "Hark, hark, my soul, angelic songs are swelling," and that as he started to go out he remarked, "That will do to die on." "Will it not do to live on, Mr. Beecher?" asked a friend at his side. "That is the way to die," said he quickly. As he passed out he saw standing by the furnace register, to warm themselves, a little girl about ten years old and her brother, only five years old, who had for some weeks been in the habit of going alone to the church on Sunday evenings. Putting his hand on the little boy's head, he stooped and kissed him, saying, "It is a cold night for such little tots to be out." The children, attracted by his kindness, walked out on either side of him to the door. "It was," said Dr. Charles H. Hall, in the funeral sermon, "a fitting close to a grand life, — the old man of genius and fame shielding the little wanderers, — great in breasting tradition always and prejudices, great also in the gesture, so like him, that recognized, as did the Master, that the humblest and the poorest were his brethren, the great preacher led out into the night by little nameless waifs."

On Wednesday evening, March 2, after a full day of shopping with his wife, for some refurnishing of the parlors of the church, and a short evening of recreation with the family, he retired earlier than usual, and when a little later Mrs. Beecher went upstairs she found him already apparently soundly sleeping. Early the next morning she was awakened from her sleep by an unusual sound in her husband's room, ran to his side, and found him suffering from nausea. To her inquiry as to the matter, he replied, " Nothing but a sick headache," and dropped almost instantly to sleep again. He slept through the following day. Not until four o'clock in the afternoon was the physician sent for. An effort was made to arouse Mr. Beecher from his sleep; the response was brief and broken; and the doctor's conclusion was soon reached: Mr. Beecher was dying of apoplexy. The end came on Tuesday morning, at half-past nine o'clock, the 8th of March, 1887.

The first Sunday in the month was the one on which the Lord's Supper was always administered in Plymouth Church. The service was held; but the sermon was omitted, and the hour was devoted to the administration of the communion, the great congregation breaking in upon the hush of this solemn service with many sobs. On Sunday, Monday, Tuesday, and Wednesday evenings prayer-meetings were held in the lecture-room, participated in by various members of the church. It was afterwards noted as a significant fact that no one prayed, even in the earlier meetings, for the pastor's recovery; it was accepted by all as a fact unalterable, that the time of his going home had come; and not one of those who loved him would have called him back. During Thursday the coffin lay in Plymouth Church, and all day long from half-past eleven in the morning until ten at night the citizens of Brooklyn moved in quiet and orderly procession by the coffin, to look upon his face for the last time, while simple music was furnished, sometimes by the organ, sometimes by the voices of singers. Members of the church and personal friends sat scattered through the edifice, engaged in silent prayer or in sacred meditation, or, in subdued tones, exchanging reminiscences. There had long been an understanding between Mr. Beecher and the Rev. Charles H. Hall, rector of Trinity Church, that, whoever should die first, the other should officiate at the funeral. In accordance with this understanding, the public services, held on Friday, were conducted by Dr. Hall. The public offices in Brooklyn were closed, by direction of the city government; the public and private schools were dismissed; and business was very generally suspended during the funeral services. Not only Plymouth Church itself, but four other churches in the vicinity, were crowded with mourners.

It is doubtful whether any death ever produced more widespread expressions of sorrow throughout the country — certain that the death of no private citizen was ever made occasion for so many and so varied memorial services, addresses, and editorials. In churches representing every phase of religious faith, Mr. Beecher's death was mentioned in prayer or sermon; by associations of every description, secular and religious, resolutions to his memory were passed; in every type of journal, from that devoted to recreation or agriculture to that voicing the sentiment of the most conservative of the religious schools, some recognition of his service to his age and nation was to be found. The New York Legislature adjourned that its members might attend the funeral service, and both the Senate and the Assembly passed resolutions of respect to his memory. Similar resolutions were passed by the Board of Aldermen of the city of Brooklyn, who directed that appropriate emblems of mourning should be displayed on the City Hall until after the funeral. A type and symbol of this universal appreciation was furnished by the memorial service held in Plymouth Church the Sabbath evening after his death, participated in by representative speakers from the Unitarian, the Presbyterian, the Lutheran, the New Jerusalem, the Universalist, the Methodist, the Baptist, the Reformed, the Episcopal, and the Congregational churches, and a Jewish synagogue, and by a letter from a Roman Catholic priest. Two weeks later a union memorial service of the African churches of Brooklyn was held in the African Methodist

Episcopal Church of the city. Nor were these
memorials confined to Brooklyn. From churches
and synagogues all over the country, North and
South, East and West, from abroad also, from
churches in London and Liverpool, from white
and colored, from Americans and foreigners, from
ministerial gatherings, political bodies, both Republican and Democratic, college associations, military organizations, and social clubs, came to Plymouth Church formal expressions of respect for
Mr. Beecher and of sympathy for his church in
its sorrow. One of the most touching of these was
a resolution spontaneously adopted by the newsboys of Brooklyn at their services in the Newsboys'
Home.

These expressions of affection were not confined
to the time of his death. While the multitude
were still filing past the dead in Plymouth Church,
the suggestion was made that a statue should be
erected by citizens of Brooklyn to his memory. In
less than two weeks after his death, a meeting of
citizens was held to forward this movement, and it
was so largely attended that many were unable to
gain admittance to the room. The money for the
purpose was easily obtained, — rather it should be
said, was spontaneously offered, — and in June,
1891, the statue, designed by J. Q. A. Ward, was
erected in City Hall Square, facing the building
where he had been put on trial as for his life, and
remaining there a perpetual witness to the judgment
of the citizens of Brooklyn between him and his

accusers. Shortly after Mr. Beecher's death, the
Rev. S. B. Halliday, who for seventeen years had
been Mr. Beecher's assistant, and to whose loyal
service, taking from the great preacher's mind
the administrative details of the great church, Mr.
Beecher's freedom for the larger public service was
not inconsiderably due, resigned his position to take
charge of a small Congregational church in the out-
skirts of Brooklyn, the services of which were held
in a vacant store on Fulton Street, small, ill-venti-
lated, and poorly lighted. He gave to this church
its new name, "The Beecher Memorial Church,"
and in 1891 an adequate structure had been raised
at a cost of twenty-six thousand dollars, which on
the 18th of October of that year was dedicated. It
was more than in name a memorial to Henry Ward
Beecher. Means for its construction had been
given by Presbyterians, Universalists, Orthodox,
Liberals, and Jews. Contributions had been received from every state and territory in the country and also from Canada, England, Scotland,
Wales, Sweden, Denmark, South America, China,
and India, almost all of them in small amounts.
Eight months after the dedication the last dollar
of debt upon the building was paid, and the
church, still in successful operation, is a monument
alike to the fidelity of Mr. Beecher's life-long
friend, Mr. Halliday, and to the spontaneous interest throughout the world which men of moderate means felt in doing something to perpetuate
the name of one who had rendered them spiritual

service. Nor is this the only church which at least indirectly perpetuates the memory of the great preacher. The Congregational Yearbook records fifty-two churches bearing the name Plymouth Church, — the name borrowed from the church which Mr. Beecher founded, the churches, let us hope, having imbibed something of its spirit. In that church itself his name is commemorated by a remarkable portrait of life size, in the lecture-room, placed as nearly as possible on the spot where he used to sit in giving his " Lecture-Room Talks," and by a tablet in the vestibule of the church containing his portrait in bas-relief, with the simple inscription, " In Memoriam. Henry Ward Beecher, First Pastor of Plymouth Church, 1847–1887. I have not concealed thy lovingkindness and thy truth from the great congregation." At the present writing, the summer of 1903, a further movement has been initiated by the present pastor of Plymouth Church, the Rev. Newell Dwight Hillis, D. D., for a larger memorial to the great preacher. The Henry Ward Beecher Memorial Association of Brooklyn has been organized and incorporated; ground has been purchased in the immediate vicinity of Plymouth Church; and it is proposed to erect thereon a memorial hall for the preservation of material relating to the life of Henry Ward Beecher and other members of the Beecher family, and to provide in connection therewith a library, reading-room, music-room, and amusement-room. For this purpose over fifty thousand dollars have already been subscribed, a large portion of it by citizens having no connection with Plymouth Church.

But next to that impalpable influence which goes on through eternity with infinite increase, the most vital memorial to Mr. Beecher is the church which he founded and inspired with his life. Those who imagined that Plymouth Church was gathered around and held together by the eloquence of a great orator, naturally surmised that the congregation would disappear and the church dissolve when the orator died. They little understood the nature of its work and the permanency of his influence. When, in the fall of 1887, I was called to supply the pulpit left vacant by Mr. Beecher's death, I found a greatly diminished congregation. Strangers no longer flocked to the edifice. The audience, which under Mr. Beecher's preaching had numbered from twenty-five hundred to three thousand, was reduced to something like half that number. But it was only the strangers who had ceased to come. Not a single eminent member of the church had withdrawn. The pewholders, with few exceptions, pledged to the church a renewal of their pew-rents at the old rate for the succeeding year. The Sunday-schools were officered as efficiently as they had been the fall before with Mr. Beecher living. Some members who had never felt that the church had need of them had emerged from their retirement and assumed active service in the prayer-meeting or the Sunday-schools. A new organization had been formed within the church for the purpose of enlisting the active coöperation of all the members, and had efficiently entered upon its varied activities. It was apparent that the pews could no longer be sold at auction, apparent that there would no longer be premiums paid for the pews on which the trustees could draw, as they had done during Mr. Beecher's lifetime, for the support of the missions. But the church had no thought of abandoning or even lessening its work. It assumed the expense which the trustees had hitherto borne. It organized an envelope fund, and by means of this envelope fund, to which every member was invited to contribute, and by means of a system of plate collections which had never before been instituted, enough money was raised to carry on and considerably enlarge the parish work in which Plymouth Church had been engaged. Nor was this the result of a mere transient enthusiasm. The last report of the committee which has this work in charge shows a receipt from the envelope fund and the plate collections of over ten thousand dollars for this mission work of Plymouth Church in the city of Brooklyn. Nor is it only these financial results which testify to the continued efficiency of the church. During the ten years which elapsed between the death of Mr. Beecher and the semi-centennial of Plymouth Church in 1897, the additions on confession of faith were but little less annually than they had been during Mr. Beecher's pastorate. A conclusive

answer to the charge sometimes brought, once
through jealousy, now through ignorance, that Mr.
Beecher's preaching promoted hero-worship, not
the worship of God, the following of a preacher,
not the following of Christ, an ephemeral emotionalism, not a life-enduring principle, is furnished
by the church which he gathered by his influence
and inspired with his spirit, — a church through
the doors of which in fifty years thirty-six hundred
and thirty-three came into the kingdom of God, —
a church in which, fifteen years after its great
preacher's death, a congregation of nearly or quite
two thousand worshipers gathers every Sunday
morning, — a church in the three Sunday-schools of
which are still gathered every Sunday afternoon
a thousand scholars studying the Bible, —a church
which, ten years after Mr. Beecher's death, on the
fiftieth anniversary day of its organization, had
every class in its three Sunday-schools supplied
with teachers, and there was in addition a waiting-
list of volunteers ready to respond to any call for
additional service.

CHAPTER XVII

ESTIMATES AND IMPRESSIONS

From 1855 to the time of Mr. Beecher's death in 1887, except for the five years which included the Civil War, I was in constant communication, and much of the time in intimate association with him. In this chapter I propose to give some personal estimates, the result of that fellowship, and illustrated by some reminiscent incidents.

During most of his life Mr. Beecher was engaged in warfare of one sort or another. He was constantly attacking what he regarded as abuses, — social, political, religious; and he was constantly under attack for what others regarded as social, political, and religious errors in his teaching. The natural consequence was that in his lifetime many false estimates of his character and few correct ones were made. His enemies exaggerated his faults and depreciated, if they did not absolutely deny, his virtues. As an almost necessary consequence, his friends were inclined to exaggerate his excellences and to ignore, if not to deny, his defects. In battle no loyal soldier criticises his general; loyalty prevented Mr. Beecher's friends and supporters from criticising their leader. In such a case the errors on the one side are not corrected by the errors on the other. On the contrary, the estimates of both friends and foes are apt to agree in statement, although antagonistic in their animus and spirit.

Thus it had been said by both critics and admirers, though with a very different meaning, that Mr. Beecher would have made a great actor, a great lawyer, a great politician, a great author, a great editor. What education might have made of him no man can tell; but take him for what he was, he would not have made a great actor, because he could not deliberately assume a part; nor a great lawyer, because he could not advocate any convictions not independently his own; nor a great politician, because he did not read character correctly, being too much possessed by the spirit which "thinketh no evil;" nor a great author, because he was not interested in art for art's sake; in what sense he was a great editor I have already considered.[1]

It is true that Mr. Beecher's interests were extraordinarily varied, and his knowledge multiform. He was an expert in horticulture, arboriculture, precious stones, Turkish and Persian rugs, — and in how many other things I know not. He was a judge of horses, and was very fond of a good one. When I was starting out in search of a parish he gave me this advice: "Look at the horses in every town you go to. If the men drive good horses, you may expect that there is progress, or at least life in the town; if they drive poor ones, the people are probably inert and lazy." The remark indi-

[1] See chapter XVI. pp. 338, 342, 344.

cates the nature of his interest. Whatever the subject, it invariably led him somehow to men, their character, their life, and the best way of reaching them with the offer of the higher life. This fact was not always recognized by undiscriminating admirers, who, from the variety of his interests, drew the conclusion that he would have excelled in all departments. But though interest is necessary to excellence, excellence is not created alone by interest. I found Mr. Beecher once, shortly after the close of the Civil War, deep in Sherman's "March to the Sea." To my expression of surprise, — for he was not merely reading, he was studying it in detail with war-maps, — he replied, "Do you know, if I were not a preacher, I would choose to be a general above anything else." But I did not take the expression seriously, and I do not think he did — except for the moment. I am certain he would have made a poor general. The jeweler who, apropos of Mr. Beecher's love for precious stones, said that he would have made a splendid salesman, was mistaken. True, he loved and understood precious stones, but he would never have cared to sell them. His interest in farming did not make him a successful farmer. When some critic attempted to arouse prejudice against him as a wealthy preacher who owned and carried on a farm of ten acres on the Hudson, he replied that if an enemy should give him ten more acres he would be bankrupted.

Varied as were his talents, kaleidoscopic as was

his mind, universal as were his interests, he gave himself to one work with a singleness of aim which I have never seen paralleled in any man of my acquaintance except Phillips Brooks. Their aims were different: Mr. Beecher's broader and more comprehensive; Phillips Brooks's more exclusively individual and spiritual. Phillips Brooks was purely a preacher. His one aim in life was to impart life. He believed correctly that he could do this best by the free use of his own personality in the pulpit. When he spoke on the platform or after a public dinner, he made the platform or the table a pulpit; his address was a sermon; his audience a congregation. For a little time in Philadelphia he took an active part in public questions, but after he went to Boston he was not active as a public teacher on social or political problems. This was not because he had lost his interest in them, or his acquaintance with them, but because he believed he could render his best service to the age by preaching: to preaching accordingly he gave himself with entire singleness of purpose. That he could write true poetry was proved by " O Little Town of Bethlehem." That he had a large knowledge of architecture and a remarkably creative as well as appreciative taste, is proved by Trinity Church, into which he put himself as truly as he put himself into his sermons. That he would have made valuable contributions to periodical literature, if he could have been persuaded to accept the numerous and urgent invitations which poured in

upon him, that as a lecturer he would have been
in great demand, had he consented to go upon the
lyceum platform, no one who knew him doubts.
He refused because he was resolved to devote himself wholly to preaching. Even as bishop his great
work was as an itinerant preacher.

Mr. Beecher's estimate of his own function was
a broader one, but it was not less clearly conceived,
nor followed with less single-heartedness. That
function was to impart spiritual life, but it was
also to instruct in the application of the principles
of spiritual life to all the various problems, both of
personal experience and of social order. His greatness consisted in his instinctive perception of moral
principles, in his practical common sense in the
application of those principles to current questions
of human experience, and in his varied literary and
oratorical ability in so presenting those principles
as not only to win for them the assent of all sorts
of men, but also to inspire in all sorts of men a
genuine loyalty to those principles. He understood
himself better than some of his friends and his
eulogists understood him. To this one work of so
inspiring, guiding, and dominating the lives of men
as to direct them in the way of righteousness, he
gave himself with absolute singleness of aim, and,
after he had fairly got an understanding of himself and his work, with undeviating purpose. He
preached, he lectured, he spoke on political platforms; he wrote, and on all subjects, social and
individual, grave and gay, secular and religious.

But always back of his work, inspiring it, controlling it, determining his choice between different phases of it, was the ambition, — if anything so unegoistic can be called an ambition, — the purpose, — if anything so unconscious can be called a purpose, — to help men to a happier, a better, a diviner life. And in his estimate diviness of spirit was of transcendently greater importance than conformity to ethical standards, and both were superior to mere happiness. His intuitive nature would have made it impossible for him to accept the utilitarian philosophy. Preaching, therefore, in the narrower sense of that term, as a heralding of Jesus Christ, Son of God and Saviour of man, always took the first place, though not the sole place, in his relative estimate of opportunities. I can best illustrate his comparative estimate of lecturing and preaching by quoting one of half a dozen similar letters sent by him to Major J. B. Pond : —

BROOKLYN, N. Y., 124 COLUMBIA HEIGHTS,
February 22, 1883.

MY DEAR POND : — I am sorry that Suffield should suffer, — but it can't be helped. All the cities on the continent are not to me of as much value as my church and its work, and when a deepening religious feeling is evident, to go off lecturing and leave it would be too outrageous to be thought of. No — No. Never — now or hereafter — will I let lecturing infringe on home work! The next week is already arranged. Several neighboring clergymen are engaged to aid, and from Sunday to Saturday every night is allotted. I take two,

— Monday and Tuesday, — and cannot be altered. I
do not know how it will be in March. If things in the
church should prosper, I will not go out, at least till
May, but I cannot tell.

> Yours,
> HENRY WARD BEECHER.

It is difficult and perhaps hazardous to speculate
on the motives which inspire men, and yet such a
character-study as this would be inadequate without a consideration of the motives which dominated
Mr. Beecher. He was almost absolutely indifferent to money. He did not care for it himself; he
did not reverence it in others. When in a widely
misquoted address he said, apropos of certain phases
of the labor problem, that he could live on bread
and water, he spoke the simple truth. This was
not because he was an ascetic. He enjoyed the
comforts and even the luxuries of life. We had
an editorial dinner at Delmonico's one spring day
in 1879; Mr. Lawson Valentine, then one of the
largest stockholders in "The Christian Union," telegraphed the office: "I like your Delmonico. Keep
at work on this line all summer;" and got from
Mr. Beecher a reply equally laconic: "You are
not the only fellow that likes Delmonico. We are
willing to patronize him all summer if you will pay
the bill." He enjoyed good living, though rather
for the social pleasures such occasions afforded than
for any mere epicurean enjoyment. Much more
than sensuous luxuries he enjoyed beauty in form
and color. But he was not dependent upon either.

And for money apart from what it could buy he cared not a jot. My first acquaintance with him illustrates his singular carelessness in money matters. I was a boy of nineteen in my brother's law office; I had been an attendant on Plymouth Church for but a few months ; he knew me only as a younger brother of one of the members of his church when he asked me one Sunday after service to call at his house the next morning. When I called he opened a drawer in his desk, took out a package of bills, gave them to me, and asked me to go to an address in the upper part of New York City to pay off a mortgage and get a satisfaction-piece. My recollection is that the amount was ten thousand dollars. I know that until I got the money out of my pocket and the satisfaction-piece in its place, I was in a dread lest my pocket should be picked and his money and my reputation should go together. He rarely came out on the right side of a bargain when the bargaining was left to him. His sermons any one was welcome to publish who wished to do so. In his later life he earned thousands of dollars by his lecturing ; but this was because he had the wisdom to put himself in Major J. B. Pond's hands, and to refer all applications for lectures to him. He was generous to a fault with his money; many were the unworthy beggars, large and small, who made off with contributions from him ; not till late in life did he learn any financial wisdom, and then not too much.

He was as indifferent to fame as he was to

money. He counseled young ministers to beware of falling into the weakness of considering how they could conserve their reputation, and satirized those who were habitually considering what would be the effect of their words or actions upon their " influence." He resented counsel to himself based on the idea that his influence would be injured by some proposed action. Partly owing to this indifference to his reputation, partly to the orator's instinct to use at the time not only that form of expression, but also that phase of truth which will produce the effect he wishes to produce, Mr. Beecher was careless of consistency, which, with Emerson, he regarded as the vice of small minds. Once called to account for the inconsistency of something he had just said with a previous utterance of his on the same subject, he replied, " Oh, yes ! Well, that was last week." Yet these inconsistencies were more apparent than real. Thus he preached one Sunday a sermon on the text, " Train up a child in the way he should go, and when he is old he will not depart from it ; " and began by saying, " This is not God's policy of insurance on children ; this is the statement of a natural law." About a year later he took the same text and began his sermon by saying, " This is God's policy of insurance on children," and proceeded to treat it as a divine promise. Yet the two utterances are really consistent, since God's promises are fulfilled through natural law.

But if he cared very little what the great public

thought about him, he cared a great deal about how those who knew him felt toward him. The expression uttered by him on his seventieth birthday represents his habitual mood: "I love men so much, that I like above all other things in the world to be loved. And yet I can do without it when it is necessary. I love love, but I love truth more, and God more yet." For great as was his love for his fellow men and his desire for their love, the dominating motives of his life were his love for God, or his love for Christ, — and in his experience the two phrases were synonymous, — and his desire for God's love. No one who knew him intimately could doubt the simplicity and sincerity of his piety. Christ was a very real and a very present Person to him. His disbelief in theology never involved in doubt his experience of vital fellowship with the living God. I do not mean that this experience was not more real at some times than at others; nor that he did not have at times the experience which in Jesus Christ found utterance in the bitter cry, "My God, my God, why hast thou forsaken me!" But if so, these experiences were rare. His prevailing mood was one of the conscious presence of Christ, to whom he would at times refer as simply and as naturally as to any other friend and companion. Yet he never, if I may so speak, traded on this experience. He never assumed it as an authority. He never said that Christ had told him to do this or that. His experience accorded with and interprets practically the philosophy of Professor William James, that mystical states are authority to the persons to whom they come, but are not to be quoted as an authority to those to whom they do not come.

I make no attempt here to analyze Mr. Beecher's power as an orator, to indicate the various elements which entered into it, or to explain its secret, further than to say that far more important than were his voice and face and gesture, his skillful though inartificial rhetoric, his opalescent imagination, his illuminating humor, his unconscious art of dramatization, his perfervid and contagious emotion — far more important than all of these were the sane judgment, the dominating conscience, and the spiritual faith which used these gifts as instruments, never in the service of self, always in the service of a great cause, or, to speak more accurately, in the service of his fellow men and his God. Here I make no attempt to compare Mr. Beecher with the famous orators of history. I attempt merely to record the impression which his oratory produced on me and on others as I had occasion to observe its impression on them. In so doing I instinctively compare him with other contemporary orators whom I have heard, — Daniel Webster, Wendell Phillips, Charles Sumner, George William Curtis, John B. Gough, William E. Gladstone, Charles G. Finney, R. S. Storrs, and Phillips Brooks. In particular qualities each of these men may have excelled him, some of them certainly did; in combination of qualities to my thinking no one of them equaled him. As I do not analyze Mr. Beecher, so I do not analyze these, his contemporaries. In respect to them all I speak only of impressions produced upon myself.

Daniel Webster impressed me by the weight of his words; Wendell Phillips by the edge of his small sword and the dexterity of his thrust; Charles Sumner by his skillful marshaling of facts; George William Curtis by the perfect finish of his art in language, tone, and gesture; John B. Gough by the combination of abandon and good sense, of dramatic impersonation, and real apprehension of the actualities of life; William E. Gladstone by the persuasiveness which captivated first your inclination and afterward your judgment; Charles G. Finney by the flawless logic which compelled your sometimes reluctant assent to his conclusion; R. S. Storrs by the more than Oriental glory of his embroidered fabric; Phillips Brooks by the sense of a divine presence and power possessing him and speaking through him, as through a prophet of the olden time. Mr. Beecher was less weighty than Daniel Webster; one was a glacier, the other an avalanche; one was a battery of artillery, the other was a regiment of horse charging with the impetuosity of a Ney. Mr. Beecher could be as clear-cut and crystalline at times as Wendell Phillips was at all times, but he was never malignant as Wendell Phillips sometimes was, and never took the delight, which Wendell Phillips often took, in the skill with which he could transfix an opponent. Mr. Beecher could, and sometimes did, marshal facts with a military skill scarcely inferior to that of Charles Sumner, as witness some passages in his English speeches, but he was never overloaded and overborne by them. He summoned facts as witnesses to confirm a truth, and when their testimony was given dismissed them, while he, with dramatic imagination and emotional power, pressed home upon his audience the truth to which they bore witness. He had not the grace either of diction or of address which characterized George William Curtis. Mr. Curtis never violated the canons of a perfect taste; Mr. Beecher often did. But Mr. Curtis spoke only to the cultivated, Mr. Beecher to all sorts and conditions of men; Mr. Curtis spoke from manuscript; his oration combined all the perfection of the written with some of the vigor of the spoken address. Mr. Beecher never spoke from manuscript. He sometimes read manuscript; he sometimes spoke without manuscript; he sometimes alternated the two methods in the one address; but he could not, or at least he did not, maintain at one and the same time an unbroken connection with the page upon the desk and with auditors in the seat. But if he lacked the grace and perfect art of George William Curtis, he possessed an inflaming, convincing, coercing power which Mr. Curtis did not even remotely approach. It is difficult to compare Mr. Beecher's dramatic power with that of John B. Gough. Considered simply as dramatic artists, Mr. Beecher was far more impassioned and moving, Mr. Gough more versatile. Mr. Gough was always dramatic. His lectures were continuous impersonations. He was the best story-teller I ever heard. He once told me that he was thinking of preparing a lecture to be entitled " That Reminds Me," which should consist of a succession of dramatic stories so contrived that each one should suggest its successor. He never did prepare such a lecture, but he could readily have done it. Mr. Beecher could hardly have conceived, and certainly could not have accomplished, such a lecture. Mr. Gough was a skillful ventriloquist. Once, when I was driving with him in a closed carriage in the country, he greatly excited a little girl, who was our companion, by the mewing of a cat, for which she searched everywhere in vain. Mr. Gough would have made a brilliant success as an actor in either farce or light comedy ; Mr. Beecher would not. I never heard him tell a story on the platform, unless the narrative of personal incidents in his own experience might be so regarded, and rarely in the social circle. I do not think he used his dramatic art for purposes of amusement. I doubt whether he was ever conscious in his imitations ; he certainly was not so ordinarily. A purpose to be achieved in the life of his audience always dominated him, and he was dramatic only incidentally and unconsciously, because in describing any incident, whether real or imaginary, his face and tone and gesture came naturally into play. He stopped at the office of

" The Christian Union " once on his way from the dog-show, and he described the dogs to me. " There was the bulldog," he said, " with his retreating forehead, and his big neck, and his protruding jaw, like the highwayman who might meet you with his demand for your money or your life; " and his forehead seemed to retreat, and his jaw protruded, and he looked the character he portrayed, so that I should have instinctively crossed the street had I met after dark a man looking as he looked. " And there was the English mastiff," he continued, " with a face and brow like Daniel Webster's; " and his whole face and even the very form and structure of his head seemed to change in an unconscious impersonation of the noble brute he was describing. For Mr. Beecher was as dramatic off the platform as on it; imitation was not with him a studied art, it was an unconscious identification of himself with the character he was for the moment portraying. I heard Mr. Gladstone but once; it was in the English House of Commons; his object was to commend and carry his motion for the use of the closure, before unknown in Parliament. It would be absurd to attempt an estimate of Mr. Gladstone's oratory from this one address. But comparing that one address with the many I have heard from Mr. Beecher, it was more persuasive, but less eloquent. As he spoke, it seemed as though his conclusions needed no argument to sustain them; I found myself saying in response to all he said, " Of course." But of the dramatic portrayal, the pictorial imagination, the warm feeling, the brilliant color, the iridescent humor, the varied play of life, catching now one hearer by one method, now another hearer by another method, converting hostility into enthusiasm, and indifference into interest, which characterized Mr. Beecher's greatest addresses, there was in this one speech of Mr. Gladstone scarcely a trace. Charles G. Finney corralled his audience; he drove them before him, penned them in, coerced them by his logic, — though it was a logic aflame, — convinced their reason, convicted their conscience, compelled them to accept his conclusions despite their resistance. His sermons are essentially syllogistic. Syllogisms are as rare in the sermons of Mr. Beecher as in the sermons of Phillips Brooks. He was not logical, but analogical. He did not coerce men; he either enticed them, or he swept them before him by the impetuosity of his nature. He sought to convince men of sin chiefly by putting before them an ideal, and leaving them to compare themselves with it. He spoke to conscience through ideality.

There were frequent opportunities for comparing Dr. Storrs and Mr. Beecher, since they often spoke on the same platform, and for forty years they ministered side by side in the same city. Dr. Storrs drew his illustrations from books, Mr. Beecher from life; Dr. Storrs was more rhetorical, Mr. Beecher more colloquial; Dr. Storrs more artistic, but sometimes artificial, Mr. Beecher more spontaneous, but also more uneven; after hearing Dr.

Storrs, the people went away admiring the address; after hearing Mr. Beecher, they went away discussing the theme. Comparing Henry Ward Beecher and Phillips Brooks, I should describe Phillips Brooks as the greater preacher, but Mr. Beecher as the greater orator. The distinctive function of the preacher is to bring home to the consciousness of men the eternal and the invisible. He may teach ethics, or philosophy; he may move men by argument, by imagination, by emotion, to some form of action, or some phase of thinking, or some emotional life; this he does in common with the orator. But the unveiling of the invisible world, looking himself, and enabling others also to look upon the things which are unseen and are eternal — this is the preacher's distinctive and exclusive function. It is this which makes him, what the Old Testament calls him, a prophet — a forth-teller, speaking by a spirit within, of a world seen only from within. This Mr. Beecher did to a remarkable degree; but he did much more and other than this — though nothing higher, for there is nothing higher that any man can do for his fellow men. This is to open the eyes of the blind and enable them to see. This was the exclusive mission of Phillips Brooks. He might have said of himself, without irreverence, " I have come that they might have life, and might have it more abundantly." Mr. Beecher was also a life-giver; but he was besides a guide, a counselor, a teacher. He moved men by his immediate spiritual power, awaking in them a power to perceive and receive spiritual life; but he also moved them indirectly and mediately through argument, humor, imagination, imitation, human sympathy, the contagious power of a passionate enthusiasm. It was his spiritual life which made Phillips Brooks the orator; Mr. Beecher would have been a great orator though he had lacked spiritual life.

To sum up in a sentence the impression on my own mind of Mr. Beecher's oratory as compared with that of other contemporary orators: in particular elements of charm or power he was surpassed by some of them; in combination of charm and power by none; but his power was greater than his charm, and his charm was subsidiary to power, and its instrument. If the test of the oration is its perfection, whether of structure or of expression, other orators have surpassed Mr. Beecher; if the test of oratory is the power of the speaker to impart to his audience his life, to impress on them his conviction, animate them with his purpose, and direct their action to the accomplishment of his end, then Mr. Beecher was the greatest orator I have ever heard; and in my judgment, whether measured by the immediate or by the permanent effects of his addresses, takes his place in the rank of the great orators of the world. I doubt whether in history greater immediate or more enduring effects have ever been produced by any orations than were produced on English sentiment and English national life by his speeches in England.

A remarkable illustration of charm and power

combined was furnished by his speech delivered at
the testimonial dinner given in New York City to
Herbert Spencer, on the eve of the latter's return
to England. The dinner was a long and elaborate
one. The diners were with few exceptions scientific
men of eminence. There were very few who were
known as active in the Christian Church or in the
religious world. Mr. William M. Evarts presided,
and lightened an otherwise heavy series of speeches
with occasional sallies of wit. But there had been
no humor, and no emotion, and little of literary
charm in the speeches. The last two speakers were
John Fiske and Mr. Beecher; their theme Science
and Religion. Mr. Fiske read an essay, clear, crystalline, coldly intellectual; he dealt with theology,
not with religion. It was nearing midnight when
Mr. Beecher rose to make the last address. The
room was filled with tobacco-smoke. The auditors
were weary and ready to go home. Not a vibrat-
ing note had been struck throughout the evening.
It seemed to me as Mr. Beecher rose that all he could
do was to apologize for not speaking at that late
hour and dismiss his audience. By some jest he
won a laugh; caught the momentary attention of
his audience; seemed about to lose it; caught it
again; again saw it escaping, and again captured
it. In five minutes the more distant auditors had
moved their chairs forward, the French waiters,
who had paid no attention to any one else, straight-
ened themselves up against the walls to listen;
Herbert Spencer on one side of him and Mr.

Evarts on the other were looking up into his face to catch the utterance of his speaking countenance as of his words. And then he preached as evangelical a sermon as I have ever heard from any minister's lips. He claimed Paul as an evolutionist; he read or quoted from the seventh chapter of Romans in support of the claim; he declared that man is an animal, and has ascended from an animal, but is more than animal, has in him a conscience, a reason, a faith, a hope, a love, which are divine in nature and in origin; he appealed to the experience of his auditors to confirm his analysis; he evoked cries of "That's so! That's so!" like Methodist amens from all over the room; and when he ended, in what was, in all but its form, a prayer that God would convey Herbert Spencer across that broader and deeper sea which flows between these shores and the unknown world beyond, and that there the two might meet to understand better the life which is so truly a mystery and the God who is so much to us the Unknown here, the whole audience rose by a common impulse to their feet, as if to make the prayer their own, cheering, clapping their hands, and waving their handkerchiefs. I can see the critic smiling with amused contempt at this paragraph, if he deigns to read it. None the less, he is shallow in his perceptions, as well as wrong in his judgments, if he is not able to recognize both the charm and the power of the orator who can win such a response, at such a time, from such an audience.

Thus far I have spoken chiefly of the impressions which Mr. Beecher's public character and conduct made upon me. What impression was left by his private life? It is somewhat difficult to answer that question, because he was a man of various moods as well as of versatile talents, and produced different impressions at different times. Every man is a bundle of contradictions; in general the greater the man the greater the contradictions. They were certainly great in Mr. Beecher.

He was most intense in his activity; the story of his life shows that. One who saw him only in his work would imagine that he was never at rest. On the contrary, in his hours of rest he was absolutely relaxed in mind and body. He was fond of horses, as I have said, and both rode and drove well; he talked eloquently of fishing and hunting; he advocated athletic sports — for others; he believed in the healthfulness of billiards and bowling; yet except croquet, he had no favorite recreation. But he loved to lie under the trees and follow his own counsel by "considering" the flowers, the clouds, the trees; in the city he would go to the house of a familiar friend, throw himself upon the sofa, and listen to the conversation of others, perhaps joining in it, perhaps not; or he would rest both mind and body by joining in a frolic with children, of whom he was very fond. His work was strenuous, but his rest was absolute.

Of his combination of courage and caution, courage in determining what to do, caution in deter-

mining how to do it, I have already spoken.[1] The
fact that the front seats of the gallery in a theatre
at Richmond are occupied by men prepared with
eggs to throw at him does not daunt him in the
least; he faces the hostile audience without a tremor.
But he disarms them by a compliment to their state
pride before he begins to give them some economic
lessons sorely needed at that time, especially in the
Southern States.

He was at once outspoken and reserved. Those
who knew him only by his public speech thought
he wore his heart upon his sleeve, because he used
his own most sacred experiences without hesitation,
if he thought they would serve his fellow men.
What father, and mother, and home, and children,
and Bible, and prayer, and Christ, and God were
to him he told again and again in public discourses,
and he urged others to make equally free use of
their experiences. Yet in private he rarely talked
of himself except as he thought the self-revelation
would help some struggling and perplexed soul into
light and freedom. Nothing in his experience was
too sacred to be used for that purpose. He was
not otherwise given to indulgence in reminiscence,
and never to narrating his achievements. He could
be as reticent and Sphinx-like as General Grant,
and could preserve a silence as impenetrable, as he
proved by being unmoved by all the misconstruc-
tion to which his silence subjected him, when speech
would have disclosed the secret of the household

[1] Chapter VII. pp. 156, 157.

whose unity and good name he was determined if possible to preserve, at whatever cost to himself. He had a way at times of abstracting himself from all around him, and becoming in appearance, and I rather think in reality, deaf and blind to everything external. When he was about to deliver his address in Burton's Theatre, by which time he knew me well, and I had done that financial errand for him of which I have already spoken, finding it difficult to get tolerable accommodation at the front, I went to the stage-door, and waited, hoping that I might get in when he entered. He brushed against me as he passed, but with that far-away look in his eyes, which seemed to say, " whether in the body or out of the body I know not ; " so my device failed. He often walked as abstracted and unobservant on the street, oblivious of all about him. Yet at other times he would pass immediately into the pulpit from what serious-minded folk would regard as unseemly frivolity. The last Sunday morning of his ministry, as he entered the church, he greeted the usher at the door, an old familiar friend, with a request for a seat. The usher caught his mood, and replied, " If you will wait here till the pewholders are seated, I will try to accommodate you." " Could I get a seat in the gallery ? " said Mr. Beecher. " You might try in the upper gallery." " But I am a little hard of hearing," said Mr. Beecher, putting his hand to his ear, " and want a seat near the pulpit." All this was done without a suggestion of a smile ; the next moment he was in his pulpit-chair turning over the leaves of his hymn-book for his hymns. Men to whom reverence and merriment are incongruous can be pardoned for not comprehending the apparent inconsistency in such a change of moods.

Quite as marked a characteristic, and to many as inexplicable, was his singular combination of self-confidence and self-depreciation. No doubt he was conscious of his power; otherwise he could not have used it. A great meeting, my recollection is on behalf of the freedmen, was gathered in the Brooklyn Academy of Music one evening during Andrew Johnson's presidency. The feeling in the Republican party against the President was already growing into bitterness. Mr. Beecher still defended him. The Academy was crowded. "They say," he whispered to me as I joined him on the platform, "that —— is going to attack the President to-night; if he does there will be music here before we get through." The attack was not made, and I did not hear the music — shall I confess it? — to my regret. Yet despite his self-confidence before speaking, he was never self-satisfied after speaking. On one occasion, when he had preached a sermon which involved a vigorous attack on Calvinism, and we were about to publish it in "The Christian Union," I went with him to his house after prayer-meeting on Friday evening, determined that he should revise the sermon. "There are expressions here," said I to him, "which were well enough when interpreted by your intonation, but they will have

a very different meaning in cold print. You must
revise this proof." He began; cut out here; inter-
polated there; again and again threw down the
proof in impatience; again and again I took it up
and insisted on his continuing the task. At last,
sticking the pencil through the proof with a vicious
stab, and throwing both upon the table before him,
he said, " Abbott, the thing I wanted to say, I
did n't say, and the thing I did n't want to say,
I did say, and I don't know how to preach anyhow."
Nor do I doubt he expressed the mood of the moment. He never wanted to read his own writings;
he rarely had enough patience with them to revise
them. It was not that he shirked the labor; it was
because the product so dissatisfied him.

But with all these contradictions he possessed
certain qualities which were always present and
potent, and which never changed with changing
moods. Among these were the spontaneity of his
humor, his love of beauty, the strength of his conscience, his chivalry toward women and children,
and his transparent sincerity.

He was humorous in the pulpit because he instinctively saw things in their incongruous relations, and described them as he saw them. He did
not crack a joke for the sake of making a laugh,
either in public or in private. But he could scarcely
write a letter, or carry on a conversation, without
that play of imagination, often breaking into
humor, which characterized his work in the press
and on the platform. He was at Peekskill; I was

carrying through the press an edition of his sermons; this is the letter he wrote me to tell me that he was going to Brooklyn, and that I should thereafter address him at that city: —

PEEKSKILL, October 24, 1867.

MY DEAR MR. ABBOTT, — Norwood is done — summer is done — autumn is most done. The birds are flown, leaves are flying, and I fly too — so hereafter send to Brooklyn.

Truly yours,
H. W. BEECHER.

He sent a check to a jeweler to pay for two rings, and this is the letter which went with the check: —

BROOKLYN, February 8, 1884.

JNO. A. REMICK.

DEAR SIR, — Please find check for amount of the opal ring and the moon-stone ring. They suited the respective parties.

The opal goes to my son's mother-in-law, who puts to shame the world-wide slander on mothers-in-law.

I think old maids and mothers-in-law are, in general, the very saints of the earth.

I looked to see you after the lecture, and to have a shake of the hand with Mrs. Remick. But you neither of you regarded the ceremony as "any great shakes," and decamped hastily.

Yours in the bonds of rainbows, opals, etc.,
HENRY WARD BEECHER.

The Brooklyn postmaster sent him formal notice that a letter had been returned to him from the Dead Letter Office, and got this in reply: —

OCTOBER 28, 1880.

COLONEL MCLEER.

DEAR SIR, — Your notice that a letter of mine was dead and subject to my order is before me.

We must all die! And though the premature decease of my poor letter should excite a proper sympathy (and I hope it does), yet I am greatly sustained under the affliction.

What was the date of its death? Of what did it die? Had it in its last hours proper attention and such consolation as befits the melancholy occasion? Did it have any effects?

Will you kindly see to its funeral? I am strongly inclined to cremation.

May I ask if any other letters of mine are sick — dangerously sick? If any depart this life hereafter, don't notify me until after the funeral.

Affectionately yours,

HENRY WARD BEECHER.

On April 1 he found in his morning mail a letter containing only the words "April Fool." " Well! well!" he said, " I have received many a letter where a man forgot to sign his name; this is the first time I ever knew of a writer signing his name and forgetting to write a letter." After I took the editorship of " The Christian Union" I urged him to give his views on public questions through its columns. "As it is now," I said, " any interviewer who comes to you gets a column from you; and the public is as apt to get your views in any other paper as in your own." " Yes," he said, " I am like the town pump; any one who will come and work the handle can carry off a pail full of

water." On one occasion I argued for Calvinism
that it had produced splendid characters in Scotland and in New England. "Yes," he replied,
"Calvinism makes a few good men and destroys
many mediocre men. It is like a churn; it makes
good butter, but it throws away a lot of butter-
milk." Charles Sumner in the Senate and Thaddeus Stevens in the House were pressing forward
the reconstruction measures based on forcing universal suffrage in the South. In conversation with
me Mr. Beecher thus diagnosed the situation:
"The radicals are trying to drive the wedge into
the log butt-end foremost; they will only split
their beetle." They did; they solidified the South
and divided the Republican party. If he had been
preaching on reconstruction, the figure would have
flashed on him then, and he would have given it to
his congregation from the pulpit as he did a like
humorous figure in the following instance. He was
denouncing the inconsistency of church members;
stopped; imagined an interlocutor calling him to
account for exposing the sins of church members
before the world, and thus replied to him: "Do
you not suppose the world knows them better than
I do? The world sees this church member in Wall
Street, as greedy, as rapacious, as eager, as unscrupulous as his companions. He says to himself,
'Is that Christianity? I will go to church next
Sunday and see what the minister says about this.'
He goes; and what is the minister saying?"
Then, instantly, Mr. Beecher folded one arm

across his breast, held an imaginary cat purring comfortably there, as he stroked it with the other hand, and continued: "The minister is saying, 'Poor pussy, poor pussy, poor pussy.'" Mr. Beecher made his congregation laugh not of set purpose and never for the sake of the laugh, but because he saw himself, and made them see, those incongruities which are the essence of humor and often the most powerful of arguments. And they flashed in his conversation as frequently and as brilliantly as in his public addresses.

Æsthetically Mr. Beecher was self-made. When he came to Brooklyn from life in the West, in what was essentially a border community, he brought with him both the unconventionality and the lack of cultivation which such life tends to develop. He never possessed that kind of taste which only inheritance and early training can impart. But he trained himself. His love of form and color, in flowers, in precious stones, in rugs, in household decorations, and in painting, was such as to make him no mean critic respecting them all. He built his house in Peekskill, as he once said to me, because he wanted to express himself in a home; he selected all the woods, the papers, the rugs, the various decorations; to that extent he was his own architect. While in church life I rather think that music always seemed to him the best which was the most effective vehicle for the expression of the emotional life of the congregation, he became a lover of the best music, and an habitual and thor-

oughly appreciative attendant on the Philharmonic
Concerts in Brooklyn.

But doubtless righteousness, and not beauty, was
his standard; ethics, not æsthetics, afforded the law of
his life. He would have taken the Latin *virtus*, not
the Greek τὸ καλόν, — valor, not beauty, — to express
his ideal of character. The Puritan is distinguished
by two characteristics : the strength of his conscience, and the will to impose it as a standard upon
others. Mr. Beecher had the Puritan conscience,
but he had no inclination to impose it on others.
He loved righteousness ; but he also loved liberty ;
and he believed that righteousness could never be
imposed from without, but must be wrought from
within. Nevertheless, though advocating liberty of
choice for others, the Puritan habits remained with
him to the end. He was a purist as regards all relations between the sexes. He did not play cards,
he did not smoke, and he was an habitual though
not strictly a total abstainer. In his later life he
occasionally took a glass of beer to induce sleep.
He went on rare occasions to the theatre, but, I
judge, rather seriously. In one of his letters he
speaks of studying " Hamlet " as a preparation for
seeing Irving. The theatre did not appeal to him, for
the same reason that it did not appeal to his friend
John H. Raymond, — because he had too much
imagination. The crude interpretation of character
and the cruder scenery offended and obstructed his
understanding of the play.

This Puritan conscience was mated to a spirit of

chivalry, and both were aroused and inflamed by
the treatment to which slavery subjected a poor
and ignorant race. He always sympathized with
the unfortunate. And this was not the professional
sympathy of the reformer. Traveling one day, he
came to a station where the passengers were to
change cars. All his fellow passengers were hast-
ening to get good seats in the adjoining train. A
woman with three children, and packages to corre-
spond, was helplessly waiting for her chance. Mr.
Beecher, standing on the station platform, took
hold of both railings of the car, braced himself
against the crowd, and said, " Is no gentleman going to help this poor woman to a seat ? " The word
was enough ; the crowd responded ; and the woman
found half a dozen willing hands to help her. Mr.
Beecher's old-fashioned courtesy to his wife, and
his chivalric attitude toward women in general, was
not less noteworthy, though it has been less noted,
than his love for little children.

No one, I think, who knew Mr. Beecher at all
intimately ever doubted his sincerity. He never
pretended ; I do not think he had the capacity to
carry a pretense out to a successful issue. He
practiced what he preached ; and he was powerful
as a preacher primarily because his preaching was
the sincere and simple expression of himself. His
literal interpretation of Christ's teaching concerning
the forgiveness of enemies has been often ridiculed
as impossible. To many men I doubt not that it is
impossible ; to him it was natural. Some year or two

after his public trial, Mr. Moulton, whose treachery had first deceived him as to the facts, and then betrayed him into writing those letters which were the only ground on which any suspicion against him was based, became involved in financial difficulties. With moistened eyes, Mr. Beecher said to me, " I wish I could help him; I would gladly loan him the money to extricate himself, but I suppose I could not. He would not understand it, — no one would understand it." And he was right. No one would have understood it. The humor, the imagination, the righteous indignation, the pleading, forgiving love of Mr. Beecher, were none of them assumed or excited for a purpose; none of them belonged to the platform or the pulpit. They were his very self.

I lean back in my chair. I close my eyes. The years that have elapsed are erased. I am sitting in the gallery pew. It is 1858. A Southern slaveholder is at my side. The preacher has declared, as he often did, that he has no will to interfere with slavery in the states; no wish to stir up insurrection and discontent in the slave. Thereupon he pictures the discontented slave escaping; portrays him stealthily creeping out from his log cabin at night; seeking a shelter in the swamp; feeding on its roots and berries; pursued by baying bloodhounds; making his way toward liberty, the North Star his only guide; reaching the banks of the Ohio River; crossing it to find the Fugitive-Slave Law spread like a net to catch him. And I see the fugitive, and hear the hounds, and my own heart beats with his hopes and fears; and then the preacher cries, " Has he a right to flee ? If he were my son and did not seek liberty I would write across his name, Disowned," and he writes it with his finger as he speaks, and I see the letters of flaming fire; and the slaveholder at my side catches his breath while he nods an involuntary assent; and as we walk out together, he says, " I could not agree with all he said, but it was great, and he is a good man."

Yes. He was a good man and a great one. Not without errors. Not without faults. But in his love for God and his love for his fellow men a good man; in his interpretation of the nature of God and the duty of man to God and to his fellow men a great man, with a clearness of vision and a courage in application which not many of us attain.

APPENDIX

APPENDIX

THE analysis of Paul's Seventh Chapter of Romans is taken from "The Christian Union," in which it was printed in March, 1887, at the time of Mr. Beecher's death, from the original manuscript in my possession. The statement of Mr. Beecher's theological views as given by him to his brethren in the ministry at the time of his withdrawal from the New York and Brooklyn Association, is here reprinted from the "Life of Henry Ward Beecher," by Lyman Abbott and S. B. Halliday. The Bibliography has been prepared by the Rev. William E. Davenport, of Brooklyn, to whom I am also indebted for other valuable information. I also acknowledge my indebtedness to the Rev. Horace Porter, of Montclair, New Jersey, for reading this volume in manuscript, verifying dates and incidents, and preparing the Index; and to the Rev. Ernest Hamlin Abbott for seeing the book through the press.

LYMAN ABBOTT.

PAUL'S THEOLOGY

AN UNPUBLISHED MANUSCRIPT ON ROMANS, CHAP. VII

By Henry Ward Beecher

[THE following notes are here printed from "The Christian Union Supplement," March 17, 1887, both as an illustration of the thoroughness of Mr. Beecher's study of the Bible and the method of his preparation for certain forms of public discourse. They formed the basis of an address before a clerical association; the date of this address I am not able to give.]

I AM to discuss verses 17, 20, and 25, in the seventh chapter of Romans (quote). Here are three distinct statements on one and the same *personal experience*.

Is the chapter to be taken literally?

Is it the experience of Paul?

Is it a universal experience of all Christians?

What is the theory of sin and responsibility?

What is Paul's theory of relief from a sense of guilt, in Christ?

Paul and *Paul's countrymen* must be understood, or we cannot interpret Romans.

Paul was a *poet* and a *dramatist*. The substance of his writing was fact, the form dramatic and in places poetic. He was not a conscious artist. As the meteoric elements, when they meet the rush of this world's atmosphere, fuse and burn, so whatever touched the soul of Paul became incandescent. The whole Book of Romans is an argument in a kind of intermitting drama, and no one can follow its course with only dictionary, grammar, and logic. To these must be added sympathy with an impetuous moral nature, whose mind *acted by intuition* — a mind that, rushing toward a goal, saw and often was detained by side-lights ; whose thoughts were opalescent, flashing, full of heavenly color.

The Book of Romans was not Paul's exposition of religion *at large*, only of so much of Christ's religion as was needful to his purposes. Romans is a grand special plea ! His audience, his countrymen ! His aim, to persuade them to new and higher methods of righteousness than they possessed. He never denies that they were seeking the right ends, but only by methods which could never insure it. Instead of a ritual, he proposed a person. Instead of conformity to a system of rules, he presented the inspiration of love. Instead of Moses dead, he presented Christ alive. His was a spiritual psychology, producing morality, not a morality hoping to blossom into spirituality.

But, Romans derives its structure full as much from what the *Jews were* as from what Paul was. It was an argument of persuasion aimed at the peculiarities of his countrymen. Abstract thought, in which order follows logical association, was not his method. He followed the minds of the men to whom he wrote. Like a surgeon, he watched the face and pulse of the patient at every motion of the knife.

Romans is not Christianity relative to its own self, i. e. in a complete scientific analysis ; but Christianity relative to the state of high-minded and conscientious Jews.

It assumes that Mosaic Jews and Christian Jews had a common ground, viz. *personal righteousness.*

The argument, then, is to demonstrate the superiority of Christ's method over that of Moses, and only so much of Christian philosophy is used as is needful for that.

The peculiarity of Jews.

1. He had before him the *best men*. He wrote to serve high purpose, deep moral conviction, sincere and earnest proofs.

2. But they were utterly blinded by *spiritual conceit*.

1. They believed they had fulfilled every condition of legal obedience.

That God was bound by His covenant to bestow certain great advantages upon them.

That these promises or honors He was precluded from bestowing on others, except they entered the nation *through the door of proselytizing*.

Romans is an argument addressed to profoundly earnest and conscientious men to convince them that they were not as good as they thought, nor possessed of the privileges they supposed, nor superior to other nations; to persuade them to try another and superior method. It was a tremendous task; it is a magnificent oration. It leaves Demosthenes far behind in grandeur of its subject, in profound materials, in grasp, and scope, and the fine finish of Cicero compares with it as the Chinese dwarf oaks with the live-oak of Carolina.

If the seventh of Romans is a logical and scientific statement we must accept the following statement : —

1. That there is a flesh-man and a spirit-man — an actual dual-man.

2. That these are distinctly at war with each other; and that through life it is an unsettled conflict.

3. That the two men, one under different laws, have separate and different characters; are so different, that the one may sin and the other be pure and blameless.

In other words, that sin does not run through, or sin in one part of a man does not involve in guilt the whole man.

4. That the " I " can retreat from the lower man and

sit apart and above, and rejoice, while the under man is sorrowing.

5. That sin is a substance, like soot in a chimney, or fungus on a plant, or a tapeworm in the stomach, a burglar in a man's house. Vs. 17 : "*Now it is no more I that do it, but sin that dwelleth in me.*"

6. Yet in 25th verse, it is stated that the flesh is part of the "I," and that the *personality* serves the law of sin.

7. The seventh of Romans is no more dramatic than the two preceding chapters, or the eighth of Romans. They are a remarkable mixture of the abstract and concrete; of feeling, imagination and fact; as simple statement and as metaphor. To interpret them by a scientific method would be as preposterous as to apply logarithm to Milton's *Allegro*, or *Il Penseroso*. We must go out into life, we must go within, to others' and our own experience, for a quick and real comprehension.

Especially one must have the sensibility to poetry.

8. Sin becomes a *power*, a conspirator and tempter.

9. A petite drama is flashed forth. A man is alive and walking in security. The commandant lying in ambush attacks him, Sin springs up as [he] passes a covert. He is slain !

10. A kind of Greek chorus comes in, a *didactic* statement of the *purpose* of the law. But, in an instant Sin becomes a person, a bandit springs up behind the law, and slays him !

12. Another chorus.

13. A strain of quasi argument.

14. *Ditto.*

15–19. A *battle* in Civil War, in which the various parts of the soul must face in conflict.

20–22. Chorus and recitation which suddenly flows forth again in vs. 23, 24 into poetic vision !

25. In a burst of feeling, he anticipates and overleaps the argument, snatches, as it were, a verse from the 8th, and yet with the cry of victory on his lips, he resumes the statement, and a wonderful statement it is (vs. 25).

Two departments in one man! Obedience reigns in one and disobedience in the other.

Under this opalescent and shifting scene, what may be regarded as Paul's psychology, if he could be kept cool long enough to make a scientific statement.

1. What is the scope of meaning in *sarx*.

It is used by Paul (1 Cor. xv. 39) to signify *flesh* — meat.

2. The body, organized physical frame, as distinguished from the spirit — 1 Cor. v. 5; Rom. ix. 8.

3. The *appetites and passions* which *strictly pertain to physical functions*.

It is in this sense that Paul uses the phrase in his argument respecting sin and guilt.

We have, in Gal. v. 19–21, *first*, *group* of *four*, *amatory sin ; second*, sins of *combativeness and destructiveness ;* third group, sins of eating and drinking — appetite; *heresies*, i. e., *factions, witchcraft and emulations*, only two not directly for passions, but they are in life so profoundly associated with the appetites and passions, that they may well be classed with them.

It is inconceivable that Paul should have meant to say that in *his flesh he could serve the law of sin* in this overt and fruitful way, while at the same time his nobler self was serving God! Nay, in Gal. v. 24, he expressly says : " *They that are Christ's have crucified the flesh with the affections and lusts.*"

But, it is conceivable, and it stands to nature, that a man's reason, conscience, and choice may be united and fixed; that they may overawe and restrain the bodily appetites and passions, and may direct the whole being toward things pure and right, and yet not to be able to withdraw from the passions, the powers of suggestion and impulse ; or even, at unwatchful moments, outbreak. The soul is kept in fear and trembling, knowing that conspirators are concealed in him. At any hour insurrection may break forth. The rebellious province is subdued, but not pacified nor won over to allegiance.

What then? When one has given his love and conscience over to a living friend, and honestly, earnestly, and intensely, seeks to fulfill his wishes, these motives of the passions, their involuntary impulses, their momentary outbreak, are not to be counted as unsettling the character, not as changing the direction from evil to good, from the flesh to the spirit, from self to Christ, and in *the judicatory of love*, they are testimonies rather of the fealty and fidelity of the soul. The instant restraint, the condemnation poured upon the evil, is a stronger proof of faithful love than would be an easy, even love, that had no tasks, no self-denial. In all this it must be borne in mind, that the question in debate is not the abstract question, whether *the casual and restricted passions and impulses* are not *violations of law* — but, whether the existence of such an experience is *inconsistent with peace of mind*.

The Apostle argues — that under the Mosaic system, as held by the best of his contemporaries with a perception of the spiritually felt law, a system of external obedience, there could never be a *sense of perfect obedience*. The ideal law will always leave actual life in the vocative.

But, under a reign of love, the whole flow and tendency of life is counted, and the incidental defections are thrown out and *not counted*. So that as a child with many faults, yet seeking to obey his parents, may be made very happy at home, so when we *become sons of*

God in a faith that works by love, disallowed sins *do not count*.

In view of this exposition:

1. Is this Paul's personal experience?
    1. He doubtless has had similar.
    2. But, *he personifies a struggle* of thousands.
2. Is it *a universal* experience?
    1. The substance matter, the elementary experiences, belong to all who seek the godly life.
    2. But they are not collected, unbattled, and brought into conscious conflict.
    3. Only in cases where the man *seeks peace*, from obedience and not from trust in love. It is the distinctive experience of *Conscience and Intellect* dealing *with real or ideal law*.

THEOLOGICAL STATEMENT

[THE theological statement here printed was given by
Mr. Beecher at a regular meeting of the New York and
Brooklyn Association of Congregational Ministers, held
October 11, 1882. It was extemporaneous, was taken
down in shorthand, and was published from the shorthand writer's report, except that portion relating to the
Atonement. For the occasion of this address, see pages
321, 322. After some autobiographic reminiscences respecting the spiritual experiences out of which his theology had grown, Mr. Beecher proceeded as follows.]

IN order to make this a little more plain, to throw
a little light on the operation of my mind, I came
to think finally that there are three fundamental ideas
of doctrine. That is to say, doctrine may be regarded
as fundamental from three standpoints. First, from the
standpoint of theology. Many things are fundamental
to a system of theology, necessary to complete the whole
chain of thinking from the beginning clear around to
the end. The most complete, interlinked, compact, and
self-consistent theology in the world is the Calvinistic —
the higher you go the better it is, as a purely metaphy-
sical and logical concatenation. Many doctrines are
fundamental to this system which are by no means
necessary to Christian life and character. A man may
be a good Christian who accepts or rejects many of the
doctrines of Calvinism. Then, secondly, you may look
at fundamental doctrines from the standpoint of ecclesiastical organization. There are a great many things

that are indispensable to the existence of a church that are not necessary to the piety of the individual member of that church. You take the Roman system. Fundamentalism there means not so much systematic theology as it does the truth necessary to the maintenance and influence of the Church as God's abode on earth; and you might take or reject a great many theological points in that system, provided you stuck to the Church and held to it firmly.

Now comes a question which I have always regarded as of special importance, viz. What doctrines are fundamental to the formation of Christian character and to its complete development? There are many things that are necessary to a system of theology that are not necessary to the conviction or conversion of men. I have called those things fundamental which were necessary for the conviction of sin, for conversion from sin, for development of faith, for dominant love of the Lord Jesus Christ, and for the building up of a Christlike character. That dispenses with a great many doctrines that are necessary for a theological system, or for an ecclesiastical system. Now, let me go into details.

A PERSONAL GOD

And, first, I believe in God, and never for a moment have faltered in believing in a personal God, as distinguished from a pantheistic God, whether it is the coarser Pantheism of materialism, believing that the material universe is God, or from the more subtle view of Matthew Arnold, who holds that God is nothing but a tendency in the universe — a something that is not me that tends toward righteousness. Well, he can love such a God, but I cannot. I would rather chew thistledown all summer long than to work with any such idea as that. I mean personal, not as if He were like us, but personal in such a sense as that those that know personality in men cannot make any mistake in attempting to grasp and conceive of God. He is more than man in the operation of the intellect, larger in all the moral relations, infinitely deeper and sweeter in the affections. In all those elements, notwithstanding He is so much larger than men that no man by searching can find Him out to perfection, yet the humblest person can conceive that there is such a Being. They know in a general way what the Being is, and that He is a personal Being, and accessible as other persons are accessible, to the thoughts, the feelings, the wants, the cares of men. So I have believed and so I do believe. Then as to the controversy as to the knowable and unknowable; I believe on both sides. It is not usual that I am on both sides of any question at the same time; but I am here. I believe that there are elements that are distinctly knowable in quality but not in quantity, in nature but not in scope. I believe that when you say that God can do so and so, or cannot do so and so, you are all at sea. What God can do and what God cannot do in the immensity of His being lies beyond the grasp of human thought. The attributes are but alphabetic letters. We spell a few simple sentences. But the greatness, the majesty, the scope, the variety that is in Him we cannot compute. It will break upon us when we shall see Him as He is, and not through the imperfection of human analogies and experiences. I thank God that there is so much that is unknowable. When Columbus discovered America he did know that he had discovered a continent, but he did not know its contents, what the mountain ranges were, nor what or where the rivers were, nor the lakes, nor the inhabitants. Yet he did know he had made the discovery of the continent. And I know God so that I walk with Him as with a companion, I whisper to Him, I believe that He imparts thoughts to me and feelings, and yet when you ask me: "Can you describe Him? Can you make an inventory of His attributes?" I cannot. I thank God He so transcends anything we know of Him that God is unknowable. People say, "Some may believe this, but can you prove it?" Suppose I were to have said in my youthful days to the woman of my choice, my honored wife, "I love you," and she handed me a slate and pencil and said, "Be kind enough to demonstrate that, will you?" She would not have been my wife if she had. Are not the finest feelings that you know those that are unsusceptible of demonstration? Certainly by analysis, description, language. Are not those things that make you not only different from the animal, but from the men around about you, that lift you into a higher atmosphere, — do they not transcend any evidence that the sense can give? And is not that the instruction that runs through all of Paul's writings?

So I hold and so I have taught of God. Not seeable, not known by the senses, the full circuit of His being not discerned except by moral intuition, by the range of susceptibility, when the down-shining of the Holy Ghost comes to me I know, by an evidence within myself that is unspeakably more convincing to me than eye, or hand, or ear can be, that there is a God and that He is my God!

THE TRINITY

I accept without analysis the tri-personality of God. I accept the Trinity; perhaps because I was educated in it. No matter why, I accept it. Are there any difficulties in it? I should like to know if there are any great questions of the structure of the universe, of the nature of mind, that do not run you into difficulties when you go a little way in them. But I hold that while I cannot analyze and localize into distinct elements, as it were, the three Persons of the Trinity, I hold them — the Father, the Son, and the Holy Ghost. The theories, such as, for instance, in part are hinted in the Nicene Creed and outspun with amazing ignorance of knowledge in the Athanasian Creed, I do not believe. The Athanasian Creed is gigantic spider-web weaving. I leave it to those who want to get stuck on it, but the simple declaration that God exists in unity and yet in the tri-fold personality, I accept. A man says, " Do you believe there can be three in one?" Yes, I do. It is not contrary either to reason or to the analogies in nature. The first forms of life, the lowest, are found to be absolutely simple and unitary. Every step of development in the succession of animal life is toward complexity, — complexity of functions, of organs, of powers and faculties, — and when we reach the higher animals the complexity of mental traits is discovered, — animal passions, then social instincts, affections, moral sentiments, — until in civilized man we find a being composed not only of multitudes of parts, but of groups, so that unity is made up by whole families of faculties. I can conceive that in a higher range of being unity may be comprised of persons, as in the lower it is made up of groups of faculties. It is not proof of trinity in unity, but it dissipates the notion that three may not be one. I do not say it is so, but it runs right along and in the line of analogies of nature, and predisposes one to accept the implication of the New Testament as to the mode of Divine existence. As to any attempt to divide the functions, — the Father to His function, the Son to another department, and the Holy Ghost to yet another function, — leave it to those who are better informed than I am.

FAITH IN CHRIST

But let me say first, that while there are, of course, no doubts as to the existence of God the Father in any Christian sect, there have been grave doubts as to the divinity of Christ; but not in my mind. I believe fully, enthusiastically, without break, pause, or aberration, in the divinity of Christ. I believe that Christ is God manifest in the flesh. Is the whole of God in Christ? Well, that is asking me, Can infinity be inclosed in the finite? What I understand by His laying aside His glory is that Christ when He came under the limitations of time and space and flesh was limited by them. I am limited. You are limited. If you go down into the Five Points to talk with men, you lay aside at home two thirds of that which is best in you. You cannot bring it before such persons. You are limited by the condition of their minds. In other words, it is quite possible that even God, though I know not how, should manifest Himself under limitations at times, and that the whole power and knowledge and glory of God should not appear during His earth life. During His life He made Himself a man, not being ashamed to be called a brother. He went through the identical experiences that men go through. He was born. He was a baby, with no more knowledge than a baby has; a youth, with no more knowledge than a youth has. He grew in stature. He grew in knowledge. I believe that Christ Himself, at times, had the consciousness of His full being. There were days when it seemed as though the heavens opened and He saw the whole of Himself and felt His whole power. But the substance of His being was divine, and He was God manifest in the flesh. That is my faith, and I never swerved from it. And I can go farther and say I cannot pray to the Father except through Christ. I pray to Christ. I must.

The way the Spirit of God works with me makes it necessary that I should have something that I can clasp, and to me the Father is vague. I believe in a Father, but the definition of Him in my vision, is not to me what the portraiture of Christ is. Though I say Father, I am thinking of Christ all the time. That is my feeling, that is my life, and so I have preached, so I have taught those that came from Unitarian instruction — never asking them to a technical argument or proof, but simply saying, "You say you can pray to the Father, but cannot to Christ. You are praying to Christ; you don't know it. That which you call Father is that which is interpreted in Christ. Since the Godhead has three doors of approach to our apprehension, it makes no difference through which our souls enter."

THE HOLY SPIRIT

Then I believe next in the Holy Ghost, or the Holy Spirit, as one of the persons of the Godhead. And in regard to that I believe that the influence, the Divine influence, the quickening, stimulating influence of the mind of God proceeds from the Holy Ghost, and that it is universal, constant, immanent. The body of man receives all the stimulus it needs from the organized physical world—feeds itself, maintains itself; the social affections receive all the stimulus and impulse they need from society; but whatever in man reaches toward holiness—aspiration, love of truth, justice, purity —that feeds upon the spiritual nature and is developed by the down-shining of the Holy Ghost. And as the sunlight is the father of every flower that blossoms, — though no flower would blossom if he had not separate organized existence in the plant on which it shines, — so "work out your own salvation with fear and trembling, for it is God that worketh in you," describes the working of the

Divine Spirit in producing right affections and good works in man.

PROVIDENCE

I hold and I teach that there is a general and a special providence of God which overrules human life by and through natural laws; but, also, I believe that there is an overruling and special providence of God in things pertaining to human life as well as to the life of the world by the direct action of His own will, by such a use of laws in the first place upon us, — such a use as may not be known to us, but is perfectly known to God, — by such a use of natural laws as is wisely adapted to effect needed results. A great thinker can employ natural laws to create conditions of life that did not exist before, to change public sentiment, to repress indolence, to stimulate activity. Every man that is acting in the world is employing natural laws with cunning, with wisdom, with skill, by which he is enabled to change the whole course and current of things. God stands behind the whole system of natural laws and can produce special results in men whenever He pleases. Such a doctrine of the special influence of the Spirit of God makes prayer of benefit to man. I believe millions of prayers are not answered and that millions are — some directly, some indirectly. Man has the feeling and should have the feeling : "I have a right to carry myself and all that concerns me to God ; it is not in vain that I pray to Him." I believe in the efficacy of prayer, partly by its moral reaction upon us, to be sure, but a great deal more by direct answer from God. I believe, then, in Divine Providence ; I believe in prayer, and out of the same view of God I believe in

MIRACLES

I believe miracles are possible now; they not only were

possible, but were real in the times gone by, — especially the two great miracles that began and ended the Christian dispensation — the miraculous conception of Christ and His resurrection from the dead. When I give those up the two columns on which the house stands will have to fall to the ground. Being of scientific tastes, believing in evolution, believing in the whole scheme of natural laws, I say they are reconcilable with the true theory of miracles.

I wrote in a book when I came to Brooklyn: "I foresee there is to be a period of great unbelief; now I am determined so to preach as to lay a foundation, when the flood comes, on which men can build;" and I have thus, as it were, been laboring for the Gentiles, not for the Jews, in the general drift of my ministry.

REGENERATION

Man is a being created in imperfection and seeking a full development. I believe him to be sinful, — universally man is sinful, — but I do not believe he is totally depraved. I believe that to be a misleading phrase. But no man ever lived, and no man ever will live, that was only a man, that was not a sinner; and he is a sinner not simply by infirmity, though much of that which is called sin is but infirmity, but he is a sinner to such an extent that he needs to be transferred out of his natural state into a higher and spiritual state. He needs to be born again. If any man believes in the doctrine of the sinfulness of man I do, and I have evidence of it every day, and if ever a man believed in being born again, I believe in that. The degree of sinfulness in men, I have always taught, is dependent on a variety of circumstances. Some persons are far less sinful than others. It is far easier for some to rise into the spiritual kingdom than for others. Heredity has a powerful influence. The circumstances that surround men by their influence lift some very high and leave others comparatively low. God judges men according to their personal and their actual condition.

[Here a member of the Association asked if a man needed to be regenerated for anything beside his personal sin.]

He needs to be regenerated to become a man. I hold that man is first an animal, and that then he is a social animal. He is not a full man and a religious being until he is lifted into that higher realm in which he walks with God. And every man needs to be lifted into that high estate, partly by parental instruction; by the secondary or reflected light of Christianity upon the morals, customs, and spirit of the age in which he lives, some men are lifted nearer the threshold. There is not a man born that does not need to be born again, and it is a work which is as impossible to men as it is for a person to come suddenly to education, to knowledge, simply by a volition. No man can ever lift himself up so. It is not within human power; it is within the power of a man to put himself under instructors and grow up into education, but I hold man has not the power to regenerate himself. He is under the stimulating influence of the present and immanent Spirit of God which is striving with every man; when he will open his mind to receive Divine influence every man is helped, and the act of surrender to God and entrance into the spiritual kingdom are the joint act of the man willing and wishing and the coöperative influence of the Spirit of God enabling him.

INSPIRATION OF THE BIBLE

As to the inspiration of the Bible, let me say that with a few exceptions I can accept the chapter in the

Confession of Faith on that subject, which I think to be a very admirable compend. I will read it : —

"Although the light of nature and the works of creation and Providence do so far manifest the goodness, wisdom, and power of God as to leave men inexcusable, yet they are not sufficient to give that knowledge of God and of His will, which is necessary unto salvation ; therefore it pleased the Lord, at sundry times and in divers manners, to reveal Himself and to declare that His will unto His church ; and afterward, for the better preserving and propagating of the truth, and for the more sure establishment and comfort of the church against the corruption of the flesh and the malice of Satan and of the world, to commit the same wholly unto writing ; which maketh the Holy Scripture to be most necessary ; those former ways of God's revealing His will unto His people being now ceased."

That is my theory. The Bible is the record of the steps of God in revealing Himself and His will to man. The inspiration was originally upon the generation, upon the race ; and then what was gained step by step was gathered up, as this says, and put into writing, for the better preservation of it. "It pleased the Lord, at sundry times and in divers manners to reveal Himself and to declare that His will unto the church ; and afterward, for the better preserving and propagating of the truth, and for the more sure establishment and comfort of the church against the corruption of the flesh and the malice of Satan and of the world, to commit the same wholly unto writing." I do not want any better definition of my view of inspiration — that is, inspiration of men, not inspiration of a book — and that the book is the record of that inspiration that has been taking place from generation to generation. [Reading] "The authority of the Holy Scripture, for which it ought to be believed and obeyed dependeth not upon the testimony of any man or church, but wholly upon God (who is truth itself), the author thereof; and therefore it is to be received, because it is the word of God." I have no objections to make to that. [Reading] "We may be moved and induced by the testimony of the church to a high and reverend esteem for the Holy Scripture; and the heavenliness of the matter, the efficacy of the doctrine, the majesty of the style, the consent of all the parts, the scope of the whole (which is to give all glory to God), the full discovery it makes of the only way of man's salvation, the many other incomparable excellences, and the entire perfection thereof, are arguments whereby it doth abundantly evidence itself to be the word of God; yet, notwithstanding our full persuasion and assurance of the infallible truth and divine authority thereof, is from the inward work of the Holy Spirit, bearing witness by and with the word, in our hearts." External arguments are good, that says, but the witness of God in your own soul is the best evidence. I believe that. No man can wrest the Bible from me. I know from the testimony of God in my moral sense. [Reading] "The whole counsel of God concerning all things necessary for His own glory." I do not believe that. Who knows what is necessary for God's glory? "Man's salvation." I believe that. The whole counsel of God concerning all things necessary for man's salvation, faith and life, "is either expressly set down in Scripture or by good and necessary consequence may be deduced from Scripture; unto which nothing at any time is to be added, whether by new revelations of the Spirit or traditions of men." Yes, I might believe that. I believe it with an addendum. "Nevertheless we acknowledge the inward illumination of the Spirit of God to be necessary for the saving understanding of such

things as are revealed in the world." That settles that
little question. It is the moral consciousness. It is the
man as he is instructed by knowledge, and then inflamed
or rendered sensitive by the Spirit of God that sits in
judgment upon the word of God. Talk about our not
being allowed to come to the Bible with our reason.
That is the only way we can go. Is a man to come with
his ignorance, through a council or somebody else's
thinking? Must we not use our reason to know what the
word of God is? When a man says, "You must not
dilute the word of God by any thinking of your own;
you must not translate the Bible or construct the doctrines of the Bible except by the Bible itself," then I
will turn and catechize that man, saying, "Will you be
kind enough to tell me from the Bible alone what a lion
is?" You cannot. "Will you be kind enough to define
from the Bible what a mountain is?" You cannot.
"Will you, out of the Bible, define a river, an eagle, a
sparrow, a flower, a king, a mother, a child?" You
cannot do it. What do you do? You go right to the
thing itself outside of the Bible. When you see a flower,
you know what the Bible means when it says a flower.
In all things that are cognizable by man's senses, he
finds what is the thing spoken of in the Bible by going
to the thing itself, outside of the Bible. It is absurd to
say that the Bible must be its own sole expounder.
Now, that which is true in respect to miracles, — in
respect to the whole economy of human life, — is it not
also true in respect to the man himself and his own
individual experience? A man says, "You must not
undertake to dictate to the word of God what conversion is." I should like to know how I am going to find
it out except by seeing it? I go to the thing itself.
Then I understand what is meant by it. And so far
from not going outside of the Bible to interpret it, no

man can interpret it without a knowledge of what lies outside of it. That is the very medium through which any man comes to understand it.

(Dr. H. M. Storrs.) You used the sentence just now, "We are not to substitute our reason for the Word of God?"

(Mr. Beecher.) Yes, and in using it, I say you are not confined to the mere comparison of texts. You have a right to go out to things that lie within the reach of human knowledge, and study outward things spoken of, and then come back to the Bible with a better understanding of what the Bible teaches. Well, I shall not have time to say much more; but, in the main, with such modifications as will be clearly understood now by what I have said, I accept the first chapter in the Confession of Faith of the Presbyterian Church as being a very wise and very full and very admirable definition of my views of the Bible.

ATONEMENT

[Mr. Beecher had spoken an hour and a half before reaching this topic. It became impracticable for the reporter to reduce it to writing both because he had become weary with the long session, and because the speaker was interrupted by a multitude of questions from all parts of the house. Mr. Beecher has been obliged to write out his views for publication without regard to the reporter's copy.]

The New Testament, instead of discussing the Atonement, — the word is but once used in the New Testament, — confines itself to the setting forth of Christ, His nature, power, relations, and commands. We hear nothing of a " plan,"of an " arrangement," of a " scheme of salvation," of any " atonement," but everything of Christ's work. I am accustomed to say that Christ is in Himself the Atonement, that He is set forth in His life, teaching, suffering, death, resurrection, and heavenly glory, as empowered to forgive sin and to transform men into a new and nobler life who know sin and accept Him in full and loving trust. He is set forth as one prepared and empowered to save men, to remit the penalty of past sins, and to save them from the dominion of sin. It is not necessary to salvation that men should know how Christ was prepared to be a Saviour. It is He Himself that is to be accepted, and not the philosophy of His nature or work. I employ the term Christ for that which systematic writers call the Atonement. But Christ is not merely a historic name. It is a group of attributes, a group of qualities, a character, a divine nature in full life and activity among men. When we accept Christ, we yield love and allegiance to that character, to those qualities, deeds, and dispositions which make his name " to be above every name." The idea of faith is such an acceptance of Christ's heavenly dispositions as shall reorganize our character and draw us into a likeness to Him. When it is said that there is none other name given under heaven whereby men can be saved, I understand it to be a declaration that man's exit from sinful life and entrance into a spiritual life, can only be through a new inspiration — a new birth — into these divine elements. What Christ was, man must become; the way and the life He was. It is by the way of those qualities that every man must rise into a regenerated state. Christ is to the soul a living person full of grace, mercy, and truth ; of love that surpasses all human experiences or ideals (it passes understanding) a love that is patient, forgiving, self-sacrificing, sorrowing and suffering not for its own but for others' sins and sinful tendencies. Christ is a living actor moving among men in purity, truth, justice, and love, not for His own sake, not seeking His own glory, but seeking to open, both by His person, presence, actions, words, and fidelity, the spiritual kingdom of God to men's understandings — in short, it is the moral nature of God manifest in the flesh — to "follow" Him, to "learn of" Him, to become His "disciple" or pupil, to "put on the Lord Jesus Christ," to be "hid in Him," to have not our own natural rectitude, but "that rectitude or righteousness which is by faith in Him," to assume His "yoke and burden" — all these and a multitude of other terms clearly interpret the meaning of faith in Christ, or receiving Christ.

I do not teach that this heart of Christ presented to men "gives them power to become the sons of God;" that the ordinary human understanding could of itself develop the energy which is needed for the revolution of human character and life. I teach that there is a power behind it — the stimulating, enlightening, inspiring spirit of God — the Holy Ghost — and that this view of Christ, when set home upon men by the Holy Spirit, this development of the Divine nature in Christ, "is the wisdom of God and the power of God unto salvation." It is asked whether I limit the effect of Christ's life and death to its relation to man, and whether it had no relation to the unseen world, to the law of God in heavenly places, to the administration of justice through the ages. In reply I would say, that I cannot conceive of the emergence from heaven of such a being as Christ, upon such a mission, without its having relations to the procedures of the unseen world. There are some passages of Scripture that bear strongly to that view. But whatever necessity there was for Christ's sacrifice apart from its influence on man, and whatever effect it may have had on Divine government, that part of the truth is left unexplained in the Word of God. If alluded to, as I am inclined to think it is, it is left without expansion or solution. The Scrip-

tures declare that the suffering of Christ secured the remission of sins. They do not say how it secures it. The
fact is stated, but not the reason or philosophy of it. The
Apostles continually point to Christ's sufferings — they
inspire hope because Christ has suffered ; they include
in their commission that their joyful errand is to an-
nounce remission of sins by reason of Christ's work.
But nowhere do I see any attempt to reach those questions of modern theology, — *Why* was it necessary ? *How*
did his suffering open a way for sinners ? I regard the
statement in Romans iii. 20–26 as covering the ground
which I hold, and as including all that is known.

"Therefore by the deeds of the law there shall no
flesh be justified in His sight : for by the law is the
knowledge of sin. But now the righteousness of God
without the law is manifested, being witnessed by the
law and the prophets ; even the righteousness of God
which is by faith of Jesus Christ unto all and upon all
them that believe : for there is no difference : for all have
sinned and come short of the glory of God ; being justified freely by His grace through the redemption that is
in Christ Jesus : whom God hath set forth to be a pro-
pitiation through faith in His blood, to declare His righteousness for the remission of sins that are past, through
the forbearance of God ; To declare, I say, at this time
his righteousness : that He might be just, and the justi-
fier of him which believeth in Jesus."

That part of Christ's mission, or that part of the
Atonement, if one choose that phrase, which flames
through all the New Testament, and which can be understood, is that moral power which it exerts and those
effects which, through the Holy Spirit, are produced
by it.

[At this point the report is resumed.]

FUTURE PUNISHMENT

I will say a few words on the subject of eschatology. I believe in the teaching of the Scripture that conduct and character in this life produce respectively beneficial or detrimental effects, both in the life that now is and in the life that is to come; and that a man dying is not in the same condition on the other side, whether he be bad or whether he be good; but that consequences follow and go over the border; and that the nature of the consequences of transgression — that is, such transgression as alienates the man from God and from the life that is in God — such consequences are so large, so dreadful, that every man ought to be deterred from venturing upon them. They are so terrible as to constitute the foundation of urgent motives and appeal on the side of fear, holding men back from sin, or inspiring them with the desire of righteousness. That far I hold that the Scriptures teach explicitly. Beyond that I do not go, on the authority of the Scriptures. I have my own philosophical theories about the future life; but what is revealed to my mind is simply this : The results of a man's conduct reach over into the other world on those that are persistently and inexcusably wicked, and man's punishment in the life to come is of such a nature and of such dimensions as ought to alarm any man and put him off from the dangerous ground and turn him toward safety. I do not think we are authorized by the Scriptures to say that it is endless in the sense in which we ordinarily employ that term. So much for that, and that is the extent of my authoritative teaching on that subject.

FAREWELL

Now, Christian brethren, allow me to say that these views which I have opened to you, and which of course, in preaching in the pulpit, take on a thousand various forms, under differing illustrations, and for the different purposes for which I am preaching — allow me to say these views have not been taken up suddenly. I might as well say my hair was suddenly got up for the occasion, or that my bones I got manufactured because I wanted to go somewhere. Why, they are part of my life and growth. I have not varied in the general line or direction from the beginning to this day — like a tree that grows and diversifies its branches, but is the same tree, the same nature. So I teach now with more fullness and with more illustrations and in a clearer light what I taught forty years ago. It is not from love of novelty that I vary in anything. I do not love novelty as such, but I do love truth. I am inclined to sympathize with the things that have been : reverence for the past lies deep in my nature. It has not been from any desire to separate myself from the teachings of my brethren in the Christian ministry. I should rather a thousand times go with them than go against them, though if I am called to go against them I have the courage to do it, no matter what the consequences may be. I have endeavored, through stormy times, through all forms of excitement, to make known what was the nature of God and what He expected human life to be, and to bring to bear upon that one point every power and influence in me. I have nothing that I kept back — neither reason, nor wit, nor humor, nor experience, nor moral sensibility, nor social affection. I poured my whole being into the ministry with this one object : to glorify God by lifting man up out of the natural state into the pure spiritual life. In doing this I have doubtless alienated a great many. The door has been shut, and sympathy has been withheld. I have reason to believe that a great many of the brethren of the Congregational faith would speak more than disapproval, and that many even in the association to which I belong feel as though they could not bear the burden of responsibility of being supposed to tolerate the views I have held and taught, and as a man of honor and a Christian gentleman I cannot afford to lay on anybody the responsibility of my views. I cannot afford especially to put them in such a position that they are obliged to defend me. I cannot make them responsible in any way, and therefore, I now here, and in the greatest love and sympathy, lay down my membership of this Association and go forth — not to be separated from you. I shall be nearer to you than if I should be in ecclesiastical relation. I will work for you, I will lecture for you, I will personally do everything I can for you. I will even attend these meetings as a spectator, with you. I will devote my whole life to the Congregational churches and their interests, as well as to all other churches of Christ Jesus.' I am not going out into the cold. I am not going out into another sect. I am not going away from you in any spirit of disgust. I never was in warmer personal sympathy with every one of you than I am now; but I lay down the responsibility that you have borne for me — I take it off from you and put it on myself. And now you can say, " He is a member of the Congregational Church, but he has relieved his brethren of all responsibility whatever for his teachings." That you are perfectly free to do. With thanks for your great kindness and with thanks to God for the life which we have had here together, I am now no longer a member of the Congregational Association of New York and Brooklyn, but with you a member of the Body of Christ Jesus, in full fellowship with you in the matter of faith and love and hope.

At the close of Mr. Beecher's address, after some informal debate, a committee of three, consisting of Messrs. H. M. Storrs, W. C. Stiles, and A. Whittemore, was appointed to draft a resolution expressive of the sentiments of the Association, which, as finally amended, was carried without a dissenting voice. It was as follows: —

Resolved, That the members of the New York and Brooklyn Association receive the Rev. Henry Ward Beecher's resignation of his membership in this body with very deep pain and regret. We cannot fail to recognize the generous magnanimity which has led him to volunteer this action, lest he should seem even indirectly to make his brethren responsible before the public for the support of philosophical and theological doctrines wherein he is popularly supposed to differ essentially with those who hold the established and current Evangelical faith. His full and proffered exposition of doctrinal views that he has made at this meeting indicates the propriety of his continued membership in this or any other Congregational Association. We hereby declare our desire that he may see his way clear to reconsider and withdraw it. We desire to place on record as the result of a long and intimate acquaintance with Mr. Beecher, and a familiar observation of the results of his life, as well as his preaching and pastoral work, that we cherish for him an ever-growing personal attachment as a brother beloved, and a deepening sense of his worth as a Christian minister. We cannot now contemplate the possibility of his future absence from our meetings without a depressing sense of the loss we are to suffer, and unitedly pledge the hearts of the Association to him, and express the hope that the day for his return may soon come.

INDEX

As clergyman, author and editor, LYMAN ABBOTT worked closely with Henry Ward Beecher, succeeding him as editor in chief of the *Christian Union* in 1881. Nine years later, at Beecher's death, he took over the pulpit of the famous Plymouth Congregational Church in Brooklyn Heights, New York. In addition to writing his friend's biography, Abbott authored *Theology of an Evolutionist, The Great Companion* and *The Spirit of Democracy*.

WILLIAM G. MCLOUGHLIN is Professor of History at Brown University. He has written *New England Dissent* and, most recently, *Revivals, Awakenings and Reform*.